RARY

D0481713

ALSO BY RICK NEWMAN

Bury Us Upside Down (with Don Sheperd)

FIREFIGHT

INSIDE

———

THE BATTLE TO SAVE

———

THE PENTAGON

———

ON 9/11

FIREFIGHT

Patrick Creed
Rick Newman

 BALLANTINE BOOKS | NEW YORK

Copyright © 2008 by Patrick Creed and Rick Newman

Maps: Adapted from maps created by the U.S. Government

Photographs by Daryl Donley, copyright © Daryl Donley.
Used by permission.

All rights reserved.

Published in the United States by Presidio Press, an imprint of
The Random House Publishing Group, a division of
Random House, Inc., New York.

Presidio Press and colophon
are trademarks of Random House, Inc.

Library of Congress Cataloging-in-Publication Data

Creed, Patrick.
Firefight : inside the battle to save the Pentagon on 9/11 /
Patrick Creed and Rick Newman.
p.   cm.
Includes bibliographical references and index.
ISBN-13: 978-0-89141-905-1 (hardcover : alk. paper)
1. September 11 Terrorist Attacks, 2001.   2. Pentagon (Va.)
3. Rescue work—Virginia—Arlington.   I. Newman, Rick.
II. Title.

HV6432.7.C724 2008
975.5'295044—dc22   2008004253

Printed in the United States of America on acid-free paper

www.presidiopress.com

2 4 6 8 9 7 5 3 1

First Edition

Book design by Liz Cosgrove

CONTENTS

Contents   ix

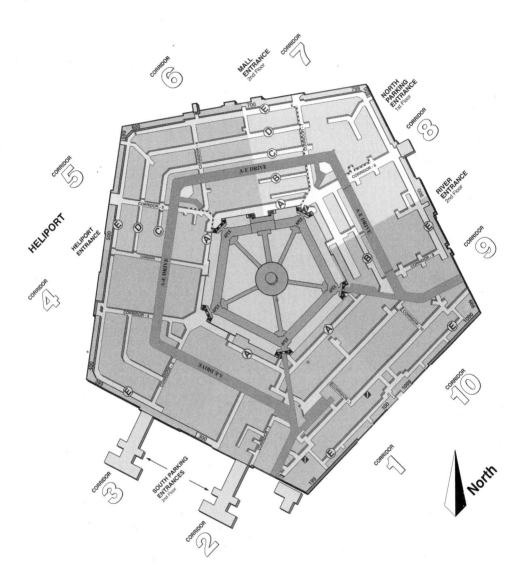

The Pentagon's floor plan, above, shows how the 10 corridors, which run from the outside of the building to the center, like spokes, intersect with the five concentric rings (A through E). A&E Drive is the service road that served as a rallying point for firefighters. The tunnel that fire crews used to get to the center courtyard begins to the right of the Corridor 2 entrance.

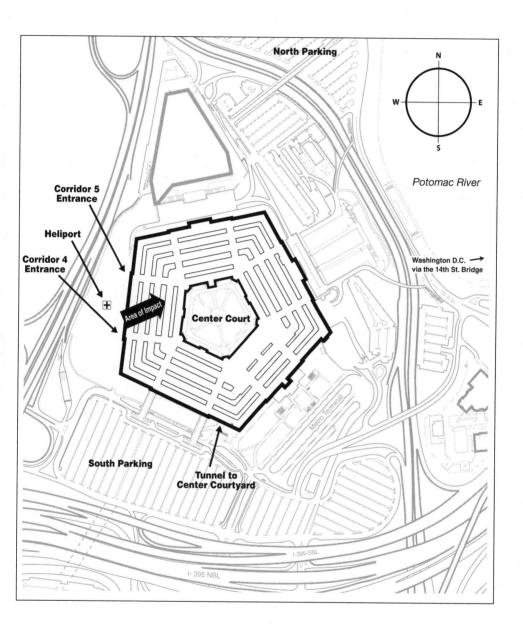

The broader map above shows where Flight 77 struck the Pentagon, near the heliport, between Corridors 4 and 5. Most of the interior fire burned in the area bounded by those two hallways and A&E Drive, where the force of the plane created the "punch-out hole" and the final remnants of Flight 77 came to rest.

RECURRING CHARACTERS

ARLINGTON COUNTY FIRE DEPARTMENT

Jim Anderson, driver of Quint 104, fought fire throughout the building and on the roof on Sept. 11.

Bobby Beer, member of Rescue 104 crew who also worked on the Technical Rescue Team (TRT).

Capt. Ed Blunt, an EMS supervisor, established the casualty triage site on Washington Boulevard, overlooking the burning Pentagon.

Battalion Chief Jim Bonzano helped run EMS and worked as one of the incident commanders.

Fred Calvert, driver of Engine 108, manned multiple water pumps into the night on Sept. 11.

Ron Christman steered the rear tiller wheel of Truck 105, the first fire vehicle to arrive at the Pentagon.

Battalion Chief Bob Cornwell set up the first command post and ranged throughout the fire ground on Sept. 11.

Chris Cox, part of a composite crew that went to the inner courtyard and fought fire near the C Ring.

Capt. Dan Fitch, TRT squad leader who helped clear debris, recover remains, and stabilize the building.

Capt. Chuck Gibbs, initially placed in command of the "River Division" responsible for the firefight on the helipad side of the Pentagon.

Dodie Gill, director of Arlington County's mental health and employee support program, counseled workers at the scene.

Capt. Bob Gray, one of the TRT leaders.

Battalion Chief Randy Gray, one of the incident commanders.

Capt. Denis Griffin, officer in charge of Quint 104, led his team into the center courtyard and fought fire throughout the building.

Capt. Ed Hannon fought fire throughout the building and on the roof with D.C. and Arlington crews.

Capt. Doug Insley, Chief Schwartz's aide at the command post.

Capt. Kenny Johnson, a medic who assisted battalion chief Dale Jerome Smith in the courtyard.

Joe Lightfoot, Bob Cornwell's aide, worked multiple duties at the command post.

Battalion Chief G. O. Lyon, one of the incident commanders.

Jason "Cub" Lyon, part of a composite crew that went to the inner courtyard and fought fire near the C Ring.

Paul Marshall, part of a composite crew that went to the inner courtyard and fought fire near the C Ring.

Capt. Steve McCoy, the officer in charge of Engine 101, one of the first to report seeing Flight 77 crash, also led his crew fighting fire throughout the building.

Capt. Scott McKay, one of the TRT leaders.

Fire Chief Ed Plaugher, delegated tactical command of the incident to his operations chief so he could coordinate with numerous government agencies sending workers to the Pentagon.

Chris Ramey, Chief Plaugher's aide.

Brian Roache, driver of Truck 105, the first fire vehicle to arrive at the Pentagon.

Assistant Chief Jim Schwartz, incident commander for the overall operation.

Battalion Chief Dale Jerome Smith directed operations in the center courtyard on Sept. 11.

Capt. Mike Smith, officer in charge of Engine 108, led his crew on multiple sorties into the burning building.

Derek Spector, acting officer in charge of Truck 105, led the first fire crew to enter the Pentagon.

Capt. Brian Spring led the composite crew including Chris Cox, Jason Lyon, and Paul Marshall, also one of the TRT leaders.

Chad Stamps, part of Bobby Beer's crew on Rescue 104, fought fire and searched for victims near the impact site.

Keith Young helped control "freelancers" running in through the Pentagon's Corridor 5 entrance.

OTHER FIRE DEPARTMENTS

District Chief Richie Bowers from Montgomery County, Maryland, led teams of firefighters on the roof on Sept. 12.

Capt. Mike Defina, acting battalion chief from Reagan National Airport, helped run the River Division command post early in the operation.

Lt. Craig Duck, from the District of Columbia, led one of the first crews to arrive in the center courtyard.

Chief Micky Fyock, from Woodsboro, Maryland, led a crew of volunteers manning an antique ladder truck in the center courtyard early in the morning on Sept. 12.

Battalion Chief John Gleske, from Fairfax County, Virginia, led teams of firefighters on the roof on Sept. 12.

Battalion Chief Denny Martin, from Reagan National Airport, in command of overnight operations in the courtyard on Sept. 11–12.

Mark Skipper, from Fort Myer, Virginia, on routine firefighting duty at the Pentagon helipad on Sept. 11 when Flight 77 crashed into the building.

Battalion Fire Chief Dick Sterne, from the District of Columbia, one of the commanders on Sept. 12.

Alan Wallace, from Fort Myer, Virginia, manned the Pentagon helipad the morning of Sept. 11 when Flight 77 struck.

Dennis Young, from Fort Myer, Virginia, manned the Pentagon helipad the morning of Sept. 11 when Flight 77 struck.

FEDERAL EMERGENCY MANAGEMENT AGENCY (FEMA)

Perry Bowser, a contractor hired to operate the "T-Rex," a huge crane used to dismantle the rubble pile at the impact point.

Domenick Iannelli, hazardous materials specialist and search team member for Virginia Task Force 1, or VA-TF1, from Fairfax County.

Elizabeth Kreitler, dog handler for VA-TF1 who searched for victims and remains with her dog, Nero.

Randy Leatherman, search team member for VA-TF1.

Buddy Martinette, one of the leaders of Virginia Task Force 2, from Virginia Beach, who helped command the overall FEMA operation.

Steve McFarland, search team member for VA-TF1.

Mike Regan, search team leader for VA-TF1.

Earl Shughart, heavy rigging expert for VA-TF1, helped coordinate trucks, cranes, and other heavy equipment.

Dean Tills, senior structural specialist for VA-TF1, helped assess the Pentagon's stability, and plan clearing and shoring operations.

Leo Titus, structural specialist for VA-TF1, on his first deployment at the Pentagon.

Kent Watts, rescue team leader and shoring expert for VA-TF1.

DEPARTMENT OF DEFENSE

Sean Boger, Army civilian working as a controller at the Pentagon helipad when Flight 77 struck the building.

Lt. Gen. P. K. Carlton, Air Force surgeon general, helped rescue survivors in A&E Drive.

Steve Carter, Pentagon assistant building manager, remained in the building doing damage control all day on Sept. 11.

Vice Adm. Scott Fry, director of the Joint Staff, responsible for keeping the National Military Command Center operating.

Specialist Dakota Gallivan, member of the Army's Old Guard regiment, helped recover remains and clear debris out of the Pentagon.

Capt. Jennifer Glidewell, Army nurse, helped manage the treatment of casualties in the center courtyard.

Kathy Greenwell, assistant to Steve Carter, remained in the building all day on Sept. 11, helping with damage control.

Maj. Gen. James Jackson, liaison between the Defense Department and fire commanders.

John Jester, head of the Defense Protective Service, the Pentagon's police force.

Gen. John Keane, vice chief of staff of the Army.

Specialist Jackie Kidd, Army soldier working as an assistant in the helipad control tower when Flight 77 struck the building.

Allyn Kilsheimer, civilian structural engineer whose assistance was requested by the Pentagon Renovation office.

Maj. Dave King, Army officer badly burned when his first floor office erupted in flames.

Col. Phil McNair, Army officer who led a group of survivors on their knees through smoke and wreckage.

Dan Murphy, Pentagon engineer, remained in the building with Steve Carter all day on Sept. 11 doing damage control.

Cmdr. Craig Powell, Navy SEAL who helped rescue survivors in A&E Drive.

Sgt. Matthew Rosenberg, Army medic who helped treat casualties in the courtyard and search for victims near A&E Drive.

Secretary of Defense Donald Rumsfeld, spent most of Sept. 11 in the Executive Support Center, a secure suite of rooms above the National Military Command Center.

Lt. Cmdr. Dave Tarantino, Navy doctor who helped rescue trapped victims near A&E Drive.

Capt. Dave Thomas, Navy doctor who helped rescue trapped victims near A&E Drive.

FBI

Special Agent John Adams, one of the supervisors in charge of evidence recovery.

Special Agent Tara Bloesch ran the morgue.

Special Agent Chris Combs helped run the overall FBI operation.

Jen Farmer, photographer who helped document evidence and remains.

Jen Hill, photographer who helped document evidence and remains.

Special Agent Garrett McKenzie helped with photography, evidence collection, and coordination with contractors.

Special Agent Jean O'Connor led an evidence recovery team, married to Tom O'Connor.

Special Agent Tom O'Connor, one of the supervisors in charge of evidence recovery, married to Jean O'Connor.

Special Agent Mark Whitworth, bomb expert who helped organize the search for the black boxes and other key evidence.

FIREFIGHT

THE TOWERS

Tuesday, September 11, 2001, 8:50 A.M.

There was one hell of a fire up in New York. Nobody seemed to know what had happened, whether it was an accident or a terrorist attack or something else. But one thing was for sure—the FDNY had a long day of work ahead.

At Fire Station 4 in Arlington, Virginia, half a dozen firefighters watched TV with a kind of professional envy as smoke poured from one of the towers at the World Trade Center. The television commentators were speculating about what had happened and what it meant. Some kind of airplane seemed to have smashed into the North Tower, in downtown Manhattan, just as the workday was getting started. But nobody knew what kind of plane. Or why it hit the building.

The firefighters, however, were more interested in what was happening inside the tower. There was very little on TV about that. They had a pretty good idea, though.

Capt. Denis Griffin was a burly 20-year veteran who had joined the Arlington County Fire Department back when canvas coats and hip-high rubber boots were the standard protective gear. He recalled some details of the 1945 crash of a B-25 bomber into the Empire State Building, which wrecked several floors and cut most of the building's elevator cables. This looked similar. With the elevators probably out, he figured, the New York firefighters would be walking up hundreds of stairs, with axes and other tools and hoses and air packs—probably 50 pounds of gear for each guy—while an avalanche of people coursed in the opposite direction.

"Imagine getting all those people down the stairs," Griffin bellowed, his usually calm voice roused with excitement.

"Just think what it must be like humping all that gear up to the top of that building," added Bobby Beer, a salt-haired West Virginian who had been fighting fires as long as Griffin.

"Goddamn," Griffin said, "that is gonna be one hell of a long walk."

Arlington had a few high-rises, but nothing like New York. That's what made the New York City Fire Department so legendary—just about any kind of fire there was, the guys in New York had seen it. Now they were fighting what was probably one of the toughest, highest fires ever, and the crew at Station 4 foresaw all kinds of problems. Even if they could climb that high, water pressure in the tower had probably been cut to a trickle. How would the New York crews put out the fire? Would they be able to carry up the heavy tools needed to extract victims who might be buried in rubble? And how would they get to people trapped above the fire? Did they have helicopters that could do rescues from the roof?

"Shit," somebody joked. "Those guys in New York get all the best fires."

A shrill chirping sound disrupted the armchair firefighting. The room went silent as a series of staccato beeps got louder. It was a fire call at an apartment building, and the dispatcher was summoning multiple units: Engine 109, Engine 101, Engine 105, Quint 104 . . . That was Griffin's unit. He and his crew of three others rushed to the truck, jumped into their turnout gear, and started the engine.

It was not shaping up as a good day to get dental work done. Vice Adm. Scott Fry, the director of the Joint Staff at the Pentagon, had orders to ship out soon for a new job as commander of the Navy Sixth Fleet in Naples, Italy. And he had to get to the dentist before he left.

Just as Fry was about to leave his office, his executive assistant called out, "Hey, you won't believe this." The TV was on. "It looks like an aircraft hit the World Trade Center."

Fry watched for a moment. That was odd, he thought. But probably just a freak accident. He told his secretary to call his cell phone if anything came up, and headed out the door for his nine o'clock appointment.

At the clinic, the news was on in the waiting room, with coverage of the incident in New York. The newscaster was asking somebody if there were any reports on the size of the plane that had hit the building. Had it been a small, private plane? "No," an analyst said. "It looks bigger than a civil aircraft."

Fry was antsy. This didn't feel right. The lean, frenetic admiral was pretty wired to start with, and he debated heading back to his office. But then the dental assistant called him in. At least we'll get this over with fast, he thought.

The dentist started prepping him for a novocaine shot when they heard a shout from an outer office; there was some kind of commotion. Then Fry's cell phone rang. It was his assistant. "Sir," he huffed, "I don't know if you saw it, but another airplane hit the World Trade Center."

That was all Fry needed to hear. "This appointment is over," he announced, pushing the dental tray out of the way and leaping out of the chair. He walked swiftly out of the clinic. Out in the corridor, he started to run. One airplane hitting a skyscraper, that was damned suspicious. But two . . . there was no doubt about it. It had to be a terrorist attack.

Fry raced to the National Military Command Center, the Pentagon's highly secure nerve center. Above the command center was a suite of rooms known as the Executive Support Center, or ESC, where the Secretary of Defense, the Joint Chiefs of Staff, and other senior officials would meet to discuss urgent matters. A video teleconference link could connect them to the White House, the State Department, the CIA, and military commanders throughout the world. Running the whole complex was Fry's job.

As he bounded up a spiral staircase that led from the command center to the conference room, a group was already gathering. Stephen Cambone, Defense Secretary Donald Rumsfeld's right-hand man, was there, for the moment the ranking civilian. He and Fry started discussing what they knew about New York: not much, except what they could see on TV. Everybody in the room knew that events were unfolding that would likely lead the nation into war. But right now there were more immediate concerns. Should the Pentagon send a hospital ship to New York? An Aegis cruiser? An aircraft carrier? What would it take to get National Guard troops into Manhattan? And what was the status of the nation's air defense network?

Like the men in Denis Griffin's company, Derek Spector, Brian Roache, and Ron Christman had raced to the Arlington apartment fire. As with most calls, there turned out to be no fire—in this case, just some burnt coffee smoldering on a stove. It had been a quick call, pretty routine—except that as they were packing up to leave, somebody had mentioned a big fire up in New York. An airplane had hit a high-rise. So when the three firefighters returned to their station in south Arlington, they went straight to the kitchen and flipped on the TV.

It was an astonishing sight. There were now *two* airplanes. Smoke poured from both towers of the World Trade Center, and the networks kept re-airing footage of the second plane—clearly a commercial airliner—roaring into the South Tower, followed by a spectacular eruption of flame and debris.

"That's weird, man!" Roache roared. "Fucking weird! This has got to be some kind of incident!"

Spector was the acting officer on the crew—standing in for another officer, who was on leave. He was the most experienced of the three, but he had never seen anything like it. Terrorism, maybe—but it seemed too big even for that. Didn't terrorists use truck bombs? And operate on the *ground*?

Spector was a part-time firefighter in Frederick County, Maryland, where he lived. A lot of firefighters did that—earned their pay in a big department, then volunteered or worked part-time locally. Spector's shift in Arlington would end at 7:00 A.M. the next day, and he was scheduled for a shift in Maryland right after that. He'd be late, so he called a colleague in Frederick, to work something out. They made a plan. Then they talked about New York.

"Hey, be careful man," Spector's friend told him. "That could happen down there."

"Nah," Spector answered. "That kind of stuff doesn't happen down here in Arlington."

Protestors were heading for the nation's capital. And law-enforcement officials were determined to avoid a melee.

Dignitaries at the International Monetary Fund met from time to time in Washington, D.C., and until recently the biggest problem had been gridlock caused by fleets of limousines blocking the streets. But global financial institutions had become a rallying point for protestors upset about poverty, economic unfairness, and a litany of other problems. Demonstrators numbering perhaps 100,000 or more were planning a huge march to greet the world bankers at the end of the month.[1] At similar protests in other cities, chaos and violence had erupted. So throughout the Washington area, public safety officials were planning how to keep that from happening in D.C.

The firefighters were FBI Special Agent Chris Combs's assignment. After joining the Washington Field Office in 1998, Combs noticed that the Bureau had solid outreach programs to local police departments, but not to the fire squads. Before joining the FBI, Combs had been a firefighter on Long Island, up in New York, where he grew up, and he still had two cousins on the FDNY. He knew that in a major emergency or terrorist incident, like the 1995 Oklahoma City bombing, it would be the fire department—not the police or the FBI—doing rescues, battling fires, and going into wrecked buildings. "We've got all these great relationships with police, but not with the fire departments," he had told his bosses. "If there was a major bombing today, the fire chief is going to own that scene. He needs a relationship with the FBI."

Combs got the go-ahead to begin a liaison program with local fire departments. He set up joint training programs, made sure the FBI understood fire department procedures, and got to know the fire officials in D.C., Maryland, and Virginia. Today he was teaching a class on crowd control, in case firefighters had to respond to an incident during the IMF meetings that involved police cordons, tear gas, or masses of people.

As Combs lectured about 50 firefighters and police officers at the Metropolitan Police Academy near Capitol Hill, he impressed the group with his energy and enthusiasm. A passion for law enforcement came across in his eager speech and animated body language. Traces of a New York accent added authenticity.

Combs's audience was silent and attentive, until one of the firefighters reached into his pocket and pulled out a cell phone. Combs scowled, thinking how rude it was to take a call in the midst of his class.

Then the firefighter blurted out, "It's my wife. She says New York is under attack!"

Combs decided on the spot to cancel class. The group moved to another room, where there was a TV. Then Combs's pager went off—

the message said to prepare for a possible deployment to New York. "I gotta get out of here!" Combs announced. "I gotta get to New York!" He sprinted out the door, jumped in his car, and headed for the FBI's Washington Field Office in downtown D.C.

This sounded like a big incident. It could last for days. Combs decided to make a quick stop at his Capitol Hill town house on the way—it couldn't hurt to toss some clean socks and underwear in his car.

When Denis Griffin and his crew returned to Station 4, the mood was a lot more somber than when they had left. The second plane had hit New York. The TV networks had footage, and kept showing it, over and over. Both towers were retching thick black smoke—typical of fuel fires. Something horrendous was happening.

Bobby Beer was on the phone with some buddies who belonged to a federal search-and-rescue task force. They didn't have orders yet, but from the looks of things on TV, they figured they were going to be sent to New York to help search for victims at the World Trade Center—or anyplace else that might get attacked. The task force was starting to muster. "Be safe," Beer implored one of his pals.

Chad Stamps, another firefighter, called his best friend in the department, Paul Marshall, who was on leave that day. The "wonder twins," as they were known, were notorious for jokes and pranks, especially when they were around each other. There was no joking now. "Are you watching this?" Stamps asked.

"What the fuck!" Marshall shouted on the other end of the phone. "How do you fight a fire like that? What are they gonna do?"

Somebody else pointed to the TV and said it looked like the top of one of the towers was askew. Then the firefighters started speculating about what sorts of landmarks terrorists might target if they were to attack northern Virginia. The most obvious was the *USA Today* complex, which included the two tallest high-rises in Arlington. They had aimed for the tallest buildings in New York, right? So wouldn't they do the same thing here?

Or they might go after CIA headquarters, somebody volunteered. Or the Pentagon. Or the White House and the Capitol, over in D.C.

The chirping sound interrupted. "Apartment fire," the dispatcher announced, "1001 Wilson Blvd . . ."

Time to get back to work.

★ 2 ★

AA 77

9:15 A.M.

It was puzzling. And worrisome. Air traffic controllers at the Federal Aviation Administration's tracking facility in Indianapolis had maintained routine communications with American Airlines Flight 77 since about 8:40 A.M., when the plane had crossed into their airspace from the sector controlled by the Washington tracking center, to the east. The Boeing 757 had taken off from Washington's Dulles International Airport, bound for Los Angeles, just a few minutes behind schedule, at 8:20 in the morning. It was a light load—just 58 passengers and six crew members.[1] The weather was clear—stellar for flying, in fact. When the plane was over West Virginia, the pilots had checked in with controllers at Indy Center, reporting an altitude of 33,000 feet. A controller directed them to 35,000 feet.[2] Perfectly routine.

At about five minutes before nine, John Thomas, the controller who was tracking Flight 77, noticed the plane turning toward the south, over southeastern Ohio—a deviation from its assigned flight path.[3] "Indy Center calling American 77," he radioed repeatedly. "American 77, Indy." No answer.

Then the plane disappeared from his tracking scope. Losing both radio contact and radar identification was never good news. Thomas tried half a dozen times to raise the pilots on the radio, and called

American Airlines, asking dispatchers there to give it a try. Nobody got an answer.

Thomas and other officials at Indy Center started scanning radar returns along Flight 77's projected flight path, to the west. There were no signs of a wayward plane. Thomas assumed the worst—that AA 77 had suffered some kind of catastrophic failure and crashed. Shortly after 9:00 A.M., Indy Center started putting out the word that an aircraft was probably down, and asked the Air Force Rescue Coordination Center at Langley Air Force Base in Virginia to begin a search.[4]

A few minutes later, however, the Indy officials started to change their minds about Flight 77. They learned that some other jetliners had been hijacked, and they saw on TV what was happening in New York. Indy Center updated its report: AA 77 was believed to be "lost," not gone. At the FAA Command Center in Herndon, Virginia, officials started looking for AA 77, scanning for telltale radar signals. A few controllers at other FAA facilities started looking too, along with dispatchers at American Airlines.[5]

The problem was rapidly mushrooming. Nobody at the FAA or anyplace else in the government knew exactly what was happening in the skies. But it was becoming clear that there was an unknown number of hijacked planes flying over the country. That was enough for the FAA to order a nationwide "ground stop," which prevented any more commercial flights from taking off.[6] Then, at about 9:30, President Bush made a terse statement before television cameras. He was in Sarasota, Florida, where he had been visiting a school. "Today we've had a national tragedy," he said somberly. "Two airplanes have crashed into the World Trade Center in an apparent terrorist attack on our country." Bush ended with the most reassuring pledge he could offer, in the midst of a surprise attack by unknown assailants: "I've ordered that the full resources of the federal government go to help the victims and the families, and to conduct a full-scale investigation to hunt down and to find those folks who committed this act."[7]

American Airlines Flight 77 was indeed still airborne—but not where air traffic controllers thought it was.[8] While Indy officials were looking to the west, trying to project AA 77's continued flight path toward Los Angeles, the jet had actually turned around and begun heading east. By 9:15 it was back over West Virginia, once again into the airspace controlled by the Washington center,[9] which controllers were unaware of. Word was spreading throughout the FAA that AA 77 had probably been hijacked. The ominous implications were settling in, and the hunt for AA 77 intensified. Still, there were hundreds of planes in the sky along the East Coast. Without the transponder data, searching for a single runaway jet among all those radar dots was like looking at mites under a microscope.

Under the cover of all that traffic, the hijackers began a gradual descent, back toward Washington—as if they were returning to Dulles. Except Flight 77 was flying faster than a plane preparing to land. By 9:30 the 757 was roaring over Haymarket, Virginia, about 35 miles west of Washington, at about 350 miles per hour.[10] It had dropped to about 7,000 feet. At about the same time the President had finished his brief remarks in Florida, controllers at Dulles noticed a fast-moving aircraft on their radars, hurtling toward the D.C. area. A moment later the tower supervisor at Ronald Reagan Washington National Airport, just across the Potomac River from downtown Washington, called the Secret Service and told them an unidentified airplane was heading rapidly in the direction of the White House—and refusing to identity itself.[11]

With only the radar data as a guide, controllers couldn't tell what flight was racing across their screens, or even what kind of plane it was. A National Guard C-130 cargo plane had taken off just before the FAA ground stop, and controllers at Reagan National radioed the pilot, asking if he could locate and follow the suspicious plane. He turned the lumbering C-130 around and was able to identify the jet as a 757. That was about all he could make out.

Then, as suddenly as it had appeared, the mysterious plane heading toward D.C. from the west began to bank to the right, turning away from Washington. Less than ten miles from the White House, AA 77 began a looping turn to the south. Controllers were closely tracking the plane on their scopes now and watching it the entire way. It flew south for about a minute, tracing Route 7 toward Alexandria, then crossing the I-495 Beltway as if heading toward Richmond.

But it wasn't heading south after all. The plane stayed in a bank and began to circle back toward Washington—descending the entire time. It skirted just north of Fort Belvoir, Virginia, cast a shadow near the Springfield Mall, and crossed back over the Beltway, heading north now. Once again it appeared to be drawing a bead on Washington. The Reagan controllers, on the phone with the Secret Service, now had a clear enough idea what was happening. With the plane once again less than ten miles from Washington, the Secret Service decided to evacuate Vice President Dick Cheney, who was in the White House, to an underground bunker. Within a minute agents had hustled him into the tunnel that led to the shelter deep beneath the White House.[12]

By then Flight 77 was just 2,000 feet off the ground, and still flying at about 350 miles per hour. The plane straightened out on a northeast heading, on a path that now led south of Washington—toward the Pentagon.

Inside the Pentagon, the daily routine of briefings, PowerPoint presentations, budget analyses, and casual chats over coffee was grinding to a halt, as the nation's military establishment began to realize that the United States was being attacked. At the National Military Command Center there was a furious hunt for information: What were the next possible targets? Who were the attackers? Were there fighter jets available to fly combat patrols over New York and Washington? The command center was beginning to fill with admirals and generals, and a videoteleconference with the White House and other agencies had begun.

Since its design was unveiled in 1941, the Pentagon's size and secrecy had made it one of the most intriguing buildings in the world. The structure was notoriously huge—its six million square feet of office space was three times larger than the Empire State Building.[13] In 1942, one magazine writer sneered, "Perhaps it will house the entire U.S. Army."[14] The building inhabited 29 acres of ground,[15] the equivalent of five city blocks in Manhattan or Chicago.

The Pentagon's severe architectural profile—along with the grave, mysterious mission of the people who worked inside—left the impression that the building had been built as a fortress. It hadn't. When President Franklin Roosevelt approved the Pentagon's design, he envisioned it as a temporary military headquarters necessary to handle a surge in staff associated with the expanding war in Europe. When the war was over and the military shrank, as it had after every other war, the Pentagon could be used as a records-storage facility, Roosevelt and other planners had reasoned. But as long as it housed the military, its vastness was a potential liability: At least one top official had argued it was the "largest target in the world for enemy bombs."[16] Roosevelt, foreseeing nothing more significant than a giant warehouse, rebuffed the worry.

Although huge, the Pentagon's design was famously rational. Five concentric hallways, labeled A through E—the "rings"—encircled the building's core. The A Ring, the shortest, was closest to the interior; the E Ring, the longest, closest to the exterior. Ten corridors, designated 1 through 10, intersected the rings at equal distances, like spokes on a wheel. Between the B and C Rings, around most of the building, a service road called A&E Drive offered motorized access for maintenance workers. The whole scheme overlaid five floors, connected by long, sloping ramps. In the center of it all was a grassy, five-acre, tree-lined courtyard, a bucolic respite from the bustle inside the walls.

The orderly layout was meant to consolidate dozens of military agencies into one relatively discreet building that wouldn't overwhelm Washington's skyline. And the ring-and-spoke system was designed so workers could walk from office to office without wearing out their shoes. The Pentagon's designers estimated that the longest point-to-point walk inside the Pentagon would be about 1,800 feet—a long way, yes, but shorter than if the building were square or rectangular.[17] At a healthy pace, that would be a ten-minute walk, at most. Eventually, the workers who serviced the Pentagon began to adopt three-wheeled pedicarts and electric buggies to ferry supplies around the Pentagon's wide, smooth hallways.

But the Pentagon's logical floor plan was broken in dozens of places, confounding all but seasoned veterans of the building. In 1989, on one of his first days in the building, Defense Secretary Dick Cheney had gotten lost in the basement, wandering for ten minutes before finding his way out.[18] Most newcomers had similar experiences. Expanded offices enveloped hallways, disrupting the hub-and-spoke system. Ever-present construction created endless detours. Secured areas, closed to most of the building's occupants, blocked entire passageways, some of them manned by armed guards. In addition to the basement, there were rumors of several subbasements that contained secret facilities and agencies the public had never heard of. Pentagon officials, of course, always declined to comment on such rumors.

Over its 50 years, the Pentagon had housed troves of secrets and was the backdrop to some of the nation's most historic—and frightening—moments. If the 1962 Cuban Missile Crisis had escalated into nuclear war, the order to launch would have come from Gen.

Maxwell Taylor, chairman of the Joint Chiefs of Staff, in the National Military Command Center.[19] Intense arguments over Vietnam strategy had taken place in the Joint Chiefs of Staff conference room—"the tank"—and many other offices. In October 1967, Defense Secretary Robert McNamara had watched from the Pentagon's roof, with growing doubt about his own war strategy, as thousands of demonstrators marched on the nation's military headquarters to protest the Vietnam War. In 1991, after Iraq had invaded Kuwait, Colin Powell, Chairman of the Joint Chiefs of Staff, had famously stood before the podium in the Pentagon's press briefing room and declared of the Iraqi army, "First we're going to cut it off, then we're going to kill it."

Most people in the Pentagon, however, had jobs more mundane than planning wars or selecting targets. Thousands of people analyzed and prepared budgets, or helped procure weapons and equipment, or greased relationships with all the other agencies in Washington.

Now the building teemed with fidgety action-takers whose adrenaline soared as they watched a terrorist attack unfolding on TV. In Room 1D516, a windowless interior office, Maj. Dave King was trying to get his boss's attention. The Special Forces officer, sent to the Pentagon for two years to do staff work before returning to the field for a command job, had been down the hall watching the devastation in New York in a neighboring office. Something told him the attack wasn't over. He had gone back to his computer and e-mailed a friend. "We should evacuate the Pentagon," he insisted. "This building is a target waiting to be hit."

King worked with a small group in the Army's G-8 division, responsible for developing the Army's future programs and equipment. About ten feet away from King, Staff Sgt. Maudlyn White worked quietly at her desk, despite the mounting hubbub. White was a single mom, with a six-year-old daughter, who had just transferred to Washington from a posting in Korea. She was a proficient worker who knew few people in the area and largely kept to herself. King walked to the door of his boss's office, where Lt. Col. Jerry Dickerson was on the phone. King waved to get his attention, and made sure the boss knew what was going on in New York. Somebody, it seemed, should give an order to get people out of the building.

Four floors up, Cmdr. Craig Powell was itching to be anywhere but the Pentagon. The towering Navy SEAL, who stood six-five, had been in the building just three days, fresh from a tour as defense attaché at the U.S. Embassy in Jamaica. He wouldn't even have been in the Pentagon except that the Navy had declined to give him a field command. Powell had figured his Navy career was winding down, so he asked for a staff job in Washington, where his father-in-law lived, and where there would be good job prospects once he left the Navy.

Powell's habit was to wear civilian clothes to and from work, and change once he got there. With the TV coverage absorbing his attention, he put off changing into his Navy khakis. As President Bush finished his short address from Florida, the elite SEAL, trained for commando operations, knew better than most what the destruction in New York signified. Yes, there would probably be a war. But before and after that, there would be clandestine operations against terrorists in some of the world's most shadowy places. His comrades would be there. He wouldn't.

Other offices were still filled with people deep into the day's work, oblivious to the attacks in New York. At the northwest corner of a 100-yard-long cubicle bay on the Pentagon's second floor, one level above Dave King's office, nearly a dozen Army officials from the Army's personnel division were in a standing, every-other-Tuesday meeting. Lt. Gen. Tim Maude ran the personnel division, and one of his staff officers, Col. Philip McNair, was chairing the session. Each staffer gave a brief update on recent activities. It was routine stuff: a retirement party, an upcoming conference. The last staffer in the rotation was Lt. Col. Marilyn Wills, the department's congressional liaison. As her turn to speak neared, she thought to herself that the meeting was running longer than usual. She glanced at her watch. It showed 9:36.[20]

Outside the conference room was a huge cubicle farm—known as "Dilbertsville"—where most workers were glued to TV sets. But the meeting in the conference room had started before any of the participants knew of the attacks in New York, and nobody from Dilbertsville had interrupted to break the news.[21]

By then thousands of people throughout the Pentagon were gathering in knots wherever there was a TV set, wondering if the twin towers would survive and reeling at the thought of the victims. In the Pentagon's Building Operations Command Center, near the center of the building, on the first floor, Steve Carter and Kathy Greenwell watched a bank of video screens, with TVs showing the reports on New York. Carter was one of the most colorful characters in the Pentagon, a portly former sailor who had been injured in a car accident and ended up with brain damage in his early thirties. The Navy discharged him, saying he'd never be able to speak without a slur or walk without dragging a foot. But he recovered fully and started working as a plumber at the Pentagon. Eighteen years later he had become the assistant building manager, charged with helping oversee a massive renovation of the entire building.

When somebody needed a problem solved fast, Carter was the man they were likely to flag down. He was well-known throughout the Defense Department, famous for his loud shirts and ties, which stood out in the sea of khaki, green, and blue military uniforms. He knew more about the Pentagon than almost anybody else who worked there. Generals would stop him in the halls to ask about upgrades to their command centers; secretaries would flag him down to report seeing a rat in a trash can. Plus, he was usually a pleasant distraction, affable, talkative, and quick with a corny joke.

But not today. The moment the second plane slashed into the World Trade Center, Carter and Greenwell, his assistant, started calling their supervisors, guessing that a terrorist attack was under way.

The Pentagon would probably raise its security posture. They got busy calling maintenance and engineering people, preparing them for unusual measures. And they started making sure plans were in place to lock down sensitive areas, like the National Military Command Center and other operational and intelligence facilities. It was going to be a busy day. Steve Carter felt like he could use a cigarette break already. He had quit smoking about a year earlier, but would have loved to go out to the courtyard in the center of the Pentagon and grab a smoke once things calmed down.

At the Pentagon helipad, on the lawn adjacent to the western facade of the building, a small fire crew was on higher alert than usual, though it was hard to imagine what for. Firefighting duty at the helipad was considered one of the dullest assignments in the whole complex. Nothing ever happened. Firefighters Alan Wallace, Mark Skipper, and Dennis Young—one of the crews from nearby Fort Myer—were expecting a routine helicopter arrival at ten that morning, and then President Bush was supposed to arrive for a visit that afternoon. That would bring a bit of excitement. But for firefighters, even VIP missions were anticlimactic. The small facility would swell with security officers for a moment or two, but the fire crew would be shuffled into the background. Then everybody would hurry off and there would be little activity for hours. Some firefighters even volunteered for helipad duty so they could catch up on their sleep in the cab of Foam 161, the fire truck stationed there.

Alan Wallace had spent the morning tidying up the truck and the station. Wallace was older and more experienced—not to mention more talkative and inquisitive—than many of the other civilian firefighters who worked at federal installations like Fort Myer. Wallace had been a Navy corpsman in Vietnam and stationed at several other locations across the country as an airport firefighter. He gave a lot of thought to his job, and had pulled Foam 161 out of the station onto the lawn, so other vehicles wouldn't block it in when the President's entourage showed up. He had been sitting in his favorite chair in the garage area, reading a book, when Mark Skipper came in to tell him about New York. Their commander called a moment later to make sure they knew what was going on. "These were intentional acts of terrorism," he said gravely—and there could be more, he stressed. If it had happened in New York, it could happen in Washington. The chief spoke to each of the three firefighters, making sure they were all on their toes and ready to respond to an unexpected incident.

Wallace and Skipper went back outside, near the truck. They talked about New York. Wallace thought about moving the truck back into the station for protection, just in case. But then he decided, no, it was fine where it was.[22]

A small control tower hovered over the fire station. Sean Boger, the air traffic controller, and his assistant, Specialist Jackie Kidd, were also talking about New York. Boger, a civilian who was working for the Army, mentioned how surprising it was that nobody had ever flown a plane into the Pentagon. It sat right along one of the approach paths to Reagan National, and planes sometimes flew so low over the Pentagon you could read the ID numbers on the bottom of the fuselages.

"You've been saying that for three years," Kidd answered.

"Yeah, you're right," Boger acknowledged.

Kidd got up. "Keep an eye on those planes," she joked.

Very funny, Boger thought. He had been planning to get some laundry out of his car, parked beside the tower, and run it down to the dry cleaners in the Pentagon's minimall. But it was turning out to be a strange day. The President was supposed to come to the Pentagon. With the attacks in New York, his return from Florida might get moved up. Maybe it would be better to put the laundry on hold until later that afternoon, Boger decided. Things should have calmed down by then.[23]

★ 3 ★

0.8 SECONDS

9:37 A.M.

The whine of jet engines was part of the daily sound track in Arlington, as familiar as the clatter of car and bus traffic. With Reagan National Airport nestled just across the river from Washington, D.C., low-flying planes buzzed over Arlington several times an hour. Visitors were often startled at the sight of a jetliner skimming toward National, just a few hundred feet above the tangle of highways that led in and out of D.C. But locals got to know the approach routes, which were mainly along the river—either from the south or the northwest, depending on the wind—and the planes became part of the bustle in a busy city. Aviation buffs would even hang out at the federal parkland just opposite the runways, gawking at the underbellies of planes as they lumbered overhead, so low you could almost bounce stones off the gleaming aluminum.

On Columbia Pike, a busy four-lane road less than a mile west of the Pentagon, Arlington County paramedics and firefighters were responding to a medical emergency. As they were loading a stroke patient onto an ambulance, a plane roared overhead. It was low and loud—and not where it should have been. Everybody looked up. If the plane had been over the river, it wouldn't have attracted much notice. But it was flying over the heart of Arlington, where there was danger of running into an office building or apartment complex.

Paramedic Claude Conde, a former chef known as "Scooter," whose cooking skills made him one of the most popular firefighters in the department, noticed that he could read the markings on the bottom of the aircraft, and even make out rows of rivets. He had never seen a plane so close. Something wasn't right. The airport wasn't far away, but the plane was already at treetop level, well below the glide path it should be on for National Airport. Conde watched the plane for another second as it followed Columbia Pike to the northeast. Then it dipped out of sight. "Shit!" he said to himself as the plane disappeared. "That doesn't look good!"

Just south of the Pentagon, the crew of Arlington's Engine 101 was in their fire truck, traveling north on I-395 toward a training session near the Pentagon. Capt. Steve McCoy, a soft-spoken southerner, was the officer in charge. When he and his crew learned of the New York attacks back at Station 1, McCoy had warned that terrorists could target D.C. or Virginia too. McCoy was unassuming and rarely got excited, but there had been quiet gravity in his voice. The crew grew somber, taking his warning seriously.

McCoy was in Engine 101's front passenger seat, the customary spot for the crew's commander. His driver was Andrea Kaiser, one of the few women in the fire department, known for her ready smiles and positive attitude. In the back were Jamie Lewis, short, stocky, and intense, with a shaved head, and Allen Becker, a Harley-riding farm boy some of the firefighters jokingly called "Jed."

Lewis, sitting right behind Kaiser, saw the jet first.

"Hey, look at that plane!" he shouted. "What's it doing?"

McCoy rapidly scanned the horizon and saw the plane off to his left. It was banking to the right and descending well short of where it should have been for a landing at the airport. His heart sank. McCoy had been on the scene in 1982 when an Air Florida 737 that had just taken off from National Airport hurtled into the Fourteenth Street Bridge, which spanned the Potomac from D.C. to Arlington. The plane had crushed several cars on the bridge, broken into pieces, and landed in the river. That horrible event—destruction everywhere, survivors clinging desperately to wreckage floating in the water—flashed through McCoy's mind as he watched another jetliner vanish beneath the trees, plunging toward the river.

In its last second of flight, American Airlines Flight 77 passed over a Citgo gas station just down the hill from the Navy Annex, a series of buildings that overlooked the Pentagon. Rooftops rose rapidly to meet the jet. To its left, the orderly white headstones of Arlington National Cemetery stood at attention. The plane crossed Washington Boulevard, a north-south expressway separating the cemetery from the western lawn of the Pentagon reservation, with both engines at full throttle. It was traveling more than 500 miles per hour and was less than 30 feet off the ground.

As it crossed the expressway, the plane's wings knocked over several light poles that lined the road,[1] like a ten-year-old toppling Tinkertoys with a slash of his hand. One light pole fell onto a taxicab, smashing the windshield, injuring the driver, and bringing the sedan to a skidding halt. Another landed on the Pentagon lawn, in several pieces.

In the small tower on the Pentagon helipad, air-traffic controller Sean Boger was contemplating his laundry when the image of an airplane began to materialize through the window, on the near horizon: first a nose, then a wing, then no doubt about it, a whole goddamn airplane. Boger froze.

At the adjacent fire station, Mark Skipper was standing in front of Foam 161, the helipad's fire truck, smoking a cigarette and talking with Alan Wallace about New York. Wallace noticed some movement out of the corner of his eye. Both men jerked their heads around in sudden disbelief. The plane was flying straight at them from the west, rapidly filling the sky like some kind of surreal 3-D video game. They couldn't hear it, but by the time they saw the plane it was only 150 yards away, a few feet off the ground—and about to fly right through them.

"Run!" Wallace screamed. He bolted to the right, sure that the plane was about to take his head off. Skipper took off in another direction.

On the lawn outside the Pentagon's western facade, construction equipment and a chain-link fence flanked the helipad—the ubiquitous hallmarks of a ten-year-long renovation program to upgrade the entire building. As Flight 77 flew nearly to ground level, its right wing sliced into a 750-kilowatt generator in one of the construction areas. The generator erupted into a fireball. The plane's right engine ripped a hole in a fence near the generator and yanked out some of the surrounding fence posts. The left wingtip dipped almost to ground level, while the left engine grazed the grass and struck a steam vault protruding from the ground. Both wings began to break apart, hurling metal fragments into the air.[2]

The instant its nose struck the outer wall of the Pentagon, Flight 77 ceased to be an airplane. The nose of the plane hit the facade just below the top of the first story, about 14 feet above the ground, going 530 miles per hour. A deafening boom shook the morning as a violent concussion tore through the air, jarring bystanders. The collision produced a force on the passengers far greater than that from any high-speed car crash. People became projectiles. Bone separated from flesh. Body parts flew as if fired from a cannon.

When it hit the building, the fuselage crumpled immediately. Its soft aluminum disintegrated as it encountered layers of limestone, brick, concrete, a blast-resistant geotextile lining, the steel-reinforced concrete columns that held up the building, and everything else in its path. In an instant the impact reduced Flight 77 to a million superheated fragments.[3]

Two-thirds of the right wing had been severed by the impact with the construction equipment, and what was left of it carved a gash in the building's second-story floor slab, before the concrete sheared it off the fuselage. At least one-third of the left wing had snapped off when the left engine hit the steam vault. The rest of it slid into the Pentagon beneath the second-story floor slab, penetrating no farther than a few feet.[4]

The airplane's tail, 45 feet tall, was still attached to the plane as it plowed into the Pentagon. But like the stubs of the wings, its soft aluminum was abruptly shredded when it collided with concrete.[5] The horizontal stabilizers, the smaller wings at the back of the plane, didn't make much of an impact either. They may have penetrated farther than the front wings, since they were being dragged into a hole, but they too broke apart quickly.[6]

The aircraft was carrying 5,300 gallons of fuel, in three fuel tanks—one in the fuselage and one in each wing. The wing tanks were spewing fuel before the plane even struck the building.[7] At the moment of impact, about 720 gallons of fuel ignited outside the building,[8] sending a fireball twice the height of the Pentagon up through the roof and out in every direction.[9] Fire instantly charred grass and trees lining the outer wall. Burning wreckage flew across the lawn. Chunks of metal rained down. A mushroom cloud followed the blast high into the sky.

As the belly of the plane penetrated the first floor, another 4,450 gallons of fuel exploded in a blast far more powerful than the initial fireball.[10] The massive concussion obliterated what was left of the airplane. Shock waves hurtled down hallways. Part of the second-story concrete floor slab buckled like a bent flap on a cardboard box.[11] Fuel spewed into every space that physics would allow. Much of it lit off instantaneously as fire raced through office space, air vents, and stairwells at nearly the speed of sound. Fire consumed all the air it could find, while the fuel coated everything in its path and burned intensely. More fuel mingled with the disintegrating fuselage as it plowed forward and became a roaring mass of fluid and debris, or escaped outward and upward, coating everything and everybody within thousands of square feet.

Where it didn't burn at first, the viscous liquid sat in wait. For the moment, the fuel was smothered by smoke or debris, and all available oxygen was being sucked into the initial explosion. But the opening of a door, or the collapse of a beam, or a fresh burst of air might create the right mix of oxygen and heat and set off a blazing booby trap.

Since the Pentagon had been designed to function as a records repository—and was able to support thousands of metal filing cabinets filled with paper—its columns, beams, girders, and floor slabs were built toward the high end of strength standards for the time.[12] That structure was now being tested to the extremes. Along the outer wall, 21-inch-wide concrete columns, each reinforced by steel rebar spiraling around its core, stood every ten feet, supporting all five stories. The impact of the plane knocked out eight of them completely, and severely damaged two others.[13] Yet somehow the upper floors held.

In the building's interior, the remnants of the airplane careened through a forest of columns, most of them 20 feet apart. The columns dismantled the fuselage, while the force of the fuselage simultaneously wiped out the columns. The 182,000-pound aircraft was morphing into an enormous mass of energy and matter, plowing forward like a horizontal volcanic eruption.[14] More than 600,000 bolts and rivets that had held the plane together, along with 60 miles of wire, became shards of searing shrapnel that fired off in every direction.[15]

The violence of the impact tore apart concrete, aluminum, steel, wood, and flesh. Walls collapsed. Ceilings crashed. Doors blew off their hinges. Elevator shafts twisted and bent. The airplane's metal deformed around the columns, the way the chassis of a car bends around a tree during a crash. Then the roaring mass swept the columns and other parts of the building forward in a superheated tidal wave of debris. The building slowed the momentum of the plane as the force of the plane carved a huge gouge into it.

On the first floor, the mass tore through a bank of administrative offices in the E Ring, which the Army occupied. Then it obliterated the Navy Command Center, which extended from the D Ring to the C Ring. The path of devastation next reached a Defense Intelligence Agency office on the C Ring. As the debris plowed through the building, it created a diagonal field of destruction that tapered like a dagger the farther it went. At the impact point, on the outer side of the E Ring, the force of the airplane had caused severe structural damage on a swath about 90 feet wide. By the time it got to the inner wall of the C Ring, the path of structural damage narrowed to a width of about 30 feet.[16] Destruction from the fires and explosions extended much farther.

At the beginning of its path, the flaming mass sliced through a newly renovated portion of the Pentagon, which had been rebuilt with modern fire protection. Where they weren't destroyed, automatic fire doors swung shut as fire alarms activated, to slow the spread of smoke and fire. But this rebuilt section had also been outfitted with light, modular office furniture, which the vortex threw around the way a tornado tosses farm equipment across a prairie. It gathered in flaming heaps wherever walls or columns caught it. Offices that remained intact lost all familiarity, their contents smashed and displaced.

In the renovated area, blast-resistant windows had replaced ordinary glass, an upgrade that dated back to the 1995 Oklahoma City bombing. These new windows were designed to withstand the force of an external explosion and to prevent deadly glass from shattering and spraying. They worked. In offices where they had been installed, the upgraded windows cracked and bulged but mostly remained intact. But the windows had been designed to protect against a blast from the outside—not from the inside, where this was happening.

Where they stayed bolted in place, the blast-resistant windows also prevented fire and explosive force from venting to the outside, trapping them in the building as they mushroomed. Worse, the impenetrable windows also sealed off escape routes.

As the tangle of airplane parts and office equipment plowed into an unrenovated portion of the building, the fire encountered fewer barriers to its territorial ambitions. Lead paint and asbestos, standard building materials 50 years earlier, released their toxic properties into the blaze. Desks, cabinets, tables, and chairs from the rebuilt part of the Pentagon abruptly bulldozed into the building's older regions.

The airplane deposited its contents throughout the Pentagon in horrible, grotesque ways, all of the destruction following the laws of physics. When the airplane had burst on impact, the blast threw many pieces backward onto the lawn by the helipad, some with such force that they landed on the other side of Washington Boulevard, nearly 1,000 feet away.[17] But thousands of pieces also carried forward and up, even over the roof of the building. In the Pentagon's inner courtyard, tiny pieces of aluminum drifted down like confetti. Other pieces landed on the roof, along with body parts from at least one of the victims.[18]

Inside the building, bodies and other contents of the plane landed in logical but macabre patterns. Material that had been in the front of the plane tended to come to rest first, since the nose section lost its structural integrity before the rest. The body of the hijacker who had been flying the plane ended up in the D Ring, about 100 feet from the impact point. The corpses of his four fellow hijackers landed nearby.[19]

Most of the bodies of the passengers, who had been huddled in the back of the plane, ended up farther into the Pentagon. As the mass traveled through the building, it began to resemble a shaped charge, a form of explosive that funnels its force into a small, directed area—like a beam of energy—in order to punch holes through armor or other strong material. With the front of the mass boring through the walls and columns of the Pentagon, the trailing portion of Flight 77 passed through the hole that was being created. The remnants of the plane flew everywhere, but body parts scattered in a gruesome pattern, becoming denser deeper along the path of the plane. People who had been working inside the Pentagon, in the path of the plane, were swept into the maelstrom. Their bodies became intertwined with those of the airplane passengers.

The Pentagon finally arrested the forward movement of Flight 77. The mass plowed through the C Ring and blew a round hole, about 12 feet in diameter, through the ring's inner wall. A pile of fiery wreckage flew through the hole and landed in A&E Drive, the utility road between the B and C Rings. But most of the wreckage piled up behind the C Ring wall.[20] By the time it came to a stop, the mass of debris that was once Flight 77 had traveled about 310 feet from the impact point, a distance twice the length of the 757. It had destroyed more than 30 columns that were holding up the building, and severely damaged 20 others. Decelerating from 530 miles per hour to a dead stop in that distance produced a gravitational force of 30 g's,[21] more than three times the force that fighter pilots are trained to withstand in the cockpit. From the moment of impact, the entire event had taken place in eight-tenths of a second.[22]

★ 4 ★

"BUMP IT TO A THIRD"

9:38 A.M.

The crash was over. But an enormous fire had only just begun.

In the Pentagon's Building Operations Command Center, the BOCC, Steve Carter and Kathy Greenwell had been watching New York on the bank of TVs when they felt the building quake. They heard a dull explosion. The TVs flickered and the signal degraded. Alarmed, both Carter and Greenwell looked at a computer monitor that tracked the fire alarm system. The number of fire alarms that had been activated was increasing rapidly, the way memory loads on a computer when you first boot it up. In an instant the computer showed that 335 alarms had gone off—including the one in the BOCC. That didn't make sense. Normally, fire spread slowly. If the computer was correct, 400,000 square feet of the Pentagon had erupted into flame all at once.

"I think we have a truck bomb!" Carter shouted. "Or some kind of explosion!" Focusing intensely on the computers, he saw that fire alarms were activating in Wedge 1, the first slice of the Pentagon to be renovated, from the building's southeast corner all the way to the innermost corridor, where the BOCC was. Yet it was strangely still in the BOCC. The fire alarm was wailing but the sprinklers hadn't come on. Carter and Greenwell both wondered the same thing: What do we do now?

"I'm gonna go see what's going on," Carter decided. He grabbed a radio and ran out the door, toward the intersection of Corridors 3 and 4, which formed the apex of Wedge 1. In one direction he saw a thick cloud of dust and smoke drifting down the hallway toward him. His first guess was that something had exploded way down across the E Ring—except that the E Ring was a football field's length away from where he was standing. It didn't seem possible that a dust cloud from that far away—especially if the explosion had been outside—could have blown that far into the building.

People were starting to flee down the escalators, into the courtyard—some orderly, some frantic. Carter saw a Navy officer he knew going the wrong way, back into the building. "Hey, can you please evacuate?" Carter hollered.

"You don't understand," the officer shouted back. "We've got people trapped!" Then he rushed off into the smoke.

Carter followed, walking hesitantly down Corridor 4, in the direction of the E Ring and the helipad on the outside. The long hallway was hazy but navigable. He pushed open a set of swinging doors that opened into A&E Drive, crossed the service road, and pushed open another set of doors. Suddenly there was nothing but acrid black smoke. The walls along the corridor were bulging. He could only stand the smoke for a couple of seconds, so he went back through the swinging doors into A&E Drive, coughing.

In A&E Drive, black smoke was rolling out of windows, but it was venting up into the open air, and at least he could see. Up ahead, in the brick wall to Carter's left, he could see a big hole that looked like a sinister dark cave, with smoke pouring out. Burning debris was everywhere, including a big smoking object that looked like the metal rim of a truck wheel. He stepped into a staircase to look around, but the concrete was so hot that it burned his feet, so he fled back out into A&E Drive.

Carter found two of his engineers, who had also come running out, and the three huddled and formed a quick plan. Before anything else, they needed to figure out which parts of the building's electrical systems were working, which needed to be repaired, and which needed to be shut off. That was critical. They needed power to run everything in the building—computer-monitoring systems, ventilation, air-conditioning—yet exposed electrical lines in the wrong places could electrocute victims trying to get out, and slow down firefighters.

In the C Ring, near where they were standing, there was an electrical room with four big transformers that each produced 13,800 volts of electricity. Ordinarily the room was locked. But the two steel doors that kept it shut had been blown off their hinges, and Carter and his engineers peered inside. They were shocked to see that the back wall had been knocked down and rescuers were starting to pass burned and injured people through the hole in the wall.

Usually, the room was dark and cool, with little sound except for a steady hum from the huge electrical feeders. Now it was hot and roiled with smoke. Shouts for help and cries of pain cut through the air. Water from dozens of shattered pipes pooled on the floor. Most alarming, all the electrical feeders were still running—and the smell of jet fuel was overwhelming. If a live wire fell into the water, or a spark hit the wrong place, everyone in the room risked being electrocuted or incinerated. Matt Morris, an electrician who worked for Carter, quickly waded through the water, reached up, and one by one pulled the big switches that shut down the flow of electricity.

Morris rushed off to check on other electrical issues. Carter fell in with a group of rescuers who were forming an impromptu human chain, passing victims forward to the door and A&E Drive. Carter's hands began to feel sticky from the blood, jet fuel, and other gunk.

The rescue effort was a slapdash effort, yet there was a surprising orderliness to it. Rescuers were dipping their shirts into the black water on the floor and holding the shirts to their faces, to help keep the smoke out of their lungs. After a minute or two, rescuers in the midst of the smoke would retreat to the back of the line, to breathe cleaner air. Others would move in and take their place. Out in A&E Drive, workers driving utility carts were screeching up to ferry victims off toward the inner courtyard, where they could then be transported out of the building on another side, where the coast was clear.

As important as it seemed to help the people suffering right in front of him, Carter had other things on his mind—if critical building systems failed, the whole Pentagon could shut down. He gathered a few of the key people he had found, and they headed out to find out what needed to be done to keep the building in some kind of working order.

Back in the BOCC, it had only stayed calm for a moment after the initial explosion shook the room. Then the phones began to light up, and Kathy Greenwell and a couple of assistants began fielding dozens of calls. Most were people calling to say that an alarm was going off in their office and asking what they should do. Remarkably, there was still a handful of routine calls coming in, from people who had no idea that the building they worked in had just endured some kind of explosion. One person called to complain about a light fixture that wasn't working. Another woman called to report that "the colonel in my office wants the carpets shampooed."

Greenwell, nervous and annoyed, tried her best to be polite. "It's on my list of things to do," she replied, "but right now we're fighting a fire."

Greenwell hadn't heard from her boss, Steve Carter, since he'd left to investigate the incident. Suddenly the footage from New York on the bank of TV screens was replaced by something even scarier: footage of her building, the Pentagon, engulfed in flames. She could see fire leaping from the windows on the E Ring, about 400 feet from where she was sitting.

Kathy Greenwell was the perfect counterweight to Steve Carter.

While her boss was talkative and colorful, she was soft-spoken and reserved. In contrast to Carter's loud ties, Greenwell favored plain pantsuits and flat shoes. There was bonhomie between the two that made them a tight team. And now Greenwell nervously wondered where her boss was—and whether she should leave.

But the calls kept her rooted to her chair. People started to phone the BOCC saying they could see people trapped, amidst smoke and flames, through the windows of adjacent offices. They were trying to bash the windows out but couldn't budge the new, blast-resistant glass. What should they do? Greenwell struggled to keep her breath. She stifled tears. Then with shaking hands she took down the room numbers where people were trapped and tried frantically to convey the information to the Defense Protective Service, the Pentagon's police force.

The Pentagon had once had its own fire brigade, but that was abandoned long ago in favor of simply utilizing the local fire department. The Pentagon was in Arlington County, which the Defense Department now relied on for fire service. The specially equipped crash trucks at National Airport, less than two miles away, were on call in case there was a helicopter accident or some other event involving fuel or hazardous materials. And the federal firefighting crews at Fort Myer, just up the hill from the Pentagon, provided coverage at the helipad whenever it was in operation.

The system was meant to provide deep, overlapping coverage in the event of a major fire. But at the helipad, for the moment, it was solely in the hands of the three-man crew of Foam 161. Though Alan Wallace had had a front-row seat as Flight 77 approached the Pentagon, he hadn't seen the plane strike the building; instead, he had turned and run the opposite direction. But he had sure heard and felt the impact. An instant after he started to run, there was a noise like a gigantic crunch. It was terrifying. A blast of heat pulsed against his back, and he felt a pressure wave sweep over him. He was sure he was on fire, and fell to the ground to roll and smother the flames.

When Wallace finally looked up, everything around him was burning. The lawn suddenly looked like a flaming trash dump. The heat was unbearable. Wallace crawled under a van parked next to the control tower for a few seconds, thinking it would protect him. But it was still too hot, and he rolled out to get farther away from the fire.

As he pulled himself up, he saw his colleague Mark Skipper out on the lawn, looking back at the Pentagon, and he ran over to his partner. When Skipper had first seen the plane, he dove under the fire truck, Foam 161, then a few seconds later ran onto the lawn. Both he and Wallace had burns on their necks and arms, and a few other injuries, although they seemed minor compared to what they could have been. Besides, there was a huge fire right in front of them. "Get your gear on!" Wallace ordered. "We've got a lot of work to do."

They ran back to Foam 161, the focal point of their little operation, sidestepping burning debris during the 30-yard dash. The rear half of the truck was engulfed in flames. So was everything around it. Still, Wallace's instinct was to get in the truck and start it up. To his amazement, the engine turned over. He thought that if he could reposition the truck a little farther from the building, he'd be able to put water and firefighting foam from the truck into the burning hole in the Pentagon. But when he pushed the accelerator, nothing happened—except that the flames on the back of the truck got bigger. Skipper ran to the front of the truck, waving his arms and yelling for Wallace to shut it off. Finally he did.

After Wallace climbed out of Foam 161, he saw Dennis Young, the other firefighter on the crew, spraying a fire extinguisher onto the flames in the back of the truck. Young seemed to be limping, but was otherwise okay. Good. Skipper was pulling EMS gear and other equipment out of the truck, to save it from getting burned up.

The firefighters still weren't wearing their protective equipment—their "turnout gear." Wallace ran into the station to put on his coat, boots, pants, and helmet. But the doors of the station had been open at the time of impact, and the interior was filled with small jagged pieces of the aircraft aluminum and other debris, which stuck out of the wall like little spears. When Wallace found his gear, his whole uniform was covered with debris; one of his elastic suspenders was even on fire. He patted it out. His firefighting boots were filled with fragments of metal and rock.

Wallace was about to turn the boots upside down to dump out the debris when he heard somebody shout, "We need help here!" He rushed back out to the helipad as rescuers started to assemble near the Pentagon's first-floor windows. The scene was surreal. There were a lot of women, terrified and screaming, their burning clothes hanging in tatters. Some had burned skin. They were missing shoes. Smoke and fumes made it hard to breathe. All around, the ground itself seemed to be burning. It was so hot, Wallace was convinced several times that his pants were on fire. There was fire in the sky too. Small burning objects kept drifting down. Wallace looked up and realized that a magnolia tree had caught fire and the plush leaves were burning and dropping to the ground. Everywhere he looked there was searing, unquenchable fire.

The crowd of people on the lawn was growing rapidly. Amidst the throng, Sean Boger, the air-traffic controller at the helipad, and his assistant Jackie Kidd, looked back at the demolition they had just escaped. From the small tower, Boger had watched the plane smash into the building, less than 100 feet away. The force of the impact shattered the windows in the tower and sent ceiling tiles cascading onto his head. Boger had dived to the floor, then leapt back up and bounded down three flights of stairs, jumping over railings and light fixtures. Kidd was in the latrine when the plane hit and she didn't know what had happened. Boger found her at the bottom of the tower, shaking, and the two raced away from the impact point. When they turned around for the first time, the Pentagon was consumed with fire. Next to the control tower, the cars they had each driven to work that morning were wrecked and consumed by flames.[1]

Arlington's Station 5 was the firehouse closest to the Pentagon, less than a mile from the building. The fire crews based there got to know the Pentagon pretty well, since it dwarfed other buildings in the area and contained so much activity. During the day, in fact, the Pentagon was the equivalent of a small city, with 25,000 occupants, a retail complex, two huge cafeterias, several fast-food joints, a bus depot, and its own subway entrance. There were lots of false alarms at the Pentagon, but also plenty of real emergencies. Firefighters typically responded to several medical calls each week, and there were occasional small fires in the building's various kitchens, laundry facilities, and heating and refrigeration plants.

As Flight 77 had been accelerating toward the Pentagon, the crew of Truck 105—Derek Spector, Brian Roache, and Ron Christman—had been jumping into their turnout gear, about to race out to the second apartment fire. The fire station's electric garage doors had just started to retract when all three firefighters heard an earth-shaking thud. The garage door, about halfway up, rattled violently, as if hurricane-force winds were beating against it. Spector felt a whoosh of air, as though the concussive force of a bomb had washed over him.

"What the fuck was that?" he shouted.

"That was a fucking explosion!" Roache answered.

"Well, I don't think we're going to that apartment fire," Spector said. A basic rule of firefighting was that you never passed one fire to get to another. Whatever had just erupted out there was very big. And it was in their backyard.

All three firefighters felt their adrenaline soar. They were not headed out to a routine call anymore. Within seconds they were on the truck, Roache in the driver's seat, Spector next to him, in command, and Christman way back in the tiller cab, ready to steer the rear wheels around corners.

Spector flipped a button that activated the radio and all the electrical systems. Immediately they heard excited chatter on the radio.

"We got a plane down!" a voice crackled. Spector recognized the voice right away—it was Steve McCoy, on Arlington's Engine 101. "We got a plane down!" he repeated. "Looks like in the Crystal City area. By the Fourteenth Street Bridge . . . We saw it go down. Engine 101 saw it go down!"[2]

Other voices began to add fragments of information. Somebody said a plane had crashed near the Pentagon heliport. Others saw smoke but weren't sure where it was coming from. "You need to be careful," the Arlington dispatcher said to everyone listening on the net. "This is a possible terrorist attack. Plane into the building."

Roache fired up the truck and roared out of the station with sirens blaring. The Pentagon was just a few blocks away, and at the first intersection they hit they could see the Pentagon's massive roofline, smoke streaming out of it. They couldn't tell much else, but back in the tiller cab, Ron Christman knew something ominous was unfolding. He had a feeling this would be something they'd be talking about for a long time.

"Truck 105 to Arlington!" Spector had begun shouting into the radio, trying to reach the dispatcher. "Truck 105 to Arlington!" Spector was one of the first firefighters to see actual evidence of a crash at the Pentagon, and he had to get that information into the system. But the emergency response network was already clogged with calls and he couldn't get through. "Truck 105 to Arlington!" he continued. "I've got smoke coming out of the Pentagon! Priority message!"

He raised his call to the highest alert level: "Emergency message! Emergency message!" he hollered. Even that didn't work. "God damn it!" he screamed, taking his thumb off the transmit button. "I can't fucking get through!"

As Roache pressed the accelerator, the Pentagon was quickly coming into fuller view. There was so much smoke in the sky now that it was hard to notice anything else. Finally they pulled into the Pentagon's huge south parking lot. People were everywhere. Truck 105 had run dozens of calls at the Pentagon, and most were false alarms. When people were forced to evacuate it was usually a halfhearted effort, with office workers sauntering out of the building, half of them annoyed about losing a few minutes of work time. This was totally different. Hundreds of people—no, thousands—were racing out of the Pentagon as if their lives depended on it. Many ran out, turned around, saw the smoke and ran even harder. "Be careful!" Spector urged, alarmed by the sight of so many people. "Don't hit anybody!"

They came to one of the Pentagon's five corners. Just around it they could glimpse some debris scattered across the helipad. To get there, Roache pulled out to Washington Boulevard, and they began to circle the Pentagon, about 500 feet to their right. Finally they started to grasp what had happened. On the grassy field surrounding the Pentagon helipad, panicking people were stampeding out of the building. Some staggered, others ran. A few fled with their clothes still on fire, trailing smoke.

On the helipad, a fire truck was burning. The entire lawn surrounding it looked like a garbage dump. Beyond the helipad, there was a huge black gash in the side of the Pentagon. The smoke spewing from numerous places was dark and black—typical of a fuel fire.

They passed a spot near a guardrail where medics seemed to be treating a couple of victims. Spector only managed a glance, but he could tell they were badly burned and not likely to survive.

All the while, he had been trying to get through on the radio. After about a dozen tries, he finally did.

"Truck 105 to Arlington!" he shouted. "I'm at the Pentagon. I've got heavy black smoke showing. Start me a second and third alarm!"

After so many failed tries at the radio, Spector was frustrated and overexcited, and it showed in his raised voice. "One-oh-one to 105," a calm, firm voice said on the radio. It was McCoy. "You need to settle down and tell us where you're going."

Spector took a breath and focused. The first officer to arrive at a fire was always responsible for providing a "size-up" of the situation, to let others know what was going on and tell them where to go. Spector was the first firefighter to call in a size-up of the Pentagon. The accuracy of his report could save—or cost—lives.

He started over. "One-oh-five is on the scene," he said. "I have a plane down at the heliport at the Pentagon." He was slower and more deliberate now—but still sure that this was a big, serious fire. "I've got heavy black smoke showing," he reported, leaving no doubt that he knew what he was looking at. "Give me a second alarm." After another glance at the smoke, he added, "Bump it to a third."

Roache, eyes on the road, was able to steal just a glimpse of the fire. "Shit," he said to himself, "that's the fucking Pentagon!"

They came to an access road that led toward the building, manned by a security guard who eagerly raised the gate and waved them through. They drove to within 20 feet of the building, until Spector ordered, "Park here. Let's go!"

Spector jumped off the truck and did his best to stay calm. They could see straight into the building through the gaping hole near the helipad. The flames inside were thick. He grabbed his portable radio and called in an update.

"We're at the heliport," he reported. "I have a plane into the building. Five stories. Give me a third alarm."

Spector saw a torn piece of shiny aluminum with a big red C on it, and recognized the lettering. It sank in: An American Airlines jet had plowed into the Pentagon, just like the two planes that had hit the towers in New York. The C was part of the word "American," which had been painted on the plane's fuselage. An old training session flashed through his mind. After a DC-10 crash-landed in Sioux City, Iowa, in 1989, tearing the fuselage apart, some of the 110 victims who died were found still strapped into their seats. Spector quickly scanned the debris field, looking for airplane seats. He didn't see any.

There weren't as many people on the lawn as they had seen streaming out of the building near South Parking, but those they did see were in bad shape. Many were limping or being helped along by colleagues. Six or seven injured people had gathered along a guardrail that was nearby, not sure where to go. Spector recalled the area along Washington Boulevard where he had seen the burn victims, and figured medics were setting up a triage area down there. He found an Army officer who seemed okay, and pointed to the other end of the lawn. "You've got to get them down there!" he shouted. A burly Marine sergeant heard the order, picked up two people, tucked them under his arms like a couple of footballs, and started walking across the field with them. The Army officer started herding the other victims in the same direction.

Spector and Christman had been fully dressed when they left the station. All they needed to do was slide air packs onto their backs and grab whatever tools they needed to bring with them into the fire. Roache, the driver, still had to put on some of his gear. It was difficult to drive wearing the thick firefighting suit, and he leaped from the truck and ran to a side compartment, pulling on his pants, coat, and helmet, a top-of-the-line Cairns leather model, patterned after the classic look of the FDNY, which he had paid for himself. As excited as he was, it was important not to miss a single snap or zipper, since any superheated air that got inside could burn him instantly. Temperatures in an ordinary house fire could easily reach 500 degrees. The jet fuel in the fire they were facing now would probably be much hotter.

Roache had been to hundreds of fires, some pretty big. Yet when he came around the back of the truck to join his colleagues and saw wreckage spread before him, his head was spinning. He had never felt this sensation before. What do we do now? he wondered, spellbound by the chaos. Then he took a few steps. The movement broke his reverie. Well, we do what we normally do, he reassured himself. We fight the fire.

★ 5 ★

JUST LIKE VIETNAM

9:40 A.M.

Fire crews from all over the Washington region were converging on the Pentagon.

Word of a plane crash immediately energized Capt. Mike Defina, the acting battalion chief at Reagan National Airport. The airport had specialized firefighting vehicles armed with foam for suppressing the kind of intense fires that occurred when airplanes crashed and the aviation fuel ignited. The fire crews at National were on call to respond to any aviation accident in the region, whether it was on the airport grounds or elsewhere.

After getting word about the Pentagon, Defina made sure the airport was closed, then jumped into his battalion chief's van. He arrived at the Pentagon seconds behind Derek Spector's unit, Truck 105, and navigated through the same swarms of rattled and injured people fleeing the burning building. Defina looked for a command post and didn't find one, so he made his way to the helipad, where there were still only two fire trucks. And one of them was on fire.

As Defina sized up the situation, his first question was, "What might get us into trouble here?" A mass evacuation was under way. One airplane had hit the building, and there might be another. He reminded himself to stay focused on the big picture and be prepared for the unexpected.

Up at Fort Myer, on the hill overlooking the Pentagon, two dozen federal firefighters were scrambling madly to get to the fire. Most of them had been taking a class on aviation firefighting in the post's firehouse when they heard a muffled explosion. A few moments later Alan Wallace called their dispatch center to report the crash, and the transmission was piped throughout the station. An order never even went out: Chairs went flying and boots thudded on the floor as firefighters raced for their vehicles.

Three Fort Myer trucks raced to the Pentagon, where the firefighters were stunned to see the damage—as well as Foam 161 in flames. Some of them began stretching hose lines from one of the trucks, to spray water on Foam 161. Dousing that fire wasn't the most urgent priority, but it would have been unbearable to work with one of their own trucks burning right beside them.

The whole apparatus of the Arlington County Fire Department—along with crews from Alexandria, Fairfax County, and other municipalities that usually lent support in a big fire—was mobilizing rapidly. Battalion chief Bob Cornwell, in charge of all the fire crews in the southern half of Arlington County, was at Station 1, less than two miles from the Pentagon, when he heard Steve McCoy on the radio, saying a plane had gone down near Crystal City. Cornwell raced to his "command buggy," a Chevy Suburban, and headed east on Columbia Pike.

He could see a wall of black smoke on the horizon. It didn't look good. If a plane had crashed into Crystal City—well, that was one of the worst places in the whole D.C. area for a plane to go down. Highrise apartments and office buildings were stacked one after the other, and pedestrian and road traffic was dense. A lot of destruction could take place in a relatively small area.

But when Cornwell topped the hill near the Navy Annex, he saw immediately that it was the Pentagon that had been hit. That was even more overwhelming. *The Pentagon.* Cornwell had been a combat infantryman in Vietnam in 1967 and 1968, and during his years as an Arlington firefighter he became known for his toughness and tactical skill. The barrel-chested, six-two veteran rarely used an air pack in a fire, and colleagues joked that he had an "oxygen-optional" switch on his chest that allowed him to go into smoke-filled buildings without having to breathe.

Cornwell had generated a great deal of quiet concern that year, when he was diagnosed with non-Hodgkin's lymphoma. Five months earlier he underwent surgery to remove a tumor, spending 11 days in the hospital. He returned to work after a month but still had to undergo four rounds of chemotherapy treatments, which he scheduled around his shifts so he wouldn't have to miss work. When his wavy salt-and-pepper hair fell out, about 40 Arlington firefighters shaved their heads in solidarity. So did his three young sons. His final chemo treatment had been three weeks earlier, and his head remained nearly bald, with white peach fuzz just beginning to sprout.

Cornwell parked his Suburban about 300 feet from the southwest corner of the Pentagon, with a good view of the helipad and the whole lawn. He talked to Defina on the radio, and they agreed that Reagan National's specially equipped fire vehicles, designed to deal with airplane crashes, would be essential to the firefight. Two foam units, able to extinguish aviation fuel fires, were on the way, Defina reported, along with a mass casualty unit designed to handle up to 150 injured victims.[1]

Nearby, Cornwell saw Arlington Capt. Eddie Blunt, who was in charge of emergency medical services for Cornwell's battalion. When Blunt had pulled his own command SUV up on the lawn, the first thing he saw was smoldering victims staggering across the lawn, their clothes still on fire. One badly burned man, holding out his arms, had lost both of his hands. Medical personnel and other volunteers from the Pentagon were trying to help, but it was Blunt's job to establish a formal medical response command. He had started setting up a triage area along the guardrail on Washington Boulevard, overlooking the flaming hole in the Pentagon, and he requested additional medical units and a bus to transport victims with less-serious injuries to hospitals.

Blunt and Joe Lightfoot, an Arlington firefighter who had driven himself to the Pentagon, came running up to meet Cornwell. As the first senior fire officer from Arlington to arrive, Cornwell would be the incident commander, in charge of the operation. But he didn't have a clear view of the scene at the edge of the building. He and Lightfoot ran around a construction fence that was blocking their view and were suddenly staring at bedlam. Firefighters who had just arrived were running back and forth, shouting to each other. A few uniformed military personnel darted past with automatic weapons. Stretcher bearers were carrying wounded victims. A helicopter buzzed overhead. After taking in the scene for a couple of seconds, Cornwell turned to Lightfoot with a grave expression on his face. "This is just like Vietnam," he said. Then he raced back to the Suburban and opened it up, preparing to direct the operation.

Cornwell knew immediately they were facing a huge, challenging fire. It would be crucial to gain control right off the bat. In Vietnam he had learned that if the leader gives the impression that things are not going well, the troops will rapidly lose faith in the mission. Like an old firefighter told him once, if you're scared, stand next to the fender when you get out of your vehicle, so you have something to lean on for support.

Cornwell quickly started pulling gear out of the command buggy and setting up the command post in the back of the SUV. "Here you go, Joey!" he shouted to Lightfoot, tossing him a blue Magic Marker. That simple act made the good-natured young fireman Cornwell's aide. He'd be responsible for handling radio communications, logging and assigning fire crews as they arrived, and tracking them as they went in and out of the building—one of the most important jobs at a fire.

The command post came to life with reassuring familiarity. Cornwell got on the radio and for the moment overruled Derek Spector's call for a third alarm. "Go ahead and start a second," he told the ECC dispatcher, with a voice as calm as if he were ordering a soda refill, "but hold up on a third. I'll let you know something in a minute." Then he asked for help coordinating with the Pentagon police force. "Check with Pentagon security," he ordered. "I'd like them to meet me at my van at the ramp to Washington Boulevard, close to the heliport."

Nobody at the command post speculated about whether the blaze had come from a plane crash or what kind of plane it might have been—just getting organized for the massive fire in front of them was challenge enough. Cornwell wanted to know if any firefighters had been in the building and could report what they saw there. None had been in yet, but fire crews were starting to arrive in droves. Cornwell began sending them into various parts of the building, to check for victims and do reconnaissance, Lightfoot writing down the names on a marker board as fast as he could. The command post was starting to swell with people, as everybody looking for guidance came running over. It was getting hard for Cornwell to do his job.

Jim Schwartz, Arlington's assistant chief for operations, arrived right behind Cornwell. Before Flight 77 had even hit the Pentagon, he was having an extremely busy day. Once it became apparent what was happening in New York, the phones at Arlington County's communications center lit up with people wanting to know what they should do. The building managers at the USA Today towers had called, wanting to know if they should evacuate, fearful their complex could be a target. As the operations chief, Schwartz was the man to initially handle requests, make the decisions, or bump them up to Ed Plaugher, chief of the department.

When Schwartz heard Steve McCoy on the radio, describing a plane going down, he dashed out of his office. In his own command vehicle, he raced toward the area where McCoy had described the plane going down. Bright and shrewd, Schwartz had earned a reputation as a skilled and aggressive line firefighter and rose quickly in the department. Under him and Plaugher, the Arlington County Fire Department was evolving from a small-town outfit into a sophisticated, urban operation trained for terrorism, riots, building collapses, and chemical or biological incidents. Schwartz had overseen joint exercises with the Defense Department, the FBI, and neighboring fire departments well-schooled in terrorism, especially after the Oklahoma City bombing. Plus, his wife worked for the CIA and offered her own worldly perspective on the threats fire and police officers were likely to face. It didn't take much imagination for him to grasp that a massive terrorist attack was under way.

When Schwartz arrived, he spotted his battalion chief right away—Cornwell was the guy towering over a growing swarm of firefighters. Schwartz rarely took over command from one of his chiefs, since it was usually best to leave a fire operation in the hands of a commander who was out in the field doing the job every day. And Cornwell was possibly the best fire commander in the department. But this fire was bigger than anything either of them had ever faced. Schwartz knew he was going to need his best fire officers right at the fire, sizing up the challenge, devising tactics, and making sure all the crews stayed safe.

"Bobby, I'm taking command," he told the strapping battalion chief. There are two priorities in the first stage of a fire: searching for victims and getting them out, and then knocking down the fire. Cornwell had already put the search-and-rescue mission into motion, and a few fire crews were preparing to get water flowing onto the fire and drag hoses into the building. But Schwartz needed a more specific plan. Most of all, he needed to know what he was dealing with. How deep was the fire? How wide? How many floors? Were victims trapped, or had most of them gotten out?

"Listen, Bobby," Schwartz said to Cornwell. "Do you feel you can take a group in there and get me a synopsis? Take some companies and check it out?" Cornwell was precisely the guy he wanted at his right hand. He had been in the department for 30 years and knew the Pentagon better than anybody on the job. But Schwartz was also asking Cornwell a question, rather than giving him an order. Everybody knew Cornwell had just finished chemotherapy treatments, and Schwartz wanted to give him an out if he felt he wasn't up to the challenge. And Cornwell knew it.

"Sure thing, Chief," he answered promptly. He started gathering up a few crews for a reconnaissance mission into the building.

On Interstate 66, the highway that led from western Virginia into Washington, D.C., a Ford Crown Victoria was tearing down the shoulder as if trying to set a land-speed record. Arlington County Fire Chief Ed Plaugher had been at a credit union in Fairfax County that morning, about 20 miles west of the Pentagon, arranging a loan for a motor home. His wife had been ill with lupus and she'd been urging Plaugher to take more time off. The motor home was the way they were going to spend more time together. In the credit union he found out about the plane crash in New York, then heard that something had happened at the Pentagon. *Terrorism,* he thought. "I gotta go," he declared. He ran to his car and strapped a flashing light to the dash of the Crown Vic. Before long he was violating every rule for safe driving he had lectured his own officers about.

★ **6** ★

"THIS IS GONNA SUCK"

9:40 A.M.

An army of firefighters was massing outside the Pentagon. But inside, burned, hacking victims still had to find their own way to safety.

In the remnants of Room 1D516, Army Maj. Dave King was clawing through piles of smoking wreckage, searching in the sudden darkness for coworkers who had vanished in a blast of flame and noise. King had been standing behind his desk, near a couple of heavy safes, when suddenly he was asking himself, Why is my head ringing? And where did these flames come from? Then he smelled the jet fuel and knew: They had been hit by a plane too.

King raced over to the desk where the new sergeant, Maudlyn White, had been sitting moments before. A thick tangle of wires and cables had spilled out of the ceiling, enveloping the desk like jungle vines. White was nowhere to be found.

King ran back to the office where his boss, Lt. Col. Jerry Dickerson, had been working, and couldn't find him either. He ran out into the hallway, then back toward his own desk, which had been somewhat protected by the safes and by a building column that was now fully exposed. After a moment he realized that he was burned, and that his polyester Army pants were melting. Drop and roll, he thought—but the floor was on fire. A water cooler was nearby, still standing. King thought of dumping it onto his pants—then remembered that water only makes a fuel fire spatter and burn more.

On his desk, he saw pictures of his three boys: one, three, and four. The frames were still sitting upright. King had been looking for his comrades, but when he saw the faces of his boys, he told himself he had to get out of there. For them.

He climbed through a hole in the wall, behind his desk, toward the E Ring. On the other side of the hole it looked like a Mad Max movie. There were no walls anymore, just columns. Ten-foot-high piles of rubble were everywhere. It was black and smoky. He heard crackling and popping. Other people started slipping through the hole, behind him. Some looked terrified, like they were on the verge of panic.

King saw daylight. "Come to my voice! Come to my voice!" someone shouted. He and the people around him staggered toward the light and the sound, helping each other navigate the shattered landscape.

One level up, in the Army personnel division's conference room, Col. Phil McNair had gone from chairing an orderly meeting to directing a frantic escape effort. Just after Lt. Col. Marilyn Wills glanced at her watch and noticed that the meeting was running late, there was a tremendous explosion. Fire poured into the room through the ceiling, followed by thick black smoke. The lights went out. In an instant it became intensely hot.

The group jumped from the table and ran to the main door. It wouldn't open. One woman screamed until an Army officer grabbed her and insisted, "I've got you! I've got you!"

A second door worked, and the group began to crawl through it, single file. McNair, unaware of the attacks in New York, figured that a bomb had gone off outside the building, and that once they got out of the conference room, into the bank of cubicles on the other side, they'd be in the clear.

They weren't. It was just as hot and smoky in Dilbertsville, and by now the smoke was banking down nearly to the floor. It was hard to breathe. "Get below the smoke!" somebody yelled, and everyone dropped to their knees. Down by the floor there were still about two feet of breathable air. McNair remembered being taught as a kid to crawl during a fire, since smoke rises. And now he could see—it was true.

Conditions were rapidly getting worse. The whole area was dark. It was hard to see anything while crawling on the floor. The air smelled like a toxic mix of melting plastic, burnt wiring, and fuel, and it seared McNair's throat.

Most of the people who worked in the new space had just moved in and were still unfamiliar with the layout. In the dark, they were unsure where to go. The group from the conference room, still crawling, scattered in several directions. Some people followed their own instincts about the best way out. Others, feeling more disoriented, followed those who seemed to know where they were going. Two of the officers from McNair's meeting, Stephen Long and Dennis Johnson, separated from the group and seemed to head off in another direction. McNair's first thought was to head for the main hallway, the E Ring, which was close to the outside of the building and safety. But when he got to the doorway he was aiming for, fire was licking through underneath, and it was hotter than where he had come from. "We've got to go the other direction!" he shouted to the few others behind him.

They groped, on their knees, toward the opposite end of the cubicle farm, which had suddenly become a huge, disorienting maze. Desks, chairs, copiers, and office equipment were in the way at every turn. Doorways that people had taken for granted were now gone. In McNair's group, everyone held tight to whoever was ahead of them. They crawled in confusion, one person or another leading the others toward an exit that turned out to be a dead end or a door that was fused shut. Over the blare of fire alarms they tried to yell encouraging words to each other and to other groups they could hear struggling nearby. Voices, lathered in smoke, became raspy and began to crack.

Bits of the ceiling started to rain down, mixed with droplets of melting plastic. Water from the sprinklers soaked them and formed dirty puddles on the carpet. McNair splashed some of the water on his face and snorted some into his nose, trying to wash smoke out of his lungs. He showed others how to do it. Lieutenant Colonel Wills was crawling with McNair, and she produced a piece of cloth that they soaked in water and took turns breathing through. It helped a little, but McNair was starting to think they were going to succumb to the smoke before they ever found their way out.

He heard somebody yell something about a window. He couldn't see who it was, but the group moved toward the voice. Light began to penetrate the smoke, and a partially blown-out window came into focus. It gave a dim glow through the haze that brightened as they drew closer, and fresh air seeping through the broken glass thinned the smoke. A soldier was perched on the windowsill, shouting back into the smoke-filled room. McNair recognized one of the enlisted men from his division. The group clambered toward the window and one by one stuck their heads through the bent opening, sucking in as much air as their lungs could ingest.

Nearby, Craig Powell, the Navy SEAL, had quickly reverted to commando training. When the explosion occurred and the building rumbled, about half a dozen people in Powell's office had hit the floor, but Powell remained standing. If you drop in an ambush, Powell knew, you get killed. The only chance of escaping is to run through it. There was no reason to go to ground. You'd only have to get up again to move.

The walls in Powell's fifth-floor Navy office had buckled but held. The ceiling started to collapse, though. Objects fell off shelves and tables. The TV stopped working and the lights flickered. It looked like the aftermath of an earthquake.

Powell's office mates ran out. He quickly scanned the room, making sure no classified material had been left out, then darted out into the C Ring, about midway between the outer wall of the Pentagon and the inner courtyard. To his left a wall of fire raged. On his right a pneumatic fire door had just closed. Powell rushed up to it, worried that it would seal shut, the way watertight doors on ships do when a hull begins to flood. But the door gave way and he plowed through it.

On the other side it was if he'd stepped into a high school fire drill. People walked calmly toward the exits, apparently unaware of the inferno Powell had just turned his back on. He joined the orderly flow. As they began to descend the stairs that led down four flights to ground level, he saw Marines standing at the entrance to each hallway, helping guide people out, as if sentry duty were instinctive.

Most people exited into the center courtyard. Powell had second thoughts. Obviously, a sophisticated terrorist attack was under way. He knew that two planes, so far, had hit New York. The last place he wanted to be was in the courtyard, out in the open.

Plus, there were obviously people trapped in the inferno, desperate for help. On the first floor, Powell headed back into the building, down Corridor 4, toward the E Ring. A woman stumbled out of a bathroom toward him. Blood trickled from her head.

"Is anyone else in there?" he asked her.

Incoherent, she couldn't answer. Powell ushered her toward the courtyard, found somebody else to hand her off to, then went back to where he'd found her.

A young female Navy officer in a black sweater was staggering down one of the hallways—the wrong way, toward the fire. "They're still in there," she muttered. "They're still in there . . ." Powell rushed up to her. She seemed stunned but not hurt. He hustled her out toward the courtyard, then returned to the hallway she had been heading down, to see if he could reach anybody who was trapped. He encountered smoke that was gray at first, then black, and then he hit fire. He could smell fuel burning. There was no way to get through. Well, that doesn't work, he decided.

He tried to figure out if there was a back way into the same suite of offices, but he had only been in the Pentagon for three days, and hadn't yet mastered the intricacies of the peculiar building and its start-and-stop hallways, so he ran into A&E Drive.

It was an apocalyptic scene. About 40 feet away, burning wreckage was plowed up against the brick wall to his right. One big piece looked like the hub of a wheel. Guessing it was a plane that had smashed through the building, Powell figured the piece was part of the landing gear. It had a pink hue. Was the sun glinting off of it? Or was it blood? He couldn't tell.

To his left the blast had blown three big smoking holes in the wall, each as big as the mouth of a cave. Powell guessed that the trapped people the female officer had been trying to reach were inside those holes. He looked up. Above one of the holes, one flight up, he could see two faces sticking through a crevice where a window had been pried loose from the frame. Lips puckered, trying to coax in as much air as possible.

In the service road, half a dozen people were trying to build a scaffold that could reach the people trapped behind the window. They weren't getting very far—there was hardly anything in the alleyway to build a scaffold with. Somebody was trying to push a trash bin toward the window, but it was too heavy and too far away. "Look," Powell said to them, his authoritative voice—and towering stature—quickly getting their attention. "By the time you build a scaffold, these guys are gonna be toast."

He gathered several people around. "Form a net," he instructed them. "Like you see rescuers do." Five or six others gathered around and extended their arms. Above, a couple of people had been banging on the window with hands and feet, working to pry it all the way off so people could jump out and escape the fire. Finally, they created a big enough opening.

"Jump!" Powell shouted up at them. "We'll catch you as you come out!"

A petite woman appeared at the window and came down like she was jumping off a diving board into a swimming pool, arms and legs together. The moment she jumped, however, the human net disintegrated. Some of the people jumped back—human instinct, Powell knew. Unless you were trained for it, it was extremely difficult to overcome bodily instincts and stand in the path of a heavy object descending upon you. Others just didn't seem to know what to do. The woman ended up coming straight down at Powell, who caught her by the hips and brought her to the ground, roughly but safely.

A second woman appeared in the window. "Come on!" Powell shouted, even though he was now a one-man net. As she climbed out, he could see that she was very large. "Oh, man," he said, preparing himself. "This is gonna suck."

Rescuers rushed the injured people from A&E Drive into the Pentagon's center courtyard, which usually was the equivalent of a city park—a bucolic respite in the midst of a bustling urban center. The five-acre courtyard was literally surrounded by the vital business of America's national security, yet it was lined with benches and wooden Adirondack chairs where people smoked and chatted and catnapped. The grass was as groomed as a country club fairway. Towering pine trees provided a kind of tranquility that many Pentagon employees never found inside the building.

Capt. Jennifer Glidewell, an Army nurse, was adjusting to a different scene in the courtyard than she was used to. Glidewell was chief nurse at the acute-care section of the DiLorenzo clinic, a health-care facility that served members of the military and was situated on the eastern side of the Pentagon. Glidewell and other staffers at the clinic had been watching the news from New York in their offices, on the side of the building opposite the heliport, when a man ran through the clinic screaming, "Get out! Everybody get out!" It was a bizarre moment at the usually staid clinic, and Glidewell wondered if he was for real. But he seemed dead serious, and so supervisors started evacuating people.

Glidewell and one of the medics who worked for her, Sgt. Matthew Rosenberg, walked out of the clinic into a hallway more than 1,000 feet from the spot where Flight 77 had bashed into the Pentagon. They hadn't heard any explosion, noise, or shudder, and Glidewell and Rosenberg thought the evacuation was a fire drill.

They had joined a flow of people walking toward the nearest exit, down Corridor 8, which emptied into North Parking, when somebody said that there was a patient in the center courtyard. As medical responders, patients were their business, so Glidewell said, "Let's go and see what's happening in the center court."

They turned around and rushed toward the middle of the Pentagon, pushing through a thickening throng of people who were going in the opposite direction and evacuating the building. "Medical! Out of the way!" they yelled. A few people—medics themselves, of one sort or another—turned around and followed Glidewell and Rosenberg back into the building.

When they entered the courtyard, the first thing they saw was smoke, billowing up out of the opposite side of the building. They ran toward it and ended up near the entrance to Corridor 4. The first person they saw fleeing the building was running with his arms up in the air, screaming, his clothes hanging off him like rags. When Glidewell saw his face, her first thought was that it was the best moulage job she had ever seen. Moulage was the makeup medical practitioners put on mock patients during exercises, to simulate injuries. But this wasn't moulage. The skin on the man's face was literally hanging off, and his face was burnt black. The reality hit home. Glidewell grabbed her radio. "This is not a drill! This is real!" she hollered, as Rosenberg got the burnt man onto the ground and started cutting off his clothes.

People started spilling out of Corridor 4. Glidewell's radio erupted with urgent pleas: "I've got patients over here! I've got patients over here!" Suddenly it was hard to tell who was talking on the radio and where anybody was.

As a captain, Glidewell was a junior officer at a place that teemed with generals and admirals and the most senior people in every discipline. But she looked around and for the moment was the ranking medical officer in a capital emergency. This is big, she thought. I shouldn't be doing this.

Rosenberg, the medic, kept glancing up at the entrance to Corridor 4. There was trouble inside. "Can I go in and see if there's anybody in there?" he asked his boss. Fit and tall, with blond hair, in his early twenties, Rosenberg, wearing fatigues, was primed for action. He was a good medic who liked to show off what he knew, and he wanted to get to the heart of the battle, wherever that was. But no firefighters or EMS personnel had shown up yet, and he was the only helper Glidewell had.

"Sorry, Rosie," she said. "I need you here."

Patients were beginning to surround them. Glidewell sent the walking wounded into the middle of the courtyard, where she hoped others would direct them out of the building. She tried to treat more serious patients on the grass, right outside the Corridor 4 entrance. Rescuers brought one woman out, using a door as a litter. Her leg appeared to be broken; somebody said she had jumped out a window. The burned man they had first encountered was lying on the grass, in bad shape. He desperately needed to get to a hospital. Glidewell had radioed for some kind of evacuation transport, but nothing had arrived yet. Another woman was struggling to breathe and screaming hysterically. She needed a breathing tube, but it was impossible while she was conscious. Glidewell was wearing a white lab coat, but she had nothing more than a pair of scissors in her pockets. What she needed was rapid-sequence drugs that would sedate patients in seconds. There were plenty in the clinic just a brisk walk away. But there was too much going on to go back and get some.

After a few minutes, doctors and other medical caregivers started running up. Many outranked Glidewell, but she had become the de facto commander of medical operations in the courtyard. "I'm a doc," one said. "Where do you need me?" She looked around and directed him to the serious patients on the grass. Other doctors started to take care of the hysterical woman and to shuffle the walking wounded toward the exits. Vehicles were showing up too—motorized carts, construction lorries, people's personal cars—to whisk victims off to area hospitals.

The flow of patients was just starting to ebb when a three-star general, in a blue Air Force uniform, approached Glidewell, said he was a doctor, and asked where she needed him. P. K. Carlton was the surgeon general of the Air Force, the service's top doctor, a tall, athletic man who could have passed as a wide receiver, except for the streaks of gray in his black hair. He had been at a meeting on the other side of the building from the heliport when the building shook. Nobody could tell what had happened, but Carlton headed straight for the DiLorenzo clinic to see what kind of help was needed.

The clinic was being evacuated when he arrived, so Carlton had gathered a group of medical personnel and led them toward the courtyard. On the way, they ran into two burn victims, their clothes and skin still smoldering. Carlton was wearing a flame-retardant vest, and he hugged each of them to put out the remaining fire. The two patients kept going, able to make their own way out.

By the time Carlton found Glidewell, most of the initial urgent-care patients had been evacuated. Carlton was sizing up the situation when an enlisted man came racing out of the building. "General," he sputtered, "if you want to see where the dying is, come with me."

Carlton looked into the building for a second, then back at the scene in the courtyard. "I'm going in," he announced decisively. "Who's going with me?"

Rosenberg, the medic, jumped at the chance. "Ma'am, can I go in now?" he asked Glidewell.

The nurse didn't want him in there; she had a feeling he wouldn't come out. But she could tell it was important to him, and there was enough help in the courtyard by now. "Be careful!" she implored her medic. Rosenberg could tell by the look on her face that she felt like she was speaking to him for the last time.

With Rosenberg and three other volunteers, Carlton formed a litter team to carry out victims. They walked down Corridor 4, following the same path Steve Carter had followed moments earlier, and ran into the same wall of smoke. Since they couldn't go any farther in that direction, they backed up and turned into A&E Drive.

The first thing Carlton saw in the service road was a large woman—airborne, her arms and legs flailing. She came down smack upon a huge man in jeans and a golf shirt, landing on him like a sack of cement. He didn't catch the woman exactly; he just broke her fall with his body. Both of them tumbled into a heap, shouting in pain.

Before the catcher had time to get up, another woman jumped at him. Since he was still on the ground, he dove into the path of the jumper, just in time to knock her sideways, so that she skidded into the ground horizontally instead of plopping straight into the pavement. A group of people ran over to help the two women who were now writhing on the ground.

A man appeared in the window. Unlike the other two, he jumped away from everybody on the ground and landed in a crouched stance, as if he were a paratrooper trained for hard landings. He fell over and seemed to be hurt, but was able to get up when people came to help. Carlton shuddered as he imagined terror so powerful it was driving people to jump frantically out of windows. What a mess, he thought. This is serious.

Up in the window there were just two people left, Colonel McNair and Lieutenant Colonel Wills. McNair tried to crawl back into the office area, to see if anybody else was still trapped in there. But it was too hot and smoky. Air from the window, it seemed, was feeding the fire and intensifying it. He went back to the window and told Wills it was time to get out. They both shouted back into the room a few times, one last call to any survivors, and then Wills climbed out.

By now they didn't have to jump. The people below had finally pushed a trash bin beneath the window, but it was still far beneath the window, so the huge man who had been catching people climbed onto the bin. Somebody put a ladder on his shoulders and tried to hold it steady. It reached almost to the base of the window. McNair helped lower Wills onto the ladder, and she climbed down into the arms of people below. McNair followed. He finally hit the ground, smoky and shaken, but okay.

Carlton, the Air Force general, had been amazed to see the huge man pop up after rolling into the second jumper, then climb up on the trash bin to help the two others down from the window. Craig Powell had searing pain in his legs and his back, from the impact of the jumpers landing on him. But when he saw the general, he came right up to him.

"Boy, am I glad to see you," he hastily greeted Carlton. "I think there are live people on the other side of that," he shouted, pointing to one of the smoking holes. Powell's main concern was still the Navy personnel trapped inside.

Even though Powell wasn't wearing a uniform or any kind of rank insignia, Carlton took for granted that he was a military man. Towering and muscle-bound, he had an unmistakable command presence, and it was clear he knew how to focus in the midst of chaos.

Carlton followed Powell toward one of the holes, adjusting to the dramatic scene. The hole seemed like an exit point for the fire raging behind the wall. Huge licks of flame were coming out, like a blowtorch that was three feet wide. It vented 15 or 20 feet into the air, and was so powerful that at times it singed the wall on the other side of the service road, 30 feet across.

Carlton was the senior officer on the scene. He was sizing up the odds of a rescue attempt into the hole. You've got to be kidding me, he thought. Nobody can survive going in there.

Then he saw two people in khaki Navy uniforms rush up to the hole from the other side of the service road. Just as he was thinking it was impossible, the two Navy officers ducked down and disappeared into the hole. To Carlton's eyes, they seemed to burrow in like rabbits. There was nothing to do but follow them.

7

"SEND NOBODY INSIDE"

9:50 A.M.

The first fire crews to arrive at the Pentagon didn't know where their commanders were. But they didn't need to. When a building was burning and people were trapped inside, you didn't stand around waiting for orders. You went inside to get people out.

The first priority was search and rescue. Once that was under way, and more crews arrived, firefighters would begin "suppression" efforts—hosing down the fire and beating it back.

The crew of Arlington's Truck 105—Derek Spector, Brian Roache, and Ron Christman—could tell by all the people staggering out onto the lawn that there were probably still victims trapped inside the rubble. After pulling on their protective gear and air packs, they hurried toward the nearest entrance, about 100 feet away. Spector, the acting commander, reminded them not to run. Walking would give the crew a few crucial seconds to focus on what was in front of them. And running would only make them winded and raise their adrenaline levels. They needed to be steady.

Military personnel were gathering with backboards to help transport people who couldn't walk. Defense Secretary Donald Rumsfeld materialized briefly, in his jacket and tie, and helped carry a victim on one of the stretchers. Rumsfeld had been in his third-floor office on the other side of the building when the plane hit, and walked out the grand River Entrance doors, facing the Potomac, with a couple of aides to see what was going on. They had turned left out of the doors and circumnavigated half the building before they saw the flames and the debris scattered across the lawn. With so much chaotic activity outside the Pentagon, few people seemed to even notice his presence.

Spector, Roache, and Christman had arrived at the entrance to Corridor 5, at the northwest corner of the building, about 150 feet north of the smoking hole. Like a lot of firefighters, Spector qualified as a "supertick," a lifelong fire hound who lived for the adrenaline of going on calls. He first joined the fire service as a teenager, in Gaithersburg, Maryland, where the department had been manned by gruff, old-school guys who thought little of getting singed in a fire or picking up a few blisters. The roughneck ethos rubbed off on the stocky, gregarious fireman. But Spector was careful and professional too, a good candidate to be promoted to captain and on the track to commanding other firefighters.

As his crew entered the building, they saw that both of the eight-foot-high oak doors that guarded the entrance were blown off their hinges, singed and splintered. The rush of people fleeing the building had slowed, but as the firefighters hustled up the steps and passed through the entranceway, a few burned, blackened victims still staggered past.

The crew pushed through a second set of doors, into the building itself, air masks still dangling from their hoses—it didn't make sense to turn on the air until absolutely necessary. Inside it was dark and full of commotion. A handful of officers from the Pentagon's police force, the Defense Protective Service, were darting in and out of smoky offices, looking for people. In the haze, they looked like frantic shadows. There was muffled shouting.

"I think I hear somebody over here!" came one cry.

"Check this office! Hurry!" somebody else implored.

In the chaos, Spector knew that he needed to sound clear and authoritative to his crew and to anybody else they encountered. He gathered a few of the Pentagon police officers together and tried to get them to focus on the search-and-rescue mission. "Don't let anybody else back inside the building," he told them. "It's too dangerous. We'll be the ones who search for survivors." The DPS officers got the message and began pushing survivors and others out the doors.

Roache was a supertick too. His father was a doctor, but Roache had no interest in white-collar work. He had gravitated to firefighting since he was a kid, volunteering for the local department when he was 16, the youngest eligible age. This was a "career fire," he knew—the experience of a lifetime. But it was still a fire. They'd fight it just like all the others.

Spector had told his crew to pull on their air masks and start their air. While Roache was getting his mask on, an Army officer came running up to him, hollering about somebody on the second floor they needed to rescue. "There's a general up there!" the man pleaded. "He's important. You've got to get him!"

"We're doing what we can," Roache answered. "Now you gotta get out of here."

The Army officer wouldn't give up. "He's important! He's a general!" the officer kept repeating.

Roache, anxious and wired, lost patience. "As far as I'm concerned, everybody's important!" he snapped. "We can't just run in and save the whole building. You're wearing me down, man! You need to get out of the building!"

The soldier relented. "I'm sorry, you're right," he glumly acknowledged, beginning to hack from the smoke. He backed away, then darted out the Corridor 5 doors.

The three firefighters had their masks and air packs on and managed to persuade everybody they saw to leave the building. Then they briefly discussed where they should go first to look for survivors. They were standing in the office-building equivalent of a four-way intersection. In front of them was Corridor 5, which led to the center of the Pentagon and the courtyard. On the left, the E Ring ran away from the fire, and on their right it ran straight into the impact zone.

Then there was the third dimension—the floors above and below, laid out in the same hub-and-spoke fashion. In the smoke and pandemonium, it wasn't obvious where they should look first. "Should we try the second floor?" Roache asked—knowing that there were possible victims up there.

Somebody else materialized out of the gloom. "I heard a lady screaming down there," a security officer choked out, pointing straight down the E Ring, in the direction of the fire. That sealed it— they were already on the first floor, and it made sense to head for the core of the fire, where they were most likely to find people needing help.

"Let's go this way," Spector directed.

They pushed open another set of doors, these leading into the E Ring. Black smoke suddenly engulfed them, as dark and murky as if they were navigating the bottom of the ocean. They had trained in conditions like this, but rarely experienced anything like it in a real fire. Spector reached for the flashlight strapped to his shoulder, then held his left arm out and pointed the beam at the reflective stripes at the end of his sleeve. He could barely see them. Visibility was less than two feet.

The Arlington County Fire Department had recently issued thermal imagers to some of its crews—sophisticated and expensive new equipment similar to the night-vision devices military units carried in the field. They allowed firefighters to see in dark areas with zero visibility, and they could penetrate the thickest smoke to spot victims by sensing their body heat. Truck 105 had a single imager, which Spector had with him now. He had trained with it but never used one in a live fire.

The imager, shaped like a handheld spotlight, worked like a digital camcorder, except that everything appeared in black, white, and gray images. Hot areas were bright white, while cooler areas were darker. The screen showed only a thermal representation of images— but it would be enough for Spector to guide his crew through the smoke.

He told Roache to take the left side of the hallway and Christman the right. They both began feeling their way blindly down the hall-way, using their hands to make out doorways. Spector stayed a few paces behind, in the middle of the hallway, watching both of his men through the thermal device, the bright white figures like spirits from a science-fiction movie. Down the hallway somewhere the fire hissed and popped like an unseen monster. But despite the smoke, the fire, for the moment, didn't threaten them; they didn't see a lot of flame. And they were able to communicate by voice without using their ra-dios.

The impact of the plane, however, had created a fun-house ver-sion of an office building. Instead of the usual flat, predictable con-tours, the walls were bowed and caved in from the explosion. The firefighters stumbled over random debris and had to crawl over ob-stacles. But the undulating walls were the only guideposts they had, so they clung to them, moving as quickly as they could through the bewildering maze.

Spector didn't want his men disappearing into dangerous spaces, and it was standard procedure to conduct a quick scan of each room with the thermal imager. If no heat from a living body registered after a few seconds, they'd move on. "I've got a doorway!" Roache called on the left.

Spector poked his head into the room and used the imager to scan from corner to corner. He saw no signs of life. "Okay, let's go!" he an-nounced, and they continued down the mangled hallway.

"I've got an office here!" Christman bellowed on the right. Spec-tor sidled over and went through the same drill. On the thermal imager there was plenty of heat but none of the white splotches that usually indicated a living being. They resumed their forward crawl down the hallway.

Roache called out an office on the left. Spector approached with the imager and suddenly felt a rush of excitement. "Hey, I got something here!" he yelled. He dimly saw a person moving right in front of him. Then he realized he was looking into the glass of a bent door—it was his own image reflecting back on the scanner. "Oh, that's me," he muttered. "Forget it!"

They checked a few more offices as they struggled down the hallway, breaking through a couple doors that were jammed or locked. Nobody was there, which seemed puzzling. Had everybody gotten out? It seemed unlikely, given the demolished offices they were encountering. Still, the rescuers weren't finding any victims, dead or alive.

The hallway was getting thicker with debris. Cables and wires, pipes, and pieces of the ceiling dangled from overhead, making it hard to walk upright. To move forward, they had to duckwalk, squatting down on their haunches and waddling beneath the overhanging hazards. As they clambered through the mess, Spector, the veteran of the group, felt proud of his men. Roache and Christman were probably shaking in their boots. But they carried themselves like ten-year veterans.

Spector started to hear occasional thumps, like snowballs splattering on asphalt. He pointed the thermal imager upward and could see that bits of the ceiling were melting and falling down around them in globs. Some of the chunks were as big as baseballs and looked like red-hot hail. Not good, he thought, as his heartbeat quickened.

There was something even more alarming in the imager. Spector pointed the scanner straight ahead, and through the tangle of cables and wires saw a glowing heap of debris—it looked like a mountain of garbage that had been doused with gasoline and torched. Even though it was blazing only about 25 feet away, Roache and Christman were essentially blind in the smoke and couldn't see it. "Hey guys," Spector called out. "I've got a huge debris pile right in front of us. It's probably three-quarters of the way to the ceiling." He paused, wondering what they should do. Should they try to go around it, or go somewhere else?

Christman, the rookie, sounded eager to push on. "Let's go around it," he said.

Roache didn't want to turn back either. Having wriggled this far down the E Ring without finding anyone, none of them wanted to give up. The heat was still bearable, and if there were people trapped nearby, they were probably up near that pile.

But Spector had a bad feeling. He didn't know how big the pile was on the other side, what was beyond it, or how stable the building was around it. The bits of melting cement falling on their heads were unnerving. "I don't think we need to be on the other side of that pile," he told his men. "I don't want to get someplace we can't get out of. Let's get out of here." Roache and Christman nodded silently. But both felt a sense of relief.

They backed out the way they came, crawling over wreckage and feeling their way, Spector issuing guidance gleaned through the imager. In a few moments they were standing back in Corridor 5. The excursion down the E Ring had probably taken less than ten minutes. They decided to head into the building and turn down the D Ring, in the same direction, to see if they could find anybody there.

But as they pushed deeper into the building, Spector tried his radio. "One-oh-five to Command," he called out. There was no answer, so he repeated the call. Then a shrill tone told him he was out of range, cut off from communications with the outside. That was enough. "Our radios are out," he told Roache and Christman. "Let's go," he said, gesturing toward the exit. They weren't going to help anyone by pushing too far into the building and getting trapped or cut off.

They walked outside, past the huge oak doors lying on the grass. The bright sun stung their eyes but helped them regain their bearings. After removing their face pieces, Nomex hoods, and helmets, it was a relief to inhale freely and not try to conserve air with every breath.

Spector knew he needed to reach a command officer and report what they'd seen inside, especially the crumbling ceiling. He looked around, searching for a command post. "I wonder who's in charge around here?" he asked himself out loud. He couldn't see the command post that was taking shape at the other end of the Pentagon's western facade, about 500 feet away, across waves of people moving every which way on the grass. There seemed to be no sense of order or control to the operation yet.

So he tried the radio again. The operations frequency was overwhelmed with traffic. "One-oh-five to Command . . . Chief," he said, not knowing which chief he might be talking to, "we've been on the inside. The structural integrity of the building is severely compromised. My recommendation is, send nobody inside."

A medic unit interrupted, calling in a request for all available rescue units. "Okay," a voice from the command post crackled back. "Where are you at?" Spector wondered if the voice was talking to the medic unit, or to him. It was impossible to tell in the confusion.

Not far from Spector, the crew of Arlington's Engine 108 was about to make its own first foray into the burning building. The crew from Station 8, about three miles west of the Pentagon, had pulled onto the helipad lawn shortly after Truck 105. Capt. Mike Smith, the officer on the truck, heard Spector's call for a third alarm on the radio.

Short and trim with a bushy mustache, Smith was a respected 28-year veteran, aggressive when a rescue was on the line but never foolhardy. His driver, Fred Calvert, himself a 20-year veteran, knew all the shortcuts to the Pentagon and had gotten them there in less than five minutes. But the other two firefighters on the crew, Justin

Scott and Greg Gulick, were younger. It was Smith's job to make sure they didn't get in over their heads.

Calvert had cut through the Pentagon's North Parking lot to get to the helipad, and was irritated to find Truck 105 parked in the way of other trucks starting to arrive on the scene. He eased around it and pulled up next to a hydrant at the north end of the helipad. Rescue Engine 161, a Fort Myer truck, was nearby. Its crew had started to lay hose on the ground, preparing to get some water flowing into the Pentagon. Smith quickly found James Angerett, who was in charge of Engine 161, and began making a plan.

Clearly, it was a huge fire. One or two engine companies, with half a dozen firefighters, weren't going to make any difference trying to put out the flames. But Smith wanted to bring a hose line into the building anyway, so they could turn it on for protection, if needed, while looking for victims.

When not on shift with the fire department, Smith was a small-scale builder who had constructed several homes. When he looked at the fire raging on all five floors of the Pentagon, he could tell the floor slabs had been damaged by the flames reaching up through them. What was the risk they'd get trapped in a collapse? At a minimum, he figured the standpipes and other fire-protection systems inside the building were wrecked. They'd have to get their water from outside, and drag a hose with them all the way in.

Smith hadn't heard Spector warn against sending anybody else into the building, and he quickly developed a plan with Angerett to hook up some hoses while they did reconnaissance and rescue. He had nosed the truck up to within a few feet of a hydrant so he could use a ten-foot sleeve to feed water to the truck's pump, which would increase the pressure, to assure that it flowed forcefully to the firefighters on the other end of the hose. Calvert had learned through the years how to get the distance between the truck and the hydrant down to a few inches and run the sleeve from the hydrant to the engine's intake valve without any kinks that might impede water flow.

Smith, meanwhile, tried to reach somebody at the command post. "One-oh-eight on the scene," he called into his radio, competing with multiple units for the attention of the battalion commander. "Engine 108 to command," he repeated. "Be advised the floor has collapsed. Structural integrity is compromised. Will give more of a report when I get to the interior."

Cornwell was still on the radio, in the final moment before he relinquished command to Chief Schwartz. "Be aware of the structural condition inside the building," he warned Smith. Evidently, he'd heard Spector's report.

Smith expected to find carnage inside, with bodies everywhere. It was never easy—dealing with dead victims. Just a single victim, he knew, could haunt you for months. There were things he'd seen that had caused nightmares. Things he had never told anybody, not even his wife, Doris. And it hit everybody differently. Smith wondered how the two younger guys on his crew, Scott and Gulick, would react. He found a moment to pull his crew aside. "Listen," he told them. "You guys are going to have to stay together. Be professional. Get done what we have to get done." He didn't say what was really on his mind—that the scene might be so disturbing, the younger guys would be traumatized—but his short lecture got the crew focused.

The plan was for Calvert to stay outside, manning the pumps. Smith would go in with his crew, Scott and Gulick, along with the Fort Myer crew from Rescue 161. They entered through the same Corridor 5 entrance that Spector's crew had used, and walked to the D Ring, the fourth of the five concentric hallways around the building. Smith walked ahead, and Scott and Gulick followed, dragging a three-inch-wide supply line, a thick hose that could channel water to a couple of smaller hand lines. Even without water coursing through it, the supply line was heavy and unwieldy. As the firefighters pulled the big hose forward, it unraveled from a storage space on the truck, where it was folded accordion-style. Occasionally it caught or snagged, and one of the firefighters would lumber back to free it. On the end of the hose was a "gated wye" coupling, in the shape of a Y, that split into two feeds; hose could be connected to each. Several of the firefighters also carried 300 feet of narrower hose, packed so they could rapidly uncoil it and hook up hand lines that would extend the reach of the supply line.

Once inside, Smith quickly determined that they were in an area of imminent danger. He told his men to "Scott up"—pull on their masks and turn on their Scott air packs.

The smoke in the D Ring wasn't as thick as Spector had encountered in the E Ring—it seemed it was being vented out someplace. There were no flames where they were either, but it still felt hot. Smith reverted to an old firefighter trick. He held his arm up in the air and pulled down the sleeve of his fire suit, to expose his wrist. Modern gloves had wristlets that were supposed to cover your skin, but Smith didn't use them. It was better, he reasoned, to be able to spot-check the heat of a fire by seeing how warm it felt on a small patch of skin on your wrist, instead of taking off a glove and burning the more sensitive skin on your fingers or hand. This fire wasn't warm. It wasn't hot. It was superhot. The heat was as intense as anything he had faced in 28 years as a fireman.

The Engine 108 and Engine 161 crews went down the D Ring, much as Spector's crew had, except without a thermal imager. The same kind of debris began to pile up in the hallway. They pushed through, muscling the supply line over wreckage, like dragging a drugged python through a dense jungle. They found the same perplexing thing as Spector—lots of demolished offices, but no victims. Smith was shocked. God damn it, he thought, where is everybody? They lifted debris and looked underneath. Nothing.

Part of the way down the D Ring they stretched the supply line to its limit. They attached two of the smaller hoses to the gated wye and began to unravel those as they went. Since Smith couldn't get through on the radio, he sent a firefighter out to find Fred Calvert, on the engine, and tell him to charge the line—start the water flowing.

As they got closer to the impact point, they saw that the walls were completely flattened. Smith had been in the Pentagon dozens of times, and never imagined it could look like this. Instead of office space, the building looked like a warehouse that had been filled with wreckage and set ablaze. The only things standing were some columns and partitions.

The heat was getting even more intense. Smith guessed the fire was close to the flashover stage, when the temperature of everything in the room rises to its natural combustion point and the only thing preventing a sudden eruption is a shortage of oxygen. In that stage, the incipient fire smolders until it finds sufficient oxygen, then the accumulating gases and superheated contents of the room light off like a cloud of napalm. But for the moment the hoses stayed off. There were no flames to squirt, just searing heat all around.

Outside, in front of the fire, foam units from the airport were starting to go to work. The hulking trucks, each with two large nozzles—one mounted on the roof, one on the bumper—looked like armored military vehicles lumbering into urban warfare. Foam units are designed to operate close to jet-fuel fires, and they're equipped so firefighters inside can manage the turrets remotely, directing water where they want it while protected from any fire outside. In addition to more than 3,000 gallons of water, each truck carried 210 gallons of foam concentrate meant to smother liquid petroleum fires that would be largely impervious to water. And unlike most fire engines, which had to park before they could pump water, foam units were able to douse a fire while advancing on it or backing away.

Two foam units were now sending powerful streams of water deep into the impact hole. Other nozzles spewed foam, which looked like globs of white suds being shot from a cannon. The foam turned gray when it hit the burning building, and covered the whole exterior wall.

The volume of foam and water, and the precise aim of the turrets, was far more firepower than individual fire crews manning hand lines would have been able to muster. In some places, where the new blast-resistant windows had been installed, the foam and water merely bounced off the surface, unable to penetrate to the fire beyond. But plenty of older windows had been blown out, which let the foam and water through. And where the older glass was still intact, the high-pressure streams of water smashed right through. The onslaught was starting to work, knocking down the visible fire, at least in the area surrounding the impact point.

From Fred Calvert's vantage point, however, the force of the water being pumped into the fire seemed to be pushing the flames farther down the E Ring. As he tended half a dozen different hoses attached to the pump panel on Engine 108, he could see the fire near him intensify as the airport foam units attacked it head-on where the plane had entered the building. He was about 100 feet north of the smoking hole, looking into it at an angle, and it seemed the high-pressure water being applied by the foam units was also driving air into the building, and feeding the fire just beyond the flow of the water. Right in front of him the fire started to spread rapidly down the E Ring, on all five floors, jumping five windows at a time as it spread from its core. Calvert worried that before long he might have to move the truck to avoid the flames, which would force him to shut down all the hoses until he got repositioned. Disconnecting all the hoses and moving the truck would be a huge job for one person. But it would be better than watching Engine 108's paint start to bubble up—or letting the truck to catch fire.

The foam and water were also weighing down the section of the building right over the hole, which was already severely weakened by the fire that had consumed all five floors. Defina, the airport fire officer, had directed his crews to apply foam sparingly, so as not to push the fire deeper into the building. But as the white cloud started to settle, firefighters noticed a seam in the building's structure, forming to the left of the hole and going all the way up to the roof. It looked like a part of the building was starting to crack off from the rest. Atop the hole, the floors and roof were drooping, as if the building was getting too tired to hold itself up.

Defina was watching it all from the lawn. He got on the radio, calling out an emergency. "I'm fearing an imminent collapse at the point of impact," he warned. "I recommend you evacuate the area."

8

FOURTH DOOR ON THE LEFT

10:00 A.M.

Standard procedure for fighting a big fire like the one at the Pentagon was to attack it from two directions at once: from the outside of the building inward, and from the center courtyard outward. The first part of that strategy was under way, with firefighters and fire trucks massing at the helipad. But in the courtyard it was taking longer for things to develop. Plus, sporadic reports had been flowing into the command post about victims in the courtyard and in A&E Drive. It was critical to get fire crews into the courtyard.

Capt. Ed Hannon had been at a training session with other Arlington County fire officers, just south of the Pentagon. When word of the plane crash arrived, Hannon drove himself and several others to Station 5, his home station, where he got his gear and caught a ride to the Pentagon. Once he found the command post, his assignment was to go to the inner courtyard and help with firefighting there.

Hannon was lean and focused, with a long brown mustache. He had two kids, and in his spare time ran a small farm with his wife in West Virginia, where they lived. Though he was religious, Hannon could joke with the bawdiest of his fellow firefighters. And he knew the Pentagon well, since, like Derek Spector's crew, he was based at the Arlington station closest to the Pentagon.

When Hannon got his orders, he hurried toward a tunnel that led directly into the courtyard. Just as he was about to turn left into the tunnel, a man came stumbling out, reeking of jet fuel. His clothes were burned and he was covered in black soot and gray foam from a fire extinguisher. He seemed okay, but Hannon found somebody to escort him, and pointed them both to the triage area back near the command post.

The tunnel was designed to allow fire engines and other emergency vehicles quick access to the center of the building. But when Hannon came out on the other end, about 500 feet away, there was hardly any sign of the fire department. Doctors, nurses, and medics were hustling around, tending to injured people who were still staggering out of the building. People ran across the grass, bringing medical supplies. One ambulance was waiting, ready to race to the hospital. And groups of military personnel were clustered at the entrances to Corridors 4 and 5, senior officers giving orders. Some were holding litters to carry patients. Others rushed in and out of the building, with towels or T-shirts wrapped around their faces.

The only fire vehicle, however, was the command buggy belonging to Battalion Chief Dale "Jerome" Smith, who was Cornwell's counterpart, in charge of all the fire crews operating on the north side of Arlington that day. At the command post outside, the one Cornwell established, Smith had already been designated the commander of "A&E Division." But his division, for the time being, existed in name only. Hannon appeared to be the first Arlington firefighter to arrive.

When Hannon found the battalion chief, Smith was battling to get through on the radio, like everybody else seeking guidance. "A&E Division to Pentagon command," he said repeatedly. His radios only worked sporadically, obstructed by the Pentagon's thick walls. There was hardly a second when somebody wasn't jabbering on the net, yet Smith only picked up fragments of the radio traffic. Finally, the connection improved and Smith announced to the command post, "We are set up in the court. People are still coming out into the center court. We're probably gonna need some more EMS help back in here."

A unit from the District of Columbia, Truck 4, had gotten to the Pentagon a moment before. But their vehicle was a ladder truck with a tall tiller cab in the back, and it was too big to fit through the tunnel leading into the courtyard. In the early 1940s, when the Pentagon was built, the tunnel could accommodate virtually every kind of fire truck in service. But trucks had gotten bigger, and years of repaving inside the tunnel had reduced its clearance. So Lt. Craig Duck, the officer on Truck 4, told the five other men on his crew they'd have to leave the truck where it was and carry everything in with them. They hoisted their air packs onto their backs and picked up all the axes, pry tools, power saws, and other devices they could carry.

They lacked one important thing: hoses. Ladder crews such as Truck 4 usually worked with an engine. The usual tactic was for the ladder crew to focus on search and rescue, and handle any work that needed to be done on the roof, like punching holes to vent smoke and heat. Engine crews were usually tasked with extinguishing the fire, since their trucks carried thousands of feet of hose and had internal pumps to push the water forward. But Truck 4's usual partner truck, D.C.'s Engine 6, was away on a training mission—so Duck's crew was on their own.

They faced daunting work without hose lines to protect them from the fire, and Duck dearly wished Engine 6 were on the scene to back them up. Instead, while preparing his crew to enter the building, he found some civilian and military volunteers eager to help and told them to start gathering hoses that were stockpiled in the building. "Stack them there," he said, pointing to the entrances to Corridors 4 and 5. They were getting somewhat organized, but it felt like a wild scene from some kind of thriller. Military personnel zigzagged everywhere, still leading smoky victims out of the building. Smoke drifted down from the roof, adding an apocalyptic backdrop to the chaos.

Duck found some of the Pentagon officials who seemed to be giving orders and pointed out that the military personnel running into the building had no protective gear or firefighting training—if they kept venturing into the fire, they would need to be rescued themselves. It was time to get out of the building, he stressed, and let the firefighters do their work.

The Pentagon was a mysterious building to Duck, who had never been on a call there; he had no concept of its layout, and the numbers and letters used to designate rings and corridors were meaningless to him. Hannon was more familiar with the building and, with no unit of his own, fell in with Duck's crew as they were about to walk up the steps to Corridor 5. He'd be a helpful guide if they needed one.

They were at the opposite end of the hallway from where Derek Spector and Mike Smith had walked past the splintered oak doors and turned into the smoke-filled E Ring. The helipad end of Corridor 5 was a good 400 feet away, yet the smoke was the same black, bitter cloud that Spector had first encountered.

Hannon and the D.C. crew pulled on their face pieces and turned on their air as soon as they entered the building to search for victims. They weren't sure where to start looking, but they quickly got some guidance. A Navy officer was in the hallway, shouting and hacking into a radio. He ran up to the firefighters. "There's a whole group of people trapped in there!" he yelled.

Hannon could see the panic on his face. The man pulled out a piece of paper and drew a rudimentary map directing the firefighters down Corridor 5, then left into the C Ring. He said the people were trapped behind the fourth door on the left. "I've talked to them on the radio! Hurry!" he implored.

"Okay, listen," Hannon said to the Navy officer through his face piece. "If we get these guys, I'm sending them your way. You need to have some guys here to assist them. Understand?"

"Roger," the man coughed.

With air tanks on, they had no problem walking down Corridor 5. There was a lot of smoke, but it hung at head level and they could navigate it easily. Once they turned into the C Ring, however, the smoke thickened and banked all the way down to the floor. Nearly blind, the firefighters felt their way forward along the walls, keeping in hand contact with each other. It was difficult moving forward while trying to hold onto one another, but it was crucial not to get separated in wrecked, smoke-filled spaces. Hannon and Duck, the most experienced guys in the group, knew how easily you could get disoriented in areas where doors and windows and other basic features of a room weren't where you expected them to be.

They could hear the fire popping and banging in front of them as the flames chewed away at the building and its contents. It was hard to talk over the din. As they felt their way past the doorways, it was getting hotter; they could feel it even through their protective suits. They encountered the first office on the left and went inside to do a quick search, shining hand lights through the smoke, lifting rubble to see if they could find any victims, and breaking through walls with axes and other tools they carried. There was nobody. On the way out they pulled the door shut—or as far as it would close—to try to slow the spread of the fire. They passed two more offices and did the same thing. It was hard to believe people could still be alive, but they had to check.

The fourth office on the left was just up ahead. Fire was beginning to roll over their heads. Without any hose lines to beat back the flames, the most they could do was inch forward through the roiling murk when the fire allowed an opening. They couldn't see the fourth door, but Hannon was guessing how far away it was, based on the spacing of the first three doors. Fifteen feet, maybe. Then ten. It was almost in sight . . .

Then part of ceiling came collapsing down on the whole group, in a hail of sparks and fire. Pipes flew. Light fixtures and ceiling tiles fell. Building materials ricocheted like shrapnel. The firefighters, who had been staying in hand contact, leapt out of the way to protect themselves, and were suddenly separated. Instinctively, Hannon went to all fours. Through the smoke, down low, he could see one D.C. guy on the floor with his helmet knocked sideways.

"Everybody get to the wall!" he shouted. "Get to the wall!" There was more protection against the walls than in the middle of the hallway, he reasoned. "Is everybody okay?" he called out. Since he was the ranking officer, he ordered everybody to sound off, shouting out their names so the others would know they were okay. They were all there, and unhurt. But Hannon was scared. He was sure the other guys were too. He realized they were deep into a thick fire, in a huge, unstable building, far from other fire crews.

There was no way they could move forward. They'd be lucky if they could back out without getting trapped. The fire was on top of them now, and it threatened to push the collapse straight down the hallway, burying them if they didn't move soon. Hannon ordered a retreat, and the D.C. crew agreed, even though they all had the same thought in mind: We've got to go back and find those people.

When they got back to Corridor 5, the Navy officer was still there. He looked shocked and saddened all at once—heartbroken not to see his comrades emerge, but amazed that the firefighters had gotten out alive. "I couldn't get to your people," Hannon told him, dejected.

"It's okay," the officer said, nodding gravely.

Hannon and the Truck 4 crew tried to regroup and go back down the C Ring. Fire cut them off. They found a set of steps and went up to the second floor, pushing down the same part of the C Ring, one flight up. It was even hotter, and they made even less headway. They were getting nowhere. The offices that weren't totally enflamed were so hot that nobody could still be alive in them. And the places where people thought there might still be victims were completely ablaze and unreachable. Without hoses, they weren't going to rescue any-body. It was maddening. There was nothing they could do except walk toward the flames until the fire turned them around and sent them back. If only he'd been a little quicker, Hannon kept thinking. He would have gotten them out.

9

EVACUATE?

10:00 A.M.

Arlington Capt. Chuck Gibbs, a brusque and dedicated fire officer, arrived at the Pentagon just as Chief Schwartz was getting to the command post. Gibbs was known for saying whatever was on his mind, no matter who he offended. He lacked the polish and college credits required to rise higher than captain, but he was a fire expert who endlessly studied the craft—one of the best tacticians in the department.

"You have your gear?" Schwartz asked him. Gibbs said yes. "Well, get up there and let me know what the hell's going on," the operations chief directed. Then Schwartz looked up and saw a green highway sign that directed traffic to the "River Entrance" of the Pentagon. "You're River Division," he told Gibbs—even though the river entrance was on the opposite side of the building, where the Pentagon overlooked the Potomac. Schwartz was stratifying his command system and giving Gibbs command responsibility for all the firefighters going into the building near the helipad. That level of command usually went to a battalion chief in a fire like this, not a captain. But Schwartz knew Gibbs had the experience and knowledge to handle it.

When Gibbs got close to the helipad, Arlington's Rescue 104 was just showing up. Bobby Beer, the senior firefighter on the truck, asked Gibbs where they should go. "Go where the plane went in!"

Gibbs told him. "Start searching for victims." Gibbs suited up for his own look into the building, joining up with a Fort Myer unit that was about to enter through a doorway to the left of the impact hole. They crawled toward the crash site looking for victims, just as Spector and Smith had. A few of the Fort Myer firefighters tried to knock out some of the windows, to vent the smoke and heat. But after bashing away for five minutes they hadn't even dented the blast-resistant panes and gave up.

After stumbling around for a few minutes and finding nobody, Gibbs decided they needed another plan. "This is crazy," he told his Fort Myer colleagues. "There's too much debris. Let's get outta here."

They began to regroup outside, near the helipad. As the ranking officer, Gibbs used a Fort Myer vehicle as an impromptu command post. Firefighters, military officers, and lots of other people were forming a crowd around him. An Air Force three-star general approached Gibbs. "What do you need?" he asked.

The throng was thick on the grass near the helipad. Firefighters were racing to the scene, while workers from the Pentagon were still milling around, trying to get back into the building or do anything else to help. "I need the military people to get out of the way," Gibbs bluntly told the general. "They're making it hard for us to do our jobs."

The general knew how to get results. To Gibbs's surprise, the teeming crowd of uniforms began to drift away from the building, like a fog bank lifting.

While Gibbs was establishing the River Division command post around the Fort Myer SUV on the helipad, Schwartz was rapidly trying to staff the broader incident command system. Battalion chief Bob Cornwell was getting ready to head into the building, and no other senior fire officers had arrived yet. Schwartz quickly scanned the faces around him.

Capt. Doug Insley, a young officer with an innocent, cheeky face and big, round metal glasses, had just arrived and was busy helping at the command post. Schwartz grabbed him the moment he saw him. "Come with me," he ordered. "You're gonna be my aide." He then turned to Joe Lightfoot, Cornwell's aide. "Joey, you're gonna be comms, logistics, support . . ." he said intently, rattling off a number of other duties Lightfoot didn't hear.

A second earlier Lightfoot had been a standard-issue battalion aide, writing names on a whiteboard, trying to track the firefighters who had gone into the building. Schwartz had just upgraded his responsibilities to those of a much more senior officer. Among other things, Lightfoot would be handling the radios for the whole command post, talking to the other fire commanders and issuing orders. It took him a moment to absorb the battlefield promotion. The enormity of the situation and his new responsibilities were almost overwhelming.

With Schwartz busy setting up an incident command structure and trying to gauge the range of the fire, and Cornwell on his way into the building, the two young captains found themselves running the swelling command post, still clustered around Cornwell's SUV. Lightfoot's first job was to open a separate radio channel for the EMS crews, to ease the gridlock on the main channel. "All EMS go to One Charlie," he announced. That would help with communications, but Lightfoot's job was getting more complex by the minute. He'd have to monitor two radio channels just to know what was going on.

They didn't have a firm handle on who was in the building either. Standard procedure was for firefighters to check in with the command post before going into a fire and to hand over their "passports"—Velcro-backed tags with each firefighter's name and unit. Somebody at the command post, usually an aide, would line up the passports to keep track of who was inside fighting the fire and who was outside. It was crucial to account for everybody, in real time, so if something went wrong, commanders would know if anybody was trapped inside.

At big events, however, firefighters often got the "Big Eye," as

Cornwell liked to say—they were so eager to get inside and attack the fire that they'd sometimes bypass the command post, which was occasionally necessary, if it was urgent to get in and rescue people. The command post hadn't even been set up when Derek Spector and Truck 105 screeched up to the Pentagon. Mike Smith and Engine 108 had driven straight up to the building too, as had the Fort Myer units. Lightfoot and Insley could hear those guys on the radio but didn't know exactly who was down there and whether they were inside the building or not. Insley started cataloguing which units were on the scene or on the way, while trying to gauge how big the fire was and how many units they'd need.

There were other things they didn't understand. Gibbs kept coming back on the radio, identifying himself as "River Division."

"What the hell is he talking about?" Lightfoot asked Insley. "The river is way over there."

"I don't know," Insley answered. "What's the River Division?"

They both wondered if there was another fire or some other problem on the opposite side of the building, adjacent to the Potomac. If so, the incident was even bigger than the catastrophe they saw mushrooming before them.

Ed Plaugher, Arlington County's fire chief, finally arrived after a harrowing, high-speed sprint down I-66 in his Crown Vic. During his race to the Pentagon, Plaugher had been weighing whether to take over command of the incident or leave it with Schwartz. From what he could tell on the radio, it was certainly a big enough fire to warrant the chief's direct involvement. It was also an extraordinary event that would require a top fire official to deal with dozens of other government agencies, Pentagon leaders, and the press. If those pressures landed on the incident commander—whose most important job was to oversee the firefighting plan—they could interfere with the fire and rescue efforts. They would need a buffer between the incident commander and the frantic outside world.

When Schwartz saw Plaugher, he took off the blue command vest he was wearing and handed it to his boss. Plaugher hesitated. "Is everything under control here, Jimmy? Do you know the magnitude of what we've got?"

"We don't know yet how much of the Pentagon is involved," Schwartz replied, "whether it's all five rings or not, or how many floors." He quickly updated Plaugher on what else he knew. It wasn't much. Then Schwartz asked, "Are you gonna take over command?"

"No," Plaugher decided. "You're the incident commander." The situation at the fire ground was still extremely fluid, bordering on chaotic. But Plaugher could tell that Schwartz had a grasp of the challenge. Besides, Schwartz knew the Pentagon better than he did. Plaugher would worry about other things—and there would be plenty to keep him busy. It was a tough decision for Plaugher; the largest operation of his entire career was occurring right in front of him, but instead of taking over, he knew he'd be most effective as chief if he let Schwartz continue as incident commander.

Chris Combs, the FBI agent, was at the command post too. Combs had arrived at the Pentagon in six minutes, driving across the Fourteenth Street Bridge before traffic had come to a standstill and roaring down the exit that led to South Parking. The lot was filled with people by then, and Combs parked his car in the midst of the crowd. He grabbed a radio, a bulletproof vest, and some other gear from the trunk and started looking for the command post. His immediate responsibility was to get an FBI operation up and running.

Combs wasn't thinking about fire. He was thinking about what was coming next. The FBI had done a lot of counterterrorism training with Israeli security forces. One standard terrorist tactic they had learned about was the follow-on attack. In one suicide bombing attack the Israelis told them about, the incident commanders arrived on scene and started to huddle together, when another suicide bomber walked right up to them and blew himself up, killing several of the commanders. Combs looked at the high-rises in Crystal City nearby, and the hill overlooking the Pentagon. Were there any shooters? Or snipers?

Combs knew Schwartz from planning and training sessions they had attended together. He spotted Schwartz and ran up to him. "Thank God you're here, man," Schwartz replied, putting his hand on Combs's shoulder.

"You know we're under attack?" Combs asked.

"Yeah."

"Okay, whaddya got here?" Combs asked. His guess was that a small plane had hit the Pentagon, because the impact hole was along the approach route smaller planes typically used when landing at National Airport. Plus, when Combs first called back to his boss, Jim Rice, at the Washington Field Office, Rice told him a small commuter plane had crashed into the Pentagon.

Even from the remove of the command post, about 300 feet from the fire, Combs could tell it was hot down there. He had been a firefighter back home in New York, and he knew that was a lot of heat for a small plane, or even for a truck bomb.

When people noticed the FBI vest Combs was wearing, they started to come up to him, telling him what they had seen. There were several eyewitnesses who said they had watched a big passenger jet slam into the building. Their stories were all similar. Within five minutes of arriving at the command post, Combs knew it hadn't been a commuter plane after all. He radioed Rice again, saying it was a commercial jet. Just like New York.

On the periphery of the command post, firefighters were beginning to gather three and four deep, waiting for assignments. Capt. Denis Griffin knew to stay out of the way while the officers in charge got the operation up and running. As eager as he and his unit—the crew of Quint 104—were to get into the flaming building and start working, it was important for commanders to impose some order on the operation and begin to track where each unit was.

Griffin knew they were embarking on an extraordinary event. Chuck Gibbs liked to say that a fire was ten minutes of work, then you were done. This was not going to be a ten-minute fire. "Look, guys," Griffin said to Jim Anderson, his driver, and Brian Mosely, his backseater. "This is going to be something we've never seen before. We're really going to have to pace ourselves."

The "quint" Anderson was driving was a hybrid fire truck with an internal water tank that could pump water like an engine, but it also had a 75-foot ladder. This was shorter than the 100-footers on tower trucks, but could still reach a couple of stories up. A hose and nozzle could be attached to the aerial device to shower water onto or over a roof.

Griffin's first plan was to park as close to the fire as possible, so they could use the quint to pump water or reach into the building, whatever was needed. He knew the Pentagon well and directed Anderson to a construction road that ran right up alongside the wall near the helipad. But debris blocked their way. Plus, it sounded like bombs were going off up there—propane tanks in the construction area were exploding, shaking the earth and rattling the quint. The fuel tank that fed the generator was on fire too, spewing smoke even darker than what was coming from the building.

Griffin knew he needed another plan. If they weren't going to be able to use the truck, he wanted it parked out of the way. He told Anderson to pull up on a grassy area, where they wouldn't be blocking any other vehicles. They jumped out and found the command post quickly, turning in their passports, for tracking purposes. Then they waited.

Steve McCoy and the Engine 101 crew, which watched Flight 77 descend beneath the horizon, followed by a huge ball of black smoke, had just arrived too. Andrea Kaiser had driven, and she was terrified. She knew this was connected to the attacks in New York, and kept telling herself this couldn't be happening. As the crew was on their way to the command post, McCoy stopped the group and offered to say a quick prayer. The four of them leaned in together, forming a small huddle. McCoy asked for strength and safety during the operation. "Amen," they all said, then continued on their way.

Battalion chief Bob Cornwell was about to head into the building and take his first look around. Schwartz had designated him "Interior Command," in charge of all operations inside the building on the heliport side. Cornwell saw McCoy and Griffin, and told them to get their crews ready. They were coming with him. They headed for the Corridor 3 entrance, which emptied into South Parking, around the corner from the helipad and the smoking hole. Cornwell grabbed a few other firefighters along the way.

By the time they walked up the steps toward the entrance, there were about a dozen of them. Several of the firefighters carried "high-rise packs," bundles of tightly folded hose and nozzles that could be carried into a building and up stairs. The hose could be attached to a standpipe inside the building whenever the firefighters needed water, saving the trouble of running lines all the way from outside. They also had axes, pry bars, saws, and other tools with them. It was the most organized fire team to enter the Pentagon so far.

Near the Corridor 3 entrance the air was relatively clear, and their first goal was to climb the stairwells and see what kind of smoke and fire conditions existed in the hallways on various floors. After that, if conditions seemed safe, they'd work their way down the hallways, toward the impact point, and start searching for victims. They went up to the second and third floors, looking down the hallway off the corridors. The smoke was relatively light, and they were able to proceed without putting on face pieces.

Cornwell's radio was only working sporadically, and transmissions that did make it through were garbled. He heard Joe Lightfoot say there were reports of people on fire, trapped in A&E Drive. But the reports of collapsed floors and structural damage didn't reach him.

On the other side of the fire, near the helipad, Bobby Beer and his crew from Rescue 104 were bashing through wreckage and digging for victims. Beer was a stand-in for Rescue 104's usual captain, who was at home taking care of his sick daughter. Compact and muscular, with thick hair and a country accent, Beer was a skilled fire tactician who felt uncomfortable around the brass and had no interest in climbing the department's leadership ladder. But he loved hanging out with the dozens of line firefighters he knew, from all over the region. He was willing to break the rules every now and then to reach a victim or get the upper hand on a fire, but he was going by the book this time. A technical rescue specialist, he had trained for operations in collapsed buildings. Typical scenarios included terrorist events like the Oklahoma City bombing. And this, he knew, was terrorism. Who knew what was coming next? It wasn't the time to take unnecessary risks.

Beer led his group into the building as close to the fire as they could get, stepping through a bent doorway between Corridors 4 and 5—the main access point to the helipad. They pulled on their masks and turned on their air as soon as they entered the building. Having grown up as an Air Force brat, always around airplanes, he noticed the odor of jet fuel right away. Then he noticed something peculiar— shoes, everywhere. From the luggage, he guessed.

Beer kept a tight rein on the younger guys behind him. He carried the radio and an axe, out in front. Fred Kawatsky, a tall, earnest rookie who had been on the job for less than two years, held a thermal imager. Chad Stamps, one of the jocular "wonder twins," wielded a sledgehammer.

They moved closer to the impact point. Through their protective gear, they could feel the heat rising. Beer called a situation report into the radio. "We're in a fully involved area," he said, meaning that the entire portion of the building was consumed with flames. Unlike Smith's crew, they hadn't taken a hose line. If flames started to surround them, their only option was to turn around and rush out.

Farther down the Pentagon's splintered facade, on the other side of the hole, the crew of Arlington's Engine 107 had just set up a deluge gun—a water cannon able to shoot 500 gallons of water per minute—and gotten a thick stream of water flowing onto the blaze. Capt. Brian Frantz, the officer on Engine 107, was closely eyeing a fissure in the structure that looked like it might split wide open. He had situated the gun in a spot close enough to reach the fire but far enough from the building to keep his crew safe if the walls started to crumble. Off to the side, a nasty plume of inky black smoke was rising from the 5,000-gallon tank of diesel fuel that had been ruptured by the airplane's right wing and caught fire. Frantz told his crew mates, Juan Cano and Harold Cook, to turn the gun on that for a few minutes. But it hardly did anything, which wasn't surprising—water was usually an ineffective way to extinguish burning fuel. So Frantz directed the stream back onto the flames inside the Pentagon.

They were peering into the building when Cano and Frantz thought they spotted some movement inside one of the windows on the ground floor, to the right of the impact hole. Am I seeing things? Frantz wondered, peering into the smoky, fiery morass. He and Cano ran up to the window while Cook stayed on the gun. Sure enough, somebody was moving inside.

"Somebody's in there!" Frantz shouted. Then he began yelling at the staggering form, "We're over here! Here's the way out!"

The shape moved toward them. Frantz looked up at the crack in the building. He was sure it was going to collapse any minute. He looked back at the person inside. It was a woman, he could now tell. She seemed to be making her way toward them, following their commands. Frantz and Cano leaned into the window, coaxing her forward. If she stopped or fell over, or if flames appeared to threaten her, they were ready to dive in and drag her out. But with the building so fragile, Frantz first wanted to see if he could draw her out, without endangering himself or Cano any more than necessary, and possibly forcing somebody else to go into the building to rescue *them*.

The woman went in and out of view as smoke thickened, then blew clear. When they caught glimpses of her, she seemed to be staggering, disoriented. She was clearly in shock. But she moved steadily toward them. "You're doing good! Over here!" the firefighters kept shouting.

Finally, the woman got to the edge of the window, and the two firefighters reached in and hauled her through. She had burns on her arms and possibly elsewhere. She was so sooty Frantz couldn't tell if she was black or white. They pulled her out a few feet, then called over some military personnel who had backboards that could be used as stretchers. The litter-bearers carried her off toward the triage point, near the guardrail on Washington Boulevard. Then Frantz and Cano hustled back toward the deluge gun. When Frantz looked back at the building, the upper floors were teetering. He and Cano had gotten away just in time.

Frantz was right. Gibbs, Defina, Lightfoot, and others had been watching the ominous crack widening to the left of the impact point, and decided everybody needed to evacuate. "Command to all units inside the structure on the heliport side," Lightfoot called over the radio. "Be advised, go ahead and back out. We've got a potential collapse."

Bobby Beer, clawing his way into the building with Chad Stamps and Fred Kawatsky, did an about-face. "Shit!" he exclaimed. "Okay, let's go guys!" he told Stamps and Kawatsky. "We need to evacuate!"

Evacuate? Stamps thought, looking at the destruction all around him. Man, where the fuck are we going to go? The Rescue 104 crew turned around and started to clamber out the same way they had come in, pushing through the same wreckage all over again.

Mike Smith, Greg Gulick, and Justin Scott had worked their way about 100 feet down the D Ring, close to the seat of the fire. Now it was a long route back to safety, with tons of soft, superheated concrete suspended precariously over their heads. When they heard the radio dispatch, they started backtracking, following the hose line they had carried into the building. They traced it up and over debris, and around the remnants of the bent walls of the D Ring. Corridor 5, which Smith had deemed an immediate danger when they first walked in, now seemed like an island of safety—if they could reach it.

Most of the firefighters were hurrying out of the building. But where was Cornwell? He hadn't responded to the evacuation call. At the command post, Lightfoot tried raising Cornwell on the radio.

"Command to Interior . . ." Lightfoot called, summoning the Interior Division commander.

There was a truncated response from Cornwell. "We're in the process of working our way to . . ." Then Cornwell's voice faded.

"Command to Interior," Lightfoot continued. "We're a little broken up . . . advise to back up and hold your position."

The message didn't get through. Cornwell and his team kept moving.

HELLHOLE

10:05 A.M.

The same cauldron of flame that had driven Ed Hannon and Craig Duck out of the C Ring was now incinerating the holes on A&E Drive. Yet P. K. Carlton, the Air Force surgeon general, had just watched two men—Navy officers Dave Thomas and Dave Tarantino—duck underneath the flames and go into one of the holes. He and Craig Powell and a group of about five others dashed over to follow them in, wading through ankle-deep water and kicking chunks of debris out of the way.

Carlton still didn't know who Powell was. But despite the civilian clothes the SEAL was wearing, Carlton knew he was a military man—and a good one. He ordered Powell to stay outside the hole and told him he was in command out there. It was important to have a capable leader outside, since everybody inside might get cut off.

A few others had leapt into the hole ahead of Carlton. Matthew Rosenberg, the medic, couldn't see anything when he jumped into the hole except for smoke. Then he realized people in the hole were digging like miners, clearing debris, and he did that for a few moments, pushing it to the left and the right, trying to open a path to where the people might be. Smoke seared his lungs with every breath. He did what he could, then turned around and groped for fresh air outside the hole, rotating out into A&E Drive.

When Carlton finally crawled through, it was like crossing into an industrial nightmare. He tried to stand at first, and got singed by crackling, electrified wires that melted and dripped like solder. It felt like a jolt of electricity zapped his head. He ducked down to get below the wires and see beneath the smoke, which hovered in a thick bank about two feet off the floor.

Carlton started pushing his way through the debris, shoving rubble out of the way. They seemed to be working in some kind of wire cage that had been torn and bent. He scooped up a handful of debris to pass back, helping clear a path into the room. He noticed lots of plastic computer parts and other bright red objects—a color used to designate documents and computer components that are highly classified, even higher than top secret. It made sense—they had to be clawing through a SCIF, a sensitive, compartmented information facility. These were supersecure rooms inside the Pentagon where the most sensitive information, clandestine intelligence sources, and elite commando tactics were discussed. To prevent electronic eavesdropping, SCIFs were enmeshed in wire cages that disrupted the kind of sensors that the Russians, for instance, might have pointed at the Pentagon, hoping to pick up valuable information.

As Carlton was wading through the debris, one of the men up ahead of him came reeling backward, overcome by smoke. Carlton passed him back, and others grabbed him and pulled him out of the hole. Squatting beneath the smoke, Carlton inched forward. He could make out one of the Navy guys who had plunged into the hole. Tarantino, a doctor, found two women who had been knocked unconscious, and revived them. The two women now came crawling toward Carlton, thrust forward by their rescuers. He shuffled them back toward the daylight at the opening of the hole, just as he had the first man.

Out in A&E Drive, Rosenberg did a quick assessment and decided the two women didn't need emergency treatment right there; they could be moved into the courtyard. He helped roll them onto litters, while others carried them off toward the courtyard.

From inside the hole, Carlton yelled back toward the opening, "We need some T-shirts! Soak them in water!" In the service road, a couple of men took off their T-shirts and started rolling them in the fetid water, tearing them into strips of cloth and passing them in. Carlton grabbed one and pressed it against his face. It helped a little.

Thomas and Tarantino, the Navy officers, had climbed over a piece of landing gear and other parts of the airplane fuselage as they crawled into the cramped space, using fire extinguishers to help clear a narrow path through the flames. Deep into the work space, they found a Navy colleague who was trapped in the chair he had been sitting in, pinned by the weight of his collapsed desk, the surrounding cubicle, and parts of the ceiling that had crashed onto him. Tarantino was on his back, trying to free the man by leg-pressing the mass up and off him. As Carlton watched through the smoke, he could see that fire filled the room, and that some of it poured onto the wrecked desk like a flaming waterfall. It must have been molten material or burning liquid. Some of it flowed down off the desk and pooled on the floor, just inches from Tarantino's face.

Tarantino finally freed the victim, and he and Thomas dragged the man toward the hole. Carlton, meanwhile, found another man who was unconscious on the floor and slapped a soggy T-shirt onto his face. The man shuddered and started to regain consciousness. "Get moving or you're dead!" Carlton ordered in the sternest military voice he could muster. That seemed to work; the man started to pull himself up, enough for Carlton to grab him by the shirt collar and heave him toward the opening of the hole. Others grabbed him and dragged him out.

By then Craig Powell had climbed into the wrecked room, helping pry the wire cage open, to create a bigger opening and pass out debris. At six-five, Powell had a hard time ducking beneath the smoke, especially since his legs and back were pounding with pain from catching the jumpers. As a SEAL, he was an expert diver, able to breathe pure oxygen, and he knew air. What he was breathing now was sludge. He could feel his body rejecting it like poison. It burned his throat and his nostrils.

He couldn't back out, though. Since he was standing over the other people in the room, Powell could see that the ceiling was falling down. He stood as tall as he could and pressed upward on the wire cage with his arms, hoping that if he held the cage up, the metal framing would keep the ceiling intact long enough for others to rescue everyone who could be saved. His lungs sucked in the black gunk. Around him all the walls were burning. He felt like he was in *The Towering Inferno*. The metal cage, he could tell, was getting soft and starting to wilt. Live wires kept bumping the cage, sending shocks through his fingers.

Behind Carlton, other people had found fire extinguishers and were spraying them onto the flames around the hole. It accomplished virtually nothing. The streams vaporized the moment they hit the fire. There was a lot of shouting, on top of the clamor of the fire, which seemed to be getting louder. Carlton wedged a fire extinguisher under the table Tarantino was trying to lift, allowing the Navy officer to relax his legs. Then, pushing aside what looked like a body part, Carlton edged deeper inside, where all three of them listened intently for signs of other victims. "There's more this way!" Tarantino shouted, pointing into the darkness.

"Let's go," Carlton agreed.

The three were about to head deeper into the hellhole when a booming voice roared, "Get out! Get out!" It was a military voice, and there was no mistaking how serious it was. Carlton was still crawling on the floor, and he reached up with his hands to see if he could feel parts of the ceiling falling down. Through the smoke, he caught a glimpse of Powell holding up the ceiling. The SEAL looked like Paul Bunyan.

Powell looked down at Carlton. "Guys, you gotta get out!" he grunted. "I don't know if I can hold the building up much longer."

Carlton was convinced. "Let's get out of here," he shouted to Tarantino and Thomas. They all realized time was running out. Crawling toward daylight, they ended up tumbling back toward A&E Drive in a tangled mass, tripping over each other and all the rubble in the way. Carlton lost track of where the hole was. He couldn't see light anymore and ran into what felt like Powell's legs.

Overhead, Powell's strength was finally about to give. He pushed up against the wire cage as hard as he could. But flames were licking at his face, he couldn't breathe, his body was screaming in pain, and the cage was starting to droop and crumble. Powell looked out of the hole and lined up his escape route, expecting the whole room to collapse the second he pulled his arms away. He let go and dived out of the hole. When he looked back, the building sagged—but held.

Powell was crestfallen, thinking he didn't have to let go, that they could have gotten a few more guys out. Then there was a terrific roar. Everything inside the hole suddenly flared up. The room completely collapsed. The entire area they had been crawling through erupted in flames.

Just inside the hole, Carlton was on his knees, trying to guess how to get out. Suddenly he felt a powerful force, like tornado winds. He and the two Navy men were churning together in the fiery haze, then all three bodies got slammed together and went flying. Somehow, they got blown out of the hole, landing in a puddle at Powell's feet. Carlton drew himself up on hands and knees, then raised himself out of the muck. He had no serious injuries. A young soldier patted him on the back. "Way to go, sir," he told the general.

"River Division to Command. Priority," Chuck Gibbs was saying into the radio with incongruous calmness. "We have structural collapse . . ."

Nobody needed to announce it. Everybody who had gathered on

the heliport lawn or the hill overlooking the Pentagon watched the spectacle with awe and disbelief. The upper floors of the Pentagon had been sagging, severely weakened by explosions, fire, and thousands of gallons of foam and water. Finally, the lower floors gave way, and once the concrete began to crumble, nothing could have stopped it. A whole chunk of the structure cracked off along a building seam to the left of the impact hole, creating a raucous avalanche of stone and metal. Roof panels snapped. Window frames crumpled. Beams and girders buckled as five floors of the Pentagon thundered to the ground.

A cloud of smoke and ash mushroomed outward from the bottom of the pile, blocking the view of the damage. Behind the smoky curtain there was now a gash in the Pentagon 70 feet wide.[1] As the dust began to clear, the insides of E Ring offices, all the way up to the fifth floor, were suddenly visible from the outside. Some seemed strangely intact. In a third-floor office, a desk, on narrow legs, held a dictionary, just feet from where the building dropped off. On the right-hand side of the gash, portions of the fractured floor slabs still clung to the structure, like broken branches hanging from a tree. The wreckage sloped steeply from right to left, forming an ugly V-shape that seemed on the verge of further collapse.

Most of the fire units had gotten out, but a group from Fort Myer, led by firefighter Jon Culberson, never heard the evacuation order, and they hadn't known a collapse was coming. They were just starting to search inside the E Ring when the building began to shake all around them. They glanced anxiously at each other, trying to decide what to do, when the smoke that had been hovering over their heads suddenly banked down all the way to the floor. Visibility dropped to nothing. Then a blast of air shot through the area, followed by a loud crashing noise. That left no doubt: They had to get out. Startled and scared, the firefighters instantly spun back the way they had come and sprinted out of the building, chased by waves of dust.

Gibbs took the turn of events in stride. A few seconds after initially announcing the collapse on the radio, he came back on to describe what he saw. "River Division to Command," he said. "Okay, in reference to the collapse, we've had a five-story collapse. A pancake collapse. A section approximately 75 . . . looks like two corridors in—everyone out of the interior." He called for more deluge guns to pour water into the building.

From the outside it was hard to tell how far into the building the fresh damage went, although a chunk of the E Ring was clearly wrecked. In fact, the force of the collapse penetrated deep into the building. It had been a blast of high-pressure air, generated by the collapse, that blew P. K. Carlton and the two Navy rescuers out of the hellhole in the C Ring, back into A&E Drive. The same rush of air was now feeding the fire that engulfed the room they had been searching. The rescuers who had plunged into the flaming hole were now regrouping in A&E Drive, a knot of disheveled people in tattered clothes, reeking of smoke.

Colonel McNair, who had crawled through Dilbertsville to get to safety, was there, trying to figure out what he could do to help. After squeezing out of the second-floor window and clambering down the ladder onto the trash bin, McNair went into one of the holes along A&E Drive, digging through rubble and passing it back, trying to reach voices coming from behind a huge piece of machinery. He ingested too much smoke and could no longer breathe, so he rotated back out into the service road. When he could breathe again, he went back and saw an arm poking out of the rubble. With another soldier, he pulled out a woman struggling to free herself. Despite being buried in debris, she seemed okay.

At one point, when he was back in the service road getting air, McNair went to look for flashlights and other tools that might be helpful. He opened maintenance closets and dug through service carts, but all he could find was one painter's mask. When he got back to A&E Drive, conditions were far worse. Smoke and fire were getting thick inside all the office spaces. He saw one group of people with a hose trying to connect it to a faucet on the wall, but the handle had been removed. To turn on the water, they needed pliers, which they didn't have.

Someone handed McNair a fire extinguisher. He ducked back into the hole and sprayed the extinguisher onto the fire where the smoke seemed thickest. The stream sizzled and evaporated on contact, the fire mocking his efforts. McNair was in a tightly confined space and felt he was blocking what little light was coming in from the service road. He climbed out again and handed the painter's mask to somebody inside.

In A&E Drive most of the people who had been trying to rescue victims in the C Ring were starting to drift away. A Defense Protective Service officer came up to McNair and said he had to leave. It was unsafe. Plus, there were reports that another plane was headed toward the Pentagon.

"Another plane?" McNair asked, confused. "What do you mean?"

The officer explained that a plane had hit the Pentagon. McNair had thought it was a bomb somebody planted in the building. When he asked more questions, the officer told him about New York. It was the first McNair had heard about the terrorist attack unfolding along the East Coast. He was stunned. "You need to move along now, sir," the police officer insisted.

11

CIGARETTE BREAK

10:20 A.M.

The command post was on overload. Jim Schwartz, the operations chief, and the others manning the command post had just watched a huge chunk of the Pentagon come crashing down. They weren't certain that all the firefighters had cleared the building before it collapsed. Cornwell and his group hadn't been heard from. Now there was an even more urgent problem: Another aircraft was heading toward the Pentagon.

Chris Combs, the FBI agent, was getting updates from Jim Rice, his boss at the Washington Field Office. At first all Rice knew was that a second hijacked aircraft was heading toward the Washington area. It might be headed for the Pentagon—the kind of follow-on attack the Israelis had warned about. Or it might be heading for another Washington landmark, like the White House or the Capitol Building. There was no way of knowing.

Combs found Schwartz. "Jimmy," he said, "there's another airplane that's 20 minutes out." Schwartz looked at him, not sure what Combs was saying. "Did you hear me?" Combs asked, leaning in. "There's another hijacked airplane, 20 minutes out!"

After a second or two it registered "Are you sure?" Schwartz asked.

"Yeah," Combs nodded.

"Okay," Schwartz said, swinging his head around. "We gotta get our guys out. Where are we going?" He was scanning the area for someplace safe to relocate the command post. He and Combs both saw two underpasses where I-395 crossed over local roads.

"How about there?" Combs said.

"Okay," Schwartz decided, "let's put everybody under there."

Schwartz found Joe Lightfoot. "We're moving the command post," he told the aide, pointing to the new spot. "Take the buggy and meet me over there."

The only firefighters remaining inside the Pentagon were with Bob Cornwell. They were making their way up the stairwell near the Corridor 3 entrance, surveying the smoke and fire conditions and assessing the damage. The edge of the collapse zone was about 400 feet away. When the building fell, they had felt a shudder but were not harmed.

The group was spread out, and a few firefighters at the front had started to trek down the E Ring, toward the impact point. Cornwell had a radio, as did Griffin and McCoy, both captains. But there was so much chatter that it was hard to tell what was going on, especially with so many things happening at the same time. Some of the transmissions were garbled, and there was a lot of noise and confusion in the building, as firefighters shouted back and forth and other people rushed around. On the radio, Griffin could hear something about a collapse but couldn't make out exactly what.

Near the front of the group, Cornwell suddenly froze. His radio had been undependable, but this time he heard Joe Lightfoot, at the command post, loud and clear. "Command to all units on the fire ground," Lightfoot was saying. "Evacuate the building and reposition! We have a report of another hijacked aircraft."

Cornwell didn't hesitate. "Everybody out of the building!" he shouted to the group. "Drop everything and go!"

A few of the firefighters couldn't believe it. "You've got to be kidding me," Jim Anderson muttered to himself. When he first arrived at the Pentagon with Griffin, there were so many walking wounded that he'd worried they would get stuck doing triage outside—and miss fighting the fire. Now, after the tedious wait near the command post, they were finally inside the building. There might be victims needing help right around the corner. If another plane was going to hit the Pentagon, Anderson figured, they were stuck.

He and a few of the other firefighters hesitated on the steps. Farther down, other firefighters hadn't heard Cornwell's order over the din and kept trudging upward. Cornwell drew himself up and mustered his deepest command voice. "Another airplane is coming!" he roared. "I want everybody to evacuate the building—now!"

The protests stopped. Griffin knew that Cornwell had been in combat in Vietnam, and he always seemed unflappable under pressure. But now the battalion chief looked wide-eyed and anxious, an expression Griffin had never seen on him. If this rattled Cornwell, he thought, it had to be serious.

As Griffin led his crew out of the building, he was thinking that if another attack was coming, the goal would be to kill as many of them as possible. He told his crewmates Anderson and Mosely to leave their gear near the building, including their air packs; they'd retrieve it all later. As he tried to figure out where to go, Griffin began lumbering toward the underpass where I-395 crossed over Washington Boulevard, making sure his crew followed. If a follow-on attack was coming, Griffin thought, terrorists would be looking for big groups. He'd lead his crew to someplace remote, away from the visible crowd.

But when he turned around to check on his crew, he saw dozens of others following him. Well, there goes that idea, he told himself. There's no place to hide out here.

Other firefighters were also unsure what to do when they came out of the building, so Cornwell stayed on the landing at the bottom of the stairs, ushering everybody out. When he finally came outside, a number of firefighters were standing near the exit, as if merely leaving the building would keep them safe. They still had air bottles on their backs and all their turnout gear on. It was extremely awkward and strenuous to run in the thick, heavy gear, and firefighters were trained to walk quickly when they had to, but to run only as a last resort.

Cornwell invoked the last resort. "Drop that shit and run!" he yelled to the dawdling firefighters. That was all the motivation anybody needed. Cornwell never cursed. And he never ran, or told anybody else to. So if he said run, they would run. Air packs, helmets, and face pieces fell to the ground, and fire crews began to scatter in different directions.

Gibbs came on the radio, reporting that all of the units under his command had evacuated and moved out to the highway, Washington Boulevard. But Arlington battalion chief Dale Smith, the A&E Division commander in charge of operations in the courtyard, seemed to be falling behind the pace of events. Lightfoot had been trying to reach Smith and stress the importance of getting all his people out, but radio contact was sketchy. Smith finally answered. "A&E Division," he said, identifying himself. "We're still in the center courtyard. We have four firefighters still in the building."

"I want them all out," Lightfoot said, finding his command voice. "Step it up." Protocol was to speak calmly and clearly into the radio, no matter how dramatic the situation. But Lightfoot was getting agitated.

Smith still didn't seem to understand that a second plane might be about to crash into the Pentagon. "When we get these firefighters out," he asked, "do you want us to clear the center courtyard?"

"We want all personnel 500 yards clear of the building," Lightfoot answered firmly. "Are you aware of the report of a second plane?"

Gibbs broke in. Defina, from the airport, was with him, and they were able to communicate on Defina's radio directly with the tower at Reagan National. "River Division with priority," Gibbs said. "Okay, security is in contact with the tower. They report a plane is in the air a few minutes out, destination unknown, and they are saying 'take your guess.' So we need to watch out."

Lightfoot tried Smith again. "Command to A&E Drive sector," he barked. "Are all of your units clear of the building?"

"We have two or three firefighters exiting," Smith answered.

"Copy," Lightfoot acknowledged. "Get those folks out now!"

"At this point," Smith said back, "be advised that people from the Pentagon are still entering the building."

Doug Insley had now replaced Lightfoot, who was preparing to move the command buggy. "That doesn't matter," Insley told Smith. "Just get our people out."

Smith weighed his options. The command post was telling him to order his fire crews out of the building—but it was a long way out, and he wasn't sure they'd make it before the plane hit. Besides, how would it look if the firefighters fled, while all the military people stayed behind, doing rescues and treating patients? Smith decided the best course was to ride out the evacuation in the courtyard.[1]

While those with radios were learning about the inbound plane, most of the people in the courtyard were still in the dark. P. K. Carlton had just returned to the courtyard from A&E Drive, smoky, wet, and rattled from his ordeal in the inferno. "We can't find anyone else," he told Jennifer Glidewell, the nurse. Carlton saw a woman lying on the grass—one of the jumpers—who looked like she needed help. He ran over to her.

Just then one of the DPS officers started yelling, "Another plane is coming! It's 20 minutes out. We don't know if it's hijacked or not, but it's not responding so it probably is!" Everybody who was working on a patient looked up. Their faces all said the same thing: *Not again.* Then, almost in unison, everybody started working faster.

"Okay, 20 minutes," Glidewell said to Rosenberg, her medic. "Let's see who else we can get up and out by then."

The DPS officer started shouting again. He had an urgent update. The plane wasn't 20 minutes away, it was 20 *miles* away. Glidewell went numb. They could get wiped out any second. Nobody around her said anything. "Well, it's not here yet," she finally muttered. "Let's see if we can help somebody else out."

The woman Carlton was working on, an Army officer, was gasping for air. Her vocal cords had swelled from the smoke, and she couldn't breathe. Carlton had pulled out his pocketknife to perform a rudimentary tracheotomy when she looked at him in panic and managed to suck in a little air. He put away the knife and called for one of the motorized carts, to rush her to an ambulance or hospital.

But there was no way the doctors or nurses could evacuate the courtyard, with patients still in need. And Carlton had a strategic position he didn't want to give up—if there was another crash, he was in the center of the Pentagon, the best place to take care of more patients. As the senior military officer on the scene, he decided he would send the people working with him to different corners of the courtyard. If there was a second strike, part of the group might be killed, but not everyone, he hoped.

Craig Duck, Ed Hannon, and the rest of the D.C. Truck 4 crew had used up their air looking for victims in the fiery confines of the C Ring. Sweaty and tired, they got back into the courtyard just as one of the guards was warning of the second plane. It took a moment to sink in, then they realized that the building was about to be attacked—*again.* Nobody was telling them to leave the courtyard, and they didn't know what else to do, besides wait.

Ed Hannon knelt down beside a tree and prayed. He noticed a few others doing the same thing. That made him feel better. "Dear God, please watch over my wife and two kids," he implored. When he finished, he waited. It didn't make sense to flee. If the plane was just a couple minutes away, it would take too long to run back through the tunnel, especially with all his gear on, into South Parking. And once out there, where would he go? Since he had no idea where the plane was coming from, he'd be just as likely to run into its path as away from it. Hannon simply looked to the sky, watching for whatever was coming.

If the incoming plane didn't destroy the building altogether, Craig Duck's group would still need more tools and hoses than were available in the courtyard, so Duck decided he might as well use the break to fetch some equipment from South Parking. He brought Mike La-Core, a tall, muscular firefighter who was known for his moves on the basketball court—and a high-pitched voice that rose a couple of octaves when he got excited. They trekked out through the tunnel to find South Parking filled with unattended fire trucks. They rummaged through several engines and found some hose packs, nozzles, a deluge gun, and other gear.

It was heavy, and in a normal situation firefighters would have taken turns carrying the dense, bundled hose and the cumbersome deluge gun into the building. But nobody else was around. Duck was an avid cyclist, in good shape, and he figured he'd just muscle his share of the burden back through the tunnel. LaCore would follow with whatever he had scrounged.

As Duck was huffing and puffing under the load, he heard an unmistakable squeaky voice and glanced to the side. LaCore was pulling up next to him on one of the motorized carts used to shuttle workers around the Pentagon. "Hey, Lieutenant," he squealed, "let's just load it all on here and drive it back." It was an improbable moment for a laugh. But the firefighter, perched on the cart like he was out for a day of golf, made Duck chuckle. He tossed his load onto the cart and hopped on, and they whizzed through the tunnel, back to the courtyard.

In the tunnels beneath the Pentagon, Steve Carter, the assistant building manager, was trying to devise the best way to save his people. The engineering spaces in the Pentagon basement were old, subterranean caverns, but they were usually clean, well-lit, and orderly. Like the overall Pentagon design itself, there was a circular central area, with tunnels that fanned out like spokes on a wheel. Huge plastic tubes ran over the whole warren, color-coded based on what they carried. Green tubes carried chill water for cooling, blue tubes carried drinking water, and red tubes supplied water for firefighting. Smaller orange pipes carried steam for hot water and heating, and yellow pipes carried natural gas. A variety of other conduits carried electrical lines, copper and fiber-optic cables, and compressed air. The crisscrossing tubes, in bright colors, looked like a three-dimensional rendering of the New York City subway map.

After helping pass victims out of the flooded electrical room on A&E Drive, Carter and one of his engineers, Dan Murphy, had raced to the basement. Water was gushing out of dozens of shattered pipes, and Carter had gotten word that the building's water pressure was dangerously low. If it dropped much further, the air-conditioning throughout the building would fail, including all the cooling systems that kept banks of computers and other electronic gear from overheating. There would be a meltdown, literally—in the midst of a national crisis, just when the government most needed the vital equipment housed in the Pentagon. Sprinklers and hydrants would conk out too. And the system couldn't just be restarted once there was more water. It would have to be reprimed and repaired, which could take hours or days.

Carter and Murphy plunged into a basement they now barely recognized. The tunnels were filled with a foot of standing water and teeming with smoke. They couldn't see the colored pipes overhead and had just one flashlight between them—so they had to feel around above them for the valve handles. Some they could reach with their hands. Others were too high, and had to be operated by pulling on a chain that turned the handle. Either way, it took both hands to do the work, so they breathed through the armpits of their coats to keep the smoke out of their throats. Carter's nose started running and he didn't have a free hand to wipe it. The gunk he was breathing felt like a gooey mass of ash in his mouth. His eyes watered, adding to the slop oozing down his shirt.

Carter and Murphy finally got the water valves in the burning part of the Pentagon turned off. Then they turned off other valves that controlled steam, gas, and electricity, and stumbled back up the stairs to the ground floor of the Pentagon.

Carter's assistant, Kathy Greenwell, was still answering phones in the Building Operations Command Center, and running hard hats, batteries, and other supplies out to the staff as they needed them. A dozen engineers and other workers were roaming throughout the building, troubleshooting wrecked or damaged systems. When Carter's radio delivered the news of the second plane and the orders to evacuate, he faced a conundrum: He was obligated to get his people to safety, yet they were essential to the operation and survival of the building. They were the only ones who knew how to turn the air flow up and down through vents on the ceiling, how to turn the water on and off, how to find the breakers that would shut down the electricity.

Carter summoned his people on the radio and gathered them in the courtyard. The majority he sent outside, half toward North Parking and the rest toward South Parking; he was concerned for their safety but also wanted to make sure that if another plane hit, there would be some survivors to help save the building. A skeleton crew of six remained in the courtyard. Carter dispersed them too, employing the buddy system and relying on his knowledge of the tunnels in the basement—probably the safest place to ride out a follow-on attack. He sent Kathy Greenwell and one engineer to the tunnel beneath the apex of Corridors 5 and 6. Two other engineers went beneath Corridors 3 and 4. Carter and Murphy settled at a spot beneath the entrance to Corridors 1 and 2.

On the radio there was a somber countdown. The incoming plane was 15 miles out, then 10. Carter fidgeted in the smoke-filled tunnel. Murphy had always pestered him about quitting smoking. Now, Murphy looked at him and said, "What are you gonna do?"

Carter paused for the first time since Flight 77 had hit the building and he had felt the shudder in the BOCC. "I'm gonna go have a cigarette," he decided. He had kicked the habit a year earlier but had been craving a smoke. Why not?

He walked up the steps to the courtyard, Murphy behind him. It was eerily quiet. Bandages and other detritus were scattered about. Smoke drifted in and out. A few people seemed to be hugging the walls, but otherwise the courtyard seemed strangely empty, especially considering the chaos Carter had seen throughout the building just moments before.

He asked for a cigarette from a Pentagon worker hurrying from the building, and was rewarded with a whole pack of Marlboro Lights. Carter sat down on a curb, shaking, and lit one. Murphy sat down next to him. They both gazed at the smoke-filled sky, waiting for whatever was coming.

★ 12 ★

SPECTATORS

10:25 A.M.

It had been about 45 minutes since Flight 77 smashed into the Pentagon. The first firefighters had arrived within 10 minutes of the impact. Yet all of the firefighters and rescue experts inside the Pentagon had been driven out.

Frustration seethed along a long line of sweaty firefighters as they baked in the sun, fanned out in an L-shaped arc overlooking the fire. They watched the smoke and flame like spectators, from the underpasses beneath I-395 and the stretch of Washington Boulevard adjacent to the heliport lawn.

When Denis Griffin and his crew finally made it to the underpass, Griffin turned around and saw several D.C. fire trucks that were just arriving and driving past them. Their crews looked puzzled by the people standing around, doing nothing. Griffin imagined what they must be thinking, that they knew nothing about the plane and were probably wondering what the hell was wrong with these firefighters.

Nearby, some medical people were setting up a triage area. "Well, guys," Griffin told Anderson and Mosely, "drop your fire gloves and grab your medic gloves. Let's assist with triage." Anderson and Mosely groaned. There were plenty of medics there to give assistance. If they got involved with patients, they might not be able to go back in and fight the fire. That's not what they were there to do. But he and Mosely followed Griffin's instructions.

Everybody was fixated on the second airplane. How far away was it? Where was it headed? What should they be doing to plan for it? Information was scarce. While FBI agent Chris Combs was heading to the underpass, he passed one of the National Airport fire trucks. It dawned on him that the airport fire crews might be getting information directly from the FAA's air-traffic controllers. "Hey!" he shouted to one of the firefighters. "Can you contact the tower on your radio?"

"Yeah," the fireman answered.

"Okay," Combs instructed him. "Tell your chief the FBI has taken you, and you ain't leaving."

"Sir?" the firefighter asked, confused.

"If you need to say you've been detained by the FBI," Combs explained, "well, you have. You've gotta tell me about these freakin' airplanes!"

"Oh, shit," the firefighter sighed. Being attached to the FBI, manning a radio, was pretty much a guarantee he wouldn't be fighting the fire.

Out on Washington Boulevard, closed to traffic now, dozens of fidgety firefighters sat on the guardrail, watching the Pentagon burn. Mike Smith was angry. All his career he had trained to run into burning buildings—not away from them. And here they were—at the Pentagon, of all places—and nobody could protect them so they could go in and do their jobs.

The busiest people on Washington Boulevard were the medics. The highway overlooking the helipad was the closest hardtop to the smoking hole in the side of the Pentagon, a natural rallying point not just for ambulances, but for a handful of helicopters from the U.S. Park Police and other agencies that had landed to help transport patients. When Ed Blunt, the EMS supervisor for Cornwell's battalion, arrived at the scene, he had seen burned victims, some still trailing smoke, staggering across the helipad lawn toward the highway. Military doctors and nurses were already kneeling over patients on the grass, while volunteers stood holding IV bags. It was the obvious place to set up triage and medical aid.

Blunt, sober-minded and calm, had established an orderly if extremely busy EMS operation. He quickly got the police to clear stalled or parked cars off the highway and remove debris like the light poles knocked over by Flight 77. More than a dozen ambulances had been lined up, all facing north, so they would depart for area hospitals traveling in the same direction and nobody would get blocked in. Firefighters Scott Hagan and Mike Alvarado, from Arlington's Rescue 109, had used saws and blowtorches to cut away a section of guardrail between the highway and the Pentagon lawn, so medic units could easily move victims onto ambulances. And Blunt made sure that one lane of the highway was kept clear as a landing zone for helicopters.

But now he dropped his orderly plan. If a second airplane was about to smash into the Pentagon—or someplace nearby—it was time to get every patient who could be moved out of there.

Blunt was feeling the stress. In addition to the Arlington County medics, military personnel and volunteers were crowding the scene, trying to help. The noise from the helicopters made it damn near impossible to hear anything over the radios. And the helicopters' rotor wash blew dust and debris onto patients, forcing stretcher teams to lean over the victims and protect them.

Blunt had personal matters on his mind too. His wife, Kay, an accountant, was scheduled to be flying back to D.C. that morning from a conference in Chicago. As far as he knew, she was in the air at that very moment. He worried about her safety, but also about what he would do when his two sons got out of school later in the afternoon. What if Kay wasn't around to pick them up? Who would take care of them?

He tried to focus on the demanding job he had to do, but it was a struggle. He told a couple of colleagues that he was worried about his wife. Firefighters kept coming up to him, offering rumors and other information that might or might not be true. At one point an FBI agent heard about Blunt's wife and announced, "We think there might be hijackers trying to seize planes and fly them into the Sears Tower in Chicago." Fellow firefighters shouted down the agent.

Blunt told himself to stay busy, knowing it was better to focus on what was right in front of him instead of something he couldn't control. He knew there was nothing he could accomplish by worrying.

As busy as it seemed before, Washington Boulevard was now beginning to overflow with people, as everybody responded to the evacuation order to move 500 yards from the building. Blunt made a command decision, and ordered a "load-and-go": The medics would grab everyone who looked injured, cram them into every available emergency transport vehicle, and head for the hospitals as quickly as possible.

Arlington County firefighter John Delaney had seen his share of burn and accident victims during his years as a firefighter. Yet as he loaded patients from the Pentagon, he was stunned by some of their grotesque injuries. Short and stocky with a mischievous grin, Delaney was always the comedian in the group, able to break up a room with a funny, unexpected quip. But not today.

He was working overtime, driving Arlington's Medic 106. As he and his partner, Jody Marker, were driving toward the Pentagon, the usually cheerful and sanguine Marker had erupted with anger at the terrorists who hadn't even been identified yet. "Those motherfuckers!" Marker screamed, pounding on the dash. "This is war! We need to find these fuckers and bomb their sorry asses!" Delaney just listened to the tirade. He was still trying to comprehend the morning's events, and couldn't even begin to calm Marker down.

They had pulled into the Pentagon's North Parking lot to figure out where they were most needed. A soldier walked up to the ambulance, all bloodied. They pulled him into the back of the unit, along with an Army nurse who offered to help treat his injuries, then continued toward the triage site on Washington Boulevard—where they parked and sent the soldier off toward some medics gathered on the lawn. It was against protocol to release a patient to find help on his own, but the soldier qualified as walking wounded, and Marker and Delaney both knew there would be more seriously injured victims needing their attention.

Their first patient at the triage site was a large woman who was lying facedown on one of the backboards the military rescuers had been using to carry people out of the building. They set her in the grassy area inside the guardrail on Washington Boulevard. She had been wearing a full-length dress, but the back of it was burned off. The front remained, but her body was burned from the top of her head to her heels. Delaney and Marker rushed over to her with a wheeled stretcher from their ambulance. They struggled to lift her from the backboard to the stretcher and finally got her into the ambulance with the help of several volunteers.

A second later somebody tapped Delaney on the shoulder. It was a flight medic, pointing to a helicopter Delaney hadn't noticed. "We're here to take the worst," he told Delaney.

"Well, you're taking her," Delaney said without hesitating. They enlisted some military help once again, and started wheeling the woman toward the helicopter on the stretcher.

Delaney jumped into the helicopter to help haul her inside, and leaned over the woman to ask how she was dong. He didn't expect an answer, and doubted she was even conscious. But she mouthed a response. He couldn't hear what she said but realized she could hear him, so he told her to think happy thoughts. "Sing 'You Are My Sunshine,' " he encouraged her. That was Delaney's family's song. He knew that when a patient had burns this bad, there wasn't a lot of hope for recovery, but at least she was still with them. Now they just needed to get her to a burn center, and fast.

Another team of medics carried a second patient to the helicopter just as Delaney and Marker finished loading theirs. It was a man who had been burned on his belly and chest. His arms were injured too. But most striking were the man's eyes. The whites had been burned, and turned a sallow green and yellow color. Delaney was still in the helicopter, and he helped pull the fresh patient inside. It took just a moment, and then he hopped out of the chopper. But the eyes stayed with him.

Debbie Walker's ambulance, Medic 102, was about as full as it could get. There was only room for one patient to lie on the stretcher in back, although a few more could sit on the two bench seats, as long as they weren't hurt too bad. Normally, Walker and her partner, Tom McAllister, would transport no more than two patients at a time. There were now five in the back of the ambulance. The two medics were trying to figure out what hospital they should go to. Burn victims and other trauma cases would ordinarily go to George Washington, over in the District. But if another plane was coming, and it was headed for D.C., then those hospitals might end up swamped. They decided to head for Arlington Hospital instead.

Mark Skipper, the Fort Myer firefighter, was one of the patients being loaded onto an ambulance. When he saw Flight 77 barreling straight toward him, he dived under the fire truck for protection. He was being treated for scrapes and cuts he suffered when he rolled under Foam 161—which was now completely burned. Other firefighters were rapt as he told them what it had been like seeing the plane come from nowhere and hearing the crash.

Army Maj. Dave King was being treated for his injuries too. After failing to find his office mates and deciding he needed to hurry out of the building, King had followed the voices guiding people to safety and eventually stumbled onto the Pentagon lawn. Both of his arms were burned, and he held them out in front of him, looking like a mummy covered in soot and dust. King saw an officer he recognized,

Lt. Col. Bill Delaney, who had a stack of three-by-five note cards and a Sharpie and was taking down names of everybody who might still be trapped in the building. King offered the names of his office mates. He also gave Delaney the phone numbers for his wife and parents, and asked his colleague to call them and say he was okay. Delaney promised he would, then wrote the phone numbers on King's shirt, in case he ended up unconscious or incoherent. "Hey, while you're at it," King said, "write 'O pos, no meds, no allergies.' "

Delaney pointed King to the triage area, on Washington Boulevard, and King walked over there. Two other Army officers saw the condition he was in and started to help, taking off his shoes and pants, pouring water on his burned arms and wrapping them in towels. People were still being carried away on stretchers. There seemed to be a lot of women on the stretchers, some still smoldering. King didn't want to ask for any extra help until they had been taken care of.

Something was strange, though. Nothing hurt. It should have— his arms were seared, with skin hanging off. King realized he was probably about to go into shock. "Damn, I'm feeling no pain," he said to himself. "Pretty soon, this is gonna hurt real bad."

An Army medic was working nearby. "Yo, Sarge," King called out to him. "Can you jack me up with something here? 'Cause I'm gonna go into shock real soon."

That got the medic's attention. "How long have you been here?" he asked King. One of the officers with King said about 20 minutes. "You—on a stretcher now," the medic ordered.

The others helped King into an ambulance. A news cameraman noticed the drama and came over to shoot some footage. King saw him, raised his bandaged arms—and gave the finger to the camera with both hands. "Tell him I'm dead," King muttered. He didn't like the press during normal times. Injured or not, he wasn't about to become fodder for a TV spectacle.

★ 13 ★

HELO RIDE

10:30 A.M.

Jim Schwartz had a lengthy to-do list. The threat of another airplane hitting the Pentagon was his top worry. But Schwartz also needed to know how big the fire was and exactly where it was burning. Finding people who might be trapped and getting victims to hospitals was still a top priority. Beyond that, fire commanders still didn't know which fire crews were on the scene. Then there were all the other agencies with which Schwartz and his command had to coordinate. A small army of state and federal agencies was descending on the Pentagon, and he needed to devise a system to make sure everybody could work together, instead of getting in each other's way and making a tough job even harder.

Schwartz had been in the Pentagon numerous times, starting with a two-alarm fire that broke out in a storage area close to the courtyard during his rookie year, in 1984. He had come to think of the Pentagon as not one huge building, but as five buildings in close proximity to each other. Each building formed a wedge, shaped like a piece of pie with a bite taken out of the pointy end, where the courtyard was. During a fire, the courtyard would be the best place to stage trucks and firefighters, since it offered the shortest distance to the greatest number of points in each of the five wedges. Fire crews could cover more distance working from the inside out, instead of the other way around.

But that's not how this fire was unfolding. Many units had shown up on their own and gone into the burning building on their own initiative, following the smoke and fire from the outside in. Few of the arriving firefighters headed for the center courtyard, where they were needed most. Schwartz was getting only pieces of information from Dale Smith, the A&E Division commander in the courtyard. Since he first set eyes on the blaze, Schwartz had assumed that the fire went all the way from the E Ring to the courtyard, and consumed all five floors. But he wasn't sure how wide it was. He also knew that engines, which pump water and carry hose, could fit into the courtyard, but that taller ladder trucks, with a telescoping ladder or other aerial device mounted on top, couldn't squeeze through the tunnel. Ladder trucks usually carried all the axes, sledgehammers, ceiling hooks, and power tools firefighters might need, which meant lots of heavy gear would have to be carried in—and it was a long walk.

Of everybody in the department, Gibbs and Cornwell probably knew the Pentagon best. That's one reason Schwartz had placed Gibbs in command of the misnamed River Division and Cornwell in command of the Interior Division, and why he sent Cornwell in to scope out the fire. The evacuation had cut short Cornwell's reconnaissance mission. But when he got back to the command post, Cornwell was able to put a boundary on the southern edge of the fire.

They didn't yet have a map of the building, so they drew a five-cornered rendering of it on a Plexiglas whiteboard. "The fire extends to about here," Cornwell said, drawing a line just south of Corridor 4. Flight 77's right wing had clipped the outside of the Pentagon near that entrance, and the collapse stopped just before reaching the mouth of Corridor 4, which was now charred and half buried in debris.

Schwartz and his aides knew from Gibbs and the firefighters who had gone down Corridor 5 that that part of the building was smoky but navigable. There was enough information now to start bracketing the problem. The seat of the fire, where it burned most intensely, was between Corridors 4 and 5. Thick smoke probably ranged from Corridor 3 to Corridor 6. If firefighters didn't get back in soon, fire might claim that broader area too. They still didn't know whether the fire burned all the way to the courtyard or all the way to the roof. They didn't even know how big the collapse was. Did it just take out a section of the E Ring? Or go deeper, into the D and C Rings? Whatever the case, it seemed likely that at least two wedges, from Corridor 3 to Corridor 6—the equivalent of two buildings, in Schwartz's rationale—were fully affected by the fire. The crash had effectively taken out 40 percent of the Pentagon.

Plaugher, the fire chief, decided to conduct his own reconnaissance. Unlike many others in the Arlington County Fire Department, Plaugher had spent most of his career working elsewhere. Arlington County had hired him from the adjacent Fairfax County Fire Department, where he was a deputy chief, in 1993, and his new bosses charged him with modernizing a relatively small department. Plaugher and Schwartz had worked with other government officials to pioneer a locally based terrorism-response plan for the D.C. area, following the sarin gas attacks on the Tokyo subway system in 1995. One pillar of this plan was a synchronized incident-command system that created a structure for numerous agencies to work together in the event of a similar attack on the D.C. area subway system—the Metro—or any other kind of terrorist attack.

Plaugher had also pressed for better cooperation with law-enforcement officials at the Pentagon. When a steel security barrier in a Pentagon driveway had popped up beneath a limousine bearing the Japanese defense minister in 1998, sending the car flying and injuring the minister, there was conflict between Arlington EMS officials and medical teams from the Pentagon about who had primary responsibility for the incident. Plaugher worked out an agreement with the Defense Department clarifying everybody's role. Arlington would be the first responder, with Pentagon teams in support.

Firefighters who had been around for a while could tell the difference. Bob Cornwell had run calls at the Pentagon for years, and there were times when guards escorting them into the inner recesses of the Pentagon, usually for medical calls, took forever. There would be byzantine detours and marches so long that the guards themselves got tired. "Man, I don't want to get sick in the Pentagon," Cornwell once said. "I'll die before I get out of there." Pentagon officials became much more cooperative after Plaugher started reaching out to them.

Among his peers, Plaugher had a reputation as a big-picture guy. And he focused on the big picture now. He knew the general layout of the Pentagon but not the structure of the floors or the various hallways. Plus, there was so much confusion, it was hard for anybody to gauge the scope of the fire. Anybody sitting at home watching TV, he thought, probably knows more about what's going on here than I do. He needed to get a better understanding of the building and the situation his commanders faced. Fast.

After checking in with Schwartz and deciding to leave his operations chief in charge, Plaugher left the command post and headed toward the triage area on Washington Boulevard. He walked up to a Park Police helicopter that had just dropped off a patient and was on standby for further missions. Approaching the pilot in the cockpit, and pointing to the words FIRE CHIEF on his helmet, Plaugher asked, "Are you waiting to evacuate casualties?" The pilot shook his head no. "Good!" Plaugher yelled over the din of the engines. "Now you're working for me." He pointed to the sky. "I need to go up!"

While Schwartz and Cornwell were sketching out the fire on the whiteboard in the command post, Plaugher was above it, getting an aerial view of the damage. He still didn't know for sure that it was a jetliner that had wrecked the building. He knew what had happened in New York, but hadn't seen the devastating footage on TV. And when he saw the Pentagon from above, he was surprised how much of it remained intact. The thick black smoke had become gray now, and it continuously wafted beneath the helicopter, blocking his view. But he could see that the walls on four of the Pentagon's five sides stood as erect as ever, their rows and rows of windows as orderly as soldiers in formation. Many of the satellite dishes and pieces of machinery on the roof seemed undisturbed. When the smoke blew out of the way, even the courtyard, with its evergreens and other trees reaching nearly as high as the surrounding roof, seemed placid from overhead.

The part of the building facing west was a disaster, though. It resembled a gaping wound. The collapsed area looked like part of the building had been snapped off. From the south, looking north, Plaugher could see into office spaces that were now exposed to daylight, as if looking at a cross section of a model in an architect's office. It was also clear that only the E Ring had collapsed. From the D Ring inward, the roof was still intact.

But there was plenty of other bad news. The Pentagon's penitentiary-gray walls were scorched all the way to the C Ring. Black stains marked the fire's path, showing where it had burned hottest. It looked like A&E Drive, the open section that ran between the B and C Rings, had stopped the fire from progressing all the way to the courtyard. Still, smoke was pouring out of windows on all floors, well beyond what looked to be the impact area. That meant the fire had spread far inside the building.

Plaugher kept asking the pilot to fly lower so he could get a better look. In addition to the scale of the fire, he wanted to know everything he could about the building's structural integrity, so that nobody sent firefighters into parts of the building that might collapse. As they descended, Plaugher could feel the heat. They started flying in the smoke, which was risky. Helicopters need air in their engines, like all other gas-powered machines, and the smoke could seize the motor. Finally, the pilot told Plaugher he couldn't get any lower.

"Okay," Plaugher agreed. "Take 'er up one more time. I just want one more look around." As they rose, he scanned the whole scene. The area beneath was filling with vehicles and people. They were going to be there awhile. They'd need to set up a security fence, to keep people out. He called the emergency control center on his radio. "We're going to need some fence," he told the dispatcher. "Get me 2,000 feet."

When the helo landed, Plaugher hurried to the grassy area where he had first found Schwartz at the makeshift command post. Nearly everybody had moved to the underpass by then, but Joe Lightfoot was still packing up Cornwell's Suburban. Lightfoot closed the door of the Suburban and began to drive off toward the underpass where Schwartz had gone when a stocky, commanding figure stepped in front of the Suburban with his arm out, giving the halt signal. It was Plaugher. The fire chief rushed around to the passenger-side window, expecting to see Cornwell. When he realized it was Lightfoot, he barked, "Where's the command post?"

"Chief Schwartz and the command post are down there," Lightfoot said, pointing to the underpass.

Plaugher climbed in. "Go!" he ordered.

The fire chief passed his fresh intelligence to Schwartz and Cornwell. They began to refine their plan of attack. Once they got back into the building, they'd flood the E, D, and C Rings with fire crews on all five floors. Most would come from the outside, where hundreds of firefighters were now staged, waiting out the evacuation. But they'd work on getting crews and trucks to the courtyard too. Cornwell would get in there and coordinate with Chief Smith. One vital part of the plan: Make sure fire crews working their way toward each other, from the inside and outside, didn't end up with opposing hose lines. Being on the receiving end of a fire hose was always unpleasant, and it could be deadly. The force of the water could push a fire right on top of somebody on the opposite end of the stream.

Back on Washington Boulevard, Chuck Gibbs and Mike Defina

were facing an unusual problem: Too many firefighters were showing up. In virtually every fire, the department for that jurisdiction had responsibility for calling in units from other departments if they were needed. Sometimes different departments would share responsibility for buildings that were close to both. Arlington County, for instance, had mutual-aid agreements with fire departments in neighboring Alexandria and Fairfax County, which placed units in each department on call to the other. But racing to somebody else's fire without being summoned—"self-dispatching"—was bad form. And it complicated the job of commanders on the scene. In an unpredictable event like a fire, it could be challenging just coordinating and keeping track of your own people. Throwing another department's units into a blaze could produce opposing hose lines, endanger crews, and make it impossible to track everybody going in and out of the burning building.

Yet all around Gibbs, self-dispatched units were showing up, most from the D.C. Fire Department. Nobody had called for any D.C. units yet, and when the Arlington commanders realized they were coming, a dispatcher had gone on the radio and asked the D.C. crews to stage on the Fourteenth Street Bridge, which crossed from D.C. into Virginia and was about a mile from the Pentagon. But the D.C. crews had ignored that request and headed straight for the Pentagon. Some called in to the command post, but others just followed the orders of their own battalion chiefs and gathered near the building's entrances. Gibbs was annoyed but not surprised. This was a "career fire," the biggest most of them would ever see, and everybody wanted in on the action.

Still, he was in charge on the helipad side, and he was not about to lose control of the fire ground and allow random units to go racing into the building just to grab a piece of glory. The evacuation and the lull in the firefight provided an opportunity to get organized and develop a plan. He and Defina started sketching out what they knew about the fire, and figuring out how to use all the units that were showing up—and make sure they didn't get in each other's way.

There was still a huge unknown in the sky, though, and the tension was getting to people. Near one of the underpasses, Allen Becker, one of the crew members on Engine 101, watched a police officer pull up with a gun in his holster—but without the vest that Arlington police officers usually wore to identify themselves. Half a dozen other cops suddenly drew down on him, pointing their pistols and yelling for him to raise his arms. "Hey, I'm a police officer!" the man shouted, eventually convincing them.

"Man, what a mess," Becker muttered.

FBI agent Chris Combs was hastily trying to get security in place. He called John Jester, head of the Pentagon's security force, and asked him to send a SWAT team to surround the command post and protect it from threats on the ground. He also wanted snipers posted in surrounding high-rises, to look out for suspicious cars or anything else that might be coming.

Combs kept getting the updates on the second airplane from his boss, Jim Rice. The FAA was no longer able to track the precise location of the plane; somehow it seemed to have slipped beneath radar coverage. But based on its last known position, heading, and airspeed, the FAA was estimating the time until it reached Washington and passing that on to the FBI and other authorities.

Rice had been giving Combs updates every five minutes, telling him in a calm, professional voice how many miles away the plane was. Then Rice broke the pattern. "Chris, you got four minutes," he said somberly. There was personal concern in his voice. Combs felt it, and realized it wasn't just a countdown. It was the last pregnant moment before another unstoppable catastrophe. He passed the update to Schwartz. They each stopped what they were doing and looked to the sky.

14

1,000 DEGREES

10:40 A.M.

T-minus-zero came and went. On Steve Carter's radio, the security people were saying that the incoming plane was due any second. As Carter peered through the smoke into the sky over the courtyard, he put in a call to some of his maintenance people outside the building, who had evacuated. "If you see the plane," he said, "could y'all let us know what direction it's coming from?" If he knew at least that, he figured, it might give him and his people a few seconds to run away from it.

The courtyard was practically silent. Everybody was waiting for the same thing. It was hard to see through the smoke, so they were listening as intently as possible. In the distance there was a buzz. It quickly got louder. It was the unmistakable roar of a jet engine winding up. Carter tensed, expecting to feel a shudder or hear an explosion. Or worse.

Then an Air Force F-16 zoomed low and fast over the courtyard. Panic became relief. Carter exhaled like he had been holding his breath for an hour. "Okay!" he cheered. "No more bad things are going to happen!" He and Dan Murphy hurried to find their colleagues, still huddling in the tunnels beneath the building.

On Washington Boulevard, frustration was suddenly transformed into jubilation. When the F-16 flew over, it appeared to dip its wing, as if signaling to the people on the ground that the cavalry had arrived. Cheers went up. "Thank God that guy's there!" Mike Smith shouted. "Where has he been?" Now they could get back to work, he told himself, planning his next foray into the fire.

At the command post, Chris Combs was on the radio again to Jim Rice, his FBI boss, who had an official update on the second hijacked aircraft. "You're all clear," Rice informed him. "The plane hit Camp David."

Holy shit, Combs thought to himself. Camp David. He wondered if the President was there. He realized that for a while he had been operating as if this were a typical incident. It wasn't. If Camp David had been hit, this was a serious attack on the whole country.[1]

Gibbs and Defina were getting the same information from the tower at National Airport. "River Division to Command with priority update," Gibbs announced on the operations channel, in his usual deadpan. "Per the airplane operations center, there is no additional threat. No additional threat per the airport operations center. Okay?"

Behind Gibbs, firefighters who had overheard his report were shouting, "We can go back in! We can go back in!"

The command post was preparing to resume firefighting operations—but this time it was going to be orderly, more or less, with a thorough accounting of which units were in the building. Doug Insley, operating the radios, told Gibbs, near the helipad, and Smith, in the courtyard, that he needed an "accountability check"—a list of all units on the scene under their command.

Smith had only two fire units in the courtyard, both from D.C., totaling seven people. "I need hose," he pleaded. "Okay for us to go back in the building?"

Gibbs had many more units at his disposal. He ticked them off.

Schwartz finally approved the all-clear over the radio. Gibbs and Smith were now free to resume the firefight inside the Pentagon.

The firefighters who had been displaced onto Washington

Boulevard hurried back to their trucks to grab fresh air packs or change soggy socks or replace tools they dropped on their forced exit from the Pentagon. Mike Smith, Justin Scott, and Greg Gulick got some new air bottles from their truck, Engine 108. Smith found James Angerett, the Fort Myer firefighter he was working with before, and they started making a plan for getting back to the area they had abandoned 40 minutes earlier. Derek Spector's crew from Truck 105 joined them too. Instead of operating as single crews, they reasoned, they'd be able to accomplish more as a larger group.

There were vast amounts of demolished office space that still needed to be searched, under demanding, tedious conditions—it was like pawing through the aftermath of a tornado with fire at your back. Yet now they all knew it was unlikely they'd find any living victims. Crews had already searched portions of the E and D Rings and hadn't found anyone alive. In much of the wrecked area it was simply too hot for anybody to have survived this long. And areas that hadn't completely burned up were so smoky, it would have been impossible to breathe for more than a minute or two.

What they needed to do, Smith argued, was continue to look for victims, but switch from a rescue phase to offensive firefighting. It was time to start beating back the fire and reducing its spread. To do that they needed a lot more water power than the high-rise packs could muster, with openings just 1¾ inches in diameter. "We're gonna have to throw more water at this," he told Angerett. "Forget it with the little hose lines. That's not gonna do it."

Instead of the high-rise hoses, which put out a limited stream but were easy to carry, they'd need another thick supply line, and some bigger hand lines too. Gulick and Scott started unraveling another supply line from Engine 108, while others found bigger hand lines elsewhere. Then the group went back to the Corridor 5 entrance for another foray into the building.

Smith and the other officers led their teams back to where the hose lines had been dropped during the first evacuation. The whole group went back down the D Ring, using the leader line that Engine 108 had left in there the first time as a guide. Smith still couldn't raise Gibbs or anybody at the main command post on the radio—the channel remained clogged with traffic. So he acted on his own authority as an experienced captain, equal in rank to Gibbs.

They followed the hose up and over debris, climbing on top of desks, cabinets, and other objects they couldn't identify. Smith led, while the firefighters worked the second supply line up over the mess and carried additional hand lines to extend its reach. These were 2½-inch lines, considerably heavier than the hoses they had carried before. It took two firefighters working together to advance them through the jumbled mess, and they grunted and heaved as they dragged the hoses and other tools over the tangles of debris. Sweat poured into their eyes. Snot ran from their noses. Heavy breathing fogged their face pieces, further narrowing their vision through the smoke. Yet there was no way they could remove the face pieces to wipe their noses or clean their masks—the smoke would rapidly overcome them.

Adrenaline helped propel them forward, and they soon reached the point where they dropped the end of the hose the first time. Before, it had been extremely hot but there was little actual fire in the area. Now the whole space was ablaze. The fire had spread while all the firefighters were out waiting for the hijacked plane that never came. One of the hand lines they carried in had been dropped and burned and was unusable.

Smith called a halt and looked around. The whole area was dark, lit only by flames. Unlike the part of the D Ring that was behind them, filled with cluttered pieces of office equipment, the area up ahead looked to be swept clear. Nothing was there—no walls, no furniture—just a big, open area. What happened to all the offices? Smith wondered. And all the stuff that was in them?

Overhead, Smith could see through a big hole in the ceiling, two or three levels above where the fire was burning. The surroundings reminded him of the sniper scene from *Full Metal Jacket*, the Vietnam movie, in which a squad of Marines crawls through the remains of a bombed-out building, crunching rubble with every step, searching through flames for a sniper who has picked off three of their men. Shit—this is just like wartime, Smith thought.

He decided they'd stop there. Any farther and they might end up buried in another collapse. The hand lines were connected to the supply line by then, and Fred Calvert out on Engine 108 had charged the line. The firefighters dug in and opened the hoses, dropping to their knees to steady the lines and stay out of the heat above, which was several hundred degrees hotter than down by the floor.

Their nozzles were dialed down to tight, narrow streams. Spraying water toward a fire drives air into it—the wider the spray, the more air, and the greater the chance the fire will flare. So they concentrated their streams, to minimize the amount of air they pushed onto the flames.

The superheated fire devoured the water at first, spitting out clouds of smoky steam. Physics was working against them. Water turns to steam at 212 degrees Fahrenheit, and they were attacking a fire that was well over 1,000 degrees in places.[2] At such temperatures, water can evaporate in midair, before it even hits the burning contents of the room. But they kept the hoses steady, and in a few minutes the water started to find its mark and the fire began to retreat. For the first time all day, Smith and his crew were making a small amount of progress against the unrelenting blaze.

While Gulick, Scott, Christman, Roache, and the others worked on the fire, Smith was keeping close track of time—and the air they had available. Each tank provided about 45 minutes of air. It took them about 10 minutes to clamber down the D Ring and reach the end of the supply line they had dropped. That meant it would take about 10 minutes to get back outside, with a cushion of five minutes or so, in case they got hung up or something happened. That meant they had about 20 minutes to work on the fire before they'd have to turn around and head back out for more air.

Firefighters were flooding into various hallways around them. It was a hodgepodge firefight—not nearly as organized as the commanders wanted. Some of the crews were taking guidance from Gibbs, others were moving through the hallways on their own. A number of D.C. crews were filing in, and their radios operated on different frequencies than those of the Arlington firefighters—the D.C. units could talk to each other on the radios but not to anybody else. Crews that never worked together passed each other in hallways, curious who the other guys were, yet keeping to themselves.

Arlington Capt. Bob Gray was working near Mike Smith, with a crew of six others. Gray and dozens of other off-duty firefighters had first been sent to Arlington's Station 1, about two miles from the Pentagon. Then they were bused up to the fire as Schwartz and other commanders called for them. Gray was a technical rescue specialist, trained to operate in collapsed buildings. When he first saw the pancaked E Ring and the astounding pile of wreckage, he had the awful feeling that it would be a grim day for the Arlington County Fire Department. If there was a collapse already, he thought, there would probably be two or three more. They were going to lose somebody.

When Gray led his group into Corridor 5, he did a quick assessment of the hallways to the left, away from the fire. The walls had all buckled. Where there should have been right angles, there were fissures and bends instead. Nothing was uniform. There weren't signs of fire in that direction, but a massive pressure wave had clearly pushed walls in or out wherever there was give. "Hey guys," Gray warned his crew, "this building is under tremendous stress. We need to be on our toes. Listen for creaking and any other signs of additional collapse."

Their assignment was search and rescue: Get as close to the fire as they could, on all five floors, and look for people. Conditions were horrible. There was no stable footing anywhere. Everything was slick from the water cascading down from overhead. Close to the collapse zone, where the walls were blown down, Gray could see where the building's huge support columns were damaged and wrecked. As a technical rescue specialist, he knew that getting the fire out would be just the beginning of the job. After that there would be days of work to shore up the destroyed columns and make it safe to operate in there.

Bobby Beer and the crew from Rescue 104 were on the lawn preparing to enter the building again. Their truck didn't usually carry hose, so they borrowed some from a D.C. crew and connected it to Engine 108, still being manned by Fred Calvert. They entered the building and began advancing their hose up a stairwell off of Corridor 5, for a reconnaissance and firefighting run on the second floor. Beer had the dry hose on his shoulder, with a couple of others lugging sections of it behind him, when he heard a hiss. He knew right away the hose had just been charged, and since they hadn't yet put a nozzle on it, water was about to come spewing out like rocket exhaust, at a rate of more than 100 gallons per minute.

The force knocked Beer over. "Goddamnit!" he blared into the radio. "Who charged that line without me telling you to?" Just below, meanwhile, his crewmates, eager to snatch a moment of levity from the foul-up, guffawed at the sight of Beer being manhandled by the hose.

He wrestled the hose under control while Calvert, outside, quickly got the water turned off. Calvert was tracking half a dozen different hoses attached to the panel of Engine 108, each requiring a different water pressure. To make sure there was no more confusion, he decided to jot info about each hose onto the pump panel with a grease pencil.

Beer and his crew entered the second floor, on the E Ring, in an area that was burning fiercely. They got the supply line recharged and opened up hand lines right away, spraying desks and other office furniture that was blazing, looking for victims underneath and behind the debris. Arlington firefighter Chuck Guice, who had joined Beer's crew, couldn't believe how hot it was. Guice discovered that he couldn't even put his arms down; any tight spot on his fire suit, without a cushion of air between the liner and his body, felt like it would burn instantly.

The water they were spraying had little effect. They'd hit a burning pile of broken furniture, and the flames would die down, only to flare back up the second they turned the stream of water in another direction. All they were doing was lowering the temperature at the edges of the burning material for a few seconds. The extreme heat of the fire burning deeper in the pile caused the water to evaporate; anything that had been burning would simply reignite. To tame this fire, they would have to thoroughly douse and soak everything, which was not possible with flames roaring everywhere and just a few hand lines to attack them.

Through the smoke and flame, they saw a couple of other crews pass by in the hallway. Chad Stamps was amazed to see one crew walk right past them, carrying two packs of hose line, evidently on their way to fight fire someplace else. Firefighters are trained *never* to go through a fire without putting it out, since it might seal off your exit. You might as well walk into a burning room and lock the door behind you. Yet there they went. This is totally disjointed, Stamps thought.

Crews couldn't stay in the Pentagon for long. Where the fire was, it felt like they were operating in a furnace, and they were quickly driven out by the heat. Fire-resistant turnout gear made out of Nomex and other materials was only designed to withstand temperatures of about 600 degrees, and then only for brief periods of time.

These flames were several hundred degrees hotter. Dragging hose and working with axes, ceiling hooks, and other tools loosened up protective clothing, occasionally allowing small gaps between garments. Superheated air would find the openings and sear the firefighters' skin like a branding iron. Even their own sweat became dangerous, turning into steam as the temperature inside the suits skyrocketed and scalding their skin.

Thirst was another good reason to take frequent breaks. Every firefighter knew that it was hard to replenish fluids during a long fire, and dehydration could send you to the hospital just as easily as injuries from smoke or fire. Then there was bottled air, which lasted no more than 45 minutes.

The Arlington and Fort Myer crews in the D Ring turned off their lines and headed for a breather after about 20 minutes. They got fresh air bottles and drank water and rested, then discussed how to get more water on the fire. Smith decided to bring a deluge gun into the building, something fire crews rarely did. Deluge guns, like the one Brian Frantz's crew had set up outside the building right before the collapse, were usually used to shoot water into a building from outside, since they fired powerful volleys that covered long distances.

In most buildings there wasn't enough open space to make a deluge gun useful. But there was enough room in this building, and Smith wanted to get water flowing into the big, open expanse that looked too unstable to send firefighters into.

There was another advantage to a deluge gun—it was meant to operate automatically, so they'd be able to leave it in place with water flowing the next time they came out, instead of turning off their hoses and giving the fire a chance to reclaim turf they had just won. And if there was another evacuation, they could just leave it flowing the whole time.

The gun on Engine 108 was heavy and cumbersome. It was designed to be rolled up to a building, not lifted up and over a smoking garbage dump. But everybody agreed—they needed more water on the fire. Smith and Angerett led the way into the D Ring once more, while the firefighters behind them lugged the heavy gun toward the fire. They set up the water cannon, fed it with connectors from the two supply lines, and opened up. They would just let it blast away at the fire this time, and push the cannon forward as the flames fell back.

Out on the lawn, Gibbs moved back to the Fort Myer command vehicle, at the southwest edge of the helipad, with a plan to impose order on the potluck firefight that had developed. Firefighters began to crowd around him like kids around Santa, eager for their assignments inside the building, many self-dispatchers trying to get to the front of the line. The throng made it impossible for Gibbs to operate. He found Keith Young, one of the burliest men in the Arlington County Fire Department. "Keith, you've gotta do something for me," Gibbs told him. "Clear the deck—the deck being the entire heliport. I need it cleared."

Young complied. "I need everybody off the heliport. Now!" he shouted, with as much authority as a four-star general could have mustered. Within seconds Gibbs and his aides had the heliport to themselves.

While units were charging pell-mell into Corridor 5, Gibbs and Defina had been developing a more orderly fire plan. They'd set up more deluge guns and pour all the water they could into the building, using Fort Myer and Arlington engines to pump it. D.C. units had been clustering near Corridor 5, well to the left of the hole and the still-smoking collapse zone. A D.C. ladder truck had arrived, and Calvert was running a line to it. The ladder could be used to get a hose up high, streaming water down onto the roof or into the hallways behind the E Ring.

At the same time, they'd organize individual fire crews into larger groups, by jurisdiction. Gibbs didn't want random firefighters or small groups entering the Pentagon without clear instructions or a task to accomplish. Every crew needed to fill a role in the overall fire-fighting plan, instead of running around looking for fire to squirt. Gibbs also wanted to make sure each crew was completely filled out, with all the proper equipment and tools. As he and Defina began building a list of fire groups, they told everybody who didn't have a full set of protective equipment or the right tools to go to the back of the line and straighten themselves out.

They'd start a grid search in the E, D, and C Rings on the north side of the collapse zone, on all five floors. It had been nearly two hours since the plane hit. There could still be victims trapped under debris or locked in mangled offices, but the odds were slipping. They'd still search for victims, but they were moving into the offensive phase of the firefight—it was time to seriously knock down the fire.

One problem Gibbs didn't have was manpower. The D.C. units nearby hadn't checked in with him, but once they did, they'd round out a sizable firefighting force. And more units were on the way. All off-duty Arlington firefighters had been paged and told to report for duty. Several crews from Alexandria were staging at Station 1, on S. Glebe Road, less than two miles away, ready to head for the Pentagon the moment they were needed. Crews from Fairfax and Loudoun counties, farther to the west, were on their way to back-fill for Arlington units who were massing at the Pentagon. More D.C. units were surely on the way, and probably lots of others, whether they were needed or not. At a minimum, they'd come in handy when the first-arriving units wore down and rotated out for a breather.

Gibbs also planned to make sure he had the name of every fire-fighter going into the building. Accountability in every fire—especially big, unwieldy ones like this—was critical. There would be no more "freelancers" going into the building without orders or instructions. Gibbs put the word out: If the command post didn't have the name of every firefighter in the group, the group wasn't going in. With firefighters desperate to get in and do their work, he knew, nobody would miss their chance simply because they couldn't get the details right.

15

RETREAT

11:00 A.M.

Chief Schwartz had heard sporadic reports of military personnel trying to get back into the building, but figured they were isolated events. Then he got a radio call from Jim Bonzano, one of the EMS battalion chiefs, who was on Washington Boulevard near the helipad. Bonzano said he was watching a column of soldiers forming up like they were going to assault the building. "You've got to do something about these guys," he told Schwartz. "We can't control them."

Schwartz hopped into a vehicle and zipped over to the lawn. Sure enough, he saw about 15 people in military uniforms lined up outside the Corridor 5 entrance. He went up to a one-star general at the back of the line. "What are you doing?" he asked.

"We're going in there," he told Schwartz. "We've got people in there. We've got to get to them."

"Oh no, you're not," Schwartz fired back, explaining that it was the fire department's job to mount rescues—not the military's.

Schwartz realized he had to do something decisive about all the "volunteer participants," as he called them. He hurried back to the command post and called Chuck Gibbs on the helipad. "Chuck, I need you to set up a line at the building entrances and deny access," he instructed. "We need to keep the military people and the freelancers out."

Gibbs had just the man for the job. He found Keith Young, the muscular firefighter who had cleared all the people off the helipad, and sent him to the Corridor 5 entrance. "Your job is to keep free-lancers out," Gibbs explained. The plan was to send over a battalion chief, to back Young up with some rank, and communicate with the command post about which fire crews should be allowed in. But the immediate priority was getting control of the entrance and keeping out the ad-hoc rescuers.

It wasn't Young's preferred duty. Like others, he was awed by the magnitude of the incident and the devastation. The things he had seen after first arriving on the scene near the helipad still flashed through his mind like they were playing on a Jumbotron: people shuffling across the grass, steaming, smoking, and screaming. Skin falling off. Blood everywhere. A priest with rosary beads praying over people lying on backboards. This is what a war must be like, Young thought.

He took up sentry duty at the Corridor 5 entrance, where the big oak doors were still lying on the grass. A moment later another formation of Army officers and enlisted soldiers marched up. They were led by a burly four-star general with a chestful of medals and shoulders that seemed as broad as a fireplace mantel.

The general strode to the Corridor 5 entrance with about 20 people behind him. "I need to get into this building to save my men," he told Young at the door, expecting the lowly firefighter to step aside.

Young held his ground. "Look here, General," he said, "you might outrank me every way possible in the military, but you're not going into this building. It's not safe."

The four-star, unaccustomed to mouthy subordinates, tried to ignore him and walk right past. Young stepped in his way, looking up at the man's chin. "I'm sorry, sir," he said. "I'm just following orders to keep people out."

He hated doing it. Young could see the dedication in the eyes of the general, desperate to help his people inside, no matter what the risk. It was a lesson in the ethos of the military; this was a soldier doing what needed to be done, in a state of war.

But still, he couldn't let him in the building. The general tried to slip by. Young threw his body in front of him once more. The general jumped to the other side, and Young blocked him again. A pushing match developed, with soldiers and firefighters stunned at what they were seeing. The military man was taller, but Young was thick and agile, and to the amazement of everybody watching, the general ended up on the ground. He quickly picked himself up, paused for a moment, then approached Young once more. The firefighter remained stone-faced, but prayed that he wouldn't have to do any more wrestling—and that his racing heart wouldn't explode through his chest. "I'm sorry," the general finally said, backing down. "You're right." Then he led the column of soldiers behind him back down the steps, onto the lawn.

Nearby, Joe Lightfoot was hunting down an aide for Chief Plaugher, whose to-do list was swelling rapidly. As Lightfoot had hoped, he found Arlington firefighter Chris Ramey near the helipad. Ramey came across as a beach bum compared to many Arlington firefighters, with their rural roots and country accents. He was laid-back and gregarious, calling everybody "dude." His colleagues loved to joke about his "Clint Eastwood hair," which was coiffed into a stylish semipompadour. But Ramey's bohemian good humor was infectious, and he was a popular member of the department, able to bring down the house just by being himself.

He was being treated for a chronic back injury he had sustained years earlier, while lifting a patient on a paramedic call, and was on disability at Station 4, "on T-shirt duty," as Ramey called it—helping stock and supply uniforms for the crews. He had caught a ride to the Pentagon with another firefighter, and helped out near the triage area early on. Since he didn't have an assigned unit and wasn't fit for firefighting inside the building, Ramey was hanging around Gibbs's command post, offering to do whatever was needed.

Lightfoot spotted him right away. "Dude!" he greeted his pal. "Ramey!"

"Dude!" Ramey echoed. "What do you think, man?"

"I think you should come with me," Lightfoot told him. He didn't want to tell Ramey what he had in mind for him—he was afraid Ramey might try to sneak away. Most firefighters wanted nothing to do with the brass during a fire—they wanted to be close to the action, not tucked into the hip pocket of a fire chief in a command bunker.

They climbed into Lightfoot's vehicle. When they got close to the command bus, Lightfoot broke the news. "You're gonna be Chief Plaugher's aide. Follow him around and write everything down. Stuff like that."

"Aw, man!" Ramey groaned. He didn't know Plaugher very well, and considered him to be a bland leader with a dry personality. He wished he could be back on the fire ground with Gibbs. "Oh well," he sighed, "it is what it is."

They walked inside. "I've got your aide," Lightfoot told Plaugher, presenting Ramey.

Plaugher momentarily slipped into Ramey mode. "Chris!" he exclaimed.

"Dude!" Ramey answered. Then, in a flash of spontaneity, they hugged, drawing grins from their colleagues in the command bus who knew it was probably the only time they would ever see Plaugher embrace a colleague.

Plaugher quickly got down to business. He explained to Ramey how he planned to fence in the whole area and bring in earth movers to plow some new roads they'd need to move vehicles around quickly. Ramey was impressed. They had barely started fighting the fire and Plaugher was already thinking days ahead. *Maybe he's not such a bad chief after all*, Ramey thought.

Plaugher gave him a list of things to do. They'd need all kinds of supplies and heavy equipment. Plaugher would have to coordinate with top Pentagon people, other fire chiefs, and dozens of government officials. There was already a long list of people trying to reach the chief. Ramey found a pad and a pen and started writing as fast as he could.

Bob Cornwell, still in charge of the interior firefight, decided it was time to go on a tour of his troops. First he went over to the helipad to see how Gibbs was doing and to check on his tactical plan for fighting the fire. Gibbs had things under control, as much as they could be. He was getting a handle on all the firefighters showing up and putting into place a strict accountability system. Several deluge guns were being moved up to the building to pump nonstop streams of water onto the fire from the lawn. Gibbs's grid-search scheme and his plan to rotate firefighters into the building in groups of 12 or so made good sense.

One concern was whether there would be enough water to last the day. The hydrants they had tapped into were working okay, but they worried that the water pressure might fail. Gibbs suggested that they might have to develop a system to "draft" water out of the nearby Potomac River, a firefighting tactic from the days when hydrants weren't as plentiful. Arlington didn't have drafting equipment and virtually never did it. The two men wondered aloud who in the department might be trained to draft water, perhaps from their work volunteering with smaller rural departments, and Gibbs radioed back to the command post, saying they might have to get a drafting operation in place later that day.

Next, Cornwell headed for the courtyard, driving one of the fire department's SUVs in through the tunnel. He knew that Chief Smith had been directing a poor man's firefight, with barely any water, few hoses, only a handful of firefighters, and little direction from outside.

It was Cornwell's first trip into the courtyard. He saw plenty of smoke and a lot of people—but few of them were firefighters. He found Smith's command buggy and pulled up. Smith's main concern was getting water into the courtyard, since the standpipes inside the Pentagon were practically shut down, and they weren't aware of any hydrants in the courtyard. Smith was doing everything he could to get some big supply lines run into the courtyard from outside the building, so firefighters would have fully charged attack lines to bring inside.

A few fresh units had arrived. Smith was getting some help from Capt. Kenny Johnson, an Arlington medic who had been sent in after reports went out about a number of patients who still needed treatment in the courtyard. By the time Johnson arrived, there were hardly any patients left. But Smith needed all the help he could get, so Johnson became his de facto aide. Still, Smith clearly needed more people, and the shortage could become acute as the crews that were already inside began to tire and needed to be relieved. Cornwell headed back to the command bus to give Chief Schwartz an update. Top priority: getting more firefighters and other resources into the courtyard.

That's where Denis Griffin and the crew of Quint 104 were headed. "Griff," as he was known, had never seen the main command post where Schwartz and the others were huddling in the underpass. After waiting out the evacuation, he guessed that the command post would be in the courtyard, in the center of the building. So after claiming the gear they had dropped, Griffin led his men there.

On the way they ran into Ed Hannon, who had been unable to find the victims the Navy officer told him about in the C Ring. After the second aircraft failed to materialize and the all-clear sounded, Hannon had commandeered one of the Pentagon's motorized carts and headed out through the tunnel to find some hoses and fresh air bottles. "Hey!" Hannon yelled to Griffin and his men when he saw them. "You guys need a ride?"

They were happy for a lift in the 85-degree heat. "Have you seen

Schwartz or Cornwell?" Griffin asked Hannon. "You know where the command post is?" Hannon had no idea, so they scrounged some gear from various fire trucks and headed back into the tunnel.

They passed a female firefighter who was walking the same direction and stopped while she piled on too. Anderson noticed she didn't have an air bottle. "Where's your Scott pack?" he asked her.

"You think I need it?" she asked.

"Whoa! Stop!" Griffin hollered, realizing she was in over her head. Usually, he was patient with rookies. But this wasn't the time for a training session. "You," he said pointing to the woman. "Off!"

As Hannon shuttled them down the tunnel, he told them about the victims trapped in the C Ring. He knew where they were, and would lead the group there, hopefully with functioning hose lines this time.

In the courtyard, Griffin expected to see a plane wreck—literally. He figured the plane penetrated all the way through to the center of the building, and that the courtyard would be trashed. He was surprised to see all the walls that lined the courtyard intact. The plane hadn't gotten that far. He didn't even see any fire.

Griffin had glanced around when they got there, looking for a command post. Chief Smith was there, but Griffin didn't spot him, so he decided they'd go straight into the building and follow Hannon back to where he thought the victims were.

They carried a hose pack into Corridor 4, through the A and B Rings, then turned right into A&E Drive. Smoke hung like fog and blocked out the sunlight from overhead. The service road looked like a filthy moat. It was covered in a foot of water, with papers and trash floating on top. There was a greasy sheen—jet fuel, Griffin assumed. All that standing water was a bad sign. It meant the pipes were wrecked. "We're gonna have a hell of a time getting any water pressure," he said to his crew members.

Above them the windows were blown out, with fire spilling out.

In the wall on their left they saw the three big holes, also flaming. They walked closer. At the mouth of the third hole they saw a piece of a wheel and countless shards of wreckage. Some of them looked like pieces of seats. The hole itself was almost perfectly round, big enough to stand inside. To Anderson, it was exactly the kind of hole he expected an airplane to make. Just outside the hole he saw a pair of feet. They were dark-skinned, without shoes, and weren't even burned. Nobody said anything as they stared at the carnage.

The hole answered one question for Griffin. Well, he thought, now we know how far this thing went through.

Hannon led them past the hole, then pointed to the wall on the left. "It was right here," he said somberly. "They were right here, on the other side."

They made a plan to get into the C Ring, on the other side of the wall, and bring a hose in. They found a standpipe and hooked up one of the hand lines they were carrying. Some soldiers were there, trying to figure out how to help. An officer came up to Griffin. "Is there any help we can offer?" he asked. "Can we help you search?"

"Tell you what," Griffin told him. "As we advance hose, push it through that door there." He pointed to the same door that Hannon and the D.C. crew had gone through before.

The D.C. crew from Truck 4 was back in the building too, and Griffin coordinated with Craig Duck, the officer in charge. They went back into the C Ring as a group of nine. The thick black smoke hit them as soon as they pushed through the doors. Pulling their masks on, the crews started breathing from their Scott packs. As before, it was rough going, through unpredictable stacks of debris. There were no flames at first, but they could hear the fire up ahead and feel the heat.

The whole group dropped to their knees and started crawling, the only way they could see anything beneath the smoke. Jim Anderson, intense, slight, and athletic, tried to feel for the walls as a guide.

There was so much wreckage piled up that he couldn't detect flat surfaces or right angles. As they inched forward through the jagged landscape, he worried that the hose would tear and they'd lose their only real protection against flames, which could come out of nowhere in such a hot space. He decided it would be his job to tend the hose, muscling it through the debris and checking that their lifeline to safety stayed intact. All the while he kept looking up, making sure fire wasn't rolling back over their heads.

Everybody was as quiet as they could be, trying to listen for victims through the crackle of flames up ahead. The debris clanged and clattered as they pushed through it, though. Light fixtures were everywhere. Griffin felt like he was crawling through a junkyard. And he was getting nervous. This isn't real safe, he thought. If we have to get out of here, it's not going to be a quick escape.

They finally got to the same room that Hannon and the Truck 4 crew were forced to vacate before. They turned left into the room, which looked like it had been some kind of workshop. The fire raged just as it had before. Griffin pointed to the nearest flames. "Hit it here!" he shouted to Brian Mosely, who had the nozzle. Mosely opened the hose and some water sprayed out. But the stream faded. After a few seconds Mosely might as well have been holding a garden hose, squirting roses.

He continued shooting it into the flames, although the fire only seemed to get larger and hotter. Griffin wanted to see if they could knock it back a bit and search the room. But it was futile. Fire started reaching over their heads. And it was intensifying.

The D.C. crew was starting to break up and drift back. The hose wasn't doing anything, and there was no way they were going to find anybody alive in there. We should probably pull out, Griffin thought. But with the D.C. crew there—rivals from the big city—he didn't want to be the first one to suggest a retreat. He glanced at Craig Duck, his D.C. counterpart.

Duck said it first. "It doesn't look like we're making any headway!" he shouted over the cacophony. "Maybe we ought to head out!"

"Yeah, I agree!" Griffin said—glad that Duck, not he, had been the one to make the suggestion.

The whole group returned to the courtyard, to regroup and see if they could find a chief and get a plan. Once outside, soldiers offered them water that had been poured into soda bottles. Some Army personnel had raided the courtyard's snack bar—long ago nicknamed the "Ground Zero Café," since it sat in the center of one of the Soviet Union's most certain targets in the event of a nuclear war. They'd broken into the soda machines with forced-entry tools borrowed from the firefighters. Soda and other caffeinated drinks were the wrong kind of fluids for rehydrating, the fitness-minded soldiers knew. So they dumped out the soda and filled the bottles with water from the Pentagon's faucets—which came out tinted brown, from the building's disrupted pipes. It was unappetizing, but the firefighters, drenched with sweat, guzzled the murky water.

Griffin spotted Chief Smith this time, and his crew hurried over to the chief's command buggy. On the way, Mosely and Anderson noticed little pieces of shredded metal all over the lawn. "Those are pieces of the plane," Mosely said, swallowing hard. "They're all over the place." Somehow, the force of the airplane's impact and explosion had hurled fragments of the jet over the Pentagon's roof, into the courtyard.

At Smith's command vehicle, Griffin reported in to him for the first time. "Quint 104, Chief," he told Smith. "We're here with a D.C. truck company. We had reports of live people trapped in the C Ring. We tried to get to them, but got driven back. We have low water pressure and we're low on air."

He asked what they should do next. Smith told Griffin to head down Corridor 4. His biggest concern was still getting water into the courtyard. "I want to know if there's a straight shot down Corridor 4 to the outside," he instructed Griffin. "Go find out." If they could get through, they might be able to run hoses from the heliport area, where most of the arriving fire trucks were gathering, down Corridor 4 into the courtyard, and finally have some real water to throw at the fire.

Griffin, Anderson, Mosely, and Hannon went back inside the Corridor 4 entrance, as they had before. This time they crossed A&E Drive and kept going. It was smoky but bearable, and they could see through the haze. Their Scott packs had been running low, and they wanted to conserve all the air they could, so they trudged down Corridor 4 without masks, breathing the contaminated air that hung in the hallway.

After they crossed A&E Drive, the men hit a pile of debris that looked like it had been plowed into Corridor 4 by a bulldozer. It blocked the hallway like a barricade. Griffin thought he could see through to the other side, but the pile was unstable and dangerous. There was no way they'd be able to snake hose through it. He radioed Chief Smith to tell him. They turned around and headed back toward the courtyard.

Griffin and his crew were already starting to feel the strain of the firefight. They hadn't rescued anybody and had scarcely doused a flame, but were drenched with sweat, jet fuel, and muck from the floors they'd crawled on. They were starting to hack from the smoke. Most firefighters were accustomed to the occasional big fire lasting 45 minutes, maybe an hour. But this fire had been burning for close to two hours, and the firefighters had barely even started to put it out.

Back toward the entrance to Corridor 4, they ran into the crew of Arlington's Engine 103, who delivered some major news: They had run a big supply line into the courtyard, from a hydrant out in South Parking, through the tunnel. Finally there was water. "This is more like it!" Anderson hooted. The 103 crew was bringing in a deluge gun too, to set up in A&E Drive and flood the flaming C Ring with as much water as they could pump in.

Griffin and his crew helped drag the gun and its various fixtures into the service road. They struggled to get the right adapter fixed in place. Griffin hadn't noticed the carnage outside the punch-out hole, and while they were splashing around in the flotsam, he said to Mosely, "Man, I'm surprised I haven't seen a body yet."

"Look down," Mosely replied .

Griffin was standing on a severed leg, with a shoe on the end. He stepped off it, moved away and stiffened. "Well, there you go," he said. His understatement masked a growing sense of dread.

When they finally got the deluge gun flowing, they pointed it into the flaming holes on the service road. Then they started hosing down the windows on the second and third floors, where fire still raged. They were finally getting some decent water into the fire—and it still seemed to do nothing. All of them could smell the fuel, and as maddening as it was, there was little that water could do. Without the specialized foam that the airport trucks carried, the fuel was simply going to have to burn itself out.

The Engine 103 crew took over the gun. Griffin decided his team should keep searching for victims in areas where people might still be able to survive. They found a stairwell in the service road and started ascending. This time they hit thick black smoke, but saved any remaining air in case they needed it to rescue somebody, and went without masks once again.

There were some other firefighters in the stairwell. Griffin recognized Capt. Rick Genest from Arlington's Engine 105. "Hey!" Genest called out. "What are you guys doing?"

"We're trying to knock down as much fire as we can on the exterior," Griffin explained, referring to A&E Drive. "There were some reports of people trapped. But we couldn't find 'em."

"We're going up to some higher floors," Genest told him. "We've had reports of people in that area too."

"We'll go with you," Griffin said. The two crews walked up to the second floor together, and stepped into the hallway to see what they could find. There was some fire, but they could move around without masks. The closest office was a secure room that said DEFENSE INTEL-LIGENCE AGENCY on the cipher-locked door. The firefighters started bashing through the wall next to the door with an axe. They created a narrow opening. Genest slipped through, then popped back out a few seconds later.

"It's high heat and it's pitch-black," he said. Genest and Griffin both knew those were ideal conditions for a flashover, when the contents of a room rapidly ignite. When it was extremely hot and you couldn't see any fire—that was the time to watch out. Besides, Genest was sure nobody could be alive in the room.

They both realized there was no point going back in there. Maybe other offices in the hallway were in better condition. They moved on and kept looking.

UNTENABLE

11:20 A.M.

Chief Smith no longer suffered a shortage of fire crews in the courtyard. Several Arlington and D.C. companies had finally found their
way there, along with a few from other jurisdictions. Each crew underwent a similar orientation as they entered the building: There was
a brief trudge down a smoky corridor, a sharp turn into A&E Drive,
a startled glimpse of the ominous, flaming debris, and amazement at
the raging fire that seemed impervious to water.

A makeshift crew consisting of Capt. Brian Spring, Paul Marshall,
Chris Cox, and Jason Lyon was on its way. None of them had been on
duty that day. Spring, a friendly storyteller with bushy black hair and
a Jay Leno jaw, had been scheduled to work but took a day of leave to
care for his sick month-old daughter. His regular unit was Rescue
104, which Bobby Beer was leading in his place. When Spring saw
the news, he called the school where his wife was a teacher and asked
the principal to send her home right away. As soon as she got there,
he took off for Station 4, which he reached quickly—state troopers
had shut down the highway, but Spring showed his ID and sailed
north as police officers blocking all the exits watched him fly by.

When Spring got to Station 4, the other three were already there.
Cox and Lyon had just arrived—with their own fire truck, a quint
they had commandeered on the way, from the Arlington maintenance

yard. The two were half brothers whose dad, G. O. Lyon, was an Arlington battalion chief. Jason Lyon was known as "Cub"—the younger Lyon. Both he and Cox had been on the shift that ended at seven that morning, gone home, then raced back to Arlington together in Cox's truck.

Paul Marshall, the other half of the "wonder twins," had been on leave that day too, but he rushed to Station 4 from his home in Reston, Virginia. Orders by then were that all crews should report to Station 1, on S. Glebe Road, where they'd be organized and sent to the Pentagon as needed. Cox drove them all on the quint. G. O. Lyon, who was overseeing the staging operation at Station 1, decided to keep the four together as a crew. Spring was the only captain, so he'd be in charge. They found air packs and waited.

Spring suddenly got antsy about security. Station 1, filling with firefighters, was starting to look like a good target if terrorists planned a follow-on attack. "Hey, Chief," Spring said to Lyon, "we need to get a policeman in here or something." Lyon nodded but seemed preoccupied.

Spring noticed a young man with dark Mediterranean features outside the station, wearing a backpack. Spring walked up to him. "Who are you?" he asked.

The man said he was the boyfriend of a female firefighter who was at the station.

"Yeah?" Spring said suspiciously. "What's in the backpack?"

"Clothes," the man said.

"Can I see?" Spring pressed. The man pulled off his backpack and opened it. Clothes spilled out.

Okay, Spring told himself, I need to calm down.

Chief Lyon had gotten a call from the command post at the Pentagon. They were considering starting a drafting operation, pumping water out of the Potomac to use against the fire. Did anybody at Station 1 know how to do it?

The battalion chief knew that his son Jason had some experience drafting, from his work as a volunteer. That was their ticket to the fire, so Spring, Cub Lyon, Cox, and Marshall headed for the Pentagon.

By the time they got there and checked in at the command bus, the drafting plan had been put on the back burner. In Gibbs's area, they were getting plenty of water.

Instead, Schwartz sent Spring's crew to the courtyard. The quint was too tall to fit through the tunnel, so they got off and started to walk. Off to the side they saw Arlington's Engine 105 parked, with nobody nearby. Unlike the quint, Engine 105 was small enough to squeeze through the tunnel, and it carried a wide variety of hoses they'd probably need. So they hooked up a four-inch supply line to a hydrant in South Parking and reeled it off the engine as they rolled through the tunnel. More water could never hurt.

When they reached the courtyard, Lyon, who was driving, pulled Engine 105 aside, where it wouldn't block traffic. They had all been in the courtyard before, but never seen it like this. Members of the military still ran in every direction. MPs, military police, were trying to impose order, with marginal results. Bandages and trash were strewn everywhere. Amidst it all, hundreds of small metal pieces flickered in the grass, as the sun, cutting through the smoke, glinted off them.

It took some hose work to get the supply line connected to the hydrant in South Parking up and running. They affixed it to Engine 105's intake valves so the engine could function as a relay pumper, pulling water through the tunnel and adding the pressure needed to get it into the building in force. Then they ran a section of hose to another truck nearby, giving it a water supply too.

Under normal conditions the driver of an engine would stay with the truck and monitor the pump panel, the way Fred Calvert was doing on Engine 108 out by the helipad. But there was an urgent need for firefighters inside the building. Cox and Lyon found the guy working the pump on another truck and got him to handle both.

Spring, meanwhile, found the command post, where Chief Smith gave him a straightforward assignment. "Find the punch-out hole on A&E Drive. Go in and assist."

Cox and Lyon hauled the deluge gun and some hose off Engine 105 and met up with Denis Griffin's crew, working another deluge gun on A&E Drive. Once Spring's crew got the gun set up, they checked out the punch-out hole and got their bearings.

As they took in the ghastly scene, Spring spotted something that looked like a burned torso atop the wreckage outside the hole. He looked closer and saw shoes, with severed feet still in them. Other body parts floated in the grimy water. It looked to him like one of those intense fires where anybody who survived had gotten out in the first five minutes.

After a few seconds somebody said they should check the third floor for victims, so they headed for a stairwell next to the punch-out hole. The lights were out and the smoke heavy, the same noxious air that Griffin's crew had encountered. Their Scott packs were full, so they pulled on their masks and started air flowing immediately.

Cox and Lyon got to a landing and pushed on the door that led to the C Ring hallway. It wouldn't open. They banged on it with axes, but that didn't work either. The door was bent and jammed. Spring ordered everybody back to the service road, to regroup and figure out what to do next.

They decided to break the door free with a Halligan tool, a kind of crowbar designed specifically for prying open doors, padlocks, and dead bolts. One end was forked, like a typical crowbar, while the other end had two types of prongs that extended in opposite directions, along with a flat surface that could be pounded with a sledgehammer, or the flat-head side of an axe.

Back on the smoky landing, Lyon dropped to his knees, holding the forked end of the Halligan bar in the gap between the door and the frame with both hands. Cox reared back with the axe, aiming the blunt end toward the head of the Halligan bar. It was like two people working together to drive a nail, one holding the nail and one swinging the hammer. Except the nail was two and a half feet long, they were driving it sideways, and they could barely see what they were doing through their face pieces and the smoke.

Lyon closed his eyes and held his breath, half expecting his half brother to slip or miss the mark and smash his shoulder with the axe. "You got it, right?" Lyon shouted.

"Jus' hold 'er still!" Cox answered as he reared back and swung. The concussion of the blow ricocheted up Lyon's arms, all the way to his spine. But the blow landed square on the bar. Lyon eased his grip and used the gloved fingers of one hand to feel how far the bar had penetrated the door frame. A fraction of an inch, maybe. He lined up the bar for another blow. Cox was confident in his swing—but Lyon was fighting not to flinch.

After about a dozen strikes—Lyon gritting his teeth with each one—the door popped out of the frame. They rushed in to look around. More heat and smoke. Christ, Lyon thought, usually we're breaking down a door to get into the fire from outside. Not to get from inside the fire to more inside the fire.

It was very hot in the hallway they had just broken into. There were flames, but they were mostly spot fires, not the kind of inferno Hannon and Duck had encountered. The smoke was blinding, but their masks allowed them to work in it. For a while.

They split into two groups of two, so they could search the area as thoroughly as possible. Cox and Lyon turned right, Spring and Marshall turned left.

Spring moved a couple of paces and stepped on something soft. "Oh shit." He grimaced, leaning down with a flashlight. He saw a man's back, covered with soot. He rolled the man over to make sure he was dead before leaving him in place and moving on.

The smoke in the hallway seemed to be hanging in place. A basic firefighting tactic was to open windows, or break them, to help clear heat and smoke as rapidly as possible. Firefighters would even shoot hoses out a window—the water would generate a flow of air that drew the smoke out. Spring and Marshall went into one of the offices and tried to create some ventilation. With an axe and some other tools, they started bashing a couple of windows. Nothing happened— the blast-resistant windows wouldn't give. Marshall got angry and banged even harder. Finally, he smashed one window frame so violently that it popped free. The pane never broke, but Marshall was able to push out pieces of the framing, which began to draw out a little bit of smoke. It was an exhausting effort. They had hammered away nonstop for five or ten minutes, generating rivers of sweat and wearing themselves out.

With little ventilation, it was too hot to stay in the area long. Spring called Chief Smith on the radio and told him where they were. "Chief, it's becoming untenable in here," he said. "We need ventilation, and we can't do it from the inside."

A few doors down the hall, Cox and Lyon were doing much the same thing—busting into offices, looking for live victims who weren't there, and trying to push out windows that put up a ferocious defense. Every time the heat got too intense, they'd back into the hallway, where there wasn't as much fire. But they all noticed the same thing—conditions were getting worse, not better. Down the C Ring, they could see an area where the floor had collapsed. They could smell the jet fuel, as if it was gathered in a reservoir somewhere, continuously feeding the fire.

Other crews were drifting in behind them, a few poking their heads into the same hallway, others going higher. Voices rose and faded in the crackling din. The crew of Arlington's Engine 106 had gotten to the courtyard shortly after Spring's crew and followed the same path into A&E Drive. When they got there, they saw two hose lines lying in the gray water, right outside the stairwell next to the punch-out hole. They did the natural thing and picked them up—Matt Herrera on one, Justin Tirelli on the other—and carried them into the stairwell.

Like many crews, the Engine 106 team was working without much direction. They had waited outside Schwartz's command post for what seemed like a long time without getting an assignment. Capt. Howard Piansky, the officer in charge, got impatient. "Screw it," he said to Herrera and Tirelli. "We need to help." He led them to the courtyard, where they saw hose lines stretching into Corridor 4 and followed them straight to A&E Drive.

After picking up the two hoses, Piansky led them up the stairs and into a hallway. They ended up in an office area that looked completely annihilated and was engulfed in flame.

Turning their hoses on the fire got the same result as others before them. The flames would recede while the water flowed onto them but came roaring back the moment the firefighters turned the flow in another direction. Herrera, lean and muscular, with a Marine-style high-and-tight haircut, had trouble keeping his footing, tripping over debris every time he tried to turn. There wasn't a flat surface anywhere, and he felt like he was fighting a fire in a junk heap.

Occasionally they could hear shouts, and they'd shut down their hoses and listen. It sounded like other firefighters. In the confusion, Herrera thought he heard one fire crew screaming at another after getting inadvertently hosed down.

They weren't making any headway against the fire. Herrera looked at Piansky and could tell he was getting uncomfortable. "All right, let's get outta here," the captain said. "We're getting out now."

The courtyard had become a strange hub of frenetic, disorganized activity. A lot of firefighters from different jurisdictions were starting to arrive, some doing their own thing, some working with Chief Smith. Brian Roberts was one of the firefighters who never imagined he would be traipsing through the shattered Pentagon on a sunny late summer day. Roberts was a researcher at the University of Maryland, with a master's degree in aerospace engineering, who also volunteered with the fire department in Prince George's County, Maryland, about 20 miles northeast of the Pentagon. His unit had been dispatched to D.C. to backfill for companies sent to help at the Pentagon. When D.C. commanders summoned more units, Roberts found himself on a truck heading across the river. As the group neared the Pentagon, people lined the streets to applaud them, something that virtually never happened. It felt stranger still to drive into the courtyard, then walk deep inside the nation's military headquarters.

On one sortie into the burning building, Roberts was with a crew preparing to enter a set of double doors to fight fire on the other side. A rough rotational system was in place, and one crew was already working behind the doors. When they came out, Roberts's crew would relieve them. While they were waiting, a few of the firefighters started talking about the terrorist attacks. "Whoever did this," somebody said, "man, I hope we bomb these bastards back to the stone age."

"I heard a military guy outside say we were already attacking Afghanistan," another firefighter chimed in. Voices rose as other rumors flew.

A D.C. fire officer was standing nearby, and he promptly interrupted the discussion. "You all need to stop worrying about what's going on around the country or who did this," he ordered them. "You need to concentrate on what you're gonna do on the other side of those doors." He jabbed a finger toward the fire that awaited them. The group fell silent.

When Roberts's group finally pushed through the doors with masks on and air flowing, fire was everywhere. It burned between walls and ran along the ceiling, reaching angrily for the upper levels of the building. Smoke poured from desk drawers and filing cabinets as paper and other contents burned. The firefighters pulled open every drawer and cabinet door they could find—sometimes igniting fresh fires as air hit smoldering embers—before dousing the flames with their hoses.

On the floor, standing water steamed like broth in a cauldron, heated from beneath. Floor tiles, buckling from the heat, popped up out of the water occasionally like fish trying to escape a pot before it comes to a boil. Roberts found it unnerving, knowing that a fire that hot was burning directly beneath his feet.

The crew smashed windows to vent the heat and smoke, and as the air cleared, they began to notice victims strewn around the offices. Several looked mummified in place as if they had died immediately when the initial blast sucked all the air out of the room and replaced it with toxic, superheated gas. A few victims were still seated at their desks. Other bodies lay closer to doors or in hallways, where people might have fallen as they were trying to flee.

The group rotated out after a few intense moments, took a break, and eventually made another sortie into the building. Roberts found one body that made a stronger impression than the others. On the second level, toward the outer edge of a badly burned area, a man lay on the floor near a doorway. His body had fallen as if he were running into the office, with his back toward the exit. It was impossible to know for sure what had happened, but Roberts guessed that he had rushed into the area and tried to rescue people, but succumbed to the smoke before he could get back out. Roberts looked closer and could read the name tag still pinned to the uniform: MAJ. STEPHEN LONG.[1]

Since the D.C. units in the building used different radios than the Arlington crews, Chief Smith couldn't communicate with them. Smith sent Kenny Johnson, the medic who was helping him out, to find whoever was in charge of the D.C. crews and tell him to report to the command post so they could coordinate efforts. Johnson found a D.C. battalion chief and said Chief Smith needed to see him. "Okay," the chief answered. But he continued with what he was doing, in no hurry to go find his Arlington counterpart.

Smith continually sent Craig Duck and his crew into the building to do reconnaissance and bring him fresh information on the status of the fire. On one trip, Duck was astounded to run into a group of soldiers conducting their own firefighting effort, creeping down a hallway with two hose lines fully outfitted with nozzles, fighting the fire. As Duck spotted them, the leader was shouting for a rotation, calling up one group of soldiers while another fell back. The impromptu firefighters had no protective gear whatsoever, other than soaked bandanas wrapped around their faces. Duck had no idea where they had found the hose lines or why they had such good water pressure, when his crews had only weak streams from the standpipes. As soon as the military personnel spotted the D.C. firefighters, they turned over their equipment and headed for the exits without any fanfare. Duck was dumbstruck. This would never have happened at any other fire.

Military troops were still rushing around in the courtyard as well, doing what they could to help, bringing all kinds of supplies from elsewhere in the building—some useful, some not. Johnson helped one Navy medic handle a big box, the size of an end table, that he had carried into the courtyard. When they cut it open, the corpsman started laughing. The box was filled with condoms.

Except for firefighters who needed attention for injuries, heat exhaustion, or smoke inhalation the medical operation in the courtyard was winding down. All of the victims had finally been transported to hospitals, and the medical teams were leaving to find the triage points set up outside the building. In place of injured patients and makeshift litters, mortuary teams were now laying body bags on the grass, in orderly rows.

Jennifer Glidewell, the Army nurse, was one of the last medical caregivers to leave. She was walking out with Matthew Rosenberg, the medic who had helped P. K. Carlton and others pull people out of the flaming hole in A&E Drive. Glidewell looked around, beginning to absorb the depth of the tragedy. The door that the injured woman was carried out on was still lying on the ground, along with other pieces of wood that had been used as stretchers. Debris was everywhere. The courtyard looked like a rock concert had just been held there. Glidewell's panty hose were torn, her Army Class B skirt stained with fluids. As her adrenaline drained, she felt empty and scared. Rosenberg was filthy. He looked like he had been crawling around in a muddy cave. His blond hair was speckled with soot, and there was a sad expression on his face. But neither of them said anything. They just walked out.

THE NMCC

11:30 A.M.

At the command post, Chief Schwartz had an unpleasant job to do: relieve one of his best commanders.

He was worried about Bob Cornwell. The big bald battalion chief, still recovering from chemotherapy treatments, had been bustling throughout the building for two hours in full turnout gear. Schwartz had urgently needed him at the beginning; with his tactical skill and his knowledge of the Pentagon, Cornwell was the ideal person to direct operations during the early part of the incident. But Schwartz had more manpower now, and in the interest of Cornwell's health, it was time to pull him from the lineup.

Schwartz found Randy Gray, another Arlington battalion chief. "Randy, I want you to be my operations commander," he told Gray. "I want you to start a planning section too. If you could figure out what units we have here, that would be a good start. This is really confusing us." Then he mentioned Cornwell. "And we've got to give Bobby a break. He's been out there by himself all day. I want you to relieve him."

Gray understood. Everybody knew about Cornwell's health, and Gray was concerned himself.

Gray found Cornwell on Washington Boulevard. He had stripped off his turnout coat and looked hot and tired. His crisp white battalion chief's shirt hung untucked, the white undershirt beneath stretched at the collar and drenched. Sweat moistened his face. Cornwell looked like he had been through a lot.

Relieving a fellow officer wasn't a happy duty. Everybody wanted to be in on the action, doing what they train for. Cornwell was proud, and even though he was being replaced for health reasons, not performance, Gray expected it to go hard on him. "Hey, Bobby," Gray said, with an arm on his shoulder, "I'm here to give you a break. Take a breather and get some water."

Cornwell nodded and didn't resist. "Okay, Randy," he said. "Thanks."

Next up: figuring out what was going on. Gray was cheerful and likable, with a groomed mustache, round cheeks, and gentle southern drawl. But he also had a no-nonsense command presence that loomed larger than his compact five-eight frame. Schwartz hadn't exactly spelled it out, but Gray figured that by naming him Operations Commander, Schwartz was putting him in charge of the whole incident. Gibbs would remain in charge of the River Division, or the equivalent. Gray slipped on a vest that said INCIDENT COMMANDER over his dark blue light-duty polo shirt, and started gathering other officers to tell him what they knew about the fire.

One thing was obvious: They were going to be there for more than one day. The scale of the incident dwarfed everything they dealt with on a routine basis. But just about everything else was confusing. Gray didn't know who was in charge of what. He could see fire in many of the upper windows of the Pentagon but had no idea how far into the building it went. Or who was in there, fighting it.

Cornwell had the best understanding of the fire, and he followed Gray back to Gibbs's command post. Aides were taping large maps of the Pentagon to the sides of a command buggy, and Cornwell began sweeping his hand over the maps, explaining the scale of the fire. "It's running through three rings," he reported. "There's fire on the roof. We've got Dale on the inside." Cornwell was usually unflappable, but those who knew him recognized a minor tic when he got tense: He would suck in wisps of air through his lips, real fast, like a bird hyperventilating. He was bird-breathing now.

He picked up some markers and started drawing the range of the fire on one of the maps, to help Gray understand what was happening inside the building. He outlined an area bounded by Corridor 4 to the south, Corridor 5 to the north, and the C Ring to the east. Cornwell knew from his reconnaissance mission inside the building just before the evacuation that the emergency sprinklers had been working between Corridors 3 and 4. That would check the spread of the fire on the south side of the building. But nothing seemed to be slowing the spread of the fire in the other direction. In the windows on the second and third floors, Gray could see the fire moving from south to north—despite the fire crews inside fighting the fire. Gray worried that the fire would breach Corridor 5 and begin consuming the northern portion of the building. That was where they'd make their stand, he decided: Corridor 5. Their goal would be first to contain the fire and keep it from jumping over Corridor 5, then to attack it and beat it down.

There was another problem on the roof, where gray smoke oozed from beneath ornamental slate. Gibbs had already sent Derek Spector's crew up there for a look. There were few flames, but the dense, swirling smoke suggested that fire was burning underneath, in the "cockloft," the atticlike space between the ceiling of the uppermost floor and the roof. Even if the space was small and air scarce, it was still enough room for a fire to smolder and spread, the way a mattress burns. Heat and flammable gases rising from below could provide plenty of fuel to keep it stoked. A roof fire could easily run the length of a building if left unchecked, and even spread to other parts of the structure, from the top down.

Gray surveyed the roof. They'd need to watch it. But for now, gaining control of the huge blaze in the interior of the building demanded most of their attention.

Gray picked up a radio and called Dale Smith in the courtyard. "Hey, Dale," he said, "what I need you to do is keep the fire from going into the B Ring. The fire is moving from south to north. We're gonna try to cut it off at Corridor 5." They made arrangements to talk on a separate radio channel that wasn't as crowded as the main operations frequency. Smith told Gray that his firefighters had been pleading for ways to ventilate the fire, since they couldn't knock out the windows. Gray knew about the windows. He'd see about getting power saws or other tools inside, to help with ventilation.

With the help of Cornwell, Gibbs, Defina, and others, Gray sketched out a plan of attack. They'd send in the larger groups that Gibbs had been organizing. One group would go into the E Ring with hoses to push the fire back toward the path of the airplane. Another group would go into the D Ring, and do the same thing, with a third group attacking the fire in the C Ring. Fresh groups would rotate in and relieve the prior group in place, so the hose lines could simply be handed off, without losing momentum against the fire. And they'd keep pouring water into the building from outside, using deluge guns at ground level and nozzles affixed to ladder trucks to hit it from high and low.

Even though firefighters had been in the building for more than two hours, they still weren't at the extinguishment phase of the firefight. First they had to mount a coordinated effort to stop the spread of the blaze. Gray told Gibbs to gather all the fire officers in the area and bring them to the helipad for a briefing. About 30 faces gathered around Gray, many he didn't recognize. There were crews from D.C., Fairfax County, Loudoun County, and a couple other jurisdictions. What they were all doing there, he wasn't sure. But he had a sizable force at his disposal and needed to make the most of it.

Gray introduced himself, then explained the plan. He wanted to start by consolidating efforts on the ground floor—and putting a halt to the freelancing. "I want nobody on the second or third floors, or the upper floors," he told the group. It was too risky, and the odds of rescuing anybody up there at that point were extremely low. "Let's cut this bad boy off and push it back toward the plane," Gray said. "Once we get this under control, we can start to go on the upper floors."

The D.C. contingent had their own ideas. Instead of joining up with Gray's command operation, the D.C. battalion chief wanted his own chain of command—even though parallel operations usually weren't effective, and sometimes could be downright dangerous. It was hard to coordinate efforts when orders were coming from two different sets of commanders, especially with incompatible radios. But the D.C. group wasn't asking permission to set up their own fire-fight; they were just going ahead and doing it. There was too much else going on to argue about it, so Gibbs went over and worked out an informal understanding with his D.C. counterpart: The D.C. crews would operate in the C Ring and areas farther down Corridor 5. The Arlington Incident Commander would handle all the rest.

Gray was starting to regret putting on the blue Incident Commander vest—it was attracting way too much attention. At one point he gazed out at a long line of people waiting in line to talk to him. It didn't help that he was right in front of the fire, in plain view, while the main command post where Schwartz was working was essentially hidden in the I-395 underpass. He started telling questioners to go there, or delegating duties to Gibbs and others if it involved the immediate firefight.

A military officer came rushing up, bypassing the line. "We need help!" he pleaded. "Now! There's smoke coming into the National Military Command Center. And we can't leave. You've got to help us." It was yet another novelty of this particular fire: Even though the building was burning, people were still inside, working. Gibbs and others had already encountered several service members willing to risk their lives to go retrieve files or documents from wrecked offices. The firefighters had firmly directed most of those people away from the building.

This seemed different. The officer rapidly made it clear he wasn't talking about some routine conference room or office space, but the war room where top officials were dealing with whatever was going on across the country. Evacuating from there wasn't an option. They'd have to find some way to work through the smoke.

Gray and Gibbs quickly organized a group of about 15 firefighters to go check out the problem. It was an urgent mission—yet there were groans from some of the firefighters. Getting sent on a recon mission, away from the fire, meant they might miss a rotation in the midst of the real action, battling the blaze.

The National Military Command Center was on the other side of the building from where Flight 77 had smashed into the Pentagon's western wall. It was located in a section of the Pentagon, between Corridor 8 and Corridor 9, that housed the offices of the military's Joint Staff and many top officials, including the Secretary of Defense. The NMCC complex covered several floors, with a variety of secure offices that went deep into the basement. Its location wasn't public, but anybody with access to the Internet, or a library, could easily have discovered the location of other important offices on that side of the Pentagon.

The location of the Defense Secretary's office, on the outer E Ring, had been listed in a 1992 history of the Pentagon published by the Defense Department itself. Public tours of the building routinely took visitors past the office of the Chairman of the Joint Chiefs of Staff, the nation's top military officer, one deck below the Defense Secretary's suite. Many other generals and admirals worked in the same area. Had terrorists been targeting not just the Pentagon, but the senior government officials inside, there was plenty of information available to help them figure out exactly where to aim.[1] And they might have caught many of the military's top decision makers clustered together.

Yet the VIPs in the most prestigious part of the Pentagon were strangely immune, for the moment, from the maelstrom devouring the other side of the building. In the Joint Staff's complex of offices, between Corridors 8 and 9, some people felt a shudder when Flight 77 hit the Pentagon, as if a freight elevator somewhere nearby had fallen a floor. But others didn't notice anything until people started racing toward the exits and alarms went off. And the fire consuming another wing of the building was still distant, far on the other side of the inner courtyard. Had this been New York or some other metropolis, the fire would have been more than two blocks away, with three or four office buildings in between.

Smoke was a different matter. It hung heavily over the building, fed continuously by the fire, drifting this way and that as light winds blew. The NMCC was designed to operate in an emergency, and it was largely self-sufficient, with its own electrical, heating, and air-conditioning systems. But the air that circulated through the space still had to come from the outside. Intake valves for the Pentagon's ventilation system were on the roof,[2] and the smoke was infiltrating the entire building through the air vents. In most parts of the building it didn't matter, since the occupants had been evacuated. But in a few key areas, including the NMCC, workers remained at their duty stations in a gathering haze.

It was hectic in the NMCC, but not chaotic. The watch officer, a one-star general, was gathering situation reports from commanders around the country and the world. Firm information about the terrorist attacks was hard to come by, but there were plenty of unconfirmed rumors: The State Department had been attacked. There had been an explosion on the National Mall, in downtown D.C. Several cargo trucks, possibly packed with explosives, were speeding toward Cheyenne Mountain in Colorado, where NORAD, the North American Aerospace Defense Command, was based.[3] Defense Secretary Donald Rumsfeld; Gen. Richard Myers, the vice chairman of the Joint Chiefs of Staff; and other top Defense officials were able to learn more about what was happening at the Pentagon from the reports they watched on a bank of TVs than from anything coming through official channels.

After darting out to the helipad and helping carry a stretcher, Rumsfeld, his jacket stained with blood from the people he'd helped earlier, had come to the large conference room in the Executive Support Center. A secure videoteleconference was under way in the NMCC, one flight down, connecting the Pentagon, the White House situation room, and the bunker beneath the White House. Rumsfeld and Myers came down from time to time and spoke frequently with Vice President Dick Cheney, who was in the bunker. President Bush, on *Air Force One* by now, came on the teleconference occasionally, along with officials at NORAD and the National Security Council.[4]

Cheney had already authorized the military to shoot down any other hijacked aircraft, and there were vigorous efforts under way to get fighter jets in the air over major cities. Plenty of fighters were available at bases around the country. But few were prepared for live-fire missions; arming the fighters with missiles and other weaponry was taking longer than anybody liked.

There were also other problems. Vice Adm. Tom Wilson, head of the Defense Intelligence Agency, reminded Rumsfeld and others in the conference room that for the last several days the Russians had been conducting probing missions to test U.S. air defenses. They'd send Bear bombers flying toward Alaska, to see how long it took American AWACS surveillance planes to react, then turn around just before entering U.S. airspace. It was a typical cat-and-mouse game between the Russians and the Americans. Except NORAD was now on hair-trigger alert, and any suspicious aircraft might be treated as hostile and shot down. "Somebody needs to call the Russian Embassy and tell them to knock that shit off," Wilson said.

"Do it," Rumsfeld ordered.

Meanwhile, Deputy Defense Secretary Paul Wolfowitz and several others had left the Pentagon via helicopter, which took off from the parade field on the other side of the building from the helipad, and headed for Site R, the secret backup facility in the Maryland woods. A skeleton crew usually manned Site R, which was designed as a duplicate of the NMCC. If an attack took out the NMCC, or it needed to be evacuated for any reason, Site R would become the Pentagon's primary command center.

But bringing it fully online was more complicated than just flipping a switch. It would take time—a couple of hours, at least—to get a complete staff in place, fully activate the backup center, and make sure it had robust links to the Pentagon, the White House, and other vital parts of the government. Until that happened, the NMCC would be the only facility that could keep the Defense Secretary and his top advisors in secure contact with the President, and guarantee that the National Command Authority remained intact.[5] So nobody was leaving.

When Scott Fry, the admiral who had fled his dental appointment, first joined the Joint Staff in 1998 as Director of Operations, he checked out Site R. The site had been designed during the cold war as a backup military headquarters in case the Pentagon were demolished in a nuclear strike, and Fry found creaky procedures and a lax attitude among its staff. He instituted regular drills and other measures to make sure Site R could rapidly get up to speed in an emergency, without glitches that might be fatal in a war setting.

Now he waited anxiously to see if the planning would pay off. The only way to know for sure that Site R was fully operational was to see Wolfowitz and the backup team there participating in the videoteleconference, without interruption. The authority to order major military action rested jointly with the senior civilian leaders at both the White House and the Defense Department. Only they, together, could order troops to move, or missiles to fly. If the NMCC went down before Site R was up and running, the communications link required to utilize the nation's military might be severed, for the first time since the system was put in place in 1947. The NMCC represented a single point of failure in the world's most powerful military. And the command center was looking increasingly fragile as the smoke thickened.

Noses were starting to run and eyes were watering. People were coughing, and a few were getting woozy. Some workers were fetching fans from outer offices, though they didn't do much to force the smoke out of the sealed chamber.

The conference room in the ESC, where Rumsfeld and his lieutenants had gathered, was getting hazy too. They moved to a secure room below, off the NMCC, where the air was clearer, but even though it was easier to breathe in the new room, Myers noticed that the workers in the command center were beginning to struggle.

Rumsfeld, somehow, seemed impervious to the smoke, coughing occasionally but showing no discomfort. Myers became concerned about all the military personnel staffing the facility, who were his responsibility. "Sir," he said to Rumsfeld, "you do understand, all those people out there will stay as long as you're here," implying they might have to leave the NMCC and relocate someplace else. Rumsfeld said nothing.

An engineer sent by the Pentagon's building managers brought a device that measured the oxygen in the room. His measurements showed that oxygen levels were falling. "Within an hour it may be difficult to breathe in here," the engineer warned.

While the firefighters were being escorted to the NMCC with air bottles, an unseen hand was also devising a solution. Steve Carter knew the location of every vital office in the Pentagon, including the ones that could only be evacuated as a desperate last resort. He had gotten the reports of the smoke thickening in the NMCC, and was manipulating every building system at his command like an organist working the pipes.

The huge air vents on the Pentagon's roof were connected to 50-

year-old mechanical blowers, dating to the building's birth, that sucked air in or pushed it out. The massive belt-driven machines had been wired into new computerized controls that allowed building managers to adjust the airflow remotely. Some of the computerized controls still worked, but others had been severed, which allowed smoke into places where it was unwanted, and kept fresh air out.

Carter dispatched workers into mechanical spaces near the roof, to manually start the fans and open or close certain vents. Careful manipulation of the vents and the air flowing through them drew smoke out of the populated parts of the building and forced fresh air in. Getting the mix right would require some trial and error, but in the NMCC, conditions gradually improved.

By the time the group of firefighters tromped into the area near the NMCC, they wondered what all the fuss had been about. The air was hazy, and an acrid odor hung in the room. But if people were determined to work in there, well, it was workable. Rumsfeld, Myers, and their top aides had gone back up to the ESC, where the air had cleared somewhat. Others, who had been worried about running out of air a few moments earlier, barely paid the firefighters any mind, toiling intently at their computers and phones once again.

The firefighters followed their escort back up to the ground floor, along several long corridors, and out Corridor 5 back onto the cluttered lawn. It had been an anticlimactic mission, as they expected. They promptly went back to the helipad, looking for another assignment.

THE FBI

12:15 P.M.

The debris piled and scattered throughout the Pentagon and its grounds was a nuisance to most of the people working around it. Firefighters kicked and pushed it out of the way and drove over it with their trucks. Some people pocketed bits of wreckage that looked like they might be pieces of the airplane, as morbid souvenirs of the occasion. For the FBI, the shabby treatment of the debris was an alarming problem. Valuable evidence was everywhere, even if it looked like trash. They were in a frantic race to gather as much of it as they could, before it got wrecked, scavenged, or carted away.

While it was the site of a huge fire—and still a functioning office building—the Pentagon had also become a crime scene. Federal government property had been attacked and people murdered. The remnants of a hijacked aircraft were inside. Nobody knew what kind of legal proceedings would emerge from the incident, but it was the FBI's job to gather and document every fragment of evidence, so it would be available no matter what prosecutors decided to do.

Special Agent Chris Combs had a huge job ahead of him. He had to rapidly set up an evidence-recovery operation and establish security while working around the firefighters, the medics treating the victims, and hundreds of other people who felt they had urgent business inside the fire ground. He also needed to get the FBI's own command operation up. And even though he was operating in the FBI's backyard, chaos and gridlock were gumming up the FBI's mobilization.

Combs was operating beyond his pay grade too. The four-year FBI veteran regularly established command on calls relating to suspicious packages and "white powder" letters that might contain poisons, but he had never run a huge incident involving dozens of other agencies. He expected a more senior Special Agent in Charge, an SAC, to relieve him at some point in the day, when the Bureau had a better handle on what was happening and had fully deployed its top people.

Meanwhile, he had been setting up the FBI operation with whatever was available. The FBI had a fleet of sophisticated command vehicles and helicopters and other fancy equipment, but none of it had arrived yet. Rapid-deployment gear, including everything needed to gather and document evidence, was stashed at a warehouse in D.C., ready to be on an airplane for deployment anywhere in the world within eight hours. But with the federal government evacuating nearly every building in Washington, traffic was at a standstill. Even with a police escort, it was almost impossible to get through the streets.

While Combs was with Chief Schwartz at the main command, somebody decided that a Virginia State Police barracks up on the hill by the Navy Annex would be a safer place for the FBI to set up operations. Combs didn't know who made the decision, but there was no time to dicker. He started moving the FBI up to the barracks. Meanwhile, a more senior FBI official arrived and started helping him set up FBI command.

A page went out, directing dozens of agents to the Pentagon. Combs grabbed a colleague he recognized. "Hey, I need you to set up an investigative branch," he said. Eyewitnesses with stories to tell were already swarming the FBI. The taxi driver whose windshield had been smashed by a light pole knocked over by the plane was

there, and lots of others who believed they'd seen something important. Some were even carrying objects they thought might be evidence. The FBI had to interview everybody and get contact info
before they started drifting away.

More than anything, Combs needed more agents. He kept calling
his boss, Jim Rice, at the field office, asking for more people. Every
available agent had been paged, but many were stuck in traffic. The
bridges leading from D.C. to Virginia were jammed and effectively
shut down. Police were trying to clear a lane for emergency traffic,
but agents who drove across sidewalks and grass to get out of D.C.
found themselves stymied at the bridge.

Combs asked Rice if any helicopters were available, to bypass the
traffic and get equipment there in a hurry. No luck. There were several choppers at the FBI facility in Quantico, just 30 miles to the
south, but they were reserved for specific duties during government
emergencies—and were locked down. The FBI relied on other government helicopters as a backup, but those were all tied up too.

The Arlington Fire Department had its own bomb squad, but it
couldn't get its equipment there either. The commander, Jeff Everly,
asked Combs if the FBI could help. "Jeff, I'm outta birds," Combs
huffed. "I got no birds."

Special Agent Tom O'Connor was another one of the early arrivals
helping Combs get a proper FBI operation in place. He was in charge of
gathering evidence. O'Connor was talkative and energetic, as intense as
any of his fellow agents. He could also be a jovial raconteur with a blue-
collar sense of humor, the kind of guy people gathered around at the
bar after work. In the book *Home Town*, about life in Northampton,
Massachusetts, journalist Tracy Kidder had profiled "Tommy O'Connor," a local street cop who grew up there. The book had made O'Connor a hometown celebrity before he left to join the FBI in 1997. He was
sent to the bombed embassy buildings in Africa in 1998, and also inves-
tigated the 2000 bombing of the USS *Cole* in the waters off of Yemen.

His wife, Jean O'Connor, was an FBI agent too. They had met during college and gotten married when O'Connor was still a cop in Northampton. When he applied for the FBI, the Bureau conducted a standard spousal interview with Jean, to make sure she understood the pressures her husband would face as an agent. When the interviewer learned she was an auditor—a skill in short supply at the FBI—he handed her an application. She joined in 1998.

As the agent in charge of the initial evidence recovery, Tom O'Connor's first priority was to find and gather all the airplane parts and other bits of evidence from the lawn on the west side of the building, before firefighters and other responders completely trampled it. He sent every available agent out onto the lawn, which they divided into quadrants. Working around fire trucks, medics, victims, and quasiofficial onlookers, they prowled back and forth in a semi-orderly grid search. The procedure was to stick a small flag near each piece of evidence, get a photographer to photograph it in place, then scoop it up and put it in a bag, labeling each one.

There were thousands of small pieces of evidence embedded in the grass and dirt, and some larger oddities too. Agents found what looked like a big Plexiglas windowpane on the lawn, which might have been part of an airplane window, except it was too big—it took several agents to carry it. Somebody suggested it could be one of the blast-proof windows from the Pentagon, somehow blown 500 feet from the building.

Despite rehearsals and exercises between the FBI and local governments, there was tension right off the bat between the Bureau's agents and the firefighters on the scene. The FBI was used to being in charge, and agents had already been telling firefighters not to move bodies or evidence. The firefighters had their hands full battling the blaze inside the Pentagon, and weren't in the mood to have the Feds breathing down their necks. Fred Calvert, working the pump on Engine 108, had seen a federal agent run up to a group of firefighters near the entrance to Corridor 5 and yell, "This is a crime scene! Don't touch anything!"

He's out of his mind, Calvert thought as he scanned the bits and pieces of wreckage everywhere. The firefighters would have to tiptoe around like ballerinas to avoid disturbing any of it.

At one point agents gathering evidence near the helipad asked Randy Gray's group if somebody could move one of the command buggies, so they could get to something beneath it that looked like evidence. "No," Gray said stiffly. "You're going to have to reach under."

While a few of the FBI agents were butting heads with firefighters and others on the lawn, most knew that the best thing they could do was work as quickly as possible, with minimal friction. Special Agent Garrett McKenzie was an amateur photographer whose assignment was to use his camera to document evidence. He was a gruff, burly former Marine, an officer who had participated in the 1983 assault on the Caribbean island of Grenada, then served in Lebanon a few weeks later, in the aftermath of the bombing that killed 241 Marines. He had also served during the first Gulf War in 1991. Years of hard field experience had dimmed his optimism. Yet McKenzie, a family man with three kids, was fiercely devoted to law-enforcement work and the troopers on the front lines. He was well-known for volunteering to play the bagpipes at the funerals of fallen colleagues.

He started shooting the moment he arrived on the lawn. He saw firefighters pick stuff up and toss it aside like twigs, plow hazards out of the way, and spray water everywhere. His job was to document the crime scene in as close to its original state as possible, and with conditions changing by the minute, that meant the race was on.

McKenzie focused his Mamiya 645 in close at first, shooting in an arc from south to north. He shot close-ups of the burned-out windows where Brian Frantz and Juan Cano had pulled the dazed woman out of the smoking office, then moved left, to the crater where five floors of the Pentagon lay in a smoldering pile of rubble. Then he panned the northern half of the burning E Ring, where Fred Calvert, manning Engine 108, had worried that the fire might leap from the building and threaten to singe and blister his truck.

McKenzie was shooting as fast as he could, but it wasn't fast enough. Digital photography hadn't yet been approved for evidence work, and he had to manually load and label each roll of film. Procedures also required him to keep a detailed log of every photo, which was time-consuming. Usually he would grab a younger agent as an aide—but there weren't any.

A Marine Corps major asked if there was something he could do to help, and McKenzie told him, "Here's my notebook. All I need you to do is follow me around. Everything I say, write it down." They developed a quick rapport. Before long McKenzie could speak in rapid shorthand, and the major knew what to write down without further explanation.

As other photographers—from a hodgepodge of federal agencies—began to show up, McKenzie became the de facto coordinator of the photography effort. He decided they had gotten plenty of "overalls" depicting the broad scene at the Pentagon, and it was time to focus their efforts on the technical details of individual pieces of evidence. By then O'Connor and his superiors had sent around word that there was no need to document every piece of the airplane—the smaller fragments didn't prove anything, except that there was an airplane there, which was obvious enough from other evidence. But from experience with car bombs and terrorist attacks, there were plenty of other things they knew to look for.

McKenzie gathered a dozen photographers on the lawn for a briefing. "We don't need to photograph all the plane parts," he told them, "only unique airplane parts or something specific. Like the pilot's yoke, or anything with part of a serial number on it. If we have to prove what kind of plane this was, the serial numbers will be what we need." One of the debris pieces McKenzie photographed himself was a piece of aluminum with the American Airlines twin-A logo on it.

Next he made his way toward the courtyard, and A&E Drive. Incident commanders were still trying to figure out the full range of the damage inside the building. But a number of firefighters and others who had been in there, from the courtyard side, sent back reports of the punch-out hole in A&E Drive and a debris pile nearby. It sounded like it might contain a mother lode of evidence, maybe even the aircraft's "black boxes," containing vital flight data and recordings of cockpit conversations. The punch-out hole was becoming the focal point of the catastrophe, a single place where a gruesome display of airplane wreckage, building contents, and body parts provided all the visual clues needed to tell what had happened.

McKenzie hooked up with Tom O'Connor, and the two of them headed for A&E Drive, following the trail of activity to the courtyard and the Corridor 4 entrance. When they turned right into A&E Drive, McKenzie was surprised to see that the service road itself was intact, although it was filled with water and debris. A thumping sound came from overhead, where he saw two firemen bashing with all their might on one of the blast-proof windows. One had an axe, the other a sledgehammer, and no matter how hard they pounded, their tools just bounced off the window. It seemed so futile that it was comical, and for the first time all day McKenzie laughed out loud.

As he walked to the punch-out hole, his mind reeled back to other bombings he had seen. The structural damage reminded him of the devastation in Beirut in 1983, except that unlike the Marine headquarters building there, most of the Pentagon was still standing. The Pentagon had fared better than the demolished embassy buildings in Africa too. In fact, the Pentagon hadn't been leveled at all. Not even close. It was more like somebody had poked a bloody hole in the building. In a way, it reminded him of the *Cole,* which still floated after suicide bombers detonated a boat bomb alongside its hull in open water.

Yet the carnage in the Pentagon, he could see, was more violent. Most of the victims in the *Cole* had been killed when several decks of the ship pancaked down onto one another, and the bodies pulled out by investigators had mostly been intact. McKenzie could tell there would be few intact bodies in the Pentagon, just by peering into the punch-out hole. For the most part, he saw body parts that were so mutilated they'd be recognizable only to people familiar with the aftermath of massive bombings. Yet a few looked so normal, they could have been the disassembled appendages of a mannequin, spilled from a box. He was startled to see, in the debris, a woman's hand, in perfect condition, with red nails that looked as if they had been manicured that morning. A large diamond ring gleamed from one finger.

He knew he had to put these images out of his mind, as he reached for his camera and started clicking.

EVERYBODY OUT OF THE POOL

1:30 P.M.

At the underpass, commanders were no longer working off the back of an SUV. With the operation swelling rapidly, they had moved into a command bus belonging to the Arlington County Police Department. And the bus was filling with people from government agencies that many of the commanders didn't even know existed.

Many organizations had an obvious role at the incident, like the Defense Department, FBI, National Transportation Safety Board, and local police. But it seemed that every agency with inspectors or investigators was sending them: The Drug Enforcement Administration; the Bureau of Alcohol, Tobacco and Firearms; even NASA. In the command post, Plaugher saw one man he didn't recognize, credentials draped around his neck. "Who's that guy?" he asked. "What's he here for?" Somebody told him the man was a disaster expert from the Department of the Interior. Plaugher told a police officer to escort him out. Complicating the juggling act, top officials at the White House and other parts of the government were calling frequently, asking for situation reports.

Then there were all the firefighters, swarming throughout the building whether fire commanders sent them inside or not. Earlier that morning, Steve Souder, who was in charge of Arlington's dispatch center, had contacted the Alexandria, Fairfax, and D.C. fire departments and asked them each to send identical teams consisting of seven fire trucks and their crews, four medic units, and a commander to oversee it all. He asked that the crews marshal at a staging area near the Pentagon, until Schwartz called them forward. Alexandria and Fairfax complied. But D.C. didn't. Commanders there called in three times as many units as Souder asked for, and instead of staging, they went straight to the Pentagon and started firefighting operations on their own. That was virtually unheard-of; fire departments rarely went into somebody else's jurisdiction and set up their own operation.[1]

Plaugher had little patience for grandstanding, and he wasn't shy about asserting his authority over the incident. At one point in the early afternoon, he and Schwartz were both in the command bus at the underpass when they saw a group of D.C. chiefs setting up their own command post barely 50 feet away. Plaugher's blood pressure soared. His first instinct was to kick the whole D.C. contingent out of the fire ground. Then he looked at the smoke streaming out of the Pentagon and pictured the headline tomorrow: Pentagon on Fire, Chief Orders Firefighters Home. He swallowed hard and turned to Schwartz. "Do what you can, Jim," he sighed.

"I know, Chief," Schwartz answered.

There were lots of other freelancers, in addition to the firefighters. EMS units from all over the D.C. region had converged on the Pentagon, including those from private ambulance companies. Some scooped up patients wherever they found them, and rushed them to the closest hospital, without coordinating with the Arlington dispatch center. It made sense to provide medical care as fast as possible, but in the chaos, some hospitals were getting overwhelmed, while others prepared for patients who never arrived. That added to confusion on the radio and gave commanders one more problem to untangle.

Schwartz saw several fire companies from Maryland pulling up to the Pentagon. Arlington didn't have mutual-aid agreements with *any* departments in Maryland. "Who called those guys?" he snapped, incredulous. With the radio frequencies clogged, he decided to send two firefighters out on foot to record the name, identification number, and location of every piece of firefighting apparatus they could find.

Then another urgent problem soared to the top of the priority list. At about the same time that Randy Gray's rotational plan in the E, D, and C Rings was fully kicking in, and crews in A&E Drive were starting to beat back the relentless flames, the command post got another urgent radio message from the Arlington dispatcher: The tower at Reagan National Airport was reporting that yet another "inbound unidentified aircraft" was heading up the Potomac River, from the south, at a high rate of speed. It was just minutes away from the Pentagon. Nobody knew if it was another hijacked plane. All they knew was that no aircraft, aside from military jets, were supposed to be flying, and this one wasn't identifying itself.

Schwartz looked around for Chris Combs, who had been able to get real-time info straight from FBI headquarters about the last jet, which was supposedly headed for the Pentagon. But Combs had moved to set up the FBI operation in the police barracks up the hill, by the Navy Annex, and so Schwartz had no choice but to assume that another hijacked jet might be about to plow into the Pentagon. He'd have to evacuate the entire building all over again. It was about 2:00 P.M., roughly four hours and 15 minutes since the first firefighters had arrived on the scene.

By the time the evacuation call went out, the controllers in the tower were reporting that the plane was about two minutes' flying time away. Denis Griffin and his crew were looking for victims deep inside the building, in the C Ring, when he heard the alert on his radio. There was no way they were going to get out of the building in two minutes, he immediately realized. He knew Corridor 4 was blocked to the outside, because he'd tried to go down there, and had run into a barricade of debris. Corridor 5 was as dark as a dungeon and he assumed that was blocked too. They could go back into the courtyard and run out the tunnel, toward South Parking, or try their luck down Corridor 6 or 7. But what was the point? They were still in the midst of the fire, and if they dropped their tools, ran down the stairs into A&E Drive, and tried to flee through the courtyard, they'd just end up in another part of the building.

"Hey guys!" Griffin yelled to Anderson, Mosely, and Hannon. "Another plane is coming in. Let's get down to A&E Drive." They backtracked down the stairs into the service road. "Look," Griffin continued, "here's the deal. We're cut off. We can't go anywhere. We're kinda trapped in here. If they're gonna hit this thing again, it's probably gonna be on the other side. They're saying it's two minutes out. In two minutes we're not gonna get out. We're gonna stay with the fire."

They looked at him with a mix of worry and anger. "You've got to be kidding," Anderson complained. "We're inside one of the largest office buildings in the world and they can't keep these airplanes away?"

Hannon, who had prayed near a tree during the first evacuation, was pissed off this time. This is our Pentagon, he thought, and they can't even protect us in here? What's going on?

But Griffin's crew agreed there was no point in trying to leave. They'd wait it out. Still, Griffin wondered if that was the right choice. Mosely didn't have any kids, but Anderson and Hannon both did. He did too, for that matter. What the hell were they doing, waiting idly inside the Pentagon for a terrorist attack to happen?

A group of military personnel milled around looking for ways to help, and Griffin found it a comfort to have them there as the seconds ticked away. As he looked around, he didn't see any other firefighters. He imagined that everybody in the courtyard had bugged out, leaving

Quint 104 and the military crowd as the only lonely souls left inside the Pentagon.

There were others, though. Brian Spring's makeshift crew was still on the second floor, close to the spot where Griffin's men had been when he decided to backtrack to A&E Drive. Spring made a similar call. From the moment they arrived at the Pentagon, Spring had warned his crew that this was the kind of fire some people didn't come home from. "Whatever we do," he had stressed, "we need to cover our own asses." Even though Spring had never been in the military, he figured this was going to be a little bit like combat—there would be times when they'd have to take calculated risks and put their safety on the line.

That's what he faced now. Like Griffin, he knew as soon as he heard the call on the radio that there was no chance they'd get out of the building in two minutes. But his crew still had a decent amount of air, while Griffin's crew didn't. So Spring figured they might as well just wait where they were. There was some fire nearby, but it wasn't overwhelming in the hallway, and he preferred to stay in place so they could quickly resume firefighting and search activities rather than go stumbling around on a random hunt for someplace safer.

He shouted through his mask at Marshall, Cox, and Lyon, hastily explaining that another aircraft was incoming. "Everybody stand against a wall!" he hollered. They quickly took up positions near the walls, hoping for a bit of extra protection if the structure around them started to give way. Since they all had their masks on, nobody said much. But once they were in place, Spring shouted some words of encouragement. "Listen," he huffed through his mask, "this is a huge building. The chances of another plane hitting our spot are slim." And he pleaded with his men once more to be careful. "We need to watch our asses, guys, and keep ourselves safe."

On the other side of the fire, by the helipad, dozens of firefighters were reenacting the same drill they had conducted about three hours

earlier, evacuating toward Washington Boulevard to get away from
the building they were trying to save. Except now, many of the firefighters, tired and skeptical of yet another aircraft attack, were moving more slowly. Mike Smith had bolted from the building during the
first evacuation, but this time he was in no hurry. "If a plane is coming," he told one fellow firefighter, "it's just gonna have to get me." He
was glad they had brought the deluge guns into the building earlier;
at least those would remain inside, dousing the fire.

When he finally got to Washington Boulevard, anger ricocheted
up and down the line of sweaty firefighters. "I can't believe this is
happening again," Smith vented. Compared to the first evacuation,
there was more frustration than fear this time. Instead of gathering
on the other side of the highway, firefighters lingered closer to the
building. The creeping crowd of displaced firefighters reminded
Derek Spector of the surf splashing onto the beach while the tide was
coming in—a little closer each time.

Others wondered if all the firefighters were actually out of the
building. With so many units showing up—and the D.C. crews doing
their own thing—there still wasn't a good system in place for keeping
track of everybody going in and out. Plus the radios worked so
poorly in the building, there could easily be crews in isolated office
spaces that didn't get the word.

A group of fire commanders, police officers, and FBI agents went
back to the underpass where they had waited out the first evacuation.
Tom O'Connor knew that his wife, Jean, had arrived at the Pentagon
and was working someplace on the grounds. They tried to make it a
practice not to work together, but this was an all-hands event—and
he was worried. He looked around for his wife and didn't see her. She
hadn't been there for the earlier evacuation, and O'Connor worried
that maybe she didn't know where to go. He started jogging down a
road out in front of the underpass, looking for her, then stopped himself. Whoa, he thought. He was getting carried away.

As he went back toward the underpass, he spotted his wife sitting on a curb near an exit ramp, waiting. "I went looking for you! I didn't see you!" he exclaimed. Jean could tell he was upset. She explained that she had looked for a place where she could easily get away from the building if the plane hit, and Tom calmed down.

In addition to worrying about his wife, Tom O'Connor was dealing with the disruption of his evidence-recovery operation. The FBI had contact with the tower at the airport, but that didn't give him any clearer information. At one point the airport controllers said the plane they were tracking had gone off radar, which only produced more confusion. Had it crashed? Or landed someplace? Or did the airport just lose track of it? And why wasn't the Air Force controlling the skies by now? The frustration was thicker than the smoke still rising from the Pentagon. "Don't we have any fucking planes up?" somebody shouted.

With little to do but fume, O'Connor used his radio to call FBI colleague Ed Laney, who was working the radios at the field office in the District. "Hey, Ed," he growled, "I have a question. We have any fighter jets out of Andrews?"

"Stand by," Laney replied as he checked on the status of fighter jets based at Andrews Air Force Base, in suburban Maryland.

O'Connor wasn't waiting for an answer. "Ed, can you get ahold of somebody and get some fucking air support down here?" he barked. FBI agents had no authority whatsoever to order military jets into the air, but it felt better than staring feebly into the sky, waiting for some kind of attack to materialize. Not surprisingly, Laney remained silent.

While they vented and guzzled water along Washington Boulevard, the firefighters who had spent the last four hours dealing with the fire were also getting their first updates on what 9/11 meant to the rest of the country. Brian Roache asked if anybody knew what was going on in New York. He had watched TV back in Station 5, after planes hit both of the twin towers and firefighters were presumably rushing up the stairs in both buildings. Now, he was stunned to hear that the twin towers had collapsed without warning. There were reports that 800 or 1,000 firefighters had died, along with thousands of civilians.[2] He couldn't believe it.

Mike Smith reacted the same way. And it sounded like the story was even worse. There were rumors that the Sears Tower in Chicago had been hit, and that an unknown number of hijacked aircraft were still in the air, heading for targets nationwide.[3] Adrenaline turned to rage. It seemed like the whole country was suddenly naked and vulnerable. They couldn't even fight a fire without worrying about getting attacked. "How does this happen?" Smith wondered out loud. "Why are there no fighters? Where the fuck is our protection?"

They heard reports about the Pentagon too. Somebody said that 800 people had died inside. If that was true, they were going to find piles of bodies at some point—since they hadn't found very many so far.[4]

The forced break, and the surreal news from around the country, created a powerful desire to connect with home. Many firefighters learned to compartmentalize their work, constructing a mental wall between the things they did on the job and their home life. Calls home from the site of a fire were rare, and some firefighters never talked about work with their families. It was a way of depersonalizing experiences that could be draining, even unbearable, if they became emotional. But the personal shields they had formed were crumbling as firefighters worried whether their country was protected and their families safe.

Mike Smith was able to get through to his wife, Doris, on his cell phone. Hearing about the attacks at work, Doris knew her husband would be at the Pentagon—the whole department was probably there. She had tried to remind herself how professional and experienced he was, and that he wouldn't take foolish chances. It didn't work. There were careful firefighters in New York too, and they were buried in a mountain of rubble. Plus, Mike had had angioplasty earlier that year, and two stents implanted in his arteries. The doctors had pronounced him fit to return to work—but nobody anticipated a stressful, daylong inferno.

It was a brief call. Mike sounded exhausted as he quickly explained what was going on. Doris told him what she'd been seeing about New York, then begged him to be careful.

Derek Spector borrowed a phone from Pete DePuy, another Arlington firefighter, and tried to call his wife, Betty. Spector's two boys were just five and three, but they knew their dad was a firefighter and that sometimes he worked at the Pentagon. Ben, his five-year-old, was at preschool that day, and Spector worried he'd hear something about a bomb at the Pentagon and firefighters getting hurt, and get scared. He wanted Betty to hear his voice and be able to tell everybody he was okay. But he couldn't get through. The lines were jammed.

After more than a dozen tries, DePuy finally got through to his wife. He ticked off the names of all the Arlington firefighters he saw who hadn't yet phoned their families, and she agreed to start placing calls to the wives—most of whom assumed their husbands were at the Pentagon, but didn't know for sure.

The break didn't last as long as the first evacuation. Shortly after Tom O'Connor placed his frustrated call for air support, an F-16 came screeching over the Pentagon. "Now that's what I'm talking about!" O'Connor hooted, as if his order had brought the fighter jet on demand. On Washington Boulevard, anger gave way once again to relief, and another roar went up, though more tepid than before. Moments later official word came from the airport tower and the Arlington dispatch center: The plane had been a "friendly" aircraft after all. It was safe to go back into the building.[5]

The whole crowd on Washington Boulevard—dozens of firefighters—started ambling back toward the Pentagon. "Everybody out of the pool, everybody back into the pool," Chuck Gibbs quipped as he hustled back to the command buggy on the helipad. The organizational scheme he and Randy Gray worked out was starting to pay off, with a consistent stream of firefighters keeping the pressure—and the water—on the fire. During the evacuation they were able to keep some deluge guns on the lawn firing water into the building, and the deluge gun Mike Smith and his crew had dragged into the D Ring was still pumping water onto the fire. In a lot of other places, however, they had just given the fire another 30 minutes to retrench.

The fire crews regrouped and prepared for the third fresh push into the building in five hours. The firefight had become more organized after each evacuation, as commanders used the time to refine their plans, prepare fresh crews, and gather intelligence about the fire conditions inside. But it was also a brutal war of attrition in which the firefighters and the fire fought over patches of turf that kept changing hands. And now the firefighters were charging into the battle again to reclaim territory they had already won.

★ 20 ★

MAKING THE TEAM

Early afternoon

For the crews inside the Pentagon waiting out the "inbound" aircraft, the tension abated as abruptly as it began. As Brian Spring's crew hugged the walls in the dark, smoky remnants of the C Ring, two minutes came and went. They waited some more, hearing nothing. Spring finally got the word that they could go back to work, and they resumed prying open doors and dousing the flames. The threat had been a stressful, frustrating interlude—yet it already seemed like a small episode in a bizarre day that had only just begun. A few minutes after they went back to fighting the fire, the incoming aircraft was all but forgotten.

In A&E Drive, Denis Griffin decided his crew was ready for a break. He had lost track of time, but all told, they must have been in the building for a couple of hours—most of it without masks. They were nearly out of air, and their efforts no longer felt cohesive. It was time to regroup.

When they walked back out Corridor 5, Griffin expected to find the courtyard empty. He was surprised to see that Chief Smith hadn't evacuated either. In fact, there were quite a few people milling about. He walked over toward Smith's command buggy to see what was going on. The rest of the crew dropped their air packs on the ground, took off their helmets and coats, and sank down onto the grass. They drank some more murky water. Somebody brought them sandwiches scrounged from the Ground Zero café, which they devoured.

In all their time inside the building, they hadn't found a single living victim. It was perplexing. "Man, I was expecting walking wounded all over the place," Anderson said. "I thought we'd be pulling out lots of victims."

He was also shocked at the amount of fire inside the building. Anderson had expected crash trucks from the airport to tackle the heaviest fire with the foam they carried, not realizing that those trucks couldn't fit inside the courtyard or reach the fire in the C Ring. By the time his crew got inside, he figured they'd mostly be putting out spot fires—not reeling from an inferno.

A number of fresh crews were arriving in the courtyard, which gave many of the fire crews who were first to plunge into the Pentagon a chance to rest on the grass, rehydrate, and recuperate from a morning spent battling a fire of nightmare proportions. The discolored water in the soda bottles was hardly refreshing, though. There were still military officials hanging around, looking for ways to help, and one of them asked Craig Duck if there was anything he could do. His team was exhausted from many trips into the Pentagon, so Duck thought a moment and said he could really use some Gatorade. The water was lousy, and something fresher might give his crew a boost of energy.

"Can I borrow your tool?" the officer asked, pointing at the combination sledgehammer and axe that rested at Duck's feet. The officer and a couple of others walked purposefully into one of the building entrances nearby, where half a dozen vending machines were clustered. He raised the tool and declared, "This is a national emergency!" then swung. It took only a couple of blows to smash the machine and liberate all the drinks inside, which the military group proudly delivered to the firefighters resting in the courtyard. With a new mission, they went off in search of other vending machines to conquer.

The rest and the fluids were a relief, but the fire was beginning to claim a few casualties among the firefighters—both physical and psychological. Arlington paramedic Kenny Johnson had already treated two firefighters for smoke inhalation. They had spent considerable time inside the building without masks, and Johnson decided they ought to head for a hospital. They offered no resistance.

Denis Griffin saw one of his colleagues sitting on a bench, smoking a cigarette, looking off into the distance. Griffin walked over. "This is it," the firefighter said. "I can't do this anymore." Griffin had enough experience to know that the stress of the job wasn't fleeting—it was cumulative. Exposure to trauma and other emotional strains couldn't be entirely compartmentalized. They piled up, and for some people they spilled over. His comrade had hit the wall. He was done for the day, maybe for his career.

Gear was scarce in the courtyard—especially air bottles. Many of the arriving firefighters had walked in, since their trucks wouldn't fit in the tunnel. They could only bring what they could carry, usually one air bottle on their backs and some tools and hose. And one air bottle only provided about 45 minutes of air. Whoever needed a replacement needed to scrounge his own spare.

Brian Spring's crew retreated to the courtyard as their air began to run low, and got their own distorted glimpses of what was happening beyond the confines of the Pentagon. They heard the first rumors of the collapse of the twin towers, and a military guy told Spring that U.S. fighter jets had shot down an airliner over Pennsylvania.[1] Another said somberly, "We've already sent missiles into Afghanistan."[2]

They took off their air packs and other equipment and plopped down on the grass nearby, with their backs to their gear, trying to absorb the swirl of events. A couple of D.C. firefighters walked over and inconspicuously tried to make off with their air tanks and masks. Spring caught sight of them out of the corner of his eye. "Hey!" he shouted, standing up. "What the hell are you doing?"

"Our chief sent us over to take these," one of the firefighters said sheepishly.

"Well, I'm an Arlington fire captain and you're going to leave them here!" Spring retorted. They shambled away. "What the fuck!" he shouted after them.

His whole crew had stood up, and they looked at each other in disbelief. Firefighters cadged tools from each other all the time, but rarely took each other's personal protective equipment. "They even tried to take our face pieces!" Spring said to his men, incredulous.

It quickly became clear that air was the most precious commodity in the courtyard. In big fires, air bottles were often the limiting factor that drove firefighters out of the building. But usually there were spare bottles, or light-and-air trucks able to refill empty ones. This fire was different. Not only was equipment scarce in the courtyard, but the depth and size of the fire itself still weren't fully known. Once in the building, nobody knew how much air they'd need, especially if they got trapped.

That produced a hoard mentality. In the fire, nobody wanted to go on air until absolutely necessary, to conserve as much as possible. And in the courtyard, firefighters were starting to stockpile air bottles and guard them like precious cargo. Some with half-filled bottles were walking around, checking the air pressure on other bottles they saw lying on the ground. If they found one with more air, they'd swap—providing nobody laid a competing claim on it. Chris Cox and Jason Lyon went hunting for air bottles and found an engine that had a small stockpile of them. They grabbed several and stashed them in a stand of bushes off to the side, out of sight, hoping they'd provide enough air to get them through the rest of the day.

The incident command team was still struggling to keep track of all the newly arriving crews. Just moments after arriving on the scene, Chief Plaugher had called for several of the specially trained urban search-and-rescue teams funded by the Federal Emergency

Management Agency and embedded in several local fire departments around the country. Each team specialized in the technical aspects of rescuing victims in building collapses, earthquakes, and other catastrophes. Plaugher could tell when he first set eyes on the Pentagon that there might be victims trapped in rubble for hours, possibly days, and that the structural integrity of the building would be a major issue. The collapse of the E Ring had proven that right. Arlington had a small technical-rescue team capable of dealing with collapsed buildings, but all of its members were firefighters, most of whom were already busy manning hoses or directing fire crews.

Besides, the FEMA crews had better equipment and more experience dealing with real-world incidents. The program dated to the 1980s, when an earthquake in Mexico City made it apparent that there was a need for mobile, highly trained teams capable of digging people out of the worst kinds of disasters. The federal government had partnered with several local fire departments, developing task forces able to locate people trapped deep in rubble, pull them to safety, administer medical aid, and operate the tools and machinery necessary to rapidly stabilize shattered structures.

Many task force members were firefighters or medics, but there were also doctors, structural engineers, dog handlers, and heavy rigging experts. Task force members attended specialized training sessions once a month, like military reservists, learning how to work in unstable environments and operate technical-search equipment. There were also a couple of annual exercises simulating an earthquake or other disaster. The goal was to be able to deploy by airplane with all of their equipment within six hours of being called, and to have enough food, water, tents, cots, and other equipment to live in the field for 72 hours, no matter how harsh the conditions.

The closest FEMA team, Virginia Task Force 1—or VA-TF1—was based in Fairfax, the county adjacent to Arlington, to the west. Most of their missions were out of state—or out of the country. And the

Pentagon wouldn't be their first terrorist response. VA-TF1 had deployed to Oklahoma City in 1995, and to Nairobi, Kenya, after the 1998 embassy bombings. They had also spent much of 1999 pulling victims from rubble at a trio of earthquakes—two in Turkey and one in Taiwan.

VA-TF1 had been formally mobilized at about 11:00 A.M., but most of the team members swung into action before FEMA made its official request. Those who saw the burning towers in New York on TV figured they'd probably be activated and sent there, and many raced to the staging area at one of the Fairfax fire stations. There were about 150 people on the team, but missions were usually capped at 70 or so, the optimal number for the way the team and its equipment were structured. During an incident, the team was staffed on a first-come, first-served basis. Team leaders would fill it out as members arrived and cap it off once enough people had shown up.

Just getting on the roster for an event could be as stressful as the work itself. The firefighters, canine handlers, and doctors on the task force trained intensely—in addition to their regular jobs—and missions were infrequent, so when the call went out, everybody wanted the chance to put their skills to use and have a role in a major world event. Team members would drop everything and race to the rally point, desperate to make the cut. Every now and then somebody's stress levels would be so high that they'd fail the required blood-pressure screening. Members who missed the cut sometimes ended up as distraught as if there had been a death in the family.

After the initial delays caused by traffic, the team came together quickly. Fairfax firefighter Brian Moravitz had been on the last big mission, an earthquake in Turkey. As he hurried to Fire Station 18, he figured he'd end up sitting this one out so somebody else could get a mission under their belt, but the team leaders put him on the roster.

Dean Tills was a structural engineer, a civilian, who was also the senior structural specialist for the task force. His job was to assess the safety of collapsed buildings and oversee shoring operations and other efforts to stabilize areas where rescue teams needed to work. He had gone home to prepare his gear after seeing the attacks in New York, then gone back to the office when there was no call from the task force, thinking maybe it wasn't as bad as it looked. But the call had finally come. While driving to Station 18, he heard about the second tower collapsing. It filled him with rage; he wanted to scream.

Leo Titus, also a structural specialist, was a rookie who had recently joined the task force and never been on a mission. He was the first structural specialist to arrive at Station 18—and possibly the most nervous. When he checked in, somebody told him to change into his blue military-style fatigues. Titus's clothes were in his car, out by the curb, so he changed on the sidewalk, anxiously glancing around at the homes encircling the station, worried that he'd offend the locals by stripping to his underwear in plain view.

After a few minutes the word came: He was on the roster. *Wow, I'm really going,* he thought, wondering if he was up to the job. He had been recruited to the task force by a fellow engineer, and at the first meeting, the camaraderie he felt reminded him of his fraternity house in college. It seemed like a great opportunity to do something meaningful with his skills.

But now he was facing the reality of leaving his wife, Jen, and their two young kids for a job that sounded dangerous. He had been trying to reach Jen by phone, with no luck, and being gone for more than a few days would be hard on her. Besides, he'd just finished his six months of initial training and felt barely qualified. Other structural specialists with more field experience had arrived, and he considered giving up his spot.

But task force policy was to bring nearly as many new recruits on missions as old hands, to build a broad base of experience. Another team member walked up to Titus and offered encouragement. "Leo, you've got to do this," he insisted. Finally, Titus got through to Jen.

She was frightened, but he assured her that he would be safe—
though he had no idea what they were headed into. By the time he
hung up, he felt better.

Deputy team leader Ed Brinkley was busy making sure everything
was ready to go, but he was thinking of other things too. His dad had
been a civilian Navy accountant who worked at the Pentagon for
years. As a kid, Brinkley had run through the building's wide, smooth
hallways, and scampered up and down the strange, sloping ramps
that connected the floors, dating to the days before escalators were
commonplace. Forty years later, he thought, the survival of the very
same building was at stake.

Once the roster was filled, members went through standard medical checks and got their gear. There was a quick briefing, but the
information was sketchy. Dean Tills was part of an advance team—
along with Jeff Donaldson, Garret Dyer, and Bob Dubé—that climbed
into a fire department vehicle and drove to the Pentagon ahead of the
larger group. They'd do a quick reconnaissance and coordinate with
the incident commanders, so the full team could hit the ground running once it arrived.

One of the first people they encountered at the Pentagon was an
Army officer who pleaded with them to try to rescue some people
trapped in offices on the C Ring. He gave them two office numbers,
which Tills wrote down. He and Donaldson were only wearing light
protective gear, not the heavy uniforms of ordinary fire crews. They
had no breathing devices, and Tills wasn't even a firefighter. Still, the
two men promised to do what they could.

They entered the building at the Corridor 5 entrance, still
manned by Keith Young, turned right into A&E Drive, then tried to
walk toward the impact point through Corridor 4. But smoke and
heat drove them back. They realized their team would need masks,
air tanks, and other firefighting equipment. Though it was comprised
largely of firefighters, the task force wasn't equipped to face fires on

missions. During out-of-state or overseas deployments, it typically took 24 or 48 hours before they arrived at the site. If there had been any fires, they were almost always out by the time the task force showed up.

Tills and Donaldson went up one flight and found that they could make their way down Corridor 4 on the second floor. They had circumnavigated the whole range of the fire, in a staple-shaped path down Corridor 5, along A&E Drive, then back out Corridor 4. One thing they were sure of: There was probably nobody alive in the collapse area. The fire and damage were too intense.

Outside, they found some eyewitnesses who worked for the Pentagon renovation team and had been near the helipad when the plane came in. One of the men, Michael Sullivan, told them he'd been walking on a sidewalk, heading to a meeting, when he looked up and saw the plane heading straight toward him. Instinctively, he dove to the ground to avoid getting hit. His pants were torn at the knees where the concrete had cut into them. Sullivan hadn't seen the impact, since his head was down, but watched the fireball that immediately followed, and felt its heat on his face. Thinking like an engineer, Tills considered this further confirmation that the plane had fully penetrated the building.

As Tills and Donaldson finished their initial reconnaissance, the rest of the team was pulling up in several buses. A rough security perimeter had been established, and the buses were held up near the helipad for about 20 minutes before being allowed to get through. Most of the team members were used to deployments that involved a long plane ride, which allowed time to gather information, study it, and make detailed plans. This time, they arrived at the incident less than an hour after getting the roster finalized. It still wasn't clear what was going on, but their first glimpse of the Pentagon provided more information than all the reports they'd gotten up till then.

As they looked out the windows of the bus, most of them expected to see a big field of airplane debris, like you might see on TV after a crash. But there were no big airplane parts. FBI agents, however, were scouring the grounds, picking up bits of evidence. Bandages and debris were all over the place. Fire was visible through the wrecked windows of the building. The delay on the bus dragged on. Everybody on board was dying to get off.

Leo Titus still felt nervous. But as he gazed out the window at the burning ruins, he also felt anger, patriotism, pride, and a desire for revenge. He took out a pocket camera and snapped a few pictures.

ROOKIE MISTAKE

Mid-afternoon

Chuck Gibbs had been girding for the arrival of the FEMA teams—with his teeth clenched.

The FEMA teams were an invaluable resource. They were also the media darlings of the fire and rescue world, the ones with the biggest budget, the best gear, and the most headlines in their scrapbooks. There was a natural rivalry between Arlington and Fairfax too. The two fire departments trained together, and worked alongside each other on incidents near the borders of the two counties, but they could be as competitive as jealous siblings. The Fairfax Fire Department was four times bigger than Arlington's. It encompassed some of the wealthiest neighborhoods in the D.C. suburbs, with the generous funding and gleaming facilities to match. Arlington serviced more high-rises and urban areas, with modest firehouses that dated to the 1960s or 1970s. Fairfax's FEMA designation generated esprit de corps among the task-force members, but it rankled some of the Arlington firefighters the way an older brother's Ivy League degree becomes a tiresome elitist credential.

One of the officials working near the helipad command post was Jack Brown, the assistant fire chief in Loudoun County, Virginia. He was a new arrival in Loudoun, after spending 30 years in the Fairfax Fire Department, where he also worked with the FEMA team. Brown had arrived at the Pentagon with a task force of Loudoun firefighters earlier in the day, and Schwartz put him in charge of planning for the incident. Brown knew Gibbs from his work with Fairfax, and pulled him aside for a moment. "Gibby, whatever you do," he warned, "do not give up command and let the FEMA guys run the show." Brown knew from experience that the FEMA teams were used to being the premier outfit on the scene, with other fire and rescue agencies working to support them. If allowed, he cautioned, they'd run their own operation and usurp Arlington's authority to manage the fire ground.

Task force leaders found Gibbs near his command buggy. They needed to get in and do a reconnaissance right away, they insisted. The building might be at risk of further collapse. Besides, Plaugher had ordered them to do a detailed search of the building and provide an assessment of how safe it was to work in there.

Gibbs had his own responsibilities, however, and one of them was to make sure nobody on his side of the fire, in the River Division, got in over their heads. "Now hold on," he asserted. "You don't understand the construction of the Pentagon. These are 18-inch walls. This building is a different animal." They squared off for a few moments, then agreed that the task force would send in a couple of search teams but remain under the control of Gibbs and Randy Gray, the Arlington commanders.

Leo Titus learned that he would be the structural specialist on one of the two rescue teams going into the building. One of the team leaders told him to put on his flash gear, the lightweight protective suit firefighters wear for small fires. Titus didn't even know he was supposed to have flash gear. Luckily, he found somebody who loaned him a set.

The team leader was Mike Regan, a veteran Fairfax firefighter who had grown up in Brooklyn and worked as a Teamster when he was younger. The stocky firefighter, with salt-and-pepper hair and the remnants of a New York accent, had passed up a chance to join the New York Police Department in the 1970s, and moved instead to suburban Virginia, which was growing rapidly and paying good salaries to firefighters. He had joined the task force in its early days, in the 1980s, and one of his first missions was the 1988 Armenian earthquake that killed more than 35,000 people.

Regan had seven others on his search team, including a canine handler with a dog, Nero, able to sniff out living people, along with a medic and a hazardous-materials specialist. They carried listening devices to detect human sounds beneath rubble, and a searchcam with a compact, closed-circuit camera mounted on the end of a telescoping pole. The plan was to search as close to the collapse zone as they could, on all five floors. They'd look for victims, but also evaluate the damage and try to identify areas where people might be trapped in void spaces beneath the debris. Regan knew firsthand that people could survive for remarkably long periods of time in unthinkable positions, as long as they had air to breathe.

The team leader also knew that Leo Titus, his structural engineer, was on his first mission—and it was a hell of an initiation. Titus had never seen a dead body outside of a funeral home, and the shock of it could send some people reeling. Regan had lost a team member once, during one of the earthquakes in Turkey. They had been working with a translator who was new to rescue work, and at one point she started gesticulating urgently, signaling for him to come quick. When he got to her side, she was gagging violently at the sight of a mangled body. She stayed sick for the next five days, unable to work. Regan knew he couldn't afford to lose his engineer like that. In such precarious conditions, Titus would be a vital part of the team; Regan had to look out for him.

Just before they entered the building, he gave Titus a pen. "Leo, I need you to hold onto this for me," he said. "Don't lose it! It's the only one I have." Regan had other pens in his pockets, but thought that if he gave Titus something basic to focus on, it might distract him from disturbing scenes inside the building. "Remember, you need to write down all the structural stuff you notice, so we can report back."

Regan led his team toward the door to the immediate left of the collapse zone, the same entrance Bobby Beer and the crew of Rescue 104 used when they first went into the building. The only breathing devices they had were half-mask respirators, which filter out airborne particles but not dangerous gases like carbon monoxide and sulfur dioxide. The rescue crew members strapped them on and stepped into the building.

After just a couple of paces, Regan, at the head of the group, spotted the body of a man, badly burned, who had fallen with his back to the door. The severely charred remains indicated the intense heat inside—which Regan could feel through his flash gear after only a few seconds. He worried that it could be a problem for the dog, Nero, and his unprotected paws. He noted the location of the body, but since their first priority was live victims, not remains recovery, he ushered the team forward.

Titus didn't notice the body, and Regan didn't point it out to him. But Titus was overwhelmed with plenty of other sensations. He couldn't believe how smoky and dark it was. There were no flames, but they were surrounded by glowing embers that looked as if they could combust at any moment. Water, pumped into the building by hoses and deluge guns outside, was pouring down on them like rain and pooling at their feet. As he started to follow Regan up and over smoking debris, he couldn't help imagining how his wife would react to his new volunteer job. Jen would kill me if she saw what I was doing! he thought. He kept reminding himself that above all they had to stay out of areas where the building could collapse on top of them. As the engineer, making sure that didn't happen was his job.

The first floor didn't look anything like an office building. There were no hallways or pathways or obvious places to walk, just widespread rubble, rising up from the floor and hanging down from the ceiling. Randy Leatherman, one of the team members, could see right away they were facing something the task force had never dealt with before. A few partitions stood, but mostly they saw piles of desks and walls and other wreckage that looked like it had been plowed into various corners by giant waves. Fire crews worked around them. The rescuers poked through some of the debris. "Fairfax Fire!" Regan called out over and over. "If you can hear us make a noise!" Then the team would be quiet for a few moments, listening for some kind of response. There was none.

It didn't look like they'd find victims on the first floor, so they found a stairwell and went up a flight. With no lights or windows in the stairwell, it was pitch-black. Titus had heard firefighters describe places so dark that you couldn't see your hand in front of your face. Now he knew what this sensation was like—disorienting and scary. It felt as hot as a chimney too, as if the concrete walls were holding in the heat. He followed Regan's voice and the lights mounted to the other team members' helmets.

Once they got out of the stairwell, onto the second floor, they could see better. Unlike the lower level, with its mounds of wreckage, the second floor looked like it had been bulldozed flat and then torched. Walls had been flattened and the contents of offices burned to ash. There was little visible fire, but the heat was relentless. In the direction of the collapse zone, beneath the smoke, they were able to see for at least 50 or 75 feet, with little to obstruct their view. There were some abandoned hose lines leading deep into the most wrecked part of the building, toward the collapse zone. Regan thought of the firefighters who had plunged this far into the fire and was impressed that they'd brought hoses this far in, with so much fire and heat.

Titus noticed some structural damage that he wanted to document. Among other things, a floor slab had been forced upward three or four inches, and there was a big breach where it separated from the adjacent slab. "Now that's not something you see very often," he said.

"The whole place is something you don't see very often," Regan murmured.

Titus took out his pen and paper to make some notes. The protective gloves he wore made it hard to write, so he took one of them off. Scalding water from above splattered his unprotected hand, and he flinched—and dropped his pen. It disappeared into the steaming swamp on the floor. So Titus committed as many observations as he could to memory.

A little while later, when the group stopped for a break in a room with an open window, Regan asked Titus to write down a few things. "Mike," the engineer had to admit, "I lost my pen."

"Leo!" Regan howled, "I gave you one thing to keep track of, and you lost it!" But he was grinning, and Titus knew he was being razzed. He felt foolish. But as far as Regan was concerned, the engineer's abiding concern with the pen was working—it was keeping his mind off other things. Titus borrowed another pen and continued taking notes. Next time, he told himself, bring extra pens.

The engineer was documenting cracks in the wall, the condition of the concrete, and any details he could divine about the stability of the support beams holding up the floors. There was plenty of damage, but Titus didn't see any risk of further collapse in the area where they were working. Fire conditions were another matter. Without the thick protective liners that insulated regular turnout gear, the heat was uncomfortable and dangerous.

The hazmat specialist, Domenick Iannelli, carried a multigas detector that measured levels of flammable gases, oxygen, carbon monoxide, and other substances in the air. The biggest concern seemed to be carbon monoxide. Iannelli's readings said it was mostly in the safe zone, but the levels rose and fell from room to room. The longer they stayed in the building, the more gas would accumulate in their bodies. Regan had been calling on his radio for full masks and air bottles, which would protect them from harmful gases, but it was nearly impossible to get out on the radio, and no spare Scott packs were available when they arrived.

Regan made a decision. Nero's feet were starting to get burned, so he sent the dog out with its handler, Elizabeth Kreitler. Titus too. The engineer had shown great heart, but he'd never been in a fire before, and he wasn't trained to operate in the kinds of conditions they were encountering.

Titus followed Kreitler back down the stairwell. He didn't have his own flashlight or helmet light, and in the darkness he slipped and bounced down a few steps. Kreitler heard him fall and turned around to light the way for him with her own helmet light. When he finally got outside, Titus added another mental note to his growing list: Next time, bring a flashlight.

The remaining team members turned away from the collapse zone, toward some offices that were still intact. They started opening office doors or bashing them down if they were jammed or locked. Steve McFarland came across something in one room that seemed to stand out from the surrounding debris. Then he made out a skull and a rib cage, facing down. The remains were charred black. He looked more closely and saw a chunk of flesh next to the bones. In his eight years of firefighting, McFarland had never seen a fire fatality, and it took a moment to sink in that he was looking at a human body. He breathed deeply. Okay, this is serious, he told himself. Then he asked Regan what he should do. The team leader told him to mark the body with yellow fire-line tape—and to tie the tape to something near the body, not the body itself.

Five minutes later McFarland found his second body, in some rubble on the floor. It looked like it might have been sitting in a chair, but the remains were fused with debris and it was hard to tell; he couldn't even determine whether it was a man or a woman. In the aftermath of earthquakes he had worked, it was often hard to spot bodies in collapsed buildings because everything was gray and coated with dust. In the Pentagon, he was beginning to learn, it was hard to spot bodies too—except that everything wasn't gray, it was black. The intense heat, and the ravages of the fire, made it clear this was a mission that would involve a lot more search than rescue. McFarland felt sure they weren't going to find anybody else.

Randy Leatherman and another team member, Buck Best, worked together searching locked offices. Best carried a 20-pound sledgehammer that he used for busting down doors. Leatherman followed with a listening device, slung around his neck, that could pick up sounds from people trapped deep beneath rubble. Best found one door that wouldn't budge and pounded on it with his sledgehammer. When it finally gave way, a column of heat lashed out at them like a tempest escaping a blast furnace, and both men dropped to their knees, floored by the hostile welcome. They were both experienced firefighters and knew it was typical for heat to rush from a burning room. But this room wasn't on fire—it simply held an overwhelming amount of trapped heat.

On the floor, they looked at each other with the same thought in mind: *rookie mistake*. They crawled inside to see if anybody might be trapped in the room, knowing it probably would have been impossible to survive the searing heat they had just dodged. They found no victims.

Closer to the collapse, however, near active fire, Leatherman found what looked like three sets of remains. There were only parts of skeletons, with no evidence of arms or legs. The bones almost looked as if they had been stacked in a pile—like cordwood, it seemed to Leatherman. He tried to imagine how they had ended up that way. Perhaps a small group of people were standing together when the plane hit. Or several people had been in an open area, and the force of the impact somehow pushed them all into the same corner.

With slim odds of finding anybody alive on the second floor, Regan led the team up another flight. On the third floor, it felt as if they had entered a different building altogether. There was obvious smoke damage, but not the catastrophic destruction they had seen below. Some offices were more or less undisturbed, the furniture where it ought to be, the pictures still hanging on the walls. Coffee mugs sat on desks with flecks of detritus floating in the liquid. Randy Leatherman saw one desk, lightly dusted with fine soot, but otherwise looking as it must have early that morning. An apple sat on it, along with a copy of that morning's *Washington Post*. POLL FINDS PUBLIC WARY ON TAX CUT, a headline read.

It was easier searching here, yet there were still no living victims. They made another important discovery, though: a spacious office with broken windows, which vented the smoke and heat, and chairs they could actually sit on. On the wall next to the door they saw the name of a general. The searchers temporarily took over his office, sticking their heads out the windows and sucking in fresh air. Regan decided it would be their base of operations while they were in the building doing reconnaissance.

The group searched methodically on the third and fourth floors, finding no additional victims there. As they worked up toward the fifth floor, the heat and smoke conditions became more difficult. The hot, gaseous air was getting trapped, with no place to vent at the top of the building. Leatherman and McFarland decided to look for an access point to the roof that they could open, to create a flow of air up and out.

They found a stairwell that led to the fifth floor. As Leatherman trudged up the steps, he was getting fatigued. It surprised him—he was an endurance athlete, accustomed to stressful climbs. "Man, this is ridiculous," he huffed. "My feet feel like lead weights. I run 50-mile races. Why can't I do this?"

Iannelli was closely watching the readings on his multigas meter—which had been drifting upward in the stairwell. "You don't think it has anything to do with these carbon monoxide levels I'm getting, do you?" he said to Leatherman.

Leatherman kept going, as if it didn't register. He and McFarland followed the steps up to a locked door that they guessed opened onto the roof. It was just the venting outlet they were looking for. They were about to start bashing it open when Iannelli, behind them, shouted up, "Hey, guys—we've got to get outta here. My CO readings are too high."

"Oh come on!" McFarland protested. "We're right here at the door! We just have to pop it off! We can get this done."

"Bullshit!" Iannelli yelled back. The door was thick and secured, and it might take five minutes of pounding—and heavy breathing of contaminated air—to get it off. "Don't make me come up there and drag you down!" Iannelli warned.

Leatherman and McFarland relented. As they walked back down, Iannelli held out the measuring device. "Here, look at my meter," he said. "Maybe this explains it."

All firefighters were taught the classic signs of carbon-monoxide poisoning: a cherry-red face, a pounding headache, fatigue. But with so much else going on, Leatherman hadn't even thought about the air they were breathing. "Okay, I'm stupid," he chided himself. "Now I get it—CO poisoning." Still, he didn't think it was bad enough to seek medical attention. And he certainly didn't want to abandon the rest of the team on its first trip into the building.

They regrouped at the general's office on the third floor, rested, and did more searching. There were no victims, living or dead. Then Regan got an order over his radio, which worked, for once: They were to come out of the building. Task force commanders had decided they didn't want any of their people in the building without full air masks or complete turnout gear.

Gibbs, it turned out, had intervened. He had agreed to let some of the task force searchers into the building, to do reconnaissance. But when he realized they were operating at the edge of the collapse zone, he tracked down one of the task force leaders. "You're going to have to evacuate the building until we have a better handle on what's going on in there," he declared. "I'm ordering your people out."

There was no argument from inside. As Regan led his team down the stairwell and back outside, they were all feeling woozy and tired. A break sounded like a good idea.

★ 22 ★

"DADDY'S THERE"

Mid-afternoon

Chief Schwartz had a fresh assignment for Joe Lightfoot, one of the aides in the main command post beneath I-395. "Joey, I need you to go find Chief Cornwell and bring him here." Schwartz said. "We need to make sure he's okay."

Even though Schwartz had relieved Cornwell of official command responsibility, the battalion chief continued to work the fire, helping Gibbs and Randy Gray near the helipad, checking on firefighters inside the building, shuttling around the whole fire ground in his Suburban and doing whatever else he could to help. He came on the radio every now and then to give updates on the condition of the fire or request specific equipment at certain places.

Cornwell even made an appearance on camera. By chance, a documentary crew was spending the day with some firefighters who had worked on a huge chemical fire in a Baltimore train tunnel two months earlier. The team had stumbled onto a journalistic coup: They had a front-row seat at one of the biggest news events in American history. An interviewer with a microphone found Randy Gray, in his blue command vest, and asked for a quick assessment of the fire. Gray had a thousand things on his priority list, and conducting a press briefing wasn't one of them. He quickly looked around and saw Cornwell, who had been inside and probably knew more about the fire anyway. Cornwell was more inclined to run from the limelight than seek it, but Gray called out to his colleague, "Hey, Bobby, can you talk to them?" Cornwell shot him a look that said, *You owe me.*

Cornwell turned out to be a compelling camera presence, however. Standing beside one of the command buggies, with a Pentagon map behind him, he described his early arrival, the first trip into the Pentagon to size up the fire, and the evacuation when they thought another airplane was headed their way. His bald head gleaming with sweat and his shirt half unbuttoned, Cornwell looked like a man who had already put in a full day of grueling work. He sounded optimistic about putting out the fire but was noncommittal about when. "We're getting a handle on it now," he said, "and hoping there won't be a lot of victims inside."

After the filmed interview, Gray had sent Cornwell back into the building with some D.C. units the command post was having trouble reaching by radio. Cornwell and Gray both knew they had little recourse with the D.C. crews, under the circumstances. But they thought it might rein them in a bit if Cornwell was there looking over their shoulders. He had spent a few minutes with the D.C. crews, who didn't seem interested in his assistance, come back out for a break, then plunged back into Corridor 5, to do more reconnaissance. By the time Lightfoot arrived at the helipad looking for him, nobody had heard from him in a while, and he wasn't coming up on the radio. They guessed he had walked all the way through the building, into the courtyard.

Lightfoot didn't have any turnout gear, so he couldn't follow Cornwell into the building. He'd have to head for the courtyard the long way, by driving around toward South Parking and going through the tunnel. Before he left the helipad, he looked for Mike Smith, his best friend in the department. Lightfoot was worried about Smith too, on account of Smith's recent heart surgery. He found his friend near the helipad, looking whipped. They talked about the fire Smith had been battling in the D Ring. After the setbacks of two evacuations, which allowed the fire to retrench, Smith described how they were finally starting to knock it down.

Smith had also climbed one of the aerial ladders up to the roof, at Randy Gray's behest, to check out the fire that seemed to be spreading beneath the slate shingles. "There are no flames on the roof itself, but you can see all the active smoke," Smith explained to Lightfoot, gesturing toward the gray swirls hovering over the building. "I had to Scott up, the smoke is so thick. It looks like the fire's running the cockloft. There's debris up there too that looks like it came from the explosion."

Smith was on his third air bottle. For a firefighter in good shape, going through one or two air bottles represented a good day's work. Burning through three bottles could be exhausting. Smith was nearly 50; he had done more than enough, Lightfoot felt. "Mike, you need to take a break, man," he urged his buddy. "How about calling it a day?"

"Nope," Smith answered. Now that they finally seemed to be making some progress, he wasn't about to quit.

Smith, in fact, was about to mount another attack on the fire with his crew, this time with one of the rotational groups Gibbs and Gray had put together. They suited up once more and approached Corridor 5, where Keith Young, the beefy sentry, was still regulating who went into the building. He was doing precisely what Gibbs had instructed—keeping firefighters out of the fire until they had been cleared by the command post. But it seemed like miserable work, judging by Young's apologetic tone and the pained look on his face as he turned away his fellow firefighters. "I'm just doing what I've been told," he explained over and over. "I'm following orders from the battalion chief." Nobody was giving Young a hard time anymore, but he was getting some looks of disbelief. The fire was so big that the smoke could be seen for miles, yet he was keeping fire crews—including captains and chiefs—from getting to it.

Smith and his crew were allowed to pass, and they retraced their steps down Corridor 5 toward the D Ring. Some of the smoke had lifted and they could see farther down Corridor 5, toward the courtyard. As Smith's crew approached the D Ring, Denis Griffin's crew was walking toward them, from the courtyard in the opposite direction, after taking their own break. They recognized each other through the haze. Jim Anderson walked up to Smith, who asked what conditions were like where they had been.

Anderson explained how they had tried to reach victims in the C Ring and were driven back by the fire. "It's just FUBAR,"[1] Anderson grimaced. "We couldn't even set up an organized search. Everybody's dead in here. We're not gonna save anybody."

Smith saw a lot of other Arlington units in the building. It was a relatively small fire department, and most of the firefighters usually knew who was on which shift. Smith recognized a lot of colleagues who were supposed to be off-duty and had obviously been called in for the big fire or just shown up on their own. It was an impressive showing. But with a lot of fire still to fight—and fatigue setting in—he wondered who was left to relieve the crews that had been there all day.

They went down the D Ring one more time. There were several fire crews in the area now, with four hose lines running down the cluttered hallway. They still had to climb over the same debris, and there was still fire at the edge of the impact zone, but it had finally receded. The firefighters were getting the upper hand on it at last. Smith and his men manned hoses left by crews that were rotating out, until their own air started to run low for the third time. Smith was beat. His crew wasn't complaining, but he knew they had to be tired too. As they headed out for the fourth time, he felt like he was finally ready to call it a day.

A rehabilitation bus for firefighters had been set up near the helipad, with medics checking vitals signs, administering fluids, and looking for indications of smoke inhalation, dehydration, heat exhaustion, or carbon monoxide poisoning. Old-timers would often shun such attention; they didn't feel they needed the fussing. But most firefighters in modern departments were happy to have professionals looking out for their health, and the medics in the department considered it part of their job, just as important as taking care of fire victims. Smith encouraged his crew to climb aboard and get checked out, and nobody resisted. He had a headache and his muscles were aching—likely signs of dehydration. His socks were soaked with sweat. He told one of the medics about his recent angioplasty surgery. They inserted an IV in his arm and took his blood pressure. His crewmates, Justin Scott and Greg Gulick, got IVs too.

The medics decided all three should go to the hospital. They were dehydrated, and Smith, especially, ought to be thoroughly checked out by doctors, and get an EKG. None of them wanted to go, but their protests were brief. They climbed back off the bus and walked toward the ambulances on Washington Boulevard. As Smith looked around, it was a dramatically different scene than when he had arrived. The helipad lawn was filling with all kinds of support vehicles to help the firefighters do their jobs. He could see people bringing food, and a procession of young Army troops in fatigues, from Fort Myer, less than a mile away, was pushing grocery carts filled with Gatorade toward the Pentagon. How amazing, he thought.

Medics decided that Smith should go to Alexandria Hospital, and Scott accompanied his captain there. A separate ambulance took Greg Gulick to Arlington Hospital, a bit closer, where he ran into Derek Spector. After several forays into the thick of the fire early on, Spector and his crew from Truck 105 had been sent back into Corridor 5 to clear a path through some of the areas where the fire was coming under control. While climbing over some debris, Spector fell through a piece of toppled drywall and wrenched his left ankle, causing his lower to leg to lock up. His day was over.

When Spector arrived at the hospital, he was swarmed by a full team of doctors and nurses, still on high alert and ready to receive casualties from the Pentagon. They rolled him on a gurney from room to room, doing various checks and taking X-rays. Finally they decided that even though it was just a sprain, they were going to put a cast on his ankle. But Spector was barely paying attention to his own leg after a while; at the hospital, he first learned that the twin towers had collapsed, killing thousands. It was numbing. He could barely watch the TV. By the time Gulick arrived, Spector was just about ready to leave. Doctors cleared Gulick after a quick examination, and the two of them checked out of the hospital together. An Arlington ambulance took the glum firefighters back to one of the stations.

Kenny Johnson, the medic helping Chief Smith in the courtyard, had shuttled out to the helipad lawn a couple of times to relay messages and get additional info from the Arlington commanders. He had been the one who examined Derek Spector's ankle, in fact, and sent him to the hospital. In mid-afternoon Johnson took another walk down Corridor 5, to the outside, looking for something to eat. In the courtyard, supplies—including food—were still scarce. Out by the helipad, in comparison, it was starting to look like the food court at a mall, with people handing out fast food from carts and buggies, or walking around passing it out.

For the first time, Johnson heard somebody say the twin towers had collapsed. "Bullshit!" he retorted. "There's no way! They weren't built to fail." Johnson's brother lived on Long Island and was a firefighter with the FDNY. Reports of hundreds of firefighters dead in the ruins of the twin towers seemed unimaginable. Maybe parts of the buildings had fallen down, he guessed—but surely not the whole things.

Randy Gray saw Johnson and asked if he had spotted Cornwell in the courtyard. Johnson said no. "If you see him," Gray said, "just keep an eye on him, okay?" He didn't have to explain why; Johnson knew. The medic filled his arms with food and walked back toward the courtyard with the booty.

Meanwhile, Cornwell, after tagging along with the D.C. crews, had come back out by the helipad, gotten some water, and searched anxiously for a cell phone that worked. His two boys would be getting home from school soon, and he wanted to reach his wife before then so she could tell them he was okay.

His wife, Colleen, had been a firefighter herself, before retiring to raise the family's three kids in Manassas, Virginia, a suburb about 25 miles southwest of Arlington. Yet for the time being, she wished she weren't so familiar with her husband's work. She knew that because of the territory Cornwell was responsible for, he was one of the first-due officers at the Pentagon. Watching TV, she even thought she had seen his command buggy parked on the grass as the camera panned the scene. He had probably been inside all day, leading crews, and she was desperate for some word from him, but she figured that no news was good news. If he got hurt, they'd call from the hospital right away. If he was fine, there was no need to call.

Colleen had spent the day frantically cleaning the house, worried that she'd be racing off to the hospital any minute to tend to her husband, either hurt from the terrorist attacks or weakened by the chemotherapy—for some reason, it seemed important to make sure the house was clean for the babysitter. Still, she stopped what she was doing every two minutes to catch the latest updates on TV.

When the phone finally rang, Colleen leaped for it. "Everything's fine," her husband said nonchalantly. "Tell the kids Daddy's okay." She was overjoyed to hear his voice but could tell he was tense and tired. He said he'd try to call again around ten that night, like he usually did when he was working.

The two boys, Joseph and Michael, got home from school a few minutes later. They knew that a plane had hit the Pentagon. Everybody at school had been talking about it. "Do you know where the Pentagon is?" Colleen asked, testing how worried they were.

"Yes," Joseph, the eight-year-old, said. "It's in Arlington." He had always wanted to be a firefighter like his dad, and he seemed to have uncanny intuition about what was happening. After a moment's pause, he added, "Daddy's there."

After the phone break, Cornwell plunged back into Corridor 5, heading toward the courtyard. He turned right into A&E Drive, where he closely examined the punch-out hole and the wreckage scattered outside of it. He could see the wheel that looked like part of the landing gear. Body parts bobbed in the oily water. Farther down, two civilians—Pentagon employees, he guessed—were sitting in one of the motorized carts, with about 100 dry-chemical fire extinguishers packed onboard. The small, home-style devices—suitable for a kitchen fire, perhaps—seemed pointless in such an industrial-size blaze. It seemed bizarre for civilians to be in the middle of a fire, arming themselves with such meager tools. As he passed by, he wondered what they were doing there.

Cornwell turned right again, into Corridor 4, aiming to gauge the scale of the fire. He couldn't believe that more than six hours after the fire began, he was still doing reconnaissance. In A&E Drive the fire had started to recede—partly because of the water flowing out of the deluge guns in the service road, and partly because the jet fuel finally started to burn itself out. But parts of the C Ring were still burning intensely, and there were some areas between the C and E Rings that firefighters hadn't even reached yet.

Cornwell turned around and walked into the courtyard. He called Randy Gray on the radio, to report his latest assessment. "From the C Ring out, we're still in trouble," he said. "We're in tough shape."

Kenny Johnson was back in the courtyard by then, handing out the food he'd carried in. He saw Cornwell sitting on a bench, taking a breather, and walked over. "Hey, how you doing, Chief?" he asked. Johnson knew that Gray had replaced Cornwell as operations chief, and he figured Cornwell would be deeply disappointed to have command taken from him.

"I'm good, Kenny," Cornwell answered. "I can handle this," he added, sensing Johnson's concern about his health. But Johnson noticed that Cornwell was sucking in little wisps of air—bird-breathing—the way he did when he got tense about something. Cornwell seemed like a man without a home; he had been all over the building, but with no specific responsibility. After another moment, Cornwell looked candidly at Johnson. "This is the most scared I've been since Vietnam," he confided.

Cornwell said he was going back in, to look around some more. Johnson didn't have turnout gear but said he'd go along anyway. As they were walking back into the building, they saw two gloomy-faced Navy personnel standing in the hallway, a man and a woman. The pair told the firefighters they had comrades inside and were waiting for them to come out. Could Cornwell and Johnson maybe go look for them? "We'll go look," Cornwell said. He was careful not to offer any false hope, yet the two Navy faces seemed to brighten when the firefighters offered to help.

They got the room number and headed toward the office, on the C Ring. As they got close, the whole area was completely leveled, with flames still lashing out at fire crews working to control the blaze. Cornwell and Johnson looked around briefly, but it seemed obvious that nobody in that area could have survived. It had taken the brunt of the impact and was thoroughly devastated. They went back and found the man and woman from the Navy. "If your buddies were in that area, it's not good," Cornwell told them as gently as possible. Johnson watched the two faces go ashen.

Cornwell did some more reconnaissance in the building, then went back to the courtyard. Jim Anderson saw him and walked over. Cornwell looked exhausted. "Hey Chief, why don't you take a seat?" the fit young firefighter suggested. To Anderson's surprise, he did. Then Anderson offered him some water, which Cornwell also accepted, with a weary arm. That was totally out of character. Cornwell was the kind of guy who never seemed to need anything from anybody. Anderson could see he was feeling bad, that the experience had gotten to him.

Joe Lightfoot finally pulled into the courtyard after navigating his vehicle around the two big supply lines that were now running down the tunnel, bringing water from South Parking. After spending most of the day in the command post, it was his first glimpse of the courtyard. Smoke still hung over the whole area, reminding him of *Apocalypse Now.*

When he saw Cornwell, Lightfoot hopped out of the Suburban and walked over. Cornwell's helmet was off but his turnout gear was buttoned up tight, with his fire hood around his neck as if he were about to charge back into the fire. His face was flushed and wet with sweat. "Chief, how're you doing?" Lightfoot asked, perhaps the tenth or twentieth person to inquire about Cornwell's health that day.

"Doing good, Joey," Cornwell huffed. "Doing good."

"Chief Schwartz wants you to come back to the command post," Lightfoot said.

"Nah, I'm good here," Cornwell answered.

"Uhhh . . ." Lightfoot hesitated. "I think Chief Schwartz is ordering you to come out."

"Do what you gotta do, Joey," Cornwell said softly. "It ain't happening." He was staying with his firefighters in the building.

Lightfoot offered him some more water and hung around for a few minutes, making small talk. Then he told Cornwell to be careful and climbed back in his truck.

He drove back to the command post wondering how this was going to go over with the bosses. "Where's Cornwell?" Schwartz asked the moment he saw Lightfoot.

"He ain't coming," Lightfoot said, holding his breath.

Schwartz absorbed the news for a second, then went on with his work, saying nothing.

23

TRENCH CUTS

Late afternoon

The roof of the Pentagon had been a concern since Gibbs, Gray, and Cornwell first noticed the gray smoke spewing from under the slate shingles. Gibbs had sent a couple of crews, including Derek Spector and Mike Smith, up on ladders to do reconnaissance. Nobody had doubted that fire was spreading in the cockloft beneath the slate, but with core parts of the Pentagon's interior still burning out of control, the roof seemed like a matter they could deal with later.

Not anymore. While crews had been gradually beating back the fire inside the building, the fire on the roof was turning out to be a stubborn problem that was defying firefighters' best efforts to bring it under control. By mid-afternoon Randy Gray had been sending fire crews up to the fifth floor, and to the roof itself, to conduct standard roof-fire operations. They weren't working.

One basic tactic was to pull down ceiling panels on the top floor, using specially designed hooks. Ordinarily, firefighters could get access to the space beneath the roof, typically framed by wood. It was usually the wood that burned, so firefighters would be able to douse the flames from below. As with many other things, however, the Pentagon turned out to be different. Crews working on the fifth floor reported that there was a concrete slab above the ceiling panels. The fire seemed to be burning above that, and they couldn't break through the concrete to get to it.

Other crews went up to the roof itself and tried to get to the fire underneath by cracking through the shingles. That was no easier. The roof over the E Ring was pitched, sloping down on both sides like the roofs on most houses, making it difficult for firefighters just to stand. And with the thick layer of concrete beneath the shingles on the roof of the E Ring, cutting off the fire seemed to require bashing all the way through the concrete to the open space beneath.

Fire crews had been trying to break through the nearly foot-thick concrete with raw muscle, using sledgehammers and axes—an exercise in exhaustion. After a few minutes of whacking at the roof with an axe and other hand tools, Bobby Beer called down to Randy Gray. "There's no way we're gonna vent this thing unless you send me something to cut concrete with," he gasped. Other firefighters, including many from D.C., found the same thing.

They tried using power tools, but they barely helped. The burliest firemen pounded and sawed in the afternoon sun, producing little more than rivers of sweat. Firefighters stripped down to shirtsleeves. They finally realized that if crews rotated and spelled each other, they could make meaningful holes after 30 or 40 minutes.

At the command post on the helipad, Randy Gray and Chuck Gibbs were puzzling over the roof conundrum. They were unable to find building engineers or anybody else who had blueprints of the structure or knew its construction and could help them figure out what they needed to do. So they were piecing together a roof plan based on the reports of various fire crews and other fragments of information. From what they could tell, the burning wood they were most concerned with was somehow pressed between the slate shingles and the concrete beneath. They had been using a couple of ladder tracks to spray water onto the roof, but that was turning out to be pointless—the water just ran down the shingles without touching the fire underneath.

Earlier in the day, fire commanders had assumed that dealing with the roof would be a mop-up operation, a nuisance to take care of once the larger interior fire was under control. With little notice, however, the roof fire—judging by the smoke—had migrated down the E Ring in both directions, turned the corner at Corridors 4 and 5, and started running down the roof over the "spokes" of the building, toward the A Ring and the courtyard. While fire teams inside had managed to contain the huge interior fire, the simmering roof fire was creeping over a broader portion of the building. If unchecked, it could even spread from the roof downward, and ignite portions of the building that had so far survived without any burn damage.

Randy Gray radioed his concerns to Dale Smith in the courtyard. Fire crews were already working on the roof over the E Ring, but they also needed crews up there on the courtyard side, to cut off the fire before it spread farther inward. It was possible for firefighters to walk on the roof from the E Ring to the A Ring, but it was a complicated and dangerous traverse with the fire burning. The roof was massive, and dragging hoses over that distance would be even more difficult. Ladder trucks could easily reach the roof on the helipad side, but were too tall to fit through the tunnel leading to the courtyard. Firefighters in the courtyard would have to get up to the roof . . . somehow.

Smith put Denis Griffin in charge of about a dozen firefighters from Arlington and Fairfax and gave them a roof mission. The assignment was straightforward: Get to the roof, do reconnaissance, report back, and start attacking the fire. Smith had no detailed guidance to offer, since building workers who knew how to get to the roof were in short supply. But Griffin got the point: It was critical to cut off the roof fire, whatever he had to do.

The group hiked up to the fifth floor on a series of escalators and looked for a scuttle hole or other opening that led to the roof. In addition to getting firefighters up there, they had to figure out how to run hoses up. After a frustrating 30 minutes, they hadn't found any access points, so Griffin decided they should break a window in one of the fifth-floor offices; they'd snake the hose up to the roof from the window. While a couple of firefighters got started on dislodging the window, Griffin and several others went back to the courtyard and started humping a big three-inch supply line from a Fairfax engine up the escalators.

They carried, pushed, and dragged the cumbersome hose up to the fifth floor and into the office. After preparing the hose and attaching a Y-shaped coupling to the end, so it could be used to feed a couple of smaller hand lines, they pushed the hose out the window, which the two firefighters had managed to push out after some intense pounding. One of the firefighters walked back to the A Ring and called through a window to the engine operator in the courtyard: "Charge the line!"

Griffin was standing near the escalator, on the fifth floor, when the high-pressure water started to flow through the hose. Some of the limp hose had pooled in loops on the floor, and he and a couple other firefighters were standing in the middle of it. The hose stiffened a bit as the water raced through. Then, with no warning, the hose tightened and started to fall back down the atrium, as if being reeled back into the engine. As the nozzle end came flying out of the window, into the hallway, Griffin became alarmed. He realized they had forgotten to tie the end of the hose to something near the window, and the weight of the water was pulling the hose back down the whole distance they had just carried it up. If they didn't move fast, it might take the firefighters standing inside the looped hose with it, over the edge and down five stories.

"Get out of the way!" he yelled. He and the others jumped out of the hose seconds before it would have tightened around their legs like a snare. They watched the hose, now rigid and weighted with water, uncoil itself as gravity pulled it downward. There was nothing they could do except stand clear as the whole hose plummeted over the railing near the escalator, all the way back down to the ground floor.

For the next 20 minutes the group retrieved the hose—shutting

off the water, opening the nozzle and discharging the line, then hauling the whole thing back up the escalators and into the office. This
time they tied it down securely at the window. Stop hurrying, Griffin
reminded himself over and over. Slow down and do it right.

While most of the firefighters had been working with the hose,
Jim Anderson and Ed Hannon split off to find a way to climb onto the
roof. Anderson sized up his crewmates, Griffin and Mosely. After several hours in the building, they looked spent. He surmised that they
were done. As an athlete who did long-distance runs and bike rides,
Anderson was in the habit of drinking lots of water, even when he
wasn't thirsty. He knew to keep food in his stomach even when they
were working hard, and he felt okay. But the others hadn't been
drinking enough water, even though he kept reminding them to.
Now, he thought, it was starting to show.

Hannon was keeping up, though, and they hatched a plan to get
up to the roof. Along the A Ring, on the top floor, there was a window
with a ledge underneath just big enough for them to stand on, right
below one of the parapets overlooking the courtyard. The window
was one of the older glass types, and they were able to break it without too much trouble. They climbed out and looked up. The gutter at
the edge of the roof was about ten feet above them. Back inside the
building they scrounged around until they found a small A-frame
ladder just tall enough to reach the gutter.

Anderson held it steady while Hannon climbed up. It was a nerve-
wracking escapade. There were no railings on the ledge, and falling
into the courtyard would almost certainly be fatal. They moved gingerly. But Hannon got up okay, then leaned over and held the ladder
while Anderson ascended.

They stood on the roof over the A Ring—which was not meant to
be climbed on. It was pitched, like the E Ring, and covered with the
same slippery slate tiles. They crawled on their knees toward the
apex of the roof, using small ice breakers protruding from the roof to

help pull themselves up. "Man, I hope none of these tiles break," Anderson said. If the tiles gave way under their weight and one of them started to slip, there was nothing to stop them from sliding right off the roof into the courtyard.

When they got to the crest of the roof, Hannon took a spare glove out of his pocket and marked the spot where the ladder was—in case they had to retreat in a hurry, before they found another way down. Then they straddled the apex and shuffled toward the roof over Corridor 4, where the fire seemed to be. They finally got to a flat area where they could stand safely, and looked around.

The Corridor 4 roof was pitched too, and topped with a wooden catwalk that looked like decking. Smoke swirled everywhere. Through the haze, they could see flames that seemed to be coming from the catwalk, farther along down the Corridor 4 roof. But they couldn't see to the end of it. The catwalk disappeared into the smoke like a rope bridge vanishing into a bank of fog.

Instead of one big roof that covered the whole building, like a warehouse, the roof over the Pentagon was broken into segments that covered just the rings and corridors. In between were 25-foot-wide light wells that ran down to the second or first floors, allowing narrow shafts of sunlight to slant into the windows of the B, C, and D Rings. Over those hallways, the roof was flat and topped with satellite dishes, antennas, and various kinds of mechanical equipment, and those sections were easy to walk on.

But that's not where the problem was. Based on the smoke puffing out from beneath the slate tiles, Anderson and Hannon could tell that the fire was spreading in the cockloft beneath the pitched roof. The standard tactic for battling that kind of fire was to make trench cuts in the roof—essentially, bashing or cutting out a swath of the roof and the wood framing beneath it to create a fire break that flames wouldn't be able to leap. The cut had to be big enough to get hoses in and douse the flames. To do that work, fire crews would have to step off the catwalks and railings and work on the sloping roof itself, with nothing to protect them from falling off.

They saw no other firefighters up there, although they couldn't see through the smoke or over the crest of the pitched roof to the outer edge of the building. It was an eerie sensation, but compared to hugging the pitched A Ring roof, they felt on solid footing, and they were both comfortable on rooftops. Hannon, the ranking officer, called back to Chief Smith in the courtyard to report what he saw, and to suggest they prepare for a major trench cut in the Corridor 4 roof. Smith agreed—and stressed how important it was to stop the fire before it spread any farther.

Hannon and Anderson still had more reconnaissance to do, and they started looking for doorways that led into the building below— the rickety ladder they climbed up on was way too risky to use as a primary means of access. They found a door—but it was locked, and they hadn't carried any tools up the ladder so they could force it open. They also found some 2½-inch fire hose stashed in a storage nook. "Let's toss it over the roof to one of the engines in the court- yard," Anderson suggested. That was one way to get water flowing to the roof, but first Hannon wanted to find the window that Griffin and the other firefighters had been trying to break out, so they could run the hose up through that.

It was easy to find. Hannon spotted Griffin in the window and yelled down to him. "Hey, we found some hose up here! We're going to lower it down!" They dangled the hose, and Griffin grabbed it. There was broken glass in the window, so he found a file folder on a desk in the office and used it as a sheath to protect the hose from being slashed open. Once they hooked the hand line up to the bigger supply line, there would finally be a stream of water they could use to attack the fire on the roof. Now all they had to do was reach the fire— since spraying the roof randomly would accomplish nothing besides raining more water down on the firefighters below.

Hannon also told Griffin about the door they had found. A few moments later a building engineer arrived on the fifth floor, led Griffin to the door, and unlocked it, saving a great deal of time for the next crews headed to the roof. But for now, Griffin was exhausted, and staying put on the fifth floor. "Hey, Brian, let's just take a break for a minute," he urged Mosely, who readily agreed.

The office they were in was plush and largely undamaged, except for bits of soot and debris that had floated in. There was a water cooler with a couple of crystal goblets sitting next to it, placed upside-down on a towel. Obviously some general or admiral worked there. The firefighters blew soot off the stems of the goblets and filled them with water, gulping several glassfuls. Then they plopped down in a couple of leather chairs. A jar of Hershey's Kisses beckoned from a nearby desk, and they gobbled all of them. "How funny this is," Griffin mused, his muscles aching and his throat parched. "The Pentagon is burning and we're sitting here in leather chairs, eating my man's Hershey's Kisses."

24

SENSITIVE MISSIONS

Late afternoon

On the radio, Chief Smith was insistent: It was essential to keep the roof fire from spreading any closer to the courtyard. It wasn't just a matter of putting the fire out—there was some sensitive military equipment on the roof, and it had to be protected at all costs. During one radio call, Ed Hannon could hear a military official in the background. "You cannot let the fire get beyond this point," the man implored. "We can't let it get any further."

Hannon got the point, and started developing a rapid plan to cut off the roof fire. His mission was no longer reconnaissance, it was extinguishment. The doorway from the fifth floor had finally been opened, and additional fire crews were showing up with hand tools and, Hannon hoped, a lot of muscle and energy. The main problem was the roof over Corridor 4, spanning all five rings—that's where the fire was spreading.

Hannon scrutinized the smoke coming out from beneath the soffits at the edge of the roof, and estimated that the fire underneath had spread about as far as the C Ring. When they encountered similar fires on garden apartments or strip malls, the standard tactic was to estimate where the fire was beneath the roof, back off 15 or 20 feet, and cut two slits in the roof a couple of feet apart. Then they'd collapse the roof in between, creating a gap that resembled a trench. Hannon picked a spot that seemed to be the right distance from the farthest reach of the fire. "Let's start here," he told the crews.

They developed a rotational system, with groups of two working on both sides of the sloping roof. They'd bash away with axes and sledgehammers as hard as they could for about ten minutes, then sit down for a break while another crew took over. It was exhausting and frustrating work, and difficult too; it was hard to get leverage to swing the heavy tools while standing on the sloping roof. The slate tiles and wooden planks they rested on were easy to break apart, but the concrete beneath was unforgiving. Sometimes they worked in clear air, but when the wind shifted, they'd end up in a cloud of smoke, with no choice but to pull on their face pieces and turn on their air. It was hot, and they had no drinking water. When the smoke got so thick that they couldn't see, Hannon ordered the work to stop. With no railings or handholds, he didn't want to risk anyone getting disoriented and falling off the roof.

Beneath the slate there was a layer of ancient insulation that produced a nauseating smell, like human hair, as it burned. Matt Herrera, the Engine 106 crew member who had battled the blaze in the "junkyard" on the C Ring, was one of the firefighters on the roof, and he felt his throat nearly seize as he breathed the noxious air. It was the worst thing he had ever smelled. Herrera was carefully conserving the air in his Scott pack in case he'd need it for firefighting, so when the rancid smoke blew his way, he would press his face down onto the roof, to breathe the lowest, cleanest air he could get.

After about 45 minutes the crews pounding on the roof began to break through the concrete to the space underneath. Black smoke poured out as they widened the cut. Then there was a dispiriting discovery: The fire had already spread beyond the trench cut. There was a narrow "raceway" between the slate and the concrete, and they could see small flames in there—in both directions. And smoke was starting to seep out from underneath the tiles behind the spot where they were cutting.

It was pointless to continue, since the fire had already leapt the firebreak they were trying to create. Hannon and a couple of others tried to puzzle out the problem: Once they broke through the slate, they must have fed fresh air to the fire, which caused it to burn and spread faster than anticipated. There was nothing to do but start another trench cut and try to get ahead of the fire once again.

They restarted the whole draining effort, farther down the Corridor 4 roof, closer to the courtyard. It was the same maddening start-and-stop process. After another 45 minutes of pounding they managed to make a sizable hole—when they realized the fire had spread beyond the cut once again. "What the hell is going on?" Hannon hollered in frustration. He was desperately eager to finish the mission so he and the other whipped firefighters could take a proper break and get some water and food. Chief Smith was asking for updates every few minutes, adding to the stress. It was *critical* to stop the fire from spreading, he kept saying. Did Hannon understand?

They regrouped once more. There had to be something besides oxygen fueling the fire. The whole building had been saturated with jet fuel, and after working in it for five or six hours, the smell was so familiar that it seemed like part of the ambient air. But Hannon noticed the aroma was stronger on the roof. And the smoke that poured out of the narrow raceway was much darker than the gray fumes that seeped out from under the tiles—it was the thick, black smoke typical of carbon fires. It started to make sense: There was probably jet fuel splattered throughout the raceway, coating the wood and the insulation. When they opened up holes and air rushed in, the smoldering fire must have lit off like a charcoal grill freshly doused with lighter fluid.

Hannon called Smith on the radio to report the latest developments. Then he asked for relief. "We're spent," he gasped. "We need some replacement crews up here." More troops were on the way, Smith assured him.

Meanwhile, the group started making a third trench cut, even closer to the courtyard. Hannon swung an axe along with the others. He also told a couple of firefighters to start spraying water into the second trench cut, in both directions. Maybe that would slow down the fire enough for them to finally get ahead of it.

While Hannon and his crews were chasing the roof fire, Arlington battalion chief Ben Barksdale was leading a group of Arlington and Alexandria firefighters on an odyssey from the bottom of the Pentagon to the top. Barksdale was fit and serious, with a tall military posture. He had been at the Pentagon all day, spending the early hours as part of a hazmat team testing the air for toxins. The Alexandria crew and a couple others in his group were more recent arrivals who were moving deep into the building for the first time. Their first duty had been in the pump room in the basement, where they were assigned to shut off some of the water spilling into the building through broken pipes. The water in there was knee-high, and it filled everybody's boots. When the firefighters got out of the basement, they pulled off their boots, poured out the water, then continued on with soggy feet.

Next, the group climbed to the upper floors, where they searched from office to office. Many were heavily secured, with thick steel doors and inset combination locks, and while firefighters were able to bash through a few of them, others wouldn't give. Since they hadn't been finding any victims, and there was a lot of space to search, they left many doors dented but unopened and moved on.

Barksdale, meanwhile, received a fresh assignment over the radio: Assist with the roof fire. He led his group to the fifth floor, where they began the standard procedures: pulling down the ceiling panels from underneath, to access the flames in the attic space or the cockloft. After about 30 minutes of hooking, poking, and jabbing, they realized the same things as others before them: There was a layer of concrete between them and the fire. The only way to get at it would be from atop the building.

The group found a stairwell that led to the roof, and ended up on top of Corridor 5. Some D.C. crews were already working in that area, and Barksdale's assignment was to relieve Hannon's group near Corridor 4. So they walked along the flat D Ring roof, from north to south, over to where Hannon was, carrying armfuls of supplies: sledgehammers, axes, square shovels for scooping debris out of the way, and additional hose lines. The smoldering E Ring roof, its slate tiles molting from gray to black, was immediately to their right. Barksdale and the others studied the burn patterns as they marched past. Then they gazed down onto the huge rubble pile where five floors of the E Ring had collapsed.

It had been nearly half an hour since Hannon begged for relief, and it seemed an eternity. He and his group were desperate for a break. When the new group finally arrived, Barksdale took a moment to catch his breath from the climb and the haul across the roof, leaning over with his hands on his knees.

Finally, Hannon was able to size up the situation for his replacement. He explained how the fire kept racing behind them. "We've moved back a considerable distance," he told Barksdale. "I think if we just run the trench cut down to the gutter line, we'll lick it this time."

Barksdale's crews took up many of the trench cuts Hannon's group had started, and Barksdale fanned out a few firefighters to other parts of the roof that weren't yet burning, to make trench cuts just in case. Barksdale had a few more resources than Hannon did, but it was still tedious work. The Alexandria crew had a diamond-tipped chain saw, designed to cut through stone and metal—yet even with that, it took a long time to make a narrow slit in the concrete. The Army had sent up a few soldiers to help pull and break off the slate tiles, but there

A secondary explosion erupts from the Pentagon seconds after the crash of American Airlines Flight 77. *Photo: Daryl Donley*

Parked cars sit on the highway overlooking the Pentagon, abandoned by terrified motorists after the 757, going more than 500 miles per hour, skimmed over their roofs. *Photo: Stephen Riskus*

The first fire vehicle to reach the Pentagon, Arlington's Truck 105, arrives, its crew struggling to call in the first "size-up" of the massive blaze amid frantic radio traffic. *Photo: Daryl Donley*

Firefighters deploy hose as the Pentagon's upper floors begin to sag. The white foam coating the building came from fire trucks specially equipped to battle fuel fires. *Photo: Department of Defense*

Firefighters douse a fire truck that was charred by the blast. Alan Wallace, pictured without a helmet, had been manning the helipad when he was nearly struck by Flight 77. *Photo: Jon Culberson*

Military volunteers wait to evacuate the wounded, looking into the gash left when part of the Pentagon collapsed about forty minutes after the crash. *Photo: FBI*

Firefighters work a fire engine that's feeding water to deluge guns and other fire trucks. *Photo: FBI*

Arlington firefighters Brian Frantz and Juan Cano (both kneeling) man a deluge gun shortly after pulling a burned, stunned survivor out of the Pentagon. *Photo: FBI*

Denis Griffin (kneeling) directs a stream of water into the blaze from the open-air service road that runs through the building. *Photo: Paul Marshall*

Rubble spills out of the Pentagon at the point where Flight 77 struck the building. Several bodies were buried under the rubble. *Photo: FBI*

A police officer stands guard over one of several light poles toppled by Flight 77. *Photo: FBI*

It took several hours for firefighters to snake hoses through A&E Drive, where mounds of airplane wreckage and building debris piled up. *Photo: FBI*

The "punch-out hole" blown into a wall where Flight 77 finally came to rest. The hole was created by explosive energy; the plane's soft aluminum nose and fuselage crumpled the instant it struck the building. *Photo: FBI*

Several hours after the crash, fire still raged throughout the Pentagon. The gray smoke represents a fresh problem: Fire spreading beneath a thick, reinforced roof. *Photo: FBI*

Structural engineer Dean Tills snapped this picture of the surreal gray smoke that spewed from beneath the roof. To the left, firefighters are making a "trench cut" to stop the fire's spread. *Photo: Dean Tills*

The Pentagon's inner courtyard was usually a quiet, leafy respite. By late afternoon on 9/11, it was cluttered with used bandages, airplane debris, dozens of rescuers, scattered firefighting gear, and body bags. *Photo: FBI*

The roof fire spread in several directions, creating a thorny problem for firefighters who were unfamiliar with the layout of the roof, short of water, and exhausted from the heat. *Photo: FBI*

The Pentagon burns on the night of September 11. Mindful of hundreds of firefighter deaths in New York, fire chiefs decided to pull back on firefighting efforts overnight and attack it fresh at dawn—unaware that fire was creeping toward vital parts of the nation's military headquarters. *Photo: Department of Defense*

Flight 77 wiped out more than thirty support columns that held up the Pentagon, including these two "empty baskets"—columns stripped of nearly all their reinforcing concrete. *Photo: FBI*

A piece of Flight 77's landing gear, center left, juts out from densely matted debris. *Photo: FBI*

Some offices, such as this one, escaped fire but were jumbled by explosions and the concussion of the plane crash. *Photo: FBI*

A photocopier, melted from intense heat. *Photo: FBI*

Clearing crews in protective Tyvek suits sort through debris. The surrounding filing cabinets, used for storing classified material, had their handles and combination dials melted off. *Photo: FBI*

A group of firefighters and soldiers prepare to drape a huge flag over the side of the Pentagon on September 12—unaware that it's backward. After a call on the radio they flipped it around, and drew a huge roar when they let it fly. *Photo: FBI*

A piece of American Airlines Flight 77, with the distinctive red lettering on the silver body. *Photo: FBI*

One of Flight 77's "black boxes," or on-board recorders, discovered near the punch-out hole. The black boxes were so disfigured that an FBI searcher nearly discarded one of them. *Photo: FBI*

Search experts watch for bodies while a crane pulls debris from the collapse pile. *Photo: FBI*

Workers carry a set of remains into a makeshift morgue. *Photo: FBI*

Members of a search-and-rescue team hold a departure ceremony after spending a week at the Pentagon. By this time, the collapse pile was almost completely removed. *Photo: FBI*

This aerial photo shows how the roof fire spread from the E Ring (top), down the corridors spanning the other four rings, before turning a corner again when it got to the A Ring (bottom right). *Photo: Department of Defense*

In little more than a week, work crews cleared shoulder-high debris, and recovered thousands of body parts, from 800,000 square feet of Pentagon office space. *Photo: FBI*

A view of the punch-out hole from inside the building, once clearing and recovery work was nearly finished. *Photo: FBI*

weren't any tools for them. Barksdale called down and asked for extra saws and axes, but in the meantime the soldiers worked with their bare hands.

The demanding work left little time for reflection, but some of the firefighters were thinking as much about New York as they were about the Pentagon. Like others, a group from Alexandria led by Capt. Phil Perry had been astounded to hear that the twin towers had both been completely destroyed. The toll on the FDNY felt like a personal blow: Two former colleagues, Joel Kanasky and Andy Fredericks, had left the Alexandria Fire Department and been hired by the FDNY, the premier destination for ambitious firefighters. A third, Dan McMaster, had done the same thing, then transferred back to Alexandria when a deal to get custody of his younger daughter fell through. He had dozens of friends up in New York, many of them, no doubt, on the scene in downtown Manhattan—probably including the members of his old companies, Engine 43 and Ladder 35.

McMaster, a highly respected firefighter whose father and grandfather had served in the same profession, was on the roof with Perry's group. During a break, he and Jason Wehmeyer, another Alexandria firefighter, sat down together, both worried about their friends in New York. They were all close, Kanasky and McMaster especially: Kanasky had been the best man at McMaster's wedding and was the godfather of his eldest daughter. "Man, I fucking bet Joel's dead," McMaster said.

"Yeah—and he ain't the only one," Wehmeyer added. Neither was feeling talkative, and there wasn't much else to say, so they sat in silence for a few more minutes before going back to work.

Dean Tills, the structural engineer from the FEMA task force, made his way to the roof as well. After his first reconnaissance down Corridor 5, through A&E Drive, and back out on the upper floors of Corridor 4, Tills started developing a rough plan for how to shore up the most damaged parts of the building, so they could start removing debris and recovering victims once the fire was out. He didn't know who was supposed to be in charge of stabilizing the building, but military officials and contractors with the Pentagon Renovation project kept coming up to him, asking, "How can we help? What can we do for you?" It seemed he'd become the project leader by default, at least for the time being.

Tills had asked one of the officials with the Pentagon Renovation team—known as PenRen—for a floor plan of the building, and hadn't seen him since. All he had to work with were his own observations, which he jotted down and drew hastily in a sketch pad he was carrying.

He hadn't had an air bottle or face piece during his first trip into the building—in fact, Tills had never used either, or been trained with them, since the task force had never operated in a fire before. Without protection, he hadn't been able to get close to the fire on Corridor 4 to inspect the damage there. After coming out the first time, he went back in with a second FEMA search team, led by Kent Watts, that was working its way through the building south of the collapse, near Corridor 4. Watts and his team scrounged some air bottles and masks when they first arrived, and a couple of crew members gave Tills a quick tutorial on how to use air.

The air bottle was heavy and cumbersome, and his glasses kept fogging up beneath the mask whenever he turned the air off for a moment. He stumbled in a haze for a few minutes, before getting the hang of how to turn the air on and off and remove the mask easily. Once he got comfortable with the mask, he noticed a lot of damage he hadn't been able to get close to before. There were moments when Tills could see into the heart of the fire. In addition to widespread destruction, he noted areas where support columns and beams were damaged or wiped out. The air finally ran out, and he had to leave, but he was proud of how he'd handled the air bottle—two firefighters with the group used more air than he had and left earlier.

Back outside, the Arlington and FEMA commanders asked him to go up to the roof, to check on safety conditions for the fire crews working up there. Tills also knew that from the roof, he'd be able to get a good look straight into the collapsed portion of the building and other damaged areas. PenRen had assigned Dan Fraunfelter, who worked for one of the contractors, to be Tills's guide whenever he needed to get around inside the building. Fraunfelter had spent months working on the renovation project, and he knew the ins and outs of that wedge of the building as if it were his own home. He led Tills back into Corridor 4 and up a series of stairwells to the fifth floor, where Tills checked the roof's support structure from underneath. Then they went up a final stairwell and out a door.

On the roof, atop the E Ring, Tills walked nearly to the edge of the structure, where he was able to gaze onto the crumbled roof and the big pile of rubble where five floors of the E Ring had tumbled down on one another. One of the firefighters asked him how close to the edge of the roof they could get. "To play it safe," Tills advised, "let's say no closer than five feet. But if you need to, one guy could get pretty much right up to the edge." Even though a portion of the building had collapsed just a few feet away, the roof had broken off along a seam, and the standing portion was still supported by intact columns.

He peered intently into the office spaces on the other side of the collapse, about 50 feet across. On the third, fourth, and fifth floors, there was little evidence of fire. But there were heaps of debris, as if a tornado had ravaged the contents of the offices. Tills spotted a sizable crack in one of the beams supporting the roof, a sign that there could be further collapse on that side of the building.

He then gazed down into the rubble pile beneath, where parts of the fallen roof were still hanging precariously from the building, forming a kind of lean-to over the top of the rubble. Crews from the task force would soon be working in the shadow of the huge pile, removing debris so they could start shoring up the most damaged parts of the building. He needed to gauge the risk that the pile might collapse further.

The pile looked extremely unsteady, like something as simple as vibrations on the ground or in the building could trigger a slide. There were huge pieces of broken concrete, which would be deadly if they slipped free and fell on top of workers. If the pile slid any further, it might also shoot down right into the area where they'd need to build shoring to replace destroyed columns and support the sagging floors. The avalanche of stone and metal would easily overwhelm the wooden shoring they needed to build—and might bring more of the building down with it. The work on the ground would be dangerous, the construction precarious. Tills could see that they'd have to be extremely careful not to disturb the pile.

He snapped a few pictures with his pocket camera, then turned around to head back toward the stairwell. Suddenly, his path was blocked. The Corridor 4 catwalk he had traversed ten minutes earlier was now on fire, impossible to navigate. "Hey guys!" he yelled to some nearby firefighters. "We've got fire creeping behind us!"

"Oh shit!" somebody shouted. A section of the catwalk about 15 feet long had lit off like a bonfire, sending flames shooting into the sky and sparks spattering onto the roof. Fire that had been simmering beneath the slate seemed to have broken through the roof and rapidly ignited the planking, dry and warm from sitting atop the simmering fire for several hours. The flames looked to be spreading quickly, threatening two walkways that sloped down to the flat D Ring roof, which fire crews were using as a staging area.

Firefighters rushed over to the fire with axes and hoses and started spraying. Tills watched the fireworks for several minutes, transfixed by his front-row seat at the dramatic blaze. Then he realized that the fire was blocking the way to the door they had come through. He turned to Fraunfelter, his guide. "Okay, how do we get out of here now?" he asked. Fraunfelter knew another way down, and led Tills to a door out of range of the fire.

It didn't take fire crews long to douse the flames, but now they had an entirely new problem. Part of the catwalk was charred and unstable, a fresh fire hazard and a structural danger that could break apart and crash down on firefighters who had to work around it. Fire crews began to hose down other portions of the catwalk, making sure no additional sections caught fire. They also suspended their trench cuts so they could begin the necessary "overhaul" work—dismantling the burnt timbers, to remove the danger they posed. That was more backbreaking labor with saws, picks, and axes, which would have to be done while standing awkwardly on a sloping roof five stories high. Meanwhile, pale smoke continued to puff out from beneath the slate tiles, as the persistent fire slowly metastasized beneath the firefighters' feet, unchecked yet again.

★ 25 ★

OPEN FOR BUSINESS

Late afternoon

In addition to the tension over how to protect the country and respond to the terrorist attacks, there was a battle simmering over whether to evacuate the Pentagon or keep it running.

At the beginning, it seemed that only Defense Secretary Rumsfeld and a few stalwart military officers thought seriously about staying in the Pentagon. Earlier in the day, in the Executive Support Center, one of the building technicians had been monitoring the air in the smoky room, assuming the group wouldn't be staying there. "We'll have to find you an office for tomorrow," he said.

Rumsfeld's head snapped around. "We need to show America we're functioning, and up and running," he declared. "We're staying here."

The technician, suddenly flustered, explained that the air might be filled with toxic chemicals. Rumsfeld paused for a moment. Like others in the room, his eyes were irritated and watery from the smoke. "Well," he finally answered, squinting through his wire-rimmed glasses, "I'm going to be here, and I don't care if it's with a lot fewer people than we have right now. But we need to show the terrorists that they didn't win." Nobody in the room argued.

Keeping the Pentagon open, however, involved a lot more than simply walking into the building the following morning. The fire, or its aftermath, would have to be sealed off and contained. Air, water, and ventilation systems would have to work. Security staff, building workers, and other key personnel would need to get around inside the building. The Pentagon was the equivalent of a small town, and it couldn't operate without essential services.

In the middle of the afternoon, Steve Carter, the assistant building manager, had been in the courtyard when his personal cell phone rang. It was somebody from the Joint Staff. His cell phone number was unlisted and he rarely gave it out. He wondered how in the world they got the number.

The Joint Staff officer didn't bother to explain. "The secretary wants to know," he told Carter, "whether the building is going to continue to deteriorate or stabilize. Are we going to be able to bring people back to work?"

Carter was flabbergasted. "What the hell are you talking about?" he blared. "The building is on fire!" He knew that the vital command centers needed to stay in operation. But in virtually every other part of the building, there had been a diligent effort to get people *out*, not in. Now, after a full building evacuation, a massive fire, and dozens of deaths, they wanted to go back to work the next day, as if nothing had happened?

Plaugher and Schwartz also balked at the idea of reopening the Pentagon right away. In just about every other fire, people *wanted* to get out and stay out—until it was safe to go back. If they didn't leave for some reason, it was the fire department's duty to usher them to safety. The same instincts applied at the Pentagon.

As far as Plaugher knew, the Pentagon had been totally evacuated. That's what he was told by John Jester, who ran the Defense Protective Service, the Pentagon's police force. But Jester wasn't calling the shots in the National Military Command Center—Rumsfeld and the Joint Staff were.

Besides, Jester was mostly elsewhere; he had duties all over the building. In addition to making sure people evacuated, his officers were responsible for keeping the building secure—which it most certainly wasn't at the moment. It was their job to safeguard classified material, which was haphazardly exposed throughout the building. Jester was hopscotching all over the Pentagon grounds and shuttling out to the Arlington command post to coordinate with the fire chiefs. Even to him, the NMCC was something of an afterthought.

So it was a surprise to Plaugher when an Air Force colonel in an olive flight suit—wearing a handgun in a shoulder holster—arrived at the command post in mid-afternoon and started pleading the case for the NMCC to remain in operation. Plaugher was startled to learn that anybody was still inside the building, other than firefighters.

As the fire chief listened to the colonel, he realized that Jester had been urging the NMCC staff to evacuate—while the top brass ignored his pleas.

"We've got to keep the NMCC open," the colonel stressed.

"Okay," Plaugher said. "Do you really want your people in there making decisions, possibly illegitimate decisions, under the influence of carbon monoxide?"

The colonel gave him a puzzled look.

Plaugher continued. "Carbon monoxide is odorless and colorless," he explained. "And in a hot, smoky fire, there's usually tons of carbon monoxide. One of the first side effects is, it makes you do wacky things. In house fires, people who have lived there for 50 years will try to get out by walking into a closet. Do you really want people in that situation making command and control decisions?"

The colonel paused, pondering the risks. Then he asked, "If we monitor for it, does that change the picture?"

"How many people do you have?" Plaugher asked.

The NMCC normally had a staff of more than a hundred, but the colonel said they were operating on a stripped-down crew of fewer than 50. The two men negotiated, and it struck Plaugher that the colonel had been sent out to plead the case for a decision that Rumsfeld and his staff had already made. He wasn't going to coax the military commanders out of their bunker, no matter what. Besides, Plaugher realized, as he looked at one of the fighter jets circling overhead, the military guys inside the building had a lot of other important things to worry about.[1]

They worked out a rough compromise. The colonel assured Plaugher that they'd get some equipment in place, pronto, to monitor carbon monoxide levels. The fire department, meanwhile, had some spare SCBA gear on reserve. "Let me give you enough breathing apparatus so that if something goes wrong, you can get people out of there," Plaugher offered. "It will give you an hour's worth of breathing time, which will be enough if you have to evacuate." It was a deal.

Not long after that compromise, Rumsfeld materialized on the west lawn once again, with about a dozen aides, top Pentagon officials, and security people. He left his jacket behind this time, and his tie hung loose. The group stood on the periphery of the firefighting activity near the northwest corner of the building, looking onto the smoldering roof, the charred windows, and the exhausted firefighters trudging across the grass.

Gen. Dick Myers, the vice chairman of the Joint Chiefs, was there, along with John Jester and several other top aides. Jester explained as much as he knew about the damage to the building. The wounded had all been whisked away by then, but rehab buses and ambulances were lined up to treat injured firefighters and anybody else who needed care. A small tent city was starting to spring up, as different agencies arrived to support the effort. FBI agents were milling around, still documenting the wreckage that lay everywhere.

After listening to damage-control reports for several hours—and watching the fire on TV—Rumsfeld was there to do his own size-up of the situation. The west wall of the Pentagon was breached and burned, with a gaping wound. Yet it still stood, like a stalwart fortress in the aftermath of battle. The other four sides of the Pentagon were totally undamaged. At least 60 percent of the building was unaffected by the attack, except for the irritating haze that permeated the hallways. If it had been an office building or retail complex, there'd be no question about shutting it down, until conditions were comfortable. But this was the Pentagon, the centerpiece of the nation's defense establishment, in a time of crisis. It could stay open, and it would.

Rumsfeld's tour of the west lawn was brief. As he turned to head back into the building, he reached down and picked up a twisted piece of aluminum, the size of a shoe-box lid, that looked like it might have been part of an airplane wing or tail. He studied it for a moment—then carried it into his office, a stark reminder of what the attackers had done to his building.

Jester got back in touch with Plaugher and delivered a message the fire chief had been expecting: Rumsfeld intended to officially reopen the Pentagon as soon as possible. Throughout the day, Pentagon spokespeople had been emphasizing to the press that the Defense Department was "functioning as normal," despite the hole in the building and unreported concerns about smoke in the NMCC and other sensitive compartments. Reopening the Pentagon, and making a big show of it, made sense, Plaugher decided. It was symbolically important to show the country that the Pentagon was still functioning, especially given the catastrophe in New York.

He and Jester began an informal negotiation about what would be required to allow large numbers of people back into the building.

The fire and the impact of the plane had taken out most of the office space between Corridors 4 and 5. Structural damage, and heavy smoke exposure, extended to Corridors 3 and 6. That represented roughly 40 percent of the Pentagon. Theoretically, the rest was usable.

But only under strict controls. Plaugher insisted that plywood barriers be erected to cordon off the whole area between Corridors 3 and 6. Since military personnel had been so determined to get back to wrecked offices, armed guards—with the authority to turn back even the most senior generals—would have to be placed at every juncture. And since smoke and fumes were capable of infiltrating every corner of the Pentagon, there should be plans to evacuate everybody in the building on a moment's notice.

It was a reasonable compromise, but it made Plaugher realize his control of the scene was extremely tenuous. In any other fire in Arlington County, the fire department would unambiguously be in charge. The Pentagon, in one sense, was just like any other building in Arlington, and as the on-scene commanders, he and Schwartz were responsible for any decisions that involved fire and safety.

But the building was also a crime scene—and a war zone. In an act of terrorism, the FBI had jurisdiction; it also had the bureaucratic muscle to elbow other agencies out of the way. Others had a major stake in the incident. The Defense Department obviously had important needs, including use of the NMCC. FEMA teams were accustomed to taking charge in chaotic situations. There were already command and control problems with fire crews operating outside the system, and Plaugher and Schwartz both realized that if they didn't assert Arlington's leadership on the incident, it would rapidly be usurped by any of a half-dozen agencies perfectly willing to take control. That could produce even more confusion, and turf battles likely to hamstring the fire operation.[2]

Schwartz knew when he saw all the "volunteer participants"— the military personnel trying to charge back into the building—that he needed to clarify the command structure to everybody who had a role in the incident. He called Jester. "I need a place where I can assemble the various principals from all the organizations here," he said. "Can you get me some kind of conference room inside the Pentagon?" Jester arranged it. A meeting was set for 6:00 P.M., and they sent out word to the commanders of all the various agencies operating at the Pentagon.

As the meeting time neared, Schwartz and Jester walked there together from the command post, passing the helipad and the mush-rooming tent city and arriving at the River Entrance that sat beneath Rumsfeld's office. Once inside, Schwartz's eyes itched and watered from the brown haze. People must be uncomfortable, he thought. It seemed remarkable that there was no contingency plan to leave the place.

Jester led him to a big briefing room, with several rows of chairs assembled. Schwartz felt confident, but he prepared himself for military or security officials who might challenge his authority. There were about 75 others there, from the FBI, the Red Cross, the Pentagon Renovation office, the Defense Protective Service, and several other fire and police departments.

Jester introduced Schwartz, who was eager to get started. "We've been here eight hours and everybody's done a great job," he began. "But we're going to be here eight more days," he estimated, "and we've got to get a clear command structure in place. The Arlington County Fire Department is the command agency. We need to have agreement about how we're going to operate from here forward." He explained the incident command system he intended to put in place, which would cover everybody from firefighters to evidence technicians to construction crews. There would be no parallel operations. Everybody would report into one chain of command.

Assistant Special Agent in Charge Bob Blecksmith was the top FBI official there. He had arrived at the Pentagon earlier that afternoon, and made Chris Combs his right-hand man. At the meeting, Blecksmith spoke first. "We fully support the chief," he declared, underscoring Schwartz's authority. "We're deferring to the fire department. They're in charge of life and safety." Then he turned it over to Combs, who explained how the Bureau was busy setting up a joint operations center, a JOC, which would serve as the principal facility for the commanders on the scene. If anybody wanted anything, it would have to go through the JOC, which the FBI planned to have operational up at Fort Myer, overlooking the Pentagon, by midnight.

To Schwartz's left, a lanky two-star general in fatigues and combat boots stood and introduced himself. "I'm Major General Jim Jackson," he said. "I've been identified as the secretary's liaison to the command system."

Schwartz left the meeting feeling better than when he arrived. Afterward he talked for a few minutes with General Jackson, who seemed sincere and decisive, with what Schwartz imagined to be a hard-nosed battlefield style. If any more volunteer participants got in the way, Schwartz felt confident that Jackson would rein them in.

A few moments later Rumsfeld opened his first press conference since the attacks. The briefing itself indicated that the damaged building was still functional, since the session was held in the regular Pentagon press room, with the usual pool of Pentagon correspondents ushered onto familiar, if smoky, terrain.

Rumsfeld opened by offering condolences to the victims' families. He made assurances that all possible measures were being taken to protect the country. Then he pointed out that the attack had failed to chase the nation's military leaders from their duty stations. "The Pentagon's functioning," he declared. "It will be in business tomorrow."

★ 26 ★

HOME FOR DINNER

Early evening

For some of the people involved in the rescue efforts, the end of the day was coming into view. Craig Powell, the SEAL who caught the jumpers in A&E Drive, had limped out to the courtyard with his neck, back, and legs throbbing, and hung around for a while doing what he could to help. He and a fellow SEAL helped a nurse trying to get medications out of a locked cabinet. The door was solid Plexiglas, nearly impossible to break, so the two men dragged the whole cabinet out of the building, to a triage area set up near the North Parking lot, where somebody had keys.

Powell had joined some other service members to go back into the building and look for more victims, but by then the firefighters turned them away. He looked for other ways to help and finally decided that there was little more he could do. He might as well go home.

He figured he'd get home the same way he got to work. A colleague dropped him at a nearby transit station, where he boarded a bus headed for the Park & Ride in Reston, where his car was parked. The bus was nearly empty, with fewer than half a dozen other passengers.

The strapping SEAL stood out among them. His skin and hair were dark with sooty stains, as if he'd been smeared with charcoal.

Pink patches on his skin revealed cuts and scrapes. His clothes were torn and wet from rolling in the grimy puddle in A&E Drive. Black gunk ran out of his nose. Everybody stared as he shuffled to his seat, moving like an arthritic. No one spoke to him.

As the bus drove off, Powell gazed back at the scene. He could see ambulances lined up and firefighters gathered outside Corridor 5, waiting for their turn to get into the building. Police cars were everywhere. At the beginning, it had been just Pentagon people fending for themselves, doing everything they could to save their comrades. Now there were hordes of people swarming the building. The sight cheered him. This is why America is a great nation, he told himself. No one in the world, he felt, could be doing this better.

A slide show of violent images reeled through Powell's mind. Panicked faces looking down from smoke-filled office windows. Sparks and flames in a sizzling room. In A&E Drive, he had seen a foot, with a black sock on it, the kind that went with the Navy's khaki uniforms. Had that been a Navy sock? Who had it belonged to? Had the person been atomized in the explosion, his foot the only remaining evidence of his existence? He was desperate to find out, yet it was impossible to know. The whole scene reminded him of Armageddon.

Powell hobbled off the bus at the Park & Ride in Reston and drove himself home. His wife, Christine, had just started working as a high school special education teacher in suburban Virginia. Since her husband's job at the Pentagon was brand-new, she didn't even have a phone number for him yet, and he didn't have a cell phone, so she'd heard nothing about him all day. After learning about the attack at the Pentagon, Christine tried to focus on her classes, though parents were continually rushing into the school to claim their kids and take them home.

School let out early, so she picked up her own two kids. At home, she tried to act like it was a normal day. The kids were happy to ride their bikes and play outside, and Christine took them for a walk with the dog. At one point she flipped on the news, and quickly regretted it. "He's going to come home at any time," she kept saying to herself.

Christine's father was a reluctant cook, but he offered to make dinner while she looked after the kids and tried to work off her worry. The stew he concocted was nearly ready, and the family about to sit down, when Powell walked up to the door. He looked worse than Christine had ever seen him, and smelled like burned garbage. But she didn't tell him that. Powell absently said hello to everybody, then limped to the table and sat down, as if he were home from just another day at the office.

Christine thought he might be in shock, but she didn't ask or say anything. She didn't want to know. Not now anyway. In 11 years of marriage, her husband had been on plenty of secret missions that he didn't talk about, and she'd gotten used to the mystery. She was just overjoyed that he was home. When the food arrived at the table, the kids ate, but the grown-ups didn't. They just sat silently, grateful for each other's presence.

It was an evening when husbands and wives and parents and lovers overlooked stink, filth, and inconvenience, if only they could be with each other. Not far from Craig Powell's family in Reston, Doris Smith got a call from her husband Mike. He was at Alexandria Hospital, having his heart and other organs checked. Doris raced to meet him.

When she got there, people were lined up to donate blood. She found Mike on a stretcher, in a hospital gown. Even without his clothes, he seemed to be drenched in sweat. A smoky stench rose off him like steam off a compost pile. Smith's crew mate, Justin Scott, had been treated for dehydration, given some fluids, and released. But doctors wanted Smith to stay overnight and undergo an EKG, on account of his recent heart surgery.

Smith was exhausted—yet wired. He started to tell his wife a few details of the fire. He had never been at a fire that burned so long.

And it still wasn't over, he knew—parts of it would probably burn through the night, maybe well into the next day. He might even end up back there.

He was assigned to a semiprivate room, with one other patient: a man from the Navy who was injured in the attack and barely survived. He was badly burned and sobbed frequently. Military officers and FBI agents came in and out, talking to him and asking questions. Between heaves, the man described being in a room that was pitch-black and brutally hot. He'd been searching for somebody and couldn't find him. Then the man broke down, unable to continue. Doris felt uncomfortable being in the room, as if she was invading the man's privacy. A couple of times she rose discreetly and tiptoed out.

The evening of September 11 was beautiful—balmy and dry, with clear skies and a pinkish-orange sunset. As Mike Regan's FEMA team finally walked out of the Pentagon, after several hours of searching for victims and surveying the wrecked structure, Randy Leatherman contemplated the peaceful western sky they were walking into. The sunset was spectacular, he thought. As a private pilot, Leatherman was keenly aware that for once the usual drone of air traffic around Reagan National Airport had gone silent; all the flights had been shut down. He'd never seen the skies around Washington so calm.

They were walking into a different world. When they arrived on the scene several hours earlier, there were firefighters and FBI agents milling around the helipad lawn, but aside from fire trucks and ambulances, it had still been a wide-open space. Now, the lawn was filled with tents, buses, military vehicles, and construction equipment. It was so crowded they couldn't see the task force's base of operations, the BOO, which had its own tent. They had to wander around for a few minutes before they found it.

Several hours of dodging heat and debris inside the building had inflamed their appetites. They were starving. As if summoned on demand, somebody showed up with several boxes of Domino's pizza. Steve McFarland, the rescue specialist who had been ready to break down the stairwell door when carbon monoxide forced his group to seek fresh air, grabbed a slice, but before he could swallow more than a couple bites, he doubled over. Pain tore at his belly. He felt hungry and nauseated at the same time, and his head started to pound. One of the team's medics saw McFarland clenching his gut and rushed over. "You don't look so good," he said after taking one look at McFarland's face. "Better come with me to the medic tent."

McFarland, soaked with sweat, started to shiver. Then he began to vomit. Medics handed him bottles of water. They started an IV, gave him oxygen through a mask, and drew blood to check for carbon monoxide levels. After a while a doctor came by and said that tests showed his CO levels to be okay. "You should be able to sleep your headache off in a couple of hours and go back to work," he assured McFarland, who was still shaking.

Half an hour later the doctor came back and reversed himself. "We read the CO levels wrong," he said. "They're very high. We're going to send you to the hospital." That was terrible news—once in the hospital, there was no returning to the mission. But McFarland felt too ill to object.

Mike Regan started to feel sick too, but tried to put it out of his mind—there were other things he was worried about. His father, a retired police officer for the Port Authority of New York and New Jersey, had been suffering from bladder cancer and was in a hospital on Long Island. His son Sean was up there visiting. Regan called his wife, Janice, for an update.

He got more than that. The Port Authority managed the World Trade Center and had an office there, and no doubt had lost some people. Odds were good his father knew some of them. Janice also told her husband about news reports of all the firefighters who had died in New York, including some of the top officials in the department. New York

Mayor Rudy Giuliani had announced that Ray Downey, the chief of special operations, was dead, along with several others. Regan knew Downey through the close-knit community of rescue and disaster specialists. Their wives were even friends. Regan also knew a missing FDNY fire captain, Terry Hatton, whom he had taught in rescue-specialist school.

Already feeling woozy, the devastating news was difficult for Regan to comprehend. He asked Janice about half a dozen others he knew in the FDNY. She hadn't heard whether they were safe or not.

He felt like he was about to get sick, and quickly hung up before Janice got an inkling of his condition. He also knew that if the medics saw him vomit, he'd have to pack his bags. So Regan sneaked behind the charred chassis of Foam 161, to throw up out of sight. When he finally felt like he could stand up, he shuffled as nonchalantly as he could over to the task force tent, where one of the medics inserted an IV to treat him for dehydration. "We're going to keep the fluid coming until you have to pee," the medic told him. Then the doctor checked him out. Regan insisted he was okay and pleaded with the doc not to send him to the hospital.

"We'll see," the doctor said.

For many others it was the end of one of the most draining days of their firefighting careers. When Ben Barksdale and his crews had arrived on the roof, the exhausted crew they replaced, led by Ed Hannon, headed back down to the courtyard to call it a day. Even Jim Anderson, the endurance athlete, felt wiped out.

Hannon and Anderson trudged back down to the courtyard with several other firefighters. One of them started wandering away, disoriented. There were still pockets of fire inside the building, and he was walking toward an inflamed area, his safety gear loose and his mask off. Somebody ran after him and steered him back to the group, escorting him all the way down.

A small rehab area had been set up in the courtyard, where medics were checking firefighters for smoke inhalation and dehydration and giving them fluids if needed. Hannon had a pounding headache and his throat was dry and scratchy. He dropped his gear, walked to the rehab area, got something to drink—and promptly started to vomit. A second later he passed out and tumbled face-first onto the grass.

Denis Griffin watched, astounded, as Hannon toppled over and medics rushed over to lay him out on the grass and stick an IV in his arm. "Wow," he muttered, "we've taken a beating." Griffin himself wasn't feeling a lot better. As he had walked down the steps for the last time that day, his hands started to cramp up, then curl uncontrollably. He thought he'd been drinking enough fluids throughout the day, but now he couldn't stop his muscles from contracting—classic symptoms of dehydration.

By the time Griffin got to ground level, his leg muscles were cramping up too. Like his hands, they were responding slowly, then barely at all. He started to shamble over to the rehab area, but it was difficult to walk.

A fire chief told Griffin and some others to get themselves out to a larger rehab area out in South Parking. That posed a problem: Griffin knew there was no way his legs would carry him that far. It was difficult to walk even a few steps, and South Parking was several hundred yards away.

There was a military Humvee nearby, with an open back, like a pickup truck, and the driver offered Griffin and Brian Mosely a ride out of the courtyard. Griffin tried to climb into the back of the truck and had trouble even doing that. He nearly fell over, but caught himself on the truck. "Hey, Brian," he said to Mosely, "just get me up here, man, will ya?" He didn't want anybody to notice his distress—and he sure as hell didn't want to end up in the hospital—so he acted as casual as possible as Mosely heaved him up onto the back of the Humvee.

Once in South Parking, Griffin learned what had been happening

in the rest of the country. The rumors about the Sears Tower being attacked were untrue. But it was an unthinkable scene in New York,
with hundreds of firefighters and thousands of others killed. Another
plane had gone down in Pennsylvania. Plaugher came by and chatted
with the firefighters for a moment. The chief wasn't much for pep
talks or bull sessions, so he just told the group what he knew, in his
usual dry fashion. "We think it's al Qaeda," he said, citing a villain
many of them had never heard of.

Then he explained what had happened at the Pentagon. It was the
first time Griffin heard for certain that it was a hijacked plane that
caused all the destruction. He had been working in the aftermath of
the attack all day, and seen wreckage that looked like it could be from
an airplane, but there were so many wild stories going around that he
wasn't sure what to believe. Plaugher listed all the jurisdictions that
had sent fire crews—at least those he was aware of—and gave a run-
down of other organizations that were there or on the way. Griffin
took it all in, more or less, but was too tired, or woozy, to ask questions.

Hannon, meanwhile, regained consciousness on the ambulance
ride to the hospital. He could remember walking into the courtyard
and taking off his gear, but that was it. His entire body hurt. It felt like
he'd been hit by a truck. While wincing at the pain, his mind revis-
ited the people he couldn't save. *We had a job to do and we didn't do
it*, he kept thinking, *and those people died.*

Back at the Pentagon, Cornwell found his way to the helipad and
offered another update for the video crew that was lucky enough to
be inside the wire with the fire crews. He stood, once again, alongside
the Arlington command buggy, and pointed to maps of the Pentagon
taped to the side of it. His sweat-stained shirt was still unbuttoned
and untucked.

Except for the smoke seeping from the roof, there were no longer
any signs of an active fire along the Pentagon's western facade. No

flames were visible through the charred, bent windows, and for the time being fire crews had turned off the hoses and deluge guns that had been drilling water into the building. From the outside it looked like the fire, for the most part, was out.

"We've been able to extinguish most of the spot fires," Cornwell explained. "What we're in the process of doing now is, we have a rooftop fire that we're trying to gain control of." He described how the fire was creeping along the roof over Corridor 4, toward the courtyard and other parts of the building. "Where a fire goes across into an uninvolved area, that's what we're concerned about right now. That's what we're trying to gain control of."

A reporter asked if the fire crews had checked the spread of the fire and started beating it back. "Well, we're pretty well contained," Cornwell answered. "Where a corridor goes across into an uninvolved area, that's what we're trying to get control of." He swept his hand once again over Corridor 4 on the map.

"Where's the fire going to be in two hours?" the interviewer asked.

"Well, hopefully, in two hours, the fire will be out," Cornwell said.

"Anything that's missing?"

"I don't think so right now. You know, we've got darkness that's going to become a problem. We're trying to make sure we've got enough reserve crews in place, so anything that comes up unexpectedly, we'll be able to deal with that also. We're basically preparing for our nighttime operations."

It was still hectic on the helipad, but compared to earlier in the day, it seemed that an orderly operation was falling into place. Firefighters walked calmly, no longer shocked by the magnitude of the fire. The air now hummed with the din of power tools, generators, and construction equipment. Plans were being executed. People sauntered across the grass and even joked, as if it was just another day on the job. Even the gash in the Pentagon became familiar, the longer you looked at it.

But any sense of order evaporated the moment you entered the building. There was little visible fire inside, but the burn zone was the equivalent of a massive fireplace that still held red-hot embers capable of igniting the moment a breeze blew through. Stone and metal surfaces radiated with heat that would sear flesh at the instant of contact. There were tons of paper, wood furniture, and other flammable material providing ready fuel for a fire. And flames erupted intermittently, without warning, threatening to restart the blaze all over again.

About two million square feet of office space—the equivalent of the entire Empire State Building—was uninhabitable due to fire, smoke, and structural damage. The worst of it, about 800,000 square feet, was a charnel house of dangerous wreckage. Hideously bent steel rebar protruded from walls and ceilings. Sharp-edged metal debris littered the floors, threatening to gash anybody who stumbled and put down a hand for support. Piles of rubble and half a foot of water concealed body parts and other hazards that firefighters stepped on repeatedly. Except for areas where the fading sunlight slanted in, it was pitch-black. The fire was finally receding, but its aftermath presented a whole new set of problems.

NIGHT OPS

Early evening

Ben Barksdale, who relieved Ed Hannon on the roof near Corridor 4, had a stellar view of the postcard-perfect sun as it drifted down over northern Virginia. To him, however, it was not a comforting sight. As his crews were wearily pulling apart the burned section of the catwalk on top of Corridor 4, Barksdale got some discouraging news from the command post: Once it got dark, all fire crews needed to come down off the roof. Barksdale was determined to complete his assignment and get the fire on his section of the roof under control. To him, the diminishing distance between the sun and the horizon marked not the welcome end to an awful day, but an impossibly short window of time in which to finish a demanding job.

The concern, obviously, was that the roof was dangerous enough in the daytime; in the darkness, there would be an even greater chance of somebody falling off. But Barksdale didn't see it that way. From the ground it looked like the pitched roof sloped down without any railings or other protections to prevent deadly falls. But where Barksdale was working, the Corridor 4 roof emptied onto the flat and relatively safe surfaces that topped the C and D Rings. And in between the rings there were sizable ledges on both sides, with waist-high railings. It would take a freak accident to lose somebody over the side.

Barksdale pleaded his case over the radio with Randy Gray. "In my view, we're not in danger up here," he argued. "If we fall off the pitched parts, we're not going to fall to the ground."

"Look, I understand what you're saying," Gray answered, "but the boss says no. Under no condition are you going to work under dark."

"Okay," Barksdale replied, frustrated. "Just understand, I cannot say that the fire is under control. We may have some extension. I've still got a lot of smoke showing from underneath the slate, and we haven't finished our trench cuts."

"I understand," Gray told him. "Just come on down."

As the order to stand down circulated among the firefighters, a sense of dejection set in. There was no pride in leaving a job unfinished, no matter what the reason. Plus, the fire crews knew if they simply left the roof, there was a good chance the fire they had put out would rekindle and spread beyond its farthest reaches. "Well, there goes all of our work for nothing," one Alexandria firefighter complained.

By the time Barksdale led his crews back down the stairwell, the 15-foot section of burned catwalk had been largely dismantled and there were no flames or visible fire. But that wretched white smoke was still seeping out from underneath the tiles, and there hadn't been enough time to make a trench cut that would cut it off for good, which bothered Barksdale and the others. They were leaving conditions in place for the fire to spread, when another couple hours of work might be all that was needed to take care of it.

Schwartz and Plaugher were the ones who ordered fire crews off the roof at sunset, as part of a broader plan to switch from "offensive" operations, meant to extinguish the fire and rescue any victims, to "defensive" operations, aimed at checking the spread of fire, with minimal risk to fire crews. Reports they were getting told them the fire was largely extinguished inside the building. There were hot spots and flare-ups, but mainly in a portion of the Pentagon that was already incinerated or severely damaged. The building was unstable, with numerous support columns totally wiped out. Floors and walls were liable to collapse. There were dozens of other dangers, ranging from toxins and flammable materials to falling debris and jagged metal. But now there was nobody to rescue, and all the sensitive areas that needed to be secured had been taken care of.

The two fire chiefs were also acutely aware of the devastation in New York and the brutal toll on the FDNY. At the Pentagon, several firefighters had been sent to the hospital for smoke inhalation or dehydration or minor problems. But there were no deaths or serious injuries, and Schwartz and Plaugher wanted to keep it that way. It might be the Pentagon, but still, it was just a building. If fire smoldered overnight and they had to go back in at daylight and reextinguish a few areas, well, that was better than risking the lives of firefighters just to save some office space or furniture.

Shortly after dusk Schwartz called a meeting of all the fire officers still on the scene. Word went out over the radio, and about 50 people assembled near the west lawn, overlooking the dark gash in the building with which they had all become so familiar. "We're going to stand down from offensive operations for the night," Schwartz shouted over the hum of the heavy machinery. "We're pretty confident that the fire in the interior is under control. We're going to pull everybody back and move to defensive operations."

By declaring the fire to be "under control," Schwartz was invoking fire terminology that had a specific meaning. Once a fire was "under control," commanders and fire crews knew to take fewer risks, and the dispatchers responsible for assigning units to various incidents knew they no longer had to allot every available unit to the fire in question.

They were already setting up a "surround-and-drown" operation, to drench the hot parts of the building overnight with deluge guns and hoses affixed to ladders that could reach the higher floors and the roof. Fire crews would remain on the scene all night, and commanders would have the authority to run patrols throughout the building or send fire crews in to tackle urgent problems.

There was plenty of other work that needed to be done overnight. Operations and planning cells had to develop a thorough strategy for the following day, when they'd have to put the fire out for good and start reclaiming the vast amount of space it had consumed. Schwartz had set up a safety command that would have to survey the whole damaged structure and put definitive guidelines in place. The FBI had barely even started to collect evidence or remains inside the building. And all of the agencies on the scene needed to figure out how to rotate their people and assure that they'd be fully staffed for a prolonged, around-the-clock operation—while making sure they could respond to anything else that happened over the next several days.

A massive logistical operation was just getting started too. Truckloads of lumber were on the way from various construction sites. Generators and floodlights were arriving from a warehouse at Andrews Air Force Base, in Maryland. Food providers, the Red Cross, and other support groups were setting up a complex of tents and booths in South Parking.

So many ordinary people felt helpless in the face of the terrorist attacks—and desperately eager to do something—that simple requests produced an overwhelming response. Power in the damaged areas had either been knocked out or shut off, and there was a shortage of electricians to help get lights and generators wired for the construction and recovery crews to do their work. So an Arlington fire officer had called county administrators asking for help. Most county offices had closed early, the employees sent home. But Larry Callan, an electrician for the school district, was still around, and he readily agreed to go to the Pentagon and help out. Callan ended up inside the building stringing lights throughout the smoky corridors, getting as close to the fire areas as he could without protective gear.[1]

Most of the firefighters were using rechargeable flashlights, with batteries that typically lasted about six hours and then took another six hours to recharge. That worked fine on most big fires—but not one like this, which had already lasted for hours and would go on well into the next day. So somebody called the nearest Home Depot, where the manager rallied a few employees and sent a truck with every flashlight and battery the store had in stock. The store also dispatched an assistant manager to work directly with the Arlington chiefs and help supply lumber, tools, and whatever else they needed.[2]

Other parts of the operation were moving forward despite the darkness. Chris Combs was busy helping set up the FBI's joint operations center, the JOC—and the mission had become a lot more personal. Practically everybody Combs knew back home in New York was either a cop or a firefighter, and from the moment he heard about the twin towers collapsing, he felt a twinge of dread. Then his sister Cathie got through on his cell phone, after trying for several hours. They had two cousins on the FDNY, Kenny Watson on Engine 214 and Richie Muldowney on Ladder 7. Cathie told her brother both of them were missing.

Cathie wanted to hope for the best. But Combs knew the news was bad. "Sis," he said, as gently as he could, "if they're missing, they're gone."

As Combs worked into the night, he thought of the last time he had seen his cousins. He was particularly close with Richie, whose fortieth birthday had been in January, eight months earlier. At the time, Combs had been assigned to the FBI detail preparing for the presidential inauguration in D.C., which was a demanding job. He told his family he couldn't make the party—then decided to go at the last minute. It was a quick trip, up and back in less than 24 hours. But now he felt like it was one of the best decisions he had ever made.

Tom O'Connor, one of the agents in charge of evidence recovery, was splitting his crews into day and night teams. He also had to get a temporary morgue set up. Fire and rescue crews had already come across numerous bodies, and once it was safe for recovery specialists to work inside the building, they needed to document the remains and remove them as quickly as possible.

The plan was to use a loading dock near North Parking as the first way station for remains. They'd be placed in refrigerated trucks and driven around the corner to the loading dock, where agents would log, photograph, and label them. Any identifying material, like ID cards, jewelry, the contents of wallets, even the brand of shoes and trousers, would be documented. The remains would then be driven by truck to nearby Fort Belvoir, put on helicopters and flown to Andrews Air Force Base in Maryland, then moved to airplanes and flown to Dover Air Force Base in Delaware. At Dover, the military's forensic experts would conduct DNA testing, do formal autopsies, and prepare the remains for burial.

Special Agent Tara Bloesch was assigned to set up the morgue. She had all the right experience—before joining the FBI, she'd worked as a forensic investigator near Philadelphia and as a parole officer in the city itself. With the FBI, Bloesch had helped run morgue operations in Kosovo and Serbia, documenting war crimes and mass graves, after NATO troops intervened in the war there in 1999. Her colleagues knew her as an articulate, tough Philly girl who didn't blanch at difficult jobs. She would keep the morgue under tight control.

O'Connor needed other people to work with her. He gathered several dozen agents on the lawn, near the helipad, to sort out who would deal with remains, evidence, and other aspects of the huge job. "Obviously we'll be doing a lot of human remains and body recovery," he announced to the crowd. "If you're comfortable doing that, step over here. If you're not, that's okay, because I need people doing other things too." More than half the group moved to the spot he had indicated. Then he added, "This is not a normal event. If anybody needs to talk to someone, nobody's going to think any less of you."

The FEMA teams were preparing for a busy night too. When Dean Tills had come down from the roof, he immediately started formulating a plan for stabilizing the building. He got together with the two other engineers on the task force, Leo Titus and Tony Beale, and briefed them on what he'd seen during his reconnaissance trips. Dozens of support columns had been damaged or destroyed, which would require extensive rebuilding work. Titus and Beale had seen much the same thing. For the time being, there was little they could do deep inside the structure, where spot fires were still a problem. But an obvious place to start shoring up the building was along the wall to the immediate left of the collapse.

Under the floors that were still standing, three of the outermost support columns had been demolished, creating a risk of further collapse. They'd need to work their way in toward the most dangerous spot, the edge where the building broke off along the expansion joint, erecting wooden cribbing beneath the second floor as they went. It would be extremely delicate work, with the hulking rubble pile and other precarious chunks of debris poised to tumble down on workers if they weren't careful.

Tills started taking inventory of the resources he'd have available. Another FEMA task force, from Montgomery County, Maryland, had arrived, which would double the available manpower. In addition to search and shoring, there was still a lot of detailed reconnaissance to do, on all floors, which the Maryland engineers would help with. Also, the PenRen team had a number of contractors on-site who were eager to help. A loader was pulling up in front of the collapse zone, to start clearing away debris, and construction crews had begun to build cut stations for processing the raw lumber as it arrived. As the firefight was transitioning to a new phase, an elaborate construction project was springing up inside it.

Tills was getting plenty of offers of help, including some he didn't entirely want. Allyn Kilsheimer was a structural engineer who ran a consulting firm in D.C. that did work for clients up and down the East Coast. He had done some contracting work on the Pentagon in the past, but was known more for his gruff personality and his penchant for showing up whenever there was some kind of major incident involving a prominent building. After getting a call from New York City officials, Kilsheimer had been preparing to go there to offer his services at the World Trade Center, when a contractor friend working for PenRen called him from the Pentagon. "A plane has hit the building!" he told Kilsheimer. "We need your help!"

When Kilsheimer arrived on the scene, Pentagon police were establishing a loose security perimeter around the building, and one of the officers told Kilsheimer he couldn't go in without a badge.

"Fuck you," Kilsheimer said. He kept walking.

"Sir, you've got to have clearance," the officer insisted.

"No I don't," the burly, bearded engineer snapped back. He walked through without being bothered any further.

Kilsheimer had called one of the contractors he knew, who drove around to North Parking and picked him up. They entered the construction area near the collapse zone, where Kilsheimer got his first glimpse of the damage. A couple of fire officers asked him how stable he thought certain parts of the building were. Kilsheimer offered his best guess, but said he'd have to get inside and have a detailed look around to be able to say for sure.

Tills knew Kilsheimer from various projects they had both been involved in, and Kilsheimer walked over to him with a ranking military official, asking if they could go to the FEMA command tent for a brief meeting. Once inside, Kilsheimer took the initiative. "The Pentagon wants me to watch over things," he told Tills, "and make sure the building is properly shored up. So before you start any work, I think you should let me know."

Tills was usually calm and rational, but he could also be intense, especially when his professional judgment was challenged. He still wasn't sure what the command structure was supposed to be for work that would have to be done on the building, but he did know that he was responsible for the safety of the FEMA teams as long as they were inside. "Look Allyn," he retorted, "this is a search-and-rescue operation right now. We'll be responsible for discussions involving shoring the building, since right now we're more concerned about protecting our workers than protecting the building. You can assist with our operations, but we need to make our own decisions." The meeting ended with an edgy truce.

Kilsheimer had gone off to see some other people when two men in military uniforms walked up to him. "We were told you can get things done when nobody else can," one of them said quietly.

"Yeah . . ." Kilsheimer replied. "So?"

"We need to retrieve some files from the building," the man answered. "If we don't get them, the Navy's going to be set back ten years. Can you help us?"

"Let's go," Kilsheimer said.

The two men explained that they were Navy SEALs who did planning and budgeting for the elite program. Their highly secure office had buckled and swayed when the plane hit, and the ceiling started to give way, forcing everyone to flee. They had left behind some extremely sensitive classified data, most of it stored on a number of computer hard drives. Retrieving those was crucial. Even if nobody else found them, the mere fact that they were unaccounted for could force major, costly changes in the secretive commando force.

Kilsheimer and the SEALs went in the Corridor 3 entrance, around the corner from the impact point, hooking up with a couple other SEALs along the way. The group worked its way to a shattered office that was on the fifth floor, in the E Ring, facing the interior of the building, just a couple of doorways down from where the fifth floor plunged into the avalanche of concrete and metal that had fallen into the impact hole.

As Kilsheimer gazed into the windowless office, he could see that the ceiling had partially dropped and was resting on a Compaq server unit the size of a wardrobe. The server was basically holding up the ceiling. He could see some reinforcing bars below the ceiling that hadn't yet snapped or bent, and might offer some protection if the ceiling dropped farther. Although there wasn't any fire, it felt extremely hot, and he told the SEALs to wait in the hallway as he stepped into the office.

The hard drives they needed were in the server unit, to the left of the door. Kilsheimer reached over to it and started popping out the drives, squeezing a couple of tabs for each one. Some of them came right out, and he dropped them into a duffel bag the SEALs had given him. But some got jammed and others were melted.

Kilsheimer found a pair of scissors, which he used to pop loose a couple more drives. It was taking awhile, though, and the SEALs were getting impatient. Two of them came into the room as Kilsheimer was on his knees, gently trying to move some debris on the floor that was blocking the door of the server cabinet, preventing him from opening it all the way. Leaning over next to him, one of the SEALs started yanking on the door. The motions shook the whole cabinet—which was holding up the ceiling.

"What the fuck's the matter with you!" Kilsheimer erupted, turning around. "The roof's gonna come down! Get the fuck out of here!" The two SEALs retreated back into the hallway.

After another moment, one of them called in to Kilsheimer, "Hey, you've got enough. We don't need to get any more. Let's get out of here."

But having come this far, Kilsheimer didn't want to leave without a full duffel bag. "We came here to get this stuff," he said, "and we're gonna get the job done."

He finally freed the last of the drives, and the group backtracked out the E Ring and down the stairs. When they finally hit terra firma, the SEAL who had been yanking the server door still looked rattled. Sweat ran down his forehead. "How come you were so nervous up there?" Kilsheimer asked. "You're trained for that kind of stuff."

"That was my office, sir," the SEAL answered, explaining that by chance he had walked out of the office right before the plane hit.

Kilsheimer went back to the helipad to see what else he could help with. Scott McKay, one of the Arlington technical-rescue specialists, asked him to size up the E Ring wall, to the right of the collapse. Kilsheimer said they'd need some steel bracing to stabilize that part of the structure, but McKay told him they didn't have any. So Kilsheimer found one of the contractors he knew and asked if he could get his hands on some steel I beams, flanges, and other types of bracing.

Leo Titus, FEMA's rookie structural specialist, also knew Kilsheimer, and chuckled when he spotted the burly engineer near the helipad, wearing a pink golf shirt and a baseball cap—and making plans for another foray into the building. Titus walked up and said hello, then urged Kilsheimer to don some heavy-duty protective gear before going back inside. Kilsheimer insisted he didn't need it. But some of the firefighters he'd gotten to know had taken a quick liking to him and his impolitic manner, and one of the crews agreed to loan him and Brig. Gen. Carl Strock, a top official at the Army Corps of Engineers, some turnout gear so they could take a tour of the wrecked building.

Strock's ID got them past the guards at the Corridor 5 entrance, and they walked down the water-filled hallway toward A&E Drive, every sound echoing like a catcall in a cavern. The pants Kilsheimer had borrowed belonged to a much larger man, and they kept falling down, splashing in the water as the two men sloshed down the hallway.

They turned right into the D Ring, toward the remnants of the Navy Command Center. Flames still leaped up from behind piles of debris. Hot water rained down on them. "It's like Dante's *Inferno*," Strock said in amazement.

A few fire crews were conducting patrols inside, making sure the fire stayed in check. "Hey, be careful over there," one of the firefighters warned the two men, pointing to a corner where two or three skeletons, the bones black and completely bare, lay like artifacts from an archeological dig. "Don't disturb them," the firefighter said somberly.

Farther along they came across two bodies that were more intact. One man was lying on his back, his hand on his forehead. His mouth and eyes were open, looking up at Kilsheimer as if he were about to scream. The other body had blood coming out of its mouth. After staring for a moment, Strock said, "Don't you wish you could do something for these guys?"

"We're going to rebuild this place within a year," Kilsheimer said. "That's what we're going to do for these guys."

★ 28 ★

PLANTING A FLAG

Evening

G. O. Lyon had spent the day at Station 1 overseeing "Plan B," as he called it—managing the flow of backup units to the Pentagon. The trim, thoughtful, and bespectacled Arlington battalion chief was trying to anticipate all the long-term things that would be needed to sustain the operation for an indefinite number of days. But Plan B wasn't quite gelling.

The Arlington County Fire Department, like other urban departments, was used to operations that were intense but relatively short-lived. Out West, where firefighters battled brush or wilderness fires, there were rotational systems, mobile sleeping quarters, and established procedures for operations that lasted for days. In Arlington, there was more of a surge mentality. Most fires were over in minutes, so you'd give it all you had, then go home and recover for the next incident.

Lyon was trying to impose more measured management of the department's manpower and other resources—without much success. Once the operation was in full swing, the plan had been to replace spent firefighters with fresh ones, on a one-for-one basis, more or less. Every time a bus left Station 1 with a fresh group, they were supposed to relieve crews who would rotate out, get on the bus, and come back to Station 1.

But the buses kept returning empty. When fresh units arrived at the Pentagon, the crews they were supposed to replace were often operating in the building somewhere, so both sets of firefighters stayed on the scene. There was no set policy for rotating crews in the midst of an incident, and commanders were inclined to keep all the crews they had on hand. And the firefighters themselves didn't want to leave. It was a career fire, the place was still burning, and with adrenaline flowing, it was easy to push yourself right up to the point of total exhaustion.

Arlington crews typically worked 24-hour shifts, on and off for five days, followed by a four-day break. But virtually every firefighter in the department was involved at the Pentagon—the shifts had basically been tossed out the window. Lyon had to figure out how the department was going to staff itself the following day, and thereafter. As firefighters finally did start to leave the Pentagon, where should they go? Home? Back to their stations? To some kind of staging area? Where would they get a thorough rehab and get checked out for fluids and smoke? And who would keep a roster of firefighters fit for duty the following day?

Lyon was getting very little feedback from the chiefs at the Pentagon about the disposition of the crews—who was finished, who was handling rehab, and where they planned to send all the spent troops. And there were other complications further back in the pipeline. Because so many Arlington firefighters had gone to the Pentagon, the county invoked the mutual-aid system to staff the regular Arlington stations with firefighters from Fairfax, Loudoun, and other neighboring counties. Those fire stations were filling with unfamiliar crews who would end up manning the whole overnight shift and occupying the sleeping quarters. Any Arlington crews who returned to their regular posts, hoping to crash in the bed that was supposed to be theirs for the shift, would most likely find it occupied.

Lyon and some of the county's administrative staff had decided to set up a rehab station at Thomas Jefferson Community Center—"TJ," as everyone called it—about two miles from the Pentagon, across the street from the Station 1 staging area. Medics would be there, along with counselors who practiced critical-incident stress management, CISM, meant to defuse the emotional pressure that often came from working in traumatic situations. Administrators would be able to keep track of all the fire crews that had been thrown together randomly or escaped notice during the chaotic day.

By early evening TJ was ready to go, and support staff waited for firefighters to arrive. Somebody called Lyon at Station 1. "Where are all the people?" she asked.

"I don't know," was all Lyon could say. He sent somebody to find out what was happening to all the firefighters who were ending their duty day, and called the command post, making sure firefighters understood they were to report to TJ once they left the Pentagon.

Then came Lyon's turn to go to the Pentagon. "I want you to come with the next busload," Schwartz told him. "I want you to take over night ops. Can you do that?"

Lyon was about 24 hours into his regular shift as battalion chief and had just worked the night before, with little sleep. But sleep would wait. When he arrived, he went straight to the command post, still at the I-395 underpass.

Schwartz looked tired but still brimmed with the hyperkinetic energy Lyon was accustomed to seeing. "You're gonna be ops chief," Schwartz told him. The command staff, at least, was finally being relieved in some kind of orderly way that would let them rest and recuperate and come back in force the following day.

Plaugher was there too, and the two chiefs briefed Lyon on the latest situation reports. Most of the interior fire was out. Lyon's general assignment was to keep deluge guns flowing into the building all night, but to refrain from active firefighting unless there was some kind of emergency. He would also need to work with Jack Brown, the

Loudoun chief in charge of the planning section, and the FEMA teams, to develop a detailed plan for operations the following day, September 12.

Lyon still didn't have a good feel for the fire, however. He'd seen TV footage throughout the day, but the pictures didn't offer much detail. He got in a vehicle and quickly traversed the scene, from the main command post over to the helipad.

South Parking looked like a fire-truck boneyard. Vehicles of every type, from at least half a dozen jurisdictions, were parked everywhere, helter-skelter. No fire crews tended the vehicles. They looked abandoned. As he rounded the southwest corner of the building, eerily illuminated by a few floodlights and the ambient light of the activity on the ground, Lyon could see smoke and steam gushing up out of the Pentagon's inner regions. There was no visible fire inside the building, but a few flames flickered on the roof. The courtyard, he knew, was another front, and he had no idea what was going on there. Even though he ended up standing right outside the building, he still felt like he had poor visibility into the fire he was now in charge of.

Out near Washington Boulevard, Lyon was surprised to find that Arlington's EMS division, now headed by Battalion Chief Jim Bonzano, was still on the scene—even though there hadn't been any patients for hours. Sometimes, Lyon knew, it was easier to mobilize for a big operation than to demobilize—it wasn't always obvious when the mission was over. Capt. Eddie Blunt, whose wife, Kay, had been on an airliner out of Chicago, was still working, even though there was very little to do. Blunt had spent the day suppressing panic, worrying that Kay might end up on a hijacked plane. With his wife unaccounted for, a neighbor had gotten through on Blunt's cell phone and offered to watch his two sons when they got home from school. Blunt gratefully accepted, and then thought for a moment. "Don't let them watch TV!" he begged just before hanging up.

Blunt finally heard from Kay around 6:00 P.M. She was safe in

Chicago—but unnerved, with no idea when she'd get back home. He was relieved, but his wife's anxious voice produced a new kind of stress. He could have gone home, but decided to keep working; it would keep his mind off things.

Lyon demobilized the EMS branch and told Bonzano and Blunt to head for TJ with their crews. Then he found some of the other commanders near the helipad. He got an update on fire conditions inside and started making sure all the daytime crews were rotating out and not staying on indefinitely. All the apparatus would have to be cleaned up as well, and sent back to home stations. Another priority was getting ladder trucks and other aerial devices into the courtyard, where there still weren't enough hoses that could reach the smoldering roof. And everybody was busy getting a detailed plan in place for the next day.

Battalion Chief Randy Gray, still at the helipad, finally left well after dark. He felt that, all things considered, the situation was under control. Gray knew the roof would continue to burn, but that calling the firefighters down for the night had been the right call. Hoses were pouring water onto the roof, which would slow the burn. And there would be plenty of time to attack the fire safely in the morning.

Chuck Gibbs was still there, helping to set things up for the night shift. He didn't want to leave, but Gray insisted. They were both tired and had barely eaten. It was time for a break. "Chuck, you've got to go," Gray told Gibbs. "We've been here for a very long time." Gibbs finally agreed.

Plaugher and Schwartz both knew they'd be working through the night at the Pentagon, handling an endless battery of requests and demands. General Jackson had arrived at the command post, and Schwartz introduced him to Plaugher. "This is our single point of contact for the military," Schwartz said.

Jackson asked Plaugher what the fire department needed from him. "Manpower," Plaugher answered—healthy troops who could help with the manual labor of moving debris and getting a recovery operation started. The general had several hundred soldiers at his disposal, and said he'd start calling in troops to do whatever was needed. "Great, bring 'em on down," Plaugher said. Jackson also offered a 70-person combat engineering company from Fort Belvoir that was under his command. Plaugher was happy to have it—the additional equipment and expertise would come in handy once they started clearing out and stabilizing the building.

The two men made a sound impression on each other. To Plaugher, Jackson was the kind of action-minded official he needed on the staff. It seemed he could get things done without the red tape that was already threatening to slow down the operation. And Jackson appreciated Plaugher's military-style command presence. The fire chief gave orders calmly but decisively, knew how to ask for what he wanted, and was obviously comfortable being in charge.

Jackson was a help right away. With the Pentagon set to open the next day—and war in the air—generals, admirals, and other military officials pressed to get back into the building. Many were concerned about the contents of classified safes, which were built to survive fire but, as far as anybody knew, might be sitting wide open, exposing national security secrets to anybody who happened to walk by. Jackson became the conduit for all their requests. He decided which ones seemed valid, then made arrangements with the fire chiefs to have escorts lead the military officials safely into the building.

Schwartz was busy getting a full incident-command system in place, with all of the administrative and logistical support required to sustain the operation for several days. Plaugher, among other things, was becoming an impromptu tour guide. The governor of Virginia, James Gilmore, showed up to have a look at the damage, and Plaugher showed him around. A growing list of other officials wanted tours. Hosting VIPs wasn't a duty Plaugher relished, but he knew that if he handled the visitors, it would keep the pressure off Schwartz and free him to focus on operations.

The press was also clamoring for information. Rumsfeld had provided a bit of detail when he declared that the Pentagon would open for business the following day. But he had been unable to answer many questions about casualties, the status of the fire, or the nature of the damage. A huge flock of journalists was sequestered at the Citgo gas station that overlooked the Pentagon—a natural vantage point for film crews and photographers, since it provided a direct view of the hole in the west wall. Defense Department briefers were also up there, passing on tidbits they picked up. But information trickled slowly on a day when the whole country was desperate for answers.

The Pentagon spokespeople kept asking Plaugher and Schwartz for information they could pass on, and the two fire chiefs, along with General Jackson, decided it was probably time for the fire department to make an official appearance in front of the cameras. The news out of New York was desperate, confusing, and changing constantly. At the Pentagon, at least, the situation had become fairly stable, and a public briefing might provide a small measure of reassurance. It wouldn't hurt to plant a flag either—most of the press still didn't know that the Arlington County Fire Department was in charge of the incident. So Plaugher and Jackson drove up to the Citgo station—where they were promptly mobbed.

Plaugher ended up doing most of the talking. First he had to introduce himself and spell his name. Reporters wanted to know how many casualties there were. He explained that the destroyed wing of the building had been undergoing renovation and some of the people who would ordinarily have been working there had moved out for the time being. His best estimate was that somewhere between 100 and 800 people had died, including the people on the plane. But even that broad range was a guess.

Had any of the airplane passengers survived? No.

Were there any signs that survivors were still trapped in the rubble? None that he was aware of, but rescue crews would continue searching.

What about the collapsed area? Had searchers looked there? "Obviously, in the collapsed areas," Plaugher said, "that will have to take place at a later time, after we have made the building safe."

Why were there still flames on the roof? There was "active fire" in the space between the slate roof tiles and the fifth-floor ceiling, he explained. It wouldn't be safe for firefighters to keep working up there until daylight. They'd take care of it then.

BEER RUN

Nighttime

Dodie Gill had a way of making people smile whenever she showed up. As the director of Arlington County's mental health and employee-support programs, Gill had become an unconventional fixture around the firehouses.

For several years the Arlington County Fire Department had been improving its stress-management program, to help deal with post-traumatic stress disorder (PTSD) and other issues common in fire and law-enforcement jobs. The traditional view—that the job was tough and you just had to suck it up—had been fading for years, due largely to a better understanding of PTSD in soldiers returning from combat. With improving techniques for dealing with the stress fire-fighters encountered on the job, Chief Schwartz, one of the program's advocates, had asked Gill to get involved. She studied some of the department's prevailing methods, such as peer-counseling sessions. "Well, that's not going to work," she reported back. "It's a bunch of older white guys. You need a group that's more diverse, so everybody on the force will be comfortable opening up."

With Schwartz's blessing, Gill set up some new training programs based on the latest research on PTSD and high-stress occupations. Every firefighter in the department underwent four hours of training, to help recognize and deal with stress-related issues. Formal debriefings were instituted after every incident, with a firefighter leading the sessions and counselors present. Nobody was forced to speak if they didn't want to—but attendance was mandatory.

Gill's programs got resistance from some of the firefighters, which she expected. "Nobody wants little Suzy Social Worker coming around," she had acknowledged. Besides, as a former triathlete, who wore long, flowing skirts and big, beaded jewelry, Gill stood out like a new-age guru against the traditionalism of the fire department. Old-timers would roll their eyes when she urged them to pay attention to "cortisol levels" and "brain chemistry" and the "altered states of mind" they might find themselves in after a demanding fire.

So to gain credibility, Gill put on turnout gear and a respirator and participated in a live-burn exercise at a cinder-block training facility, meant to simulate an apartment fire. She stopped in at fire stations and hung out with firefighters off the clock, getting to know many by their first names. And meanwhile, over a couple of years, her lectures began to sink in. Firefighters became conversant in some of her favorite tenets: Stress is cumulative, not episodic. It builds over time. Everybody's limits are different. Some people can hit a wall, triggered by anything, and then they're done.

G. O. Lyon had asked Gill to help get things set up at Thomas Jefferson Community Center. So Gill and her small staff of social workers spent the afternoon at TJ, trying to gauge the best way to offer support once firefighters started arriving from the Pentagon. It would be too early to conduct formal debriefings, since many of the fire crews would be going right back to the site the next morning and were still, effectively, in the middle of the mission. Yet for most of the firefighters at the Pentagon, it was the most demanding day of their careers. Gill decided she and her staff would be available for "defusings," allowing firefighters to vent or talk if they wanted to, into the night if necessary.

The debriefing program was new, and Gill got a few calls from fire officials and county administrators urging her to start debriefings right away. But it wasn't the right time, she felt, since it was such an overwhelming event and was still going on. She didn't have time to explain, though, so she yessed the county people and went back to work getting things set up.

Others had their doubts about the setup at TJ. Medic Claude Conde, who had watched Flight 77 fly overhead seconds before it smashed into the Pentagon, never made it to the huge incident. He headed toward the Pentagon several times but was continually diverted by routine medical calls elsewhere in the county. Late in the day, however, he was sent to TJ to help the employee-support teams prepare to evaluate the firefighters. As he watched cots being set up on the gymnasium floor, Conde sensed that a bunch of rambunctious firefighters, wired from the biggest fire of their careers, were never going to settle into the orderly routine the counselors hoped for. He felt sure it would never work, that none of the firefighters would want to stay there. But he kept his thoughts to himself and helped prepare for the first arrivals.

Fire crews finally started to show up sometime after dark. As Gill watched them tromp off buses, exhausted, filthy, and wet, she too wondered whether TJ was the right place for them to be after all. Most of the firefighters wanted nothing but a shower and some shut-eye. Others were dying for a beer. But they were told to pile into the bleachers in the gym, where they'd get some instructions.

As the first group straggled into the bleachers, Gill gamely spoke up. "Okay, we're going to do a debriefing later," she began, "but the most important thing is, first, get some rest. And to show you how brave I am," she continued, "I'm going to ask you all not to drink alcohol, because it interferes with your REM sleep and you all need to be okay to work tomorrow."

Groans erupted.

"Now get some rest," Gill said, flashing her warm, sisterly smile.

Other administrators stressed that nobody was allowed to leave and tried to explain that many of the firehouses were now filled with backfillers from elsewhere. Plus, the county needed all the firefighters in one place, where they could keep track of them. TJ, they pleaded, was the best solution.

Their plan was unconvincing. There were no clean clothes available, and firefighters accustomed to the routines of the firehouse weren't likely to settle in to the open-air barracks that had been set up at TJ. Conde winced as he heard county officials exhorting them, wishing he weren't associated with the TJ staff. He knew that a minor rebellion was inevitable.

The grumbling started immediately. Firefighters who happened to be on their regular shifts insisted on going back to their home stations, no matter who was there. Everybody else just wanted to go home. Jim Anderson had come to TJ after accompanying Ed Hannon to the hospital. He found Gill and let loose. "Our guys aren't going to stay here much longer," he barked. "Our clothes are soaking wet. We're getting chills. We need dry clothes."

Denis Griffin, less inclined to complain, stepped outside the community center and looked around for a way to get back to Station 4. He'd been drinking fluids steadily since hobbling out of the Pentagon the final time, and his muscles were beginning to revive. He recognized one of the county maintenance workers dropping something off, and hitched a ride, along with a few other firefighters. At Station 4, his firehouse, the garage was filled with unfamiliar equipment. Griffin walked into the day room looking for colleagues, only to find a bunch of strange faces looking up at him. When he realized there were no beds, he found the officer in charge and said he was going home. "You can't do that," the officer told him. "You have to stay here tonight."

Griffin waited a moment, slipped away, and announced to the night, "Oh yeah? Well, watch this." Then he got in his car and left.

Jim Anderson was less charitable when he found somebody sleeping in his bunk at Station 4. "Hey, buddy, hit the bricks," he ordered, shaking the man awake. "This is my bed tonight."

Bobby Beer was livid when he got back to Station 4 and found every bed full. He led Paul Marshall, Chad Stamps, and Fred Kawatsky down the road to the Courtyard Hotel, where they asked for two rooms. When the manager realized they were firefighters who had been at the Pentagon, he told them the rooms were on the house. And breakfast would be waiting when they got up.

Nobody was ready to sleep, so Beer and the others went to Ireland's Four Courts, an Irish bar a couple of blocks away. Before they knew it, drinks were stacked up in front of them, courtesy of a dozen patrons. "Wow," Marshall said to his comrades, "here we are, exhausted, filthy, and smoky, and people are saying, 'Thanks for doing that.' "

Ed Blunt, the EMS supervisor, tried to stick it out at TJ, but everybody else was leaving, so he decided to go back to Station 1, which was just across the street. Somebody on the rehab crew told him not to drink any alcohol or caffeine, and to be ready to work again in 12 hours. Blunt knew he'd be unable to sleep, and he was desperate to unwind from the stress of the incident and from the anxiety over his wife. He began to walk toward the station, then decided to go to a nearby 7-Eleven and buy a six-pack of beer. Blunt usually went by the book, but not tonight. To hell with the rules, he decided.

Inside the store, it looked like the beer cooler had been ransacked. The floor in front of it was smeared with muddy footprints. Torn cardboard boxes were everywhere. But there wasn't any beer. "What happened?" he asked.

The clerk pointed to Blunt's yellow turnout gear. "Firemen," he said.

By then Dodie Gill had realized that TJ wasn't working as planned. She hadn't known what kind of shape the fire crews would be in when they got there. Usually, after a fire, the crews might be tired, but they were still organized and disciplined. The Pentagon clearly had been a different kind of mission, with crews thrown together randomly, working with little formal guidance, and pushing themselves past their limits. She regrouped with her staff and sent a couple of her counselors to the Pentagon, to be on-scene overnight. She and the others would rotate there in the morning.

Many of the firefighters had a restless night in store, no matter where they went to bed. After corralling a bed at Station 4, Jim Anderson lay in the dark exhausted but wide-awake. He yearned to see his wife, Mary Ellen, and be near his two kids. Unlike many Arlington firefighters who lived far out in the country, Anderson lived just a few miles away, in Alexandria. He could easily get back in time to work the next day. So he got up, walked to his pickup truck outside, and drove home.

After a vigorous hug from his wife, Anderson, still sorting out the events of the day, said to her: "What the hell is going on? I'm hearing that the military shot down a plane, the towers collapsed . . . Those towers were not designed to collapse!"

They sat down and watched TV together, the first time Anderson had seen the footage of the towers crumbling. He'd heard that a "bunch" of firefighters had been killed in New York, and figured that meant 20 or 30. *Hundreds* of deaths . . . that was unbelievable. Just like somebody flying a plane into the Pentagon.

Denis Griffin also lived nearby, in Falls Church, and was standing on his doorstep just a few minutes after leaving Station 4. He didn't have a cell phone and hadn't thought to call from the station, so nobody knew he was coming. When he turned the key and rattled the door, his 13-year-old son heard the noise and ran to the basement, terrified. When Griffin and his wife, Muriel, coaxed him out, the boy told them he was afraid that Osama bin Laden had come through the door.

The commotion shook Griffin out of a dull reverie. What am I doing here? he asked himself. Muriel, while overjoyed to see him, was wondering the same thing. Her husband had just spent hours in the midst of a chemical stew that could have contained any number of toxins. He was standing in his home in the same clothes that had been drenched with the foul water cascading down on him from the upper floors of the Pentagon. Griffin, realizing he wasn't thinking clearly, looked sheepishly at his wife. "I just want to take a shower," he said.

Scott Fry, the vice admiral running the Joint Staff, finally decided that the situation in the National Military Command Center was stable. Site R was fully functional and there was no longer any obvious threat to the continuity of military command. It seemed safe to go home and get a few hours' sleep. Fry left the NMCC and headed back to his office on the E Ring, to get his hat and car keys. His office was on the opposite side of the Pentagon from the crash site, about as far from the fire as you could get without leaving the building. Yet he couldn't believe how much smoke hung in the hallways. He groped through the darkness, feeling his way along the walls until he got to his office. He found his hat and keys and ducked out.

Fry drove wearily to his quarters at the Washington Navy Yard, a few miles away—and got the ass-chewing of a lifetime when he walked through the front door. Shortly after the plane had hit the building, he'd asked his secretary, Dottie, to call his wife, Mary, to say he was okay. With that done, he went back to work and thought no more about it. But Mary didn't see it that way. "I didn't need to hear Dottie's voice," she exclaimed. "I needed to hear yours!"

Fry blinked at her for a moment—then comprehended. "I'm sorry," he said.

Steve Carter and Kathy Greenwell left the Pentagon together, just as they had arrived that morning—the two of them routinely carpooled to work. While Carter was scrambling throughout the building all day, Greenwell stayed mainly in the Building Operations Command Center, until firefighters asked for all the power to be cut, so they wouldn't have to deal with live wires or electrified water. So Greenwell spent the rest of the night running supplies around, until she and Carter decided to go home and try getting a little rest. They both knew they'd be back early the next day.

When they walked out of the Pentagon, it was the first time either had seen the damage to the building from the outside. They were shocked to see so much fire equipment, in every direction. They knew there was a big firefighting operation outside but had no idea it was this vast. It was sickening to look at the big hole in the building, and even more disheartening to watch the flames burning atop the Pentagon, untouched. Carter couldn't believe they were going to let his building burn all night. It felt like he was watching his own home burn.

They got in Greenwell's car. She dropped Carter off at a halfway point, where he got in his own car and drove home to Mechanicsville, Maryland. He told his wife, Shelly, as much as he could about the wild day, then headed for bed, pulled off his clothes, piled them on the floor, and collapsed into the mattress. An hour later he woke up, smelling smoke. He jumped out of bed, thinking his house was on fire, then realized he was only smelling his clothes on the floor. There was no way he could get back to sleep after that, so he took a shower and decided he'd head back to the Pentagon.

Meanwhile, when Greenwell walked through the door of her home in Indian Head, Maryland, she suddenly had a lot of talking to do. Her husband was a senior chief in the Navy, and his curiosity about every detail was insatiable. Her parents lived in their house too, and they wanted to hear all about her ordeal. It felt good to talk at first, relieving some of the tension and stress. But Greenwell gradually realized that she didn't have the energy to tell everything, not now anyway and finally excused herself to go to bed.

Bob Cornwell had called his wife, Colleen, that night and told her he'd probably be released sometime after midnight. It was a 40-minute drive to his home in Manassas, Virginia, on vacant roads. The couple's three boys had long been asleep, but Colleen was up when he finally got home. Cornwell usually had little to say after a fire, and he followed his custom. But this time there was an enduring embrace at the door, and the strapping battalion chief trembled. Colleen wept with relief. After a deep breath, Cornwell, smoky and spent, told his wife that he'd have to be ready to go back in the morning. Then he marched directly up the stairs and kissed each of his sleeping boys.

★ 30 ★

LADDER 16

Wednesday, September 12, 1:00 A.M.

The flames flickering on the Pentagon's roof had become a focal point for the journalists and many others on the hill, gazing at the building during the warm night. The flames didn't rage, but idled like a lazy hearth fire—taunting the firefighters looking up at them and imparting a surreal orange glow to the D.C. skyline beyond.

What most onlookers couldn't see, in the shadows beneath the smoke, was the frenetic activity aimed at reclaiming the building at first light, and making sure it would indeed reopen as Rumsfeld had promised. Several truckloads of huge generators had arrived from Andrews Air Force Base to provide power in the regions where the electricity had been shut down. But nobody knew how to operate them until Larry Callan, the school electrician, finally figured it out.

Even though no firefighters would go back up to the roof until morning, commanders were busy drawing up an aggressive plan for the roof. Aerial trucks were able to reach the roof from the outside, on the E Ring, which made it easy to get crews, hoses, tools, and supplies up there. But there was only one ladder truck in the courtyard that could reach the roof from the inside—Tower 20, from Montgomery County, Maryland, a "mid-mount" truck just low enough to fit through the tunnel. A Fairfax "telesquirt" was there too, with a boom and nozzle that could reach the roof, but it didn't have a ladder or basket capable of carrying firefighters or supplies up there. All the other ladder tracks on the scene were too tall to squeeze through the tunnel.

Commanders had figured out that the edge of the roof was about 85 feet high. That in itself wasn't a problem—most ladders were 100 feet or more. The challenge was finding a truck with a big enough ladder that was also small enough to fit through the tunnel.

At the command post, somebody mentioned to Chief Schwartz that they remembered an ancient ladder truck, smaller than modern ones, still being used by a volunteer fire company somewhere in Maryland. Staffers at the command post made a few calls and finally reached the Woodsboro Volunteer Fire Department, in rural Maryland, about 60 miles northwest of Washington.

Micky Fyock was the chief of the department, a volunteer like all of the firefighters—and a "big ol' farm boy," as he described himself, standing six-three and weighing about 360 pounds. In his regular full-time job Fyock was a supervisor at the 911 emergency communications center for Frederick County, Maryland, handling police, fire, and medical calls. It had been one of the busiest days in memory, and he'd just gotten home when his cell phone rang. A dispatcher from the same communications center where he worked was on the line. The incident commander at the Pentagon, he explained, was summoning Woodsboro's ladder truck to assist with firefighting operations. "Are you kidding me?" Fyock stuttered. The Woodsboro truck had to be one of the oldest operating in Maryland, and he wondered if one of his coworkers was joking with him. But as he listened to the explanation, he realized the request was for real.

Ladder 16, the only ladder truck in Woodsboro, was a 1954 Mack model with a 65-foot aerial ladder mounted on the top. The truck had a small profile compared to modern apparatus: Its total height off the ground, with the ladder down, was only about eight feet. Woodsboro needed a small ladder truck because the fire station's bay doors were only ten feet high. Besides, it did the job just fine, especially since there were few buildings in the district taller than three stories.

Fyock rushed to the station, thinking about how best to accomplish the mission. In an ordinary fire, procedures were straightforward. All the volunteers would be alerted by pager, and those who arrived at the station first would be the ones to suit up for the fire. That produced competition—and, occasionally, reckless driving—since volunteers would usually speed to the station, hoping to make the cut. But it was fair, and it preempted claims of favoritism.

This was no routine fire, however. Woodsboro would be in the national spotlight. Fyock wondered if he should select the most experienced firefighters in the company. Then he decided no, he'd go about it just like any other fire. Since the mission called for just one truck, the first group of fully qualified firefighters to arrive at the station would be the ones to go to the Pentagon.

The call went out, and within minutes Fyock had his four firefighters. He gathered them around and gave a quick pep talk. "Our brothers and sisters need our help," he said. "Our country needs us, and we are on the way without question."

Only two firefighters could fit in Ladder 16, since the cab had only two seats. Rob Compton, the department's assistant chief, drove the truck, with Steve Devilbiss in the passenger seat. Fyock climbed into his command vehicle, a converted police cruiser, with Michael Strausbough and Michael Cornell, a 19-year-old rookie fresh out of fire school. With the roads deserted, in the middle of the night, they got to the Pentagon in just over an hour. Fyock expected the group to be searched and interrogated before getting into the building but was amazed that they only encountered one elderly security guard, who quickly waved them past a checkpoint. As they pulled up to the monumental building, it was hard to believe they were actually going to participate in the firefight. Their hearts pounded, fearful that they'd be turned away at the last minute.

In South Parking, Fyock asked how to get to the inner courtyard. Somebody pointed toward the tunnel and told him to "follow the hose," which led to the courtyard, and report to the A&E division commander. The fat supply lines running through the tunnel had been cordoned off with wooden blocks that ran across the road, to keep vehicles from running over the hoses and wrecking them. As Ladder 16 bounced over the blocks, Fyock worried that the truck was going to bang against the top of the tunnel and not make it through. But a moment later they pulled into the open courtyard.

The ground was littered with bandages, papers, and empty water bottles. Fyock saw people laying out body bags. Flags marking evidence dotted the trampled grass. In addition to the smoke, he noticed the smell of jet fuel in the air. The other firefighters in the courtyard were wearing different-colored gear, some black, some yellow, some white, since they came from a number of departments.

It was a moving sight, and Fyock gathered his group once more. "Boys," he said, "this will be the largest and most important task this truck and crew will ever be involved with in our lifetime. God give us the strength to carry out our task, even if we have to tow the vehicle back in pieces, and me in a hearse." Ladder 16, he told his men, was "the little truck that could."

The overnight commander in the courtyard was Battalion Chief Denny Martin from Reagan National Airport, a laconic, neighborly fellow. He walked up to Fyock and offered his hand. "Chief, how can I help you help us?" he asked. Fyock was relieved by the friendly welcome. Instead of a small-time outsider, it made him feel like part of the fraternity.

The assignment was to back Ladder 16 against the building, raise the ladder, and stretch a hose up the ladder to the roof. They scouted for the best location, moved aside a van that was in the way, and backed the truck into place. Then they stretched hose onto the ladder, which was still flat, locking the nozzle onto the top rung and tying the hose to a few of the lower rungs with rope. Finally, they raised the ladder—and disappointment set in. Martin had thought he was getting a truck with a ladder tall enough to reach the 85-foot-high roof. The Woodsboro truck only had a 65-foot ladder, with another eight feet added for the height of the truck. It wasn't enough. The top rung of the ladder settled against the Pentagon's inner wall a few critical feet short of the roof. It would still help spraying water up and over the eave, onto the roof, but it was too short to transport firefighters or supplies up there.

Still, the water was needed on the roof, and they started a pumping operation. Fire crews ran a supply line from one of the other engines in the courtyard to Ladder 16 and started pumping water into the hose that went near the roof. Unlike modern fire trucks, Ladder 16 didn't have remote control to operate the hose, the ladder, or the turntable on which the ladder sat. So they rigged up a pulley system, with ropes, to manipulate the hose and direct the water stream up or down, and to turn the ladder's turntable to the left or right.

Once they got the water flow stabilized, it only took two crew members to operate the hose. So as the night progressed, Fyock rotated his men, and ventured into the building several times with those taking a break from the hose. Their eyes met the same wrenching sights that others had seen: The damage inside was far more devastating than you'd guess from the relatively intact outer facade. There was ankle-deep water everywhere. Papers marked SECRET floated in the water, and body parts appeared to bob up and down. It was dark and haunting, with the only illumination coming from the flashlights they carried.

In the courtyard, it was strangely calm, with Pentagon officials drifting in and out in small numbers. An Army captain found Denny Martin, the courtyard fire commander, and asked if he could retrieve some documents from an office in the B Ring, which had suf-

fered smoke damage but was unburned. Martin sent in a reconnaissance team to check it out. They said the area was safe enough, so he
had a fire crew escort the captain to his office, where he got what he
needed.

Two civilians approached Martin and asked if they could go into
another office on the B Ring. "How about just one of you?" Martin
asked. There was no point endangering two people if one could get
the job done.

"Nope," one of the men answered. "We both have to go." He
looked at Martin expectantly but didn't explain. The fire chief paused
for a moment, then figured they had to open a safe or secured area
that required two people, and that each of them knew part of a code
or combination. Like in the movies.

"Okay, you can both go in," he decided, and rounded up another
fire crew to escort them in.

Martin knew the roof fire was getting worse. He couldn't see the
flames from where he was in the courtyard, but the glow that ringed
the top of the building indicated the fire's presence—and it got
brighter as the night wore on. When the winds shifted, smoke wafted
down and filled the courtyard, like a desert sandstorm that came out
of nowhere. He told several of the crews on standby in the courtyard
to go down Corridor 5 and wait out by the helipad. He'd call for them
on the radio if needed, but meanwhile there was no point breathing
the smoke if they didn't have to.

As daybreak neared, more people seemed to be crowding into the
courtyard, as if anticipating a pickup in activity once dawn broke.
Fyock saw one man in civilian clothes wandering around the courtyard with tears in his eyes, and approached him. The man looked
stricken, and slung his arm around the fire chief. "Are you okay?"
Fyock asked.

The man explained that his office was in the section that had been
hit by the plane. "I was at the dentist," he said absently. "I missed

being in the attack by five minutes." He was okay—but many of his co-workers were not.

Fyock led the man to a bench. The country fire chief wasn't trained as a counselor, but he knew how to comfort a victim. They sat for a while, Fyock listening while the man cried and talked.

★ 31 ★

EXPLAIN THIS

3:00 A.M.

Fire crews were treading lightly inside the Pentagon, but the FEMA search-and-rescue teams had plenty to do. In addition to digging victims out of rubble, the FEMA teams specialized in stabilizing damaged structures, a kind of commando construction work that often had to be done rapidly, under dangerous conditions. In the aftermath of earthquakes or bombings, with debris sealing victims into airtight void spaces, it was often necessary to rapidly shore up a structure so it wouldn't come crashing down on rescuers. It was a race that pitted hammers, saws, and hasty craftsmanship against dwindling air and spilling blood: Shoring had to be erected as quickly as possible, to maximize the chance of saving people, yet flimsy work could end up costing more lives than it saved.

Despite public assurances by Plaugher and other officials, there was little hope of finding live victims inside the furnace that the Pentagon had become. But it was still urgent to start shoring up parts of the building, since there was a serious risk of further collapse around the gash in the outer wall, which threatened anybody working in the damaged area. To recover the remains scattered throughout the wreckage, searchers would have to paw through debris tied in to walls and ceilings that could fall at any moment. Just walking in some of the hallways was dangerous. Virtually everything that still needed to be done depended on stabilizing the building.

Dean Tills, Leo Titus, and some of the other structural experts had been devising a plan all day, gauging the scope of the damage and refining their options. Most of the area remained too hot to work in, with fires still burning deeper inside the building. But Tills and the others had been eyeing the eviscerated E Ring space to the immediate left of the collapse zone. It was an obvious place to start. There was no fire. Three support columns ten feet apart had been obliterated—by Flight 77's left wing, they guessed. Yet five sagging stories of the Pentagon still levitated over the empty space. If they could erect shoring where the columns used to be, it would stabilize one of the most fragile areas still standing, and give them a toehold for working their way farther into the destruction.

The engineers explained their plan to several crew members, including Kent Watts, a rescue team leader in charge of much of the construction work—the foreman, in effect. Like Mike Regan, Watts was a Fairfax firefighter and longtime task force member who had been to earthquakes and bombings all over the world. He was also a master carpenter who ran his own small contracting firm, and a cigar lover who could tell a rough joke. His gruff demeanor could rankle those who didn't know him, but Watts impressed colleagues with the passion he showed for his work.

He had already spent several hours in the building, leading a team of rescuers. He'd witnessed more widespread destruction in the aftermath of earthquakes, but had never seen a standing building as fragile as the Pentagon seemed to be. The airplane had wiped out numerous support columns, and usually when a building absorbed that much structural damage, it just crumbled entirely. Everywhere Watts had looked, conditions seemed precarious. He felt sure they were going to lose some people. It might be five, he feared—or it might be 20. He had never begun a mission with such a sense of dread.

As Titus detailed the shoring scheme, Watts's worries grew. The engineers wanted to start to the left of the collapse zone, shoring up the outer edge of the building where the three cement columns had been ripped out, working in toward the most dangerous area right at the edge of the collapse zone. "Leo, you've got to be fucking kidding me," Watts protested. "I've been through every inch of this building and there's nothing holding it up!" If they put workers in there as Titus was suggesting, Watts felt the odds were good somebody would get killed.

He appealed to Dean Tills, the senior structural specialist. "I'm not sure about this one," he said. "The damage on the inside is bad. I'm not sure we can get in there safely." Watts asked about all the contractors on the scene. They had access to the equipment and expertise to do it with minimal risk. Why not let them do the most dangerous work?

Tills walked him through the details of his plan—how he had calculated the loads that the columns needed to uphold, the precise supports that were required, procedures for dealing with the debris that dangled menacingly over the work area. Tills also argued that the FEMA team had more expertise than the contractors in terms of working in dangerous conditions—along with the best safety procedures. Watts felt reassured by the engineer's methodical calculations and gradually relented, tweaking the plan slightly and insisting that workers venture into the structure no more than five feet or so.

Prep work for a shoring operation, meanwhile, had been getting under way. General Strock of the Army Corps of Engineers asked Tills what kind of help he needed. The fire hoses and deluge guns had created a muddy lagoon near the facade of the building and Tills said they needed to get it dried out, for all the cranes and trucks that would be arriving. A short while later contractors arrived and started laying a gravel roadbed. Tills had never seen such a rapid response.

Domenick Iannelli, the hazmat specialist on Mike Regan's team, was responsible for making sure there weren't any toxins in the burgeoning work site. A storage area that was part of the PenRen project was now in shambles—muriatic acid, used to clean brick and stone, had spilled everywhere, and other unknown liquids pooled on the ground. Iannelli started clean-up procedures and asked an Army officer for help; before long, two pickup trucks arrived with about a dozen soldiers who quickly cleaned up what had spilled and hauled away the rest.

A front-end loader began to gingerly clear out a work area close to the impact zone. Lumber, steel, and other supplies arrived from Home Depot and a variety of nearby construction sites. The Army's heavy engineering company from Fort Belvoir showed up, with 70 soldiers trained for battlefield conditions. The Salvation Army delivered food. The FEMA engineers realized they were in the midst of a "luxury disaster"—whatever they asked for, they were likely to get.

Shoring operations began with a lot of grunt work. FEMA workers and soldiers from the Army's engineering company crowded in to delicately remove stone, concrete, metal, and chunks of office furniture by hand, forming the equivalent of a bucket brigade to pass it outward. Watts and a couple of safety officers watched over the removal of the debris and made sure nobody traveled too far into the building or jarred the fragile structure any more than necessary.

At the far left of the area they were focusing on, a support column had bowed out in the middle, but not collapsed. Tills told Watts to have his crews build a temporary "post shore" next to the column, a relatively simple piece of work that would help hold up the structure and give them a bit of protection while they built more robust shores closer to the collapse zone. "If the building moves," Tills instructed Watts, "the post shore will start to crackle and bend, and give you a little warning to get out."

When enough space had been cleared, Watts, the master carpenter, pulled out the pencil that was perpetually resting behind his ear and jotted down the dimensions of the wood they would need. A cut station had been set up, with power saws and other tools, and a full load of six-by-six lumber was piled up, ready for the saw. Leo Titus stood about 40 feet back from the building, squinting through a transit instrument focused on specific points near the collapse area. His assignment was to watch for any movement that might signal a further collapse, and keep a log of developments that he was required to update every 15 minutes. Titus had an air horn he could blow the moment he saw anything that looked dangerous, signaling all the workers to scramble to safety.

After the tedium of clearing out the rubble bit by bit, the construction work seemed to race along. Watts was standing back a few feet, keeping an eye on his crew, but also contemplating all the follow-on work they'd have to do deeper inside the building. There were dozens of different shoring techniques, and he was running many of them through his mind, trying to devise the most effective scheme for keeping the upper floors from pancaking down. Then, before he knew it, the first temporary shore was nailed in place. It had been a tall order, literally—the distance between the bottom of the first story and the second-story floor slab was a hefty 14 feet. But the work crew had constructed the shore in less than half an hour.

Tills, the engineer, inspected the work. It looked good. He told Watts to go ahead and start constructing a second shore closer to the collapse pile.

Meanwhile, Tills had more reconnaissance to do. A crane with a man-basket had arrived, and the engineer climbed inside to get a close-up look at some of the upper floors along the outer edge of the building where it was too dangerous to walk. The basket was about the size of a phone booth, with room for two people inside. Tills had the crane operator maneuver the basket right over the area where Watts's crews were working on the shores, so he could look at several structural stress points that were hard to see from the ground.

What he saw was distressing. In addition to the wrecked support columns and buckled floor beams, he noticed lots of loose concrete. That was a bad sign. Concrete was very strong when it was intact— but once fractured, it was liable to crumble quickly. Tills also saw that the steel reinforcing bars that had been used to construct the building were smooth, as he'd feared. That was typical of older buildings. Newer rebar was ridged and rough, which produced a stronger bond with the concrete that was poured around it. This smooth rebar wouldn't hold the concrete as well. Anchor points had been jarred loose, and huge pieces of debris hung ominously from the building. The whole structure near the collapse zone, all the way up to the roof, was extremely fragile.

The crews building the shores, meanwhile, had run into an inevitable, and grim, complication. While removing debris, they discovered some human remains tangled in with the wreckage. The shoring allowed them to get closer to the building, and the trained eyes of firefighters had spotted the remains, which were little more than gray skeletons with patches of white and red that stood out to those who knew what to look for.

Most of the rescue workers had encountered bodies before, and they knew that if you personalized the experience it could become emotionally paralyzing. It took a peculiar kind of professional detachment to deal respectfully with remains, while compartmentalizing your emotions. Leo Titus knew that too—it was part of the task-force training—yet the rookie had never encountered a body firsthand. As he peered into the rubble with a flashlight, he had trouble at first seeing what the other workers were pointing to. Then he noticed the telltale white and red splotches. As his eyes adjusted, he could make out what looked to be three or four different bodies, horribly mangled. He swallowed hard and backed away.

The FBI had made it clear that rescue workers were not to disturb or remove any remains. They were to stop what they were doing and let the FBI know immediately. So Watts called a halt to the work and summoned the FBI. One of the agents on duty was Mark Whitworth, a bomb expert whom Watts had worked with during the embassy bombings in Africa in 1998. Whitworth explained the procedures they needed to follow. "Anytime you find any piece of a body, you've got to let us know," he told Watts, "so we can mark it, photograph it, and bag it."

"Come on, Mark. You've got to be kidding me," Watts answered. "There are body parts all over. It will take forever to do that."

"Look, Kent, those are my orders," Whitworth told him. The plan seemed impossible to Watts, who figured they were going to find thousands of body parts, some no bigger than a fingernail, as they worked through the wreckage. It would take months to clear out the building if they had to stop for every grisly discovery. But for the time being they worked out a way for the FEMA crews to continue work on the outer shores, without disturbing the remains they had found. FBI agents, meanwhile, would get into the rubble and start documenting the remains.

Watts finished the discussion with a word of warning to Whitworth. "Listen," he cautioned the FBI agent, "whatever you do, I don't want you in there more than two or three feet, and only with a couple of people. There's a very good chance of collapse."

Even though it was the middle of the night, a lot of military and other officials were still milling around. FEMA rescue specialist Mike Regan had finally recovered, after throwing up behind the burned fire truck, and he persuaded the doctors to let him stay on the mission. Regan and Domenick Iannelli were out front, watching the shoring operation, when two Marines in uniform walked up to them with an American flag on a pole, the kind Iannelli and Regan had noticed standing in many of the offices. "We want to put this flag on the building," one of the Marines said. "Can you guys help?"

It seemed like a great idea. Iannelli went off to find somebody who could approve the use of the man-basket for hanging a flag over the building. The first FEMA official he asked said no, so Iannelli tracked down Dean Tills and asked him. By then, General Strock had added his support to the cause. Tills said yes.

They talked about various ways to place the flagpole atop the building, and finally Iannelli and one of the Marines got in the basket with the flag. Iannelli had some training as a rigger, working with cranes and scaffolding, and he'd be able to figure out an effective way to secure the flag. But he felt one of the Marines should be the one to actually hoist the colors. When they got to the roof, Iannelli found some cinder blocks that could form a base for the pole. While the Marine pushed the pole into place, Iannelli used wire and duct tape to attach it firmly to the blocks. The stars and stripes began to flap overtop the charred facade, just to the right of the gruesome gash.

On the lawn beneath the flag, Elizabeth Kreitler, the dog handler, was trying to get a couple of hours of sleep, with Nero, her 75-pound German shepherd, right next to her. Kreitler dozed and woke, dozed and woke. As she drifted in and out of sleep, she was aware of a crystalline, starry sky in one quadrant of her vision and a seared, crumbling building in another. She saw the flag atop the Pentagon, obscured on and off by smoke, and the continual movement of people and machinery. The nightscape changed every time her eyes creaked open, but one thing was always the same. Nero lay beside her like a sentry, his head up and his senses on high alert. Not once did he rest his chin on the grass and go to sleep. Well-trained search dogs were said to have an on-off switch, and Nero's was fully on.

For all the initial complications, the shoring work moved swiftly as the night progressed. Watts's crew began building a third shore, this one in the most dangerous spot of all, at the very edge where the building had been sheared off, right next to the five-story gash. Overhead, floor beams were bent and buckled. Holes were visible in the second-story floor. And to the right, the huge, steep pile of rubble hung like a landslide in suspended animation.

Watts was worried that the pile could slide farther and kill his workers, but he also wondered what would happen if it slid into the shoring they were about to put up right at the edge of the collapse zone. If an avalanche of debris kicked out the shoring, it might take the corner of the building with it—along with anybody who happened to be working there.

Watts and Tills discussed their options. Tills wanted the crew to build a structure called a five-member crib. But Watts felt a more robust support called a "solid crib" would be safer. "You don't need that much support," Tills assured him. "It's a waste of wood."

"I don't care about the wood," Watts said. "I'm more concerned about that big pile of rubble sliding into the crib and taking it out."

"Well, you're building it." Tills shrugged, then walked away.

Watts turned to his crew, waiting for instructions. "I want a solid crib tower wrapped in plywood," he ordered, upgrading the engineer's suggestion. The task force relied on its engineers for lifesaving judgment, but Watts and others joked that there were times when you simply had to ignore the mathematical-minded masters of reason and do your own thing. This was one of those times.

More FBI agents started coming around after Watts pointed out the remains in the rubble. With work on the third shore moving forward, Watts was talking with some of his crew members a few feet away from the building, his back to the Pentagon. He noticed that the people he was talking to had stopped paying attention to him and were looking at something over his shoulder.

When he turned around, he was startled to see about two dozen FBI agents picking through rubble, deep inside the building. He looked around for Mark Whitworth and started screaming. "Mark, what the fuck are you doing! I told you—noboby goes in there! Do you realize this building is about to collapse?"

Tills heard the commotion and came running over. Like Watts, he'd warned the FBI to be extremely careful and send no more than two people at a time into that part of the building. "Everybody out!" he shouted. "I told you—only two at a time!"

Whitworth looked around, and saw several teams of federal agents who had wandered 35 or 40 feet into the building. He wasn't in charge of all of them, but realized that he was the one FBI agent Watts knew, and could unload on. So he started yelling at everybody himself, ordering them out.

"I'm sorry," he said to Watts. "We just got carried away. Sorry. . . ."

"Don't you understand?" Watts pleaded. "You can't go in there! It's about to come down!"

Whitworth apologized some more. The evidence teams regrouped, while Watts and Tills simmered down.

The two men were about to go back to what they had been doing when a tall, imposing fire chief from the command post materialized. "Shut down your operation," he ordered Watts and Tills. "I want to talk to you."

Watts told the workers putting up the shoring to stand down until he returned. The fire chief led them to the main command post, which had been moved from the Arlington County police bus at the I-395 underpass to a more sophisticated Fairfax County vehicle near the helipad. Watts felt like he had been summoned to the principal's office.

Several chiefs were in the bus—it was the command staff managing the entire overnight operation. "What are you doing?" the big chief asked calmly.

Watts and Tills outlined the shoring operation.

"Do you realize you're in the collapse zone?" the chief asked.

The two men explained how the FEMA team was equipped and trained to operate in collapse situations, with Tills tossing in some engineering calculations and safety precautions to buttress their case.

"Okay, just one more question," the chief said. "Can you explain this?" He walked over to a TV mounted on a wall inside the bus and pushed a button. A recording of everything that had just happened began to play—the commanders had a videocamera fixed on the work site up front and were taping everything. Watts and Tills watched the whole scene they had just been a part of: the FBI agents tromping into the wreckage, the two of them running over and screaming. As structural experts, they were responsible for deciding whether the building was safe for people to work in, and they both turned red with embarrassment while watching a replay of the lapse.

The chief sent them back to work with a warning to play it safe. Watts expected a hammer to fall. "Man, I'm in big trouble," he grumbled.

Tills guessed that the commanders were just sending a message: *They were watching. No cowboys or heroes.* It was annoying to think that they were looking over his shoulder. But somehow, it also felt reassuring.

★ 32 ★

"WE CAN'T LET THEM WIN NOW"

September 12, daybreak

As the sun rose on Wednesday, September 12, Ed Plaugher was on the hillside by the Navy Annex, overlooking the Pentagon, getting his first complete view of the entire building since dusk the night before. What he saw alarmed him. The stubborn fire on the roof had not stayed in check after all. Plaugher could tell by the smoke that it had traveled down Corridor 5 a good distance, gone down Corridor 4, and turned the corner onto the roof over the A Ring, overlooking the courtyard. Having spread that far, it was a relatively short hop to other corridors, and possibly even to the other side of the Pentagon. Plaugher felt sick. It looked like the fire might go all the way around the building. That certainly wasn't what he had promised the military leaders when he decided to suspend firefighting operations overnight.

He hustled back to the command post, to make sure the roof got priority attention. He was preaching to the choir. Schwartz and the other commanders knew the roof fire had spread. Dozens of fresh fire crews were on the way, and as soon as they arrived, they'd be sent to the roof in force.

Randy Gray had gone home for the night, slept for a few hours, and was back at the Pentagon for another shift as operations commander. He was impressed to see that the FEMA teams built cribbing where the three outermost support columns had been destroyed; that was quick work. The commanders who were there all night looked beat—as Gray knew he must have looked when they relieved him the night before. One of the D.C. chiefs had been there the whole time—nearly 20 hours. He looked dreadful. Gray felt sorry for him.

G. O. Lyon was also till working, and he, Gray, and a few others developed an aggressive plan for the roof. The key spots were the juncture points on the A Ring, where Corridors 3 and 4 met and Corridors 5 and 6 met. That was where the fire was threatening to spread, and since the A Ring was the smallest of the five, it would be the fastest route for the fire to spread around the building. As a precaution, they planned to send crews far down the A Ring and the E Ring, in both directions, to make trench cuts and set up a last line of defense if the fire happened to surprise everybody—again—and spread that far. It was a big job that would take a lot of crews.

One of the first fresh fire commanders on the scene was John Gleske, a battalion chief from Fairfax County. Gleske was short and stocky, with the thick neck of a wrestler and a gregarious, back-patting manner that softened his harsher features. He had stayed back in Fairfax the day before, but gotten a call in the middle of the night at home, telling him to report to the Pentagon at 6:00 A.M. When he arrived, Randy Gray explained the operation, or at least as much as he knew about it. The overnight commanders had discarded the confusing names used earlier to identify sectors, like River Division and A&E Division, and replaced them with standard firefighting terminology. Now Division A, or Alpha, included everything in front of the crash site. Everything to the left of the crash site was Division Baker. Operations run out of the courtyard were Division Charlie, and everything to the right of the crash site was Division David. Gray told Gleske he'd be in charge of Division David.

"What do you mean, I'm in charge of it?" Gleske asked. "What kind of assessment have you done?"

"Treat the whole area as if you just arrived," Gray told him, "be-

cause I don't have a real good handle on what we've got right now."
When Gleske asked for more specific instructions, Gray answered,
"Just put the fire out."

Gleske could see that Gray had his hands full—he was still huddling with other commanders, making plans for the day. There might
not be a lot of guidance from the command post, and Gleske figured
he should be prepared to operate autonomously.

Gleske conducted his own size-up, talking to other fire commanders and looking things over. It wasn't clear whether fire was still
burning in the building, but there was fire on the roof for sure, probably underneath the tiles. Hoses attached to ladder trucks had been
pouring water onto the roof all night, but the surround-and-drown
strategy seemed to have done little good. The first thing to do was
shut down those hoses, so they could work up there.

Gleske led a group of about 25 firefighters down Corridor 4, into
the courtyard. Soot-covered fire crews who had been there all night
long were wearily starting to pack up their stuff, while eager-looking
reinforcements filtered in. Gleske found Denny Martin, the overnight
courtyard commander, and got all the hose lines turned off. Martin
gave him a quick briefing, but he didn't know a lot more than Randy
Gray. Since his orders had mainly been to keep firefighters out of
harm's way, Martin didn't have a detailed situation report. In a sense,
Gleske would be starting a new operation.

He split the Fairfax group into teams and sent them to various
floors of the building to check for fire inside and do reconnaissance.
They were duplicating some of the work done the day before but
were also able to search more thoroughly in areas that had been burning or too hot to enter. Among other things, they discovered several
bodies around a conference table that nobody seemed to have found
or marked.

With concerns heating up about the roof, Gleske got a radio call
from the command post stressing the importance of tackling the roof

fire. He did the same thing Ben Barksdale and numerous others had done the day before—he led his crews to the fifth floor, where they tried to pull down the ceiling so they could shoot water up into the space directly beneath the roof. Gleske and his crewmates puzzled through the problem just as their predecessors had, and realized that the only way to fight the roof fire was from atop the building.

Gleske led his group back to the courtyard, where there were now two tower trucks, each with a bucket that could raise three firefighters at a time onto the roof. He climbed inside one of them with two of his experienced fire captains to get a firsthand look at the roof and make a plan. They got additional input from another Fairfax battalion chief, who was overhead in a Park Police helicopter. Between them, they figured out that the fire on the Delta side was burning all along Corridor 4 and had turned the corner into the A Ring overlooking the courtyard. From there it had also spread to Corridor 3—and was heading back toward the E Ring, on a different spoke of the building. It was a complicated fire burning in several directions at once. And if it hit any other rings or corridors, the dimensions of the fire would multiply.

The firefighters would have to cut off the fire in half a dozen different places to fully extinguish it. They'd also need to run more hose lines up to the roof from the courtyard and from the outside of the building, over the E Ring. The aerial trucks in place on both sides of the building would have to be moved too, since the fire had spread beyond where they had originally been positioned the night before.

Gleske ferried his crews to the roof in the buckets on the tower ladders, along with saws, axes, and other tools. If the interior fire had been a roaring blaze, the situation on the roof reminded him of a brush fire. The flames were more of a smolder than a burn, but the smoke was so thick that when the wind kicked it up it was like working in the dark. The whole area was dangerous, and the crews started working with face pieces and air bottles right away.

They employed the same tactics as those who had come before, this time on the roof over both Corridor 4 and the A Ring roof overlooking the courtyard: The crews picked a spot several feet beyond what seemed to be the farthest reach of the fire and worked at making trench cuts. Gleske soon realized what an intractable problem he was facing, as his crews encountered the unforgiving concrete beneath the slate tiles.

As sweat started to pour down the crews' faces, they heard a huge boom. Something had exploded. Everybody stopped what they were doing. "What the fuck was that?" four or five voices shouted at once. The smoke was thick, and nobody could see more than a few feet into the distance. Frightened faces turned to Gleske. He had no idea what was happening, but he assumed the worst. Shit! he thought. How the hell did the terrorists get a bomb up here?

He grabbed his radio and called down to the commanders on the ground. Nobody knew anything. Then there was another explosion. Firefighters ducked and cursed louder. There was no way they could keep working, and Gleske thought about ordering his crews off the roof. He decided to look around to see if he could figure out where the explosions were coming from.

Gleske maneuvered down the A Ring toward Corridor 4, and discovered a small construction area on a flat part of the roof that he hadn't noticed before, right next to the part that was burning. He could see what looked like propane cylinders in the construction area. The water sprayed on the roof all night long had kept the flames and heat down, he guessed, but when they turned it off, the fire heated up again. The heat must have lit off a couple of the propane tanks.

Gleske quickly ordered crews to get hoses and spray down the construction area to prevent any more explosions. They also moved a couple of other cylinders to a part of the roof where there was no threat of fire. Then he explained to his crews what had happened.

The news was a relief, but the tension had revived fears from the day before: If terrorists could fly an airplane into the Pentagon, who knew what else they might be able to do?

Down by the command post, more fresh help was arriving. Dick Sterne, a D.C. battalion fire chief getting his first briefing on the operation, was surprised to hear that commanders had suspended offensive firefighting overnight. The D.C. Fire Department never would have done that, but suburban departments were often more conservative than those in big cities. Randy Gray put Sterne in charge of Division Baker—everything to the left of the crash site—and Sterne's crews climbed to the roof on one of the D.C. ladders, to hack through the slate and concrete and make sure the fire spread no farther than the E Ring and Corridor 5.

By the time Richie Bowers arrived at the Pentagon on September 12, incident commanders were pushing all the resources they could to the roof. Bowers was a district chief, the equivalent of a battalion chief, in Montgomery County, Maryland, a suburban community north of D.C., about 20 miles from Arlington. Like many of the other fire chiefs, Bowers blended managerial talents with a folksy, blue-collar manner. He was on a nickname basis with firefighters throughout the region, and knew Chief Schwartz and a number of others he saw in the command post. "Great job, guys," Bowers said when he checked in. "Montgomery is here. I've got 30-plus people. Where do you need us?" One of the command group officers told Bowers he was in charge of the roof division, pointed to a map of the Pentagon, and showed him how to get to the courtyard.

When the group got there, Bowers was surprised at all the fire trucks he saw, and wondered how they had gotten them all in there. There were now two tower trucks with baskets that could reach the roof, but he knew he would need several more ladder trucks for a roof operation—to get firefighters and supplies up, but also to have several ways down, in case there was an emergency and crews had to evacuate. There could be a collapse, an explosion, or an unexpected surge in the fire that might leave firefighters cut off if they weren't careful. Positioning ladders in various spots was a basic safety precaution.

Bowers found Denny Martin, the courtyard commander, and introduced himself. "I'm assigned to be the roof commander," he told Martin.

After doing little about the roof all night except watching it glow, Martin was thrilled that the cavalry was arriving. "You're assigned to the roof? Great!" he cheered. "Go put the fire out. Please!"

Bowers called out to the command post and asked for some additional ladder trucks in the courtyard. He assigned firefighters to replace the exhausted crews on the trucks that had been there all night. Then he climbed to the roof on one of the tower ladders, along with about two dozen others, to tackle the fire up top.

By the time he got up there, firefighters were climbing onto the roof from ladder trucks propped against the building on the helipad side and from a number of internal stairwells. He saw firefighters in about ten different locations. John Gleske's group was nearby, and Bowers called a huddle with them and a few other crews operating near the A Ring.

Bowers reminded the group of a basic principle of firefighting: What's burned is lost. There's no point worrying about that. Instead, try to save what isn't yet burned. So they should write off the parts of the roof that had already been blackened by fire, and focus on cutting it off before it spread to other parts. "Let's put our resources together," he encouraged the group. "We'll be remote, but working together, with the same game plan. Let's box it in." He dispersed the firefighters in small groups to various spots, mostly on the A Ring, where they would hack through the concrete, create firebreaks, and wrestle the sprawling fire until they pinned it down and defeated it.

In the command bus by the helipad, Randy Gray was busy managing the complex logistics of what had become a bigger roof operation than anybody expected. They were now using cranes to hoist saws, rope, hoses, safety lines, cases of bottled water, and even portable toilets onto the roof. There were other priorities too; fires inside the building still needed to be thoroughly doused, and the entire interior, including areas that had been unreachable the day before, had to be searched room by room to locate all the bodies that would have to be removed.

Commanders also had to spread firefighters around more carefully than the day before. The massive surge of manpower was receding, as some of the more-distant jurisdictions recalled their crews and started to put their regular shift systems back in place. Arlington command would have to set up a rotational system, relying on its own firefighters and those from Alexandria, Fairfax, and a few other mutual-aid partners. Gray and his staff were trying to throw every resource they could at the roof, but they also had to make sure fresh crews would be available for the night shift and for days to come.

It felt like a fairly orderly operation was falling into place—until a general nobody recognized walked up to the outside of the command bus, where the fire commanders were gathered. "We've got a problem," he announced, walking over to a map of the building hanging on the side of the bus. Everybody stopped talking. "If the fire gets past this or this," the general said gravely, highlighting two different spots on the roof, "they win. We'll have to shut down the Pentagon."

A hubbub erupted. Gray wondered why the hell nobody had mentioned this problem last night, when they could have been more aggressive, instead of letting the fire burn and waiting till morning. But he kept the thought to himself. Schwartz was there, and he quieted everyone and asked for details.

The general elaborated. "Over there are all the communications for the Pentagon," he said, pointing at the map, indicating a huge stack of computer and electronic equipment that was the nerve center for the building. "And over there," he continued, marking another spot, "are the satellite linkages for all of our deployed troops. We need to save both of those."

Schwartz digested the news. Then he asked, "What if I can't save both? Which one do you want?"

The general thought for a moment. "The comms," he said.

Gray felt stirred. The mission suddenly seemed even more important than before. We can't let them win now, he thought.

The fire commanders plunged into the problem. G. O. Lyon summoned a building engineer and asked him to explain exactly how the roof was constructed, so they could understand why the fire was so difficult to put out.

The engineer explained that the slate tiles were affixed to wood planking, which sat on top of concrete slabs. "And you can't get to it from the top floor," he said, telling Lyon what numerous fire crews had already discovered. "You have to get underneath the slate. Oh, and beneath that, there's horsehair insulation."

"Horsehair?" Lyon asked, leaning in toward the engineer in disbelief.

"Yes," the engineer assured him. "When they built it, they used horsehair insulation."

"I never heard of that," Lyon scoffed. The engineer quickly explained that it had been a common building material in the 1940s, before synthetic insulation became popular. If nothing else, it might explain the odd white smoke that encircled the roof.

Lyon and Gray tore up the measured rotational system they were putting in place and got on the radios to surge crews up to the roof. Schwartz made sure Richie Bowers understood the urgency. "Let's get that fire out now," he said soberly over the radio. "Put . . . it . . . out."

Gray also summoned Dick Sterne from D.C., who came over to the command post. "Look, we've got a problem," Gray said, pointing to a diagram of the Pentagon and explaining about the endangered equipment. "If fire gets to that, it will be real bad. This is critical to national security."

Like Gray, Sterne felt stirred by the gravity of the mission. "We'll get on it good," he told Gray. "I'm going to need some more people to do all that. Do you have any you can give me?"

"No," Gray said. "Can you get some from D.C.?"

"Shouldn't be a problem," Sterne answered. He got on the radio to D.C. communications and called for a "special alarm," asking for eight vehicles with their crews, plus two additional battalion chiefs.

There were other pressing concerns in D.C., where fire commanders were still bracing for possible follow-on attacks at the White House or other landmarks. But D.C. could offer six vehicles and two battalion chiefs. It was a fair compromise. "Send 'em," Sterne said.

THE WIDOWMAKER

September 12, 7:00 A.M.

By Wednesday morning Arlington fire captain Dan Fitch was one of the most frustrated people in Virginia. On September 11, Fitch had been at the meeting in D.C. where FBI agent Chris Combs was teaching crowd-control tactics. Fitch raced back to Arlington with his colleagues Bob Gray and Scott McKay, in a Dodge Ram pickup truck, all three of them holding their fire helmets out the windows to signal other cars out of the way, since they didn't have a siren or flashing light. Fitch's fellow firefighters had all ended up at the Pentagon in short order, but Fitch got trapped in a procedural no-man's-land, waiting all day for a chance that never came.

By the time he reached his firehouse, Station 4, his regular unit, Quint 104, had left for the Pentagon without him. Fitch hurried to Station 1, where all the follow-on crews were forming up. While other firefighters were being bused to the Pentagon, Fitch was told he'd be assigned to a ladder truck from Alexandria. But as his colleagues went to the fire one by one, he kept waiting. His ride never showed up.

With his home station overflowing with backfillers that night, Fitch went to Station 9, a few miles away, to spend the night and prepare for the morning shift. Lean, quiet, and intense, with a ponytail and a perpetual patch of stubble on his face, Fitch found it impossible to sleep. He spent the night pacing the floor and watching the TV footage with strangers, shocked at the deaths in New York. He wondered if his own comrades were okay and when he would make it to the firefight to do his small share.

When dawn finally arrived, Fitch went back to Station 4—where things finally started falling into place. Bobby Beer, Paul Marshall, Chad Stamps, and Fred Kawatsky had politely declined the free breakfast waiting for them at the Courtyard Hotel, and hurried back to Station 4 to see what their assignments would be for the day. When Fitch finally saw his crewmates, he hugged every one of them. "God, it's good to see you guys!" he said, smiling. Marshall and Stamps described how they had run from the building during the first evacuation, right before the section they were in came tumbling down. "Man, I'm glad you guys didn't die!" Fitch said, patting backs and shoulders.

The Arlington County Fire Department had a technical rescue team—known by its acronym, TRT—with duties similar to the FEMA teams. They were trained to operate in collapsed buildings, rescue victims trapped beneath rubble, and stabilize damaged structures so rescue crews could work. The TRT was smaller than the FEMA teams, though, with a combination of specially trained Arlington and Alexandria firefighters. It was only responsible for local incidents, and didn't have the federal funding, sophisticated equipment, structural engineers, or international renown of the FEMA teams.

Fitch, Beer, Marshall, and Brian Spring were all members of the TRT, along with about 60 others who started filtering into Station 4. The TRT was split into two shifts, with Scott McKay and Bob Gray as team leaders. Eventually they'd separate into day and night shifts, but for the time being both teams were to assemble at the Pentagon, set up a base of operations, coordinate with the FEMA teams, and size up the mission. And they'd have to plan for a much longer, more complex operation than the TRT had ever undertaken. When most of the team members were assembled at Station 4, Gray and McKay gathered them together and outlined the requirements. "If you're going to be on this job," McKay told the group, "I need a commitment to be here for two weeks." He paused and scanned the faces before him. Nobody flinched.

They worried, though. The FEMA teams would be in charge of the overall shoring and debris-removal operation at the Pentagon, and it wouldn't be surprising if the Arlington group's rivals from Fairfax treated them like the junior varsity. "I wonder if they'll just tell us to stand off to the side, since we're not FEMA," grumbled Jim Anderson, who had arrived back at Station 4 after a few restless hours of sleep at home. Others echoed his concerns.

By the time the Arlington TRT got to the Pentagon, an army of search-and-recovery specialists was forming. An additional FEMA team from Virginia Beach arrived overnight, and another one, from Tennessee, was on the way, for a total of four. Plus, there was the engineering company under General Jackson's command. Bob Gray marveled at the shoring that FEMA teams had done overnight. Having been inside the day before, and noticing how fragile the bent walls and sagging ceilings were, he was amazed that they'd done such work in a building that seemed ready to collapse.

Gray assumed that the Arlington group would get bundled into the FEMA operation, but as they were getting set up at the Pentagon, nobody offered any formal guidance. So he started formulating his own plan. Since they were unlikely to execute any rapid rescues at this point, the shoring crews would be able to take a bit more time and add a margin of safety. They'd need it: For all the engineering expertise on hand, nobody knew what happened when an airplane flew into a building. The safest assumption was that the building would collapse. "Just look at New York," Gray reasoned.

Gray met with the commander of the Army engineering unit, Capt. Aaron Barta, and they discussed strategy. The general principle in collapses was to shore from clean to dirty—start with the safest areas and work into the most fragile. As Gray and Barta stared into the ruptured wedge of the Pentagon, it wasn't hard to conceptualize a logical plan of attack. The safest approach would be to work inward from Corridor 5, to the left of the collapse pile, toward the heart of the damage, where the support columns had been totally blown out.

But others had different ideas. As the TRT was getting organized, Kent Watts, who was still on the job after working all night to get the three shores constructed, approached the Arlington group. Engineers from the Fairfax team had analyzed many of the support columns deeper inside the building and drawn up detailed shoring plans. The overnight progress had created momentum, and with daylight, task force leaders were eager to quicken the pace of operations.

Watts found Gray and told him they needed manpower to help remove debris. The Arlington group numbered about 50, and Gray said they were ready to work. "Okay, here's the plan," Watts said. "We need you to start debris removal and shoring straight through the impact zone."

That was not what Gray had in mind. The impact zone was the most dangerous place they could possibly start—it could tumble further at any minute. Plus there was nobody in there to rescue. The last thing he wanted to do was provoke a confrontation with FEMA officials, especially since he figured he was accountable to their chain of command—and was pretty far down the ladder. But if he was going to take a stand, this was the time. "That's not an acceptable way to do it," he asserted. "We're not going to put all our folks under that kind of risk for minimal gain. It's not an option."

It turned out that Watts, who had been deeply concerned about the safety of his own crews a few hours earlier, had similar worries. So did some of the structural engineers and experts from Virginia Task Force 2, who had been arguing that it was unwise to trudge into the most rickety part of the building. But somebody atop the chain of command felt it was important for the public to see rescue workers

braving the risk of tumbling concrete in the hole bored by the hijackers. Watts looked flustered, not to mention exhausted. He went back
to his commanders at the FEMA base of operations, and walked back
over to Gray a moment later. "Look, nobody's happy with this," Watts
explained. "But this is not optional. It's a sensitive issue, and it's very
political. It's very important that we show the world we're marching
in the same hole that the airplane went through."

"You know as well as I do," Gray retorted, "that there's nobody to
save in that hole."

Watts agreed. But the word had come down from many levels over
his head. "It's not an option," Watts reiterated. "These are your orders."

Gray was getting testy. He knew Watts had been in charge of
building the shores overnight and had done impressive work. But
this was going too far. "Listen, I want very badly to work on this
building," Gray said. "But I am not sending my folks in there. You
have to approach a piece of wet bread from the drier areas." That
drew a chuckle from Barta, the Army captain, who was standing next
to Gray, taking in the whole exchange.

Watts was getting exasperated too. He was only passing on orders,
not generating them himself. Plus he had been working for about 18
hours. But after a few more tense words with Gray, he agreed to go
back to the command post and press the case once more.

"Look," he pleaded at the command post, "here's one more group
that doesn't want to do it this way. Now Arlington is against it, Fairfax is against it, the engineers are not crazy about it. We need to
reevaluate the way we're gonna do this."

The debate, it turned out, went all the way to the White House.
Top government officials wanted a display of determination and
bravado by crews tackling the debris pile head-on, straight into the
hole, visible to the world via the TV cameras perched at the Citgo station. But fire and rescue commanders, with a more acute sense of the

danger, were more conservative. They wanted to start in areas they knew were relatively stable, and move inward, slowly, from there. Some of them felt the debris pile itself was the only thing holding up adjacent parts of the building. Sending workers straight in there, they argued, might be the very thing that would trigger another collapse.

Bob Gray heard nothing for about 30 minutes, and he tried to cool off. At the command post, Watts, irritated, was waiting for final orders. Finally, the officials who had been insisting on marching into the hole relented, and word was passed to Watts: Do it your way.

Watts strode back to the front of the building and called for various rescue teams to gather around. "Okay guys, listen up!" he hollered. "Here's what we're gonna do. We've decided for safety reasons to approach from the safe areas to the dangerous areas. We're going to start on the Corridor 5 side and work our way on down."

Gray and Barta exchanged glances, each surprised and relieved. Gray had prepared himself for some kind of reprimand. But instead his insistence had persuaded commanders to change the plan—even if he wasn't getting credit for it. It felt like Arlington had established itself as a legitimate part of the operation. They were part of the A Team.

With the three shores built beneath the most vulnerable part of the E Ring, the next priority was removing the remains that the FEMA workers had found in the rubble overnight. Removing them quickly, rather than letting them sit, was the decent thing to do. There was additional urgency on account of their location, so close to the outside of the building. Photographers with telephoto lenses might be able to shoot pictures of the remains from the hill overlooking the Pentagon, and the FBI was determined to prevent the unnecessary publication of gory pictures. Plus, the FEMA commanders didn't want their crews working in the vicinity of visible bodies any longer than they had to.

Even though the remains were only a few feet inside the building, it was a complicated matter getting them out. There were several body parts, and they were entangled with rubble that search crews would have to clear away. Plus, the rubble itself was lashed into the walls and other structural elements. Just moving it could cause another rupture in the building. On top of that, a huge piece of stone was suspended over the area where crews would have to work, hanging from a piece of the building's framework. If it fell, it could easily kill anybody it landed on.

Gray and a TRT colleague, Sam Short, volunteered to go to the third floor and dislodge the "widowmaker," as they called the deadly piece of stone. When they got to the third floor, they were surprised that the widowmaker was hanging outside the window of an office that seemed to have been untouched, even though it was less than 50 feet from where the plane entered the building. The blast-proof window was still intact, and they brought a battery-powered saw, Halligan bar, and a couple of axes to bash through it.

Like many of the rescue specialists, Gray and Short took pride in the quality and precision of their work. Technical rescue was an elite fraternity, and those who belonged to it were proud and competitive. They checked out each other's techniques, scrutinizing the exactitude of right angles and examining wood cuts to see if they were perfectly plumb. Crews would paint their names on shoring jobs they wanted to show off. By tackling a job outside a window on the E Ring, visible to everybody on the lawn, Gray and Short would be putting their skills on wide display.

The main challenge was breaking through the window, to get to the widowmaker, a chunk of sandstone the size of a suitcase. They started by battering the window with an axe, trying to make a hole for the saw. Short was a big roughneck, six-three, who loved bull work and every other aspect of firefighting. He swung the axe with gusto, with Gray taking a few turns. It took about 50 blows to make a two-inch hole. It was tiring, almost embarrassing. "Goddamnit, this is sturdy stuff," Gray huffed.

They finally worked the saw into the hole, but there was some kind of polymer in the glass that became supersticky the moment the saw touched it and gummed up the blade. That rendered the saw ineffective. They tried to bang a bigger hole in the window, but gave up in frustration. Finally they managed to pry off a corner of the window, which created just enough room to reach out and bang the widowmaker free. It crashed to the ground, their job finished. But it was ugly-looking work. When they got back outside and looked up at the window, it was so sloppy that they didn't want anybody to know they had done it.

With the widowmaker gone, a small crew got to work removing debris around the remains and building a couple of additional shores to make sure the structure stayed upright. Just as before, other workers continually wandered into the danger zone, to string lights or check other aspects of the structure, oblivious to the danger that concrete could come crashing down on them without notice. Gray and others repeatedly waved them out.

As the work around the remains slowly progressed, the rest of the recovery operation matured. Many of the crews that had worked overnight finally got a break and boarded buses to the Washington Navy Yard, where they could eat, shower, and sleep. There were no beds or cots, but most of the task force members were used to harsh field conditions, and they had bedrolls or sleeping bags in their gear. But Leo Titus had never deployed before and wasn't as well-prepared. After eating breakfast and watching the news on TV for a while, he went to sleep on the bare floor of an empty classroom, using a shirt for a blanket.

The search crews not working on the specific missions near the collapse zone spent the morning setting up lumber stations, planning logistics, getting oriented, and waiting for assignments. Scott McKay and Bob Gray broke the Arlington TRT into eight squads, each with about eight members. Dan Fitch was one of the squad leaders, and since he hadn't been at the Pentagon the day before, he asked a couple of team members who had been to walk through the building with him. Brian Spring and Chad Stamps led Fitch into the doorway near the helipad, to the right of Corridor 5, and they walked down the twisted remnants of the "executive hallway" that ran between Corridors 4 and 5, parallel to them.

The burn patterns looked familiar, like those Fitch had seen in dozens of building fires. But he'd never seen so much destruction. He gauged the damage in terms of the debris removal and shoring work the teams would have to do. Toward the outer edge of the building the debris was imposing, plowed randomly into shoulder-high piles. Much of it was furniture and other big objects. The debris got much denser as they went deeper into the building, as if the force of the plane had swept it all toward the interior. Cables, wires, and reinforced steel bound rubble together in unthinkable ways, and Fitch saw some materials in the mess that he didn't even recognize. There were dozens of flags marking remains, but still, they saw at least half a dozen bodies that hadn't previously been discovered and were unmarked.

"Holy shit," he murmured. He needed some help. He'd just been promoted to captain and was relatively new to technical rescue. Though comfortable being in command of the squad, he didn't feel he had enough experience to make the tactical decisions they'd need to. It was an extraordinarily complex mission for a rookie commander.

Back outside after his orientation tour, Fitch found Bobby Beer, one of his team members. Beer had done technical rescue for years, and participated in dozens of training exercises, and he even ran his own small business selling technical-rescue equipment. But because of his disdain for the brass, he'd never angled to become an officer.

Now, Fitch needed his expertise. "Hey, Bobby," he said, "I'll make a deal with you. How about you function as the squad leader, while I become the safety officer? I'll be responsible for command decisions.

But you'll call the shots on the technical stuff." Beer agreed. Both of them realized there was no need to formalize the switch. Better to just work things out without bothering the bosses.

The group working to free the body parts at the edge of the E Ring finally called the FBI. The shoring crews had built a couple of shores in the area, to prop up the weakest parts of the structure, and they'd removed the heavy debris obstructing access to the remains. It was time for the FBI to formally recover them.

Tom O'Connor was still running the overall evidence-recovery operation, which included the recovery of bodies. His group had been broken down into several teams, and his wife, Jean, was one of the team leaders. Since it was risky, Tom knew he'd have to go in with his wife. He imagined having to face his mother-in-law if something happened to Jean on his watch and he wasn't in there with her. He decided he'd rather take his chances with the Damoclean concrete in the E Ring.

They went to the edge of the building, where FEMA's collapse experts briefed them as they peered into the rubble. Jean was the shortest person in the group, and as she looked up at the building, her heartbeat raced. The FEMA briefers told them to be extremely careful about what they touched. If they pulled on the wrong thing, the ceiling might fall down on them. Then they mapped out the best approach, which everyone agreed was to enter Corridor 5 and turn right.

Tom and Jean went over procedures for tagging the remains, assigning them a number, photographing them, and placing them in body bags. Finally, in a brief private moment, Jean told her husband, "If something happens to me, make the phone call to my mother." Then she nervously chuckled at the prospect, just as her husband had. If something happens, she thought, Mom is going to kick his ass.

Jean gathered her team of eight together and gave a short pep talk.

"Don't move anything," she urged. "We're going to photograph things exactly as they are. Be careful where you step. Be conscious of where you are. Watch out for wires." They all zipped up their Tyvek suits, meant to protect them from hazardous substances, and put their respirators in place. Tom did the same. Then a couple of the FEMA workers led them into the building.

Jean was anxious. She felt honored to be doing such a solemn job but couldn't help thinking that this wasn't why she'd joined the FBI— to look for body parts. She figured everybody else on her team felt the same way. As a team leader, she knew she had to do the same uncomfortable work as everyone else and depersonalize the experience as much as possible—for her own well-being, and to set an example for the others.

They maneuvered their way into the thick of the rubble and found the remains at the bottom of a tall pile of debris. The search crews had thoroughly cleared the area, pushing furniture and other big objects out of the way, without disturbing the remains. Jean approached the pile with a couple of her team members. They still needed to move some smaller debris out of the way, and they worked around to a side of the pile that allowed them the easiest access. She and a few others got on their knees and began pulling out pieces of concrete and other building materials by hand.

The remains were in terrible shape, barely resembling a human form, and everyone was eager to get the work over with quickly. The team's photographer spent a few minutes photographing the body parts. Others noted the location of the remains and jotted information on evidence tags. Then Jean and a couple of others gently lifted the remains into a blue body bag. It was a horrible moment, impossible to depersonalize, as flesh and bone bound by little more than ash tore away from each other. No one spoke as they zipped up the bag.

The military had asked that all of the remains recovered from inside the Pentagon be formally removed from the building by uniformed troops. They would take care of their own, just like soldiers on a battlefield. The FBI agreed, and General Jackson had arranged for soldiers from the Old Guard—the elite ceremonial unit based at Fort Myer—to be on-call to carry every set of remains out of the building.

Once the body had been placed in the bag, the FBI called for a military detail to come in and carry it out. Two young soldiers arrived, with their own FEMA escort, and somberly carried the bag back through the rubble and out of the building, to a refrigerated truck waiting right at the entrance.

The rest of the group followed, drained and subdued. Jean O'Connor felt relieved to get out safely, and awed by the enormous job that lay ahead. Tom O'Connor felt relieved too. He wouldn't have to face his mother-in-law after all. But mostly he felt proud of his wife.

★ 34 ★

THE TILLER CAB

10:00 A.M.

When John Gleske first got to the roof, it struck him as a "property" operation: Their job was to save part of a building, not lives or valuables. But now the property operation was a vital national security mission. If they didn't stop the fire and put it out, key military capabilities would be lost or compromised.

They were finally getting the kind of attention a high-priority mission deserved. Firefighters were swarming the roof. Plenty of hoses and water were available: Crews had hauled up a couple of big three-inch supply lines in ladder baskets on both sides of the building and run several hand lines off the supply lines. They had also used the buckets to ferry supplies to the roof, along with lots of bottled water—and Gatorade, a luxury.

With about 50 firefighters on a relatively small portion of the roof, Gleske and Bowers still needed additional ladders placed up against the building, in case they had to get down in a hurry. The two groups were working fairly close to each other, but were separated by burned-out sections of the roof that were risky to traverse. The closest escape route for Bowers's group was via the A Ring, down into the courtyard. For Gleske's group, the E Ring would be the quickest way down. There were tower trucks with buckets on both sides of the building, but it would be slow going if they had to evacuate the whole group in a couple of buckets. Woodsboro's little ladder truck, in the courtyard, didn't reach the roof. And nobody had shown Gleske or Bowers any roof hatches leading to interior stairwells. The D.C. group up on the roof in Division Baker had better options, with a ladder truck leaning against the building and a couple of hatches in their area of the roof that led down into the building. But they were too far away to help the Montgomery and Fairfax crews.

The two chiefs both called down and asked for additional ladders, on both the courtyard and the E Ring sides. Things were busy, the command post reported, and besides, they had sent home much of the apparatus that had been on the scene the last 24 hours. But as soon as some extra ladders were available, they'd be put into place.

Meanwhile, there were plenty of other things to sort out. The A Ring was a more dangerous place to work than the Corridor 4 roof where Ed Hannon and Ben Barksdale had worked the day before, because it sloped right down over the edge of the building, with no ledge to add a safety margin. Crews worked in groups of four, with two firefighters manning saws or axes and two others anchoring them with rope, to make sure nobody fell. The horsehair insulation was a particular annoyance. It seemed to smolder everywhere beneath the slate tiles, and spread the moment you turned your back on it, stinking up the whole area in the bargain. The fire crews were improvising tactics as they went along, which produced more frustration than satisfaction. September 12 was as balmy as the day before, and as the sun rose, it started to get hot on the roof. Crews were working without rest, since getting the fire out was now an urgent matter.

And then there was a fresh complication that neither chief had anticipated: The air horns on the fire trucks surrounding the Pentagon started blaring—the evacuation signal. "All personnel evacuate the building," somebody was saying on the radio. "We have an unidentified aircraft, inbound to your location, ten miles out."

Once again air-traffic controllers at Reagan National had spotted an aircraft on their scopes that wasn't identifying itself, flying fast along the Potomac River from the south. As before, they called the Arlington dispatch center, which relayed the information to the Arlington command post at the Pentagon. Chief Schwartz, with no further information, had no choice but to assume it might be another hijacked plane, and ordered everybody out of the building—for the third time.

Neither Bowers nor Gleske had been briefed about the evacuations the day before. And they both knew that if the plane was only ten miles away, there was no way they'd get everybody down in the baskets on a couple of tower ladders. "Holy shit," Bowers muttered. "We don't need this."

They gathered their individual crews. Bowers's group was working down by Corridor 5, a good distance away from the closest tower truck. Instead of trying to get down on that, he decided to disperse his crews around the roof in the safest way possible. If the plane was coming from the south, he reasoned, and heading straight for the building, then the worst places to be would be the southern quadrant—the most likely impact point—and the northern quadrant, since that would be the general direction of the impact. He ordered his crews to position themselves on the east and west portions of the roof. Then he noticed that some of the trees in the courtyard reached as high as the building, with branches that stretched over onto the roof in places. "Get to the outside of the roof structure," he told his crews. "If necessary, jump on a tree limb if you have to get off the roof." It was the craziest order he had ever given, but he couldn't think of any other options.

Gleske's crews hurried to the outer edge of the building, where another tower truck was positioned. But when they got there, the basket was on the ground, being loaded with supplies. Gleske ordered it up. Unlike some of the other tower trucks, the aerial device on Tower 436 could operate as either a basket or a ladder, and Gleske told the tower operator to leave it in place once it got back to the roof, so the fire crews could use the ladder to climb down. Still, they had only a few minutes, and the tower ladder seemed to be moving at the speed of a Tinkertoy contraption. Then Gleske recalled his earlier request for a second ladder truck. "Hey, where's our second means of egress?" he asked, looking around. It wasn't there.

His crew lined up at the edge of the building, waiting for the ladder to rise to the roof. Once in place, it would still be a slow trek down since the ladder could only support one person every 20 feet or so. Most of the firefighters knew they'd be on the roof when the aircraft, wherever it was headed, arrived. Long, silent faces glanced down at the ground, then up at the blue sky, wondering if they'd see the plane or hear it coming.

Gleske had a cell phone in his pocket and thought about calling his wife—if this was the end, it seemed he should say good-bye. But none of the other firefighters had phones, and he knew that if they couldn't make a call, he shouldn't.

Waiting around like a trapped target started to make him angry. "Listen guys," he told those around him. "If you see a plane coming, let's make sure we flip them off before they take us out." That brought a few nervous laughs.

Finally, the ladder banged up against the roof and Gleske sent his men down—first one, then when he was about halfway down, another. It was agonizingly slow.

Gleske wasn't the only one fuming. At the command post by the helipad, Chief Schwartz was once again flying blind. Chris Combs, who had been the best source of real-time information the day before, was at the FBI's joint operations center, half a mile away at Fort Myer. With Combs elsewhere, Schwartz couldn't find out what was going on. Was it actually a hostile aircraft? Or just an unidentified one? The evacuation couldn't have come at a worse time, just as he was marshaling resources for the crisis on the roof. Schwartz vowed to tie Combs to his waist from that point on.

Like the crews on the roof, many of the firefighters in the building, bringing the remnants of the interior fire under control, were evacuating for the first time. Others stayed where they were, including Ladder 16 from Woodsboro and most of the others in the courtyard. They wouldn't leave while the comrades they were supporting up on the roof waited out a possible attack with no way to escape.

Out in South Parking, Debbie Walker, the medic who had loaded patients on Washington Boulevard the day before, fumed in disbelief. She had returned to the Pentagon that morning and hunted down her vehicle, Medic 102, which somebody had moved to South Parking. When she heard the evacuation call, she felt enraged. "How the hell can they screw us up in the head like this?" she howled to nobody in particular. She wished she could confront whoever was responsible: With all the technology you guys put into this, she wanted to shout, how can you put this thought into our heads again!?

It was a moment of high anxiety that turned out to be relatively brief. Before Gleske had sent even one five-person crew down the ladder, the evacuation was called off. The plane turned out to be a government jet, not another terrorist attack.[1] Everybody could get back to work. The sooner the better.

Since most of the firefighters on the roof had never gotten down, they quickly went back to work once they regrouped. But after the nerve-wracking propane explosions, and now a botched evacuation, a few of them were spent. One of the fire officers in Gleske's groups came up to him after the evacuation was called off. "I don't think I can do this anymore," he confided. "I'm done."

Gleske nodded. "Okay," he said, "take your crew and go to rehab." They went down the ladder. Then another officer came up to Gleske with a similar request. The battalion chief sent him down as well, with his crew. That was ten firefighters out of commission. He called down to the command post to report the development, then went around to his remaining company officers and asked them to check with their crews and make sure everybody was okay. Nobody else stepped forward.

Gleske and Bowers huddled once more, while their crews hacked at the roof again. "We kinda fucked up there," Bowers acknowledged. "We need to get more ladders here just in case." Gleske agreed. They called down to the command post and stressed the importance of getting more trucks into the courtyard. This time the answer was affirmative. Meanwhile, Bowers ordered that no more crews come to the roof until additional ladders had been set up.

Next, Bowers did something he virtually never did: call home from a fire. He was worried there would be news reports about an evacuation at the Pentagon, or about the threat of a follow-on attack. He had two teenage daughters, and didn't want them to worry. He pulled out his cell phone and dialed. His wife, Debbie, answered. "I'm standing on the roof of the Pentagon," he told her, with unintended dramatic effect. "If you hear something, don't worry."

"The roof? What are you doing on the roof?" she asked. "Get off!"

"I can't," he told her. "This is what we're assigned to do. I'm okay."

"Okay . . ." she relented. "Be careful!"   ,

Down on the ground, D.C. battalion chief Dick Sterne had a fresh problem of his own. Most of the D.C. fire crews had gotten down during the evacuation, and the additional units he'd requested had arrived, with sirens blaring. One of the new battalion chiefs, who had been at the Pentagon the day before, told Sterne that as he was driving across the bridge from D.C. the smoke swirling around the roof looked thicker and more ominous than it had right after the plane hit.

The D.C. crews were regrouping after the evacuation when one of Sterne's bosses pulled up. He approached Sterne and started yelling. "What are you doing?" he shouted. "I told the fire chief we'd be out of here, and you're calling for more help!"

Sterne explained the emergency on the roof. It was a matter of national security, he stressed. But it didn't matter. The D.C. fire chief wanted his units back, and they'd be going back. The special alarm units would return to D.C. immediately, the boss explained. The rest of the D.C. crews were expected home promptly, once the job was finished.

Sterne felt numb. He shambled over to Randy Gray at the command post to break the news. "Hey, Randy," he said, "I don't know how to tell you this, but our deputy chief said he wants our units out of here."

"What?" Gray said, as if he couldn't believe it.

"I'm sorry," Sterne apologized, reeling with embarrassment, "but there's not much I can do. We got ordered to finish up what we're doing and leave."

Gray was furious. He knew that many of the D.C. crews had busted their asses alongside everybody else over the past 24 hours. But he also had a fresh problem to solve, and there was no time for arguing. He huddled with his staff, to figure out who was going to replace the D.C. crews on Division Baker.

The evacuation had been on and off so quickly that most of the people who had come to work at the Pentagon that day didn't even know what happened. Including the press. Another news briefing was scheduled for the morning of September 12, in the same briefing room Rumsfeld had used the prior evening. This time, Chief Plaugher would be there to update the media on the firefight and make his official debut before the Pentagon press corps, in a more formal setting than the Citgo gas station where he appeared the night before.

Plaugher was late. The chief and his free-form aide, Chris Ramey, were supposed to show up before the briefing for an orientation with Torie Clarke, the Pentagon spokeswoman. But first they had to see what was going on with the airplane flying up the Potomac, which held them up.

They walked in as the press members were beginning to take their seats for the 10:00 A.M. briefing. Clarke gave them a cold, nervous glance. Ramey felt as if she were sizing them up and holding her breath, about to do damage control for a couple of bumpkins over their heads on a national stage.

The briefing began with two Defense Department officials describing the family support services put in place for victims who had worked at the Pentagon. General Jackson said a few words and explained his role. Then Plaugher stepped up to the podium.

"We are still engaged in a very stubborn firefight," the chief said to the reporters and the cameras. "We have no estimate at this time of how long it's going to take to get the fire out or how many additional resources we're going to need."

There were lots of questions about why the fire seemed to be largely extinguished the day before and was now suddenly rekindled. And what was going on up on the roof?

Plaugher explained that the roof consisted of "stout World War Two–type construction" that was extremely difficult to break through. He described what a trench cut was and how the firefighters were going about their work.

Dozens of other questions followed: Had the fire department removed any bodies? How many casualties were there? Were there visible pieces of aircraft inside the building?

Plaugher delicately parried questions he wasn't prepared to answer—like how many bodies had been removed—and said he didn't know the answer to others. When somebody asked how many firefighters had been involved in the firefight, he answered, "Believe it or not, we do not know. We just had this tremendous outpouring of help from the entire community, and we had firefighters and fire units from places that I didn't even know existed here to help with the situation."

The questions went on for another 20 minutes: How far had the airplane penetrated? How hot had the fire gotten? How bad was the flooding? What else was still burning, in addition to the roof? What exactly were the search-and-rescue crews doing at that moment? And his casualty estimate, from the night before, of 100 to 800 deaths—could he narrow that down at all? Was that still accurate?

"We don't know anything other than it might still be accurate," Plaugher said. "I mean, wow, 100 to 800? That's huge, but that's the best we can do."

Torie Clarke finally cut off the questions. "I had promised the chief he could get back to the job at hand," she told the room. Plaugher took the cue, nodded, stepped off the platform, and headed out the door.

Chris Ramey had felt lukewarm toward Plaugher up till then. But the chief's stalwart performance won him over. "Dude," Ramey said to the chief out in the hallway as they hurried back toward their vehicle, "you just gave a press conference where Colin Powell talked about Desert Storm. Man, I never thought of you as a public speaker. But you knocked it out of the park!"

While Plaugher had been talking about the roof operation—which was out of sight of the reporters in the briefing room—the firefighters on top of the building had been sweating over the smoldering slate, oblivious to the discussion about their activities. Richie Bowers had something else on his mind: the ladder truck they had ordered. There was still no sign of it, and Bowers finally lost patience. It was now broiling hot on the roof. The crews were getting exhausted. An extra ladder was a priority issue affecting life and safety. He decided to get in the bucket and go down to the courtyard to see what the holdup was.

When Bowers got to the ground, he marched over to the tunnel and walked through. Sure enough, there was the ladder he had ordered—Arlington Truck 105—parked at the entrance to the tunnel.

The cab in the back, where the tillerman sat to steer the rear wheels around corners, was too tall for the tunnel. The crew was standing outside the truck, trying to figure out a way to squeeze the truck through. It wasn't looking good.

"What's the problem?" Bowers asked the officer in charge of the truck, who explained how the tiller cab wouldn't fit. "Okay," Bowers answered. "Then take the tiller cab off."

That brought a confused look. "But—the only way to get it off would be to cut it off," the Arlington captain said.

"Well, do what you need to do," Bowers ordered. "Whatever you need to cut off, cut it off! I need that truck in here now!"

Bowers went back to the courtyard, where he told the A&E division commander, Battalion Chief Terry Kisner from Alexandria, what he had just ordered the Arlington crew to do. In a more orderly operation he would have formally run his request up the chain of command. But this was the heat of battle. Bowers had an urgent mission to complete on the roof, and the safety of his crews was at stake. If somebody had to take flak for ordering the dismantling of a fire truck, there would be time to deal with that later.

The unusual request quickly ricocheted up through Arlington command. Randy Gray fielded the request at the command post and took it to Chief Plaugher, who was back from the briefing by then. "Chief," Gray began, not sure how it was going to go over, "can they cut the tiller cab off a truck to get a ladder into the courtyard?"

The day before, the director of finance for Arlington County had secured a $50 million line of credit for dealing with the incident and told Plaugher to go ahead and get whatever he needed for the operation. The cost of repairing the tiller cab didn't concern him. "Next question?" he said, signaling his immediate approval.

Gray chuckled. "We'll try to cut it real clean, so it will be easy to fix," he assured the chief.

"Next?" Plaugher said again.

Gray guffawed, and quickly relayed the order: Cut the truck. The Army Corps of Engineers offered advice about where to cut, to avoid any mechanical or electrical problems. They measured the height of the tunnel and lined up the right place for the cut on the cab.

The unorthodox job fell to the crew of Arlington's Rescue 109, led by Capt. Gil Cook. He delegated the cutting to the two firefighters on his crew, Mike Alvarado and Leon Adams. Since Adams was a rookie, Alvarado let him have the honors—it would be a unique experience to tell his friends and family about. Adams lined up an electric saw about 14 inches from the top of the cab, and in less than ten minutes he had cut through all four posts and the Plexiglas they held in place.

Alvarado was a tillerman, and he climbed into the rear cab—suddenly a convertible—to help steer the truck into the courtyard. As the truck creeped through the tunnel, he had to duck to keep from bumping his head against the concrete above. But the truck fit through with about two inches to spare.

Once in the courtyard, Truck 105 raised its long ladder up to the roof near Bowers's group, where the Corridor 5 roof intersected with the A Ring. Bowers looked on approvingly. He would have liked another two ladders leading up to the roof, but trucks were scarce and command was swamped. It would do.

★ 35 ★

STRESS MANAGEMENT

September 12, 11:00 A.M.

When Mike Smith woke up in the hospital on the morning of September 12, he was ready to clear out. "I've got to go home," he told a nurse.

But doctors still wanted to run a few more tests to make sure his heart was in good shape. After a while a nurse came in with a device that reminded Smith, a part-time builder, of a Dremel tool used for woodworking. "It's for the stress test," she explained. Then she started shaving Smith's chest hair and roughing up his skin with the tool.

It felt like bugs were devouring his skin. "What the hell are you doing?" he asked. The nurse said they needed to run an electrocardiogram and that she was trying to get good connection points for the electrodes she needed to attach to his body. Smith gritted his teeth until she finished, then ran on a treadmill to raise his heart rate. The test came out fine, and the doctors finally discharged him. Then Smith and his wife, Doris, went out to get something to eat, and went home so he could sleep.

After passing out in the inner courtyard the night before, Ed Hannon was okay too. He had spent about six hours in the hospital, where he was treated for dehydration and smoke inhalation. He finally felt revived enough to sign himself out. A fellow fire captain drove him home to Charles Town, West Virginia, about 70 miles away. Hannon went back to sleep. When he woke up, his whole body ached and he consumed nothing but water. But gradually he started to feel better.

Army Maj. Dave King was in worse shape, like many of the people who had been working in the Pentagon when the plane hit and somehow staggered out of the inferno.[1] After he stumbled out of the building holding his burned arms out in front of him, like a mummy, King found his way to an ambulance that took him to Washington Hospital Center, in D.C., along with another victim who was burned and having trouble breathing. King's legs, arms, neck, and face were burnt, and there were blisters on his forehead and around his ears, but painkillers eased the discomfort for the time being. When a nurse struggled trying to cut two rings from his scorched fingers, King grabbed the rings himself and yanked them off—along with some pink skin that the nurse had been hoping to leave in place.

Doctors soon moved King to the hospital's burn center, where he vacillated between moments of clarity and longer spells of medicated incoherence. The doctors determined that 22 percent of King's body was burned. His condition wasn't severe enough to land him in intensive care, where other Pentagon victims were, but he faced a long recovery. The medical specialists were already planning several operations, skin grafts, and a lengthy program of physical therapy. Friends and family members started a vigil, making sure somebody was in the room with him around the clock.

There were firefighters and other workers at the Pentagon who needed attention too, even though they weren't physically injured. After giving up on the operation at Thomas Jefferson Community Center, Dodie Gill, the director of Arlington's employee-assistance program, had shown up at the Pentagon at first light on September 12. She realized that she needed to be where the firefighters were, instead of expecting them to come to her. Gill had sent a couple of her staff members to the Pentagon overnight, but it wasn't until morning that they began setting up a thorough support program.

There were two Arlington tents on the lawn, close to the building, where firefighters would rest, regroup, and get water. The grass had turned to mud, from all the hoses spraying water overnight. The Red Cross, Salvation Army, and other support organizations set up operations to support fire and rescue workers, but it was confusing trying to figure out where anything was.

Gill spent awhile looking for the two staff members who had been there overnight. Finally she found Kathy Young, who had done stress-management work in Oklahoma City after the 1995 bombing. Young looked exhausted but seemed to have her bearings. "Everybody wants a piece of this," she warned Gill, alerting her to all the wandering "experts" looking for a role to play. "Just remember, be clear who you are, or somebody else will take over." She helped explain where things were and what the firefighters seemed to need most.

The first priorities were basics: dry socks and underwear, water and food, replacement gloves—the right kind. Supplies were arriving all around the Pentagon reservation, but firefighters tired from their work inside the building weren't in the mood to go scrounging for stuff. They were more inclined to rest on the cots inside the Arlington tents, preserving their strength.

So Gill organized her staff into a minor logistics operation. A shopping mall of support services, known as Camp Unity, was springing up in South Parking. Workers could get clothing, flashlights, firefighting gear, and other supplies. Burger King, McDonald's, and Outback Steakhouse offered fast food. A relief group from North Carolina Baptist Men was setting up facilities to serve hundreds of home-cooked meals. But it was a long walk from the helipad to South Parking, through a variety of checkpoints that were unexpectedly popping up. To get the goods to the customers, Gill and her staffers started shuttling food and clothing from South Parking to the tents near the helipad.

With security tightening, firefighters suggested that Gill wear an important credential: an Arlington County Fire Department T-shirt. Somebody fished one out, and she put it on. Several times, while she was traipsing around the grounds, military officials approached her, saying they heard that she could handle critical-incident stress management. Could she come to South Parking and talk to a few people who seemed to be suffering some kind of psychological trauma? She had to say no each time. Her job was with Arlington, she explained.

Gill didn't expect to do much counseling right away, though. Too much talk, too soon, could personalize a traumatic experience. For the time being, she thought of her job as mothering—finding ways she and her staff could be available to help, without getting in the way.

One job that emerged was protecting the Arlington firefighters from help they didn't need. At one point a woman wearing a Red Cross vest came into the Arlington tent and announced, "Okay, everybody, if anybody has anything personal you want to unload on a stranger you'll never see again, you can tell me."

Gill doubted anybody would take her up on the abrupt offer, but she stepped in anyway. "This is the Arlington tent, and we don't do things that way here," she said. "But thank you for caring."

A while later another Red Cross worker walked up to her. "I've had a lot of trauma in my life," the man said. "I could help you." She brushed him off too.

None of the firefighters came up to Gill with something "personal to unload." But they reached out to her and her staff in more subtle ways. "It was really weird," one firefighter said to Gill after a sortie into the building. "There was a guy sitting at a desk, like he was working. But he was all burned up. It was really sad."

Another told Gill he had found a man on the floor. "His hands were over his face," the firefighter said. "He looked really scared."

Several of the firefighters asked Gill to come inside the building. "I want you to see what I saw," one of them said. She refused. Seeing the carnage up close, and living the trauma, would put her in an "altered state," just like the fire crews. She would no longer be a balanced, third-party resource. When Gill rode on calls with firefighters, or showed up at incidents where people had been badly injured or killed, she made a particular point never to look into the eyes of a victim, or do anything that might personalize the experience.

She had to enforce the rule on her staffers too. One of them desperately wanted to go into the building, to see what the firefighters kept talking about. "Under no circumstances are you allowed to do that," she ordered. If he did, it would undermine his value to the firefighters—and maybe create another problem for Gill to deal with.

Fire crews were still dousing flames inside the Pentagon, particularly in parts of the C Ring close to the punch-out hole. Dave Bogozi, an Alexandria lieutenant, led several crews into that area. It was routine firefighting—not nearly as hot or as tricky as the day before—except for some unusual things peculiar to the Pentagon. In a set of Defense Intelligence Agency offices, there was one hallway where the walls had been blown or burned down, but a series of metal cages was still standing—the remains of several specially hardened rooms used for discussing matters of extreme sensitivity. Firefighters found dozens of three-ring binders and other materials labeled TOP SECRET.

Their instructions were to promptly deliver anything that might appear sensitive to an area the FBI had set up for items of special significance. And to make sure nothing got smuggled out, there were FBI agents stationed at every entrance to the building, checking people for contraband as they left. Bogozi watched one firefighter he didn't know try to leave the building with an armful of bricks, as souvenirs. "Put that shit back!" a stern-faced agent barked.

Other parts of the building were becoming accessible as the fire died out, which allowed the FBI and other agencies to start a detailed recovery effort. The firefighters on the roof reported there were small pieces of airplane debris up there—along with bits of other matter that looked like it might be human remains. So the FBI sent a few agents over to the left side of the work site, where they got a safety briefing from Chief Sterne, then climbed up the D.C. ladder truck to investigate the situation on the roof.

The FBI had developed a shift system, similar to FEMA's, and broken down into day and night shifts. Special Agent John Adams was put in charge of the evidence recovery during the day, the counterpart to Tom O'Connor, who took the night shift. Adams, tall, lean, and reserved, with a trim goatee and gentle drawl from his home state of Tennessee, had arrived at the Pentagon early on September 11, in the first wave of responders. Like others, he knew the drill—he had worked the embassy bombing in Nairobi, Kenya, in 1998 and the *Cole* bombing in 2000, and also assisted with war crimes investigations in Kosovo in 1999. Now, he was overseeing several different squads that would fan out in different areas to make the grueling, tedious work go as fast as possible. It was a huge job, and it would probably take days or weeks before crews had pawed and sifted through an ocean of debris for every last body part.

Yet for the moment, Adams had more workers at his disposal than he had work for them to do. A number of investigative teams from other agencies—including several military organizations—approached him, offering their help. Adams was glad to have the reserve manpower, but he wasn't sure how to use the military teams: He didn't know what their training was or how good they were. Plus, he worried that they might be too emotionally involved to be objective—some of them probably had friends or colleagues who had been killed.

There was a lot of activity by the helipad, involving search-and-rescue teams, construction crews, and lots of heavy equipment—but it seemed to be taking a long time to get it all organized. O'Connor had briefed Adams on overnight activities: Search teams with dogs had been hunting for survivors but hadn't found any. More FEMA teams had arrived. FBI teams carried out one recovery, the one led by Jean O'Connor. But other than that, the FBI had scarcely been into the building.

After Adams took over, commanders from various agencies spent a fair amount of time just agreeing on how to refer to various parts of the building. Buddy Martinette—one of the leaders of the FEMA group from Virginia Beach, Virginia Task Force 2—was in charge of the FEMA operation for the day shift. He told Adams that there were only a couple of areas considered safe for FBI teams to work in. Much of the impact area was still unstable, and shoring teams would have to build supports before anybody else could work there. In other parts of the building there were still spot fires, or it was too hot and dangerous to operate without flash gear.

The huge rubble pile spilling out of the building was another source of gridlock, with the FEMA commanders debating different ways to handle it. The hulking pile was a potent risk to anybody in its shadow—plus, there appeared to be remains in there. The FBI put an agent in the man-basket to scan the pile up close, and he spotted pieces of clothing and other signs that several bodies were mixed in with the wreckage. But nobody had figured out how to re-move them, although the FEMA engineers were working on the thorny challenge.

Unlike the cordial, quiet Adams, Martinette was an outspoken raconteur, eager to be helpful. He had been at the Murrah Building in Oklahoma City and plenty of other collapsed structures, and he knew the Pentagon would be a deadly trap for careless workers. He pointed out all of the areas inside the building that were still consid-ered unsafe. "But you can go in Corridor 4," he told Adams. "There's one area there with a number of victims." It was one corner of the Navy Command Center. Adams asked Martinette to lead him to the spot, and Martinette agreed.

It was Adams's first trip into the building. The hallway was intact, but he saw lots of water damage to the ceiling tiles. Fire hoses snaked across the floor. They walked down to where the C Ring had been, and turned left through a set of doors. Suddenly, it was a demolition zone. The walls were blown down, and concrete and furniture littered the floor. The area wasn't burned, but it was darkened by smoke. It was as hot as a sauna. Twisted metal hung from the ceiling and jutted up from the floor, forming dozens of dangerous obstacles. The only light in the space glinted in from Corridor 4, creating spooky shadows.

As Adams's eyes adjusted, Martinette swept his hand across an area in front of them. "That's where the victims are," he said. After a moment, Adams saw them. They were intact bodies, people who looked as if they had died from smoke inhalation, not from fire or explosions. He could see that some were wearing military uniforms, while others appeared to be dressed in civilian clothes. Two were seated in chairs, around a table. Others were on the floor. Adams had prepared himself for a horror show of flesh and bone, and this first foray into the building wasn't quite as awful as he'd feared. Still, he was already thinking of the fastest way to do the work, to minimize the time his people would spend in the dismal space.

Once he figured out where he was going, Adams went back outside with Martinette and assembled a group of eight FBI agents—picking those he knew were especially skilled—to go back in and start recovering the bodies. They suited up, pulling on rubber firemen's boots, safety glasses, helmets, and HEPA respirators to filter out hazardous particles. It was important to note the exact location of every piece of remains, since they were analyzing a mass murder. Adams found a couple of PenRen officials and asked for a floor plan of the area that he could use as a diagram to mark the location of each body.

Once back in the C Ring, however, he realized that the shambles inside the building no longer resembled the floor plan. The diagram showed an orderly arrangement of hallways and offices, each with a room number or other designation. But the wrecked area they were in had no visible room numbers—or even walls, for that matter. It was just one wide-open jumble of wreckage. He couldn't even tell where on the map he was standing. "All right," Adams told the group, as he contemplated Plan B, "we're just going to have to sketch the remains the best we can."

With the work proceeding, he went back outside to deal with a number of other mounting issues. Agents were still setting up the morgue, and he went to the loading dock to check on progress there. Among other things, he made sure there was enough transportation to get remains quickly from the building over to the morgue.

Adams also realized that chasing down random PenRen people whenever the FBI needed help to navigate the building or get some construction equipment wasn't effective. He needed a permanent liaison to PenRen—and he knew just the guy. Garrett McKenzie, the photographer who had shot hundreds of pictures the day before, had a blunt, direct personality, and was rarely impressed by rank or status. Adams figured he'd get along well with the PenRen construction crews. He tracked down McKenzie and broke the news. "I want you to be my point contact for PenRen," he said. "Anything PenRen-related, you're my guy."

McKenzie thought it was a terrible plan. He was a photographer, not an administrator. "I don't think that's a good idea, John," he protested. "That's a poor utilization of my skills."

"I need somebody who can get the job done," Adams answered, "and that's you." McKenzie wasn't happy about it, but accepted the assignment.

Adams went back into the Navy Command Center, to check on the recovery team. They had already freed a few bodies and were in the process of photographing and documenting the remains. It was solemn work, and there was little chatter, yet the group seemed motivated. Still, Adams wanted them to get some fresh air and a few moments of rest. "Listen up," he said. "I want everybody to stop what you're doing. Just leave everything where it is. We're gonna go out and take a break."

Once out on the lawn, Adams checked on the crew. "How ya doing?" he asked one after another.

"Fine," the answers came back. Mostly, the crew wanted to get back inside and continue their work. That was a good sign. There didn't seem to be much to worry about. Adams sent them back in.

Then he took up another matter: how to deal with all the physical evidence on the scene. At the beginning, it made sense to gather up every part of the airplane, or anything else that might help document the crimes. But there was an overwhelming amount of debris. Plus, more than 24 hours later, there was little mystery about what had happened: Terrorists had hijacked the plane and deliberately flown it into the Pentagon. Yet agents were still gathering evidence as if the Bureau needed to piece together a giant puzzle. At one point Adams saw several agents picking up some wreckage that looked like airplane parts and bringing them over to the FBI command post. "What are they doing?" he said to a colleague. "Cleaning the lawn?"

Several FBI supervisors got together to discuss what, exactly, the recovery effort was supposed to recover. One supervisor argued that every airplane part was significant and ought to be treated as valuable evidence. "That can't be," Adams countered. "We know what happened here. Do we really need to collect every piece of the airplane?"

The National Transportation Safety Board had set up its own operation nearby—they were the crash experts who would determine exactly what had happened to Flight 77. Adams and some of the others went over to ask the NTSB officials what they thought.

"Do you guys want pieces of the plane?" Adams asked.

"No, it's clear what happened here," one of the NTSB officials answered. "We don't need pieces of the wings and stuff like that. But we do need the black boxes." Those were the two recording devices installed in the plane, meant to capture data that could help reconstruct what had happened in the event of a crash. The NTSB officials explained what to look for, and dug out some pictures to show what the black boxes looked like.

Despite their name, both devices were orange, not black. The cockpit voice recorder captured sounds in the cockpit, such as audible alarms, radio transmissions, and pilot conversations, so investigators would know what was happening at the controls during the final minutes of the flight. The flight data recorder stored electronic information on the performance of the aircraft, such as airspeed, altitude, heading, and other parameters—information that would help investigators reconstruct the jet's flight path. Each recorder was about the size and shape of a cinder block. They were hardened and designed to survive a crash, and installed in the tail of the aircraft, the most survivable section. Sometimes the recorders got damaged or destroyed, but they still represented the best chance to gather information on what had happened with the airplane.

Nobody was sure how the 757 had come apart inside the building, but one thing was clear: There was a big pile of airplane parts around the punch-out hole in A&E Drive. Agents, firefighters, and rescue crews had reported seeing pieces of the cockpit, landing gear, and all kinds of other airplane pieces in there—along with dozens of body parts. Even though the recorders had been in the back of the plane, it was quite possible they had traveled all the way through the hole the airplane bored through the building and ended up in the pile at the head of the airplane's path.

A&E Drive happened to be the one other area where it was safe for recovery crews to work. The force of the vaporized jet had blown a hole in one side of the wall, but the wall itself remained stable. So Adams organized another recovery team and sent them in to start fishing through the wreckage to see what they could find.

★ 36 ★

THE EAGLE SCOUTS

September 12, early afternoon

There was some thrilling news from the roof. Richie Bowers, the battalion chief running part of the roof operation, was calling down to the command post by the helipad. "Roof Division to Command," he said. "At this time the fire on the roof is under control."

There were a few seconds of silence. One of the officers at the command post, handling the radios, came on. "Roof Division, can you confirm your last transmission?" he asked.

Bowers repeated himself: "At this time, the fire on the roof is under control." At the command post, he could hear whooping in the background.

The job on the roof wasn't totally finished, though. Crews had finally boxed in the fire and put out most of it, but they still had to thoroughly douse the raceway beneath the tiles and make sure there was nothing that could reignite. Still, it was a triumph—they had saved the vital equipment the military was so worried about.

With the roof fire under control, commanders were able to address dozens of other priorities, including mounting requests from military officials desperate to get back into their offices. General Jackson, the DOD liaison, was the first stop, and once requests were approved, people who needed to get inside were sent to the command bus, to wait for a fire crew that would escort them. With no fire evident—except on the roof—military officials continually asked Jackson why it was taking so long to get back into the building, and now they finally could.

Then big news rippled through the command post: President Bush would be paying a visit to the Pentagon later in the day. The Secret Service wouldn't say when—unpredictability was a key element of security, which was tighter than ever—but he would probably be out on the grounds, down among the workers. Neither Schwartz nor Plaugher was a big fan of VIP grandstanding, and there had already been numerous disruptions that slowed the work of reclaiming the Pentagon. But this was different. The President's visit would be a big morale boost for all the firefighters and other workers.

As the day went on, the command post buzzed with anticipation of the President's visit. One of the officials there, Dr. Yorke Allen, who was Arlington County's medical director, had an idea. "You know what this place needs?" he asked. "More flags." The footage of the flags in New York, hanging from the ruins of the twin towers, had been poignant and stirring to those who saw it. And this was the Pentagon, the nation's most recognizable military icon. The only flag visible on the building was the one the Marines had raised overnight. It was fitting and dignified—but compared to the vast western wall of the building, it looked puny. The Pentagon called for something grander.

Plaugher asked General Jackson if he could get a bigger flag. "A flag?" Jackson grinned, energized by the idea. "Now that's something I can handle."

He called Fort Myer and ordered a garrison flag—the biggest in the inventory. Nearly five times as large as an ordinary post flag that flew on military installations, this one was normally reserved for holidays and other special occasions. Jackson asked Schwartz and Plaugher if they could make some crews available to hang the flag from the roof. Sure thing, they said.

The news from the roof, meanwhile, continued to get better. Richie Bowers came on the radio again and finally declared that the fire was completely out. Fire crews would still have to conduct patrols, with hose lines ready to go if there were unexpected flare-ups. But after eight hours, the crews that had battled the fire since dawn could finally call it a day, knowing they'd finished the job for good. Bowers led his crews to the ground and sent them to rehab.

It was time for Ladder 16, the diminutive truck from Woodsboro, to pack it up too. So the Woodsboro firefighters lowered their ladder and packed up their stuff. Several of the other fire officers in the courtyard came over and shook hands with the crew, thanking them for coming. Micky Fyock and his volunteers still felt awkwardly out of place, but proud to have been treated as equals by career firefighters battling to save the most important military building in the country.

They went back out the same tunnel they had come in, their minds reeling with images from the heady experience. Fyock kept recalling a flag that had been attached to one of the lower rungs of Ladder 16. As the sun rose over the building that morning, a hose attached to the truck was spraying water onto the roof. A rainbow formed, enveloping the flag and the Woodsboro firefighter operating the ladder in radiant light. Then there were all the people they had encountered: the worker in the courtyard overnight, mourning his lost colleagues, and all the others courageously coming to work as day broke. "America will be all right," Fyock told his men.

When they exited the tunnel, they were shocked at what they saw. Since they arrived about 12 hours earlier, a sprawling tent city had sprung up in South Parking and the grassy areas surrounding it, and cranes, construction vehicles, and news trucks were everywhere. In place of the sleepy security guard who waved them in, there were now perimeter fences, multiple checkpoints, and sentries armed with automatic weapons. Official vehicles with police escorts were caravanning through the parking lot. Activity seemed to occupy every square inch of ground. The whole scene was overwhelming. Ladder 16 suddenly seemed like a little matchbox vehicle at the Indy 500. With the chief's sedan leading, Ladder 16 headed for home.

With the fire essentially out, both inside the building and on top of it, the incident commanders had developed a comfortable rotational scheme for the roof, sending fresh crews up for watch duty every couple of hours. Unlike the earlier crews, who had tackled a mammoth job, establishing ownership of it and staying till it was done, the follow-on companies would go to the roof for an hour or two, make sure everything was fine, then come down for some rest and food while another crew took over.

Greg Lange, a Fairfax captain, arrived at the Pentagon in mid-afternoon with a crew of three others from Fairfax. The company milled around for a while, taking in the busy scene and waiting for an assignment, until commanders told Lange to lead his crew to the roof. Lange didn't expect much action, and the officer he relieved told him it was mainly babysitting duty—the earlier crews had done all the work. They'd just have to do routine patrols and make sure fire didn't flare up again.

The group climbed to the roof from a ladder truck, along with another Fairfax company, and one from Alexandria—11 people altogether. The situation was much as Lange had expected. He couldn't see any fire, and the smoke was finally gone. It was obvious from all the trench cuts and the burnt tiles, in several directions, that the earlier crews had done strenuous work. Hose lines were still in place, in case of a flare-up, but there was nothing left to do except walk around, peek inside the trench cuts every now and then, and make sure the fire was still out. Lange figured that mainly they'd end up standing around for an hour or two, until another crew came up to take the next watch.

Then he got a call on the radio from the command post. Would his group mind helping hang a flag? No problem, he said. That seemed easy.

They watched as a huge Army soldier, about 250 pounds, started to climb up the ladder on one of the trucks. He carried a big bundled flag—and looked skittish on the narrow ladder. Then another soldier, and another, climbed up behind him. The firefighters on the roof gathered around, wondering what all the fuss was about.

A young enlisted man, a sergeant, and a captain, finally got to the roof, winded from the climb. By now a crowd of people on the ground was looking up at them. Lange had figured the Army guys would come up with a small flag and hang it themselves, according to protocol, while the firefighters stayed out of their way. But when he saw how big the flag was, he realized they were becoming the center of attention. "Shit," he said to one of his crew members, "this is going to be a big deal." At a minimum, he figured, the news cameras on the hill overlooking the Pentagon would film the whole thing.

The Army captain huddled with Lange and the officer in charge of the Alexandria crew. "We can't screw this up," the captain said tensely. The moment was even bigger than Lange imagined. He and his colleagues learned for the first time that the President was due at the Pentagon shortly, and that the flag was meant to honor his visit. But there was no plan for how to hang the flag. The soldiers had carried some rope to the roof but no rigging, and they weren't sure what to do with the flag once they got there.

For several minutes a committee of a dozen dickered over how to secure a 40-foot flag to a stone roof in a stiff breeze. Finally a plan emerged. There were lightning rods on the roof of the Pentagon, with rigid cable strung between them. Through a stroke of luck, the cable ran right along the edge of the E Ring. Firefighters started tying the flag to the cable using the rope the soldiers had brought.

To secure the flag, they had to first spread it out on the roof. Nobody was sure whether the star field was supposed to be on the left

358 PATRICK CREED AND RICK NEWMAN

or the right side, or if it mattered. Plus, as they ran the flag up the roof, they were looking at it upside down from how it would look once they flipped it over, which complicated the discussion. Opinions flew. Fairfax firefighter Greg Morris, who had been an Eagle Scout, thought they were hanging it backward. But his voice was only one of many, and nobody seemed to be listening. Finally, the group got the flag secured, and prepared to drape it over the side of the building.

Down on the ground, General Jackson was watching with a number of others, including a lieutenant colonel from Fort Myer. "The flag is backward," the officer insisted. He pointed out that the star field was on the right-hand side—which was the wrong way to hang a flag.

"How do you know that?" somebody asked. "Were you a Boy Scout?"

"Yeah." The officer smiled. "An Eagle Scout."

Jackson went to the command post to get the problem ironed out immediately. On the roof, Lange's radio chirped, "You're hanging it the wrong way!" Lange had figured the Army guys would know flag etiquette, and it looked pretty good to him. But they undid the rigging and began turning the flag around. It was awkward, frustrating work. The group was working right at the edge of the roof, with no railing, and the limp flag caught the wind occasionally and threatened to take off like a kite. "I hope like hell it doesn't let loose," Morris worried aloud, "and that nobody falls off the ledge."

They finally got the flag turned around and tied to the cable once more, then pushed it over the side of the building as if relieved to be finished with a frustrating chore. But on the ground, suspense had been building, and as the flag unfurled gracefully in the breeze, onlookers were instantly stirred. The flag snapped smartly into place, caught tight by the rigging at the top, and blanketed the building in the colors that had become a singular source of comfort to many. A huge roar went up from the crowd.

Somewhere in the throng, at nearly the same time, President Bush was arriving at the Pentagon. The group on the roof had no idea where, but the buzz on the ground jolted them all into their best posture. As word of the President's arrival came over the radio, the three soldiers stood at the edge of the roof and saluted. A couple of firefighters, unsure what to do, saluted as well, while others bent down and fussed over the flag's makeshift rigging like housemaids smoothing the wrinkles out of bedsheets.

Tom O'Connor, the FBI agent working evidence recovery, was in the FBI's command vehicle, close to the impact site, sitting in the driver's seat as he watched the unveiling. When the crowd started to cheer, he tooted the bus's horn three times to express his own fervor. "Hey!" somebody yelled behind him. "That's the evacuation signal!"

"Oh shit," O'Connor yelped. Luckily, the noise and enthusiasm of the crowd seemed to have drowned out the horn.

Ed Plaugher was also moved by the sight of the huge flag that brightened the charred, wrecked facade. But as he watched from the command bus, he felt a flash of regret: There were no firefighters from Arlington on the roof to help display it. The event had taken on more significance than he or anybody else anticipated. Arlington crews had already worked as hard as anybody at the Pentagon, and Plaugher knew they'd still be there after the glory was over and many of the others had gone home. They belonged in the picture.

The flag hung from the top of the fifth floor to the bottom of the third, 40 feet in all. It formed a ready-made theatrical backdrop for the President. Rumsfeld was Bush's official escort, and together they walked out onto the lawn by the helipad, into an army of firefighters, search experts, construction crews, and federal agents. Firefighters took pride in being unimpressed by VIPs, and the steady flow of politicians and government officials at the Pentagon was already becoming tiresome. The sun was starting to fade, and most of the workers on shifts were approaching the end of a tiring 12-hour day. But the President's visit sent an electric charge into the crowd. As Bush walked up to the gash in the building and the hulking pile of rubble, workers parted. Rescue crews and military troops formed a loose cordon around the President, who shook hands and said "Thank you" as he walked somberly up to the building.

It was the first time Bush had seen the damaged Pentagon with his own eyes. After getting a close-up look, he walked back toward the command bus. There was a spot where news cameras were set up, and Bush spoke for a couple of minutes, haltingly and without a script. "Coming here makes me sad," he said, as heavy machinery clanked and buzzed in the background. "It also makes me angry. . . . The nation mourns, but our government will go on. The country will function." Behind him, the garrison flag fluttered gently, the only feature of the fractured facade that seemed to be in perfect alignment.

The President's visit was a success, Plaugher felt. It turned out to be brief and not terribly disruptive. The officers in the command post clearly felt stirred, and the workers and fire crews on the day shift suddenly had the energy of people at the beginning of a long day, not the end. After a tense, tedious day of disruptions and false starts, it was uplifting to draw the nation's attention for a few minutes. The day was ending on a high note.

Even though most of the D.C. crews had been ordered home, a few stayed through the day to extinguish their portion of the roof fire. Once the President left, they finished packing up their stuff and got ready to leave for good. Battalion fire chief Dick Sterne was walking near one of the trucks with Bill Wolf, a long-serving DCFD veteran. All of a sudden Wolf fell, momentarily disappearing from sight. Sterne looked down and saw the stocky firefighter up to his neck in water. While Wolf pulled himself out of the mud, splashing and swearing, Sterne doubled over in a fit of much-needed laughter.

Wolf saw his battalion chief laughing. "Fuck you . . . sir!" he yelled. Sterne laughed even harder, as if uncorking all the stress of a turbulent day. Once Wolf climbed out of the muck and they both composed themselves, they figured out that somebody had dug a hole to collect all the runoff water that had turned the lawn into a swamp. Orange cones and fire-line tape had probably been placed carefully around the hole at one point, but had since been trampled and knocked over and were now barely visible in the mud. The construction crews would have to come up with another way to disperse the water, Sterne could see, as, still chuckling, he regarded his muddy colleague.

LOW TIDE

September 12, evening

After the first 24 hours, each FEMA team had been assigned to either day or night work. The group from Fairfax, Virginia Task Force 1, drew the night shift. After spending the day at Washington Navy Yard, sleeping, eating, gaping at the TV, and trying to relax, everybody was eager to get back to work.

On the buses back to the Pentagon, however, there was some grumbling about the mission. As the news from 9/11 settled in and the extent of the damage became clear, everybody knew that the catastrophe in New York was far graver than the situation at the Pentagon. The Pentagon job was obviously important—but there was virtually no chance of finding any survivors. In New York, by contrast, there were news reports of people trapped in rubble, calling for help on their cell phones. A mountain of smoking debris spanned several city blocks. There could be dozens or hundreds of people desperately waiting to be rescued.

During the ride, a few of the team leaders argued that the task force should go to New York to help look for survivors instead of recovering the dead at the Pentagon. That's what their skills and training were for, after all—saving live victims.

The devastating toll on the firefighters in New York also pulled heavily on the task force crews, since many were firefighters themselves. Some had trained with the FDNY. A few knew Ray Downey, the special operations chief who had been killed. And hundreds of New York firefighters were still missing—nobody knew if they were dead or trapped. If there was anybody to save, their New York brethren might be among them. It felt like the task force ought to be there.

Jerry Roussillon, one of the task force leaders, stood up in one of the buses and gave a pep talk. He reiterated the importance of recovering the victims at the Pentagon with dignity and professionalism. Besides, there were other FEMA teams and hundreds of other rescue specialists working around the clock in New York. VA-TF1 was where it was supposed to be—helping manage a crisis in its own backyard. It was important to do the best job they could.

Roussillon's talk calmed some of the louder voices, but uneasy feelings persisted. As engineer Leo Titus took it all in, he could see anguish on the faces of some of the longtime task force members. The mission was personal.

President Bush was already at the Pentagon by the time the night shift pulled up. Since the security perimeter was sealed and nobody was allowed in, they sat on the buses, waiting for him to leave. Titus and many others were disappointed—not only because they missed the President, but also because the start of their shift was delayed. Waiting was always frustrating.

When they finally got into the site, a lot had changed. To get through security, they had to get badges for the first time, which delayed their work further. And the changeover from day to night crews took awhile, since incoming leaders had to be briefed on the latest developments, then figure out how to parcel out all their teams and experts. Most of the crews, meanwhile, waited impatiently for their assignments, wondering why it was taking so long to get to work.

Other agencies more or less adopted FEMA's seven-to-seven shift schedule. Early evening and early morning would mark a changeover from day to night crews, and vice versa. As Dodie Gill was wrapping up her day at the Pentagon, she had to deal with a new wrinkle. Gill had been in and out of the Arlington tents all day, offering support when needed and making sure her firefighters were taken care of. Earlier in the day Cingular, the phone company, had provided hundreds of cell phones that firefighters could use to call home. The Cingular tent was at Camp Unity in South Parking, a long hike for crews working by the crash site. So Gill and her staff brought phones from South Parking back to the Arlington tents, returning them for replacements when the batteries wore down.

The phones didn't work at first. But as service came online late in the day, firefighters started to line up for them. Some of the firefighters had slept at fire stations overnight before returning to the Pentagon, and hadn't been home since the attack more than 36 hours earlier. Most had gotten word to their families that they were okay, but it was still reassuring to be able to talk for a few minutes.

Gill had been watching the firefighters closely, and for the most part they seemed to be holding up just fine. But for some of the spouses, it was a different story. "Hey, Dodie," one of the firefighters said to her, holding out the phone and covering the mouthpiece, "can you talk to my wife? I'm fine, but she's kind of a mess."

Gill spoke to the spouse. Then to another, and another. She realized how helpful it was for the firefighters to be intensely involved in the work at the Pentagon—and not watching the grim, frightening footage from New York, like most of their family members were. Even though the situation at the Pentagon had stabilized, the awful news about the New York firefighters was unnerving to those sitting at home. With schools and businesses closed, many of the spouses were stuck at home with little to do besides watch the news and worry that there might be compounded tragedy at the Pentagon too. "Your husband is fine," Gill would assure the spouse, as the routine became familiar. "I'm looking at him right now. He's okay. How are you doing?"

As she counseled the family members, the first thing she tried to do was wean them off the repetitive news updates. "It's easy to get mesmerized, so let's turn off the TV," she coaxed. "Let's not get over-exposed." Then she'd probe for things they could do to clear their heads. "How do you like to spend your time?" she would ask. "Gardening? Needlepoint? Visiting with friends?" As strange as it might seem, it was a perfect time to indulge a hobby or tackle a rainy-day project, she advised.

Gill's advice seemed to work. There was something about having a third party—and a woman, at that—come on the phone to say everything was okay. Several times, Gill handed the phone back to firefighters and watched expressions of relief cross their faces as they talked to their wives and realized that things had calmed down.

Tom and Jean O'Connor had both gone home in the morning, after being at the Pentagon overnight, then commuted back to the job together that evening. Tom would take over from John Adams and run evidence recovery on the night shift. He got a briefing on the recovery operation in the Navy area off Corridor 4, where eight bodies had been removed and sent to the morgue. Much of the building was still too dangerous for FBI teams to work on their own. But A&E Drive, Adams told O'Connor, was one area that was stable—and filled with evidence, possibly including Flight 77's black boxes.

As O'Connor went over his staffing needs, he realized he needed more people to help at the morgue. While briefing his evidence teams for the night shift, he asked for volunteers. Very few hands went up, but Jean O'Connor's was one of them.

At the morgue, the job was to do the same kind of documentation as the recovery crews in the building, but more thoroughly, since they were working under controlled conditions and there was less urgency. Agents would document and photograph anything that could help identify victims, and make sure the chain of custody remained unbroken. Inside the Pentagon, the FEMA engineers were numbering every column or space where a column was missing with orange paint. As remains were bagged and assigned an ID number, recovery teams would estimate their location by measuring the distance from the closest columns, then marking the location on a floor plan of the area they were in.

Some of the remains, especially intact bodies, could be identified by badges or ID tags the person had worn, or other obvious information. But many could not, and agents at the morgue documented anything that could help with identification. They also made sure the evidence could be clearly tracked all the way through to final autopsies at Dover Air Force Base. Eventually, all remains would undergo DNA testing to help with identification, then be turned over to family members for burial services or other final disposition.

The volunteers at the morgue knew it would be demanding work, and it was. A few bodies arrived intact, but mostly the group worked up close with body parts that had been violently torn and badly burned. It was a warm evening outside, and probably ten degrees warmer inside the loading dock. The agents all wore Tyvek suits and respirators that trapped heat, and the smell from the body bags added to the discomfort. Most of them worked on the floor, hunched over the remains they were processing. There was very little talking, and when somebody spoke, it was all business.

O'Connor had enough experience to know that in tough situations you concentrate on the work and revert to the basics: Make sure you document everything properly, just like you were trained. Be methodical. Don't rush or cut corners. Double-check everything. Detach yourself as much as possible, and if that doesn't work, do the work the way you'd want it to be done if the victim were your own family member.

When her mind wandered, she thought about her father. He had been diagnosed with cancer when she was 15 years old, in eleventh grade. Two months later he was on his deathbed.

Her father had discouraged displays of emotion, and there had been little overt sadness while he was sick. Shortly before he died, he said to his youngest daughter, "You have to be strong, Jean. Be strong." She had learned since then that emotion had its place. But now was the time to be strong. She was determined to follow her father's advice and set an example for the others there: Do the work, do it well, and don't complain.

Her husband Tom came over after a couple of hours to check on things. He talked to the agents and told the group, "If anybody feels like they don't want to do this anymore, just let me know."

One after another each worker said, "No, no, I'm fine." But as he was about to leave, one agent, from a different agency, pulled him aside.

"Would you mind if I moved to something else?" she asked. It turned out she had never seen a dead body before.

"Sure," O'Connor obliged. She rode back to the command post with him to get another assignment.

There was a heavy workload at the morgue that night. With the fire out inside the Pentagon, search-and-recovery teams were now making rapid progress in the stable parts of the building, and the shoring crews expanded the zone they could work in. The refrigerated trucks made regular deliveries to the morgue.

Bob Gray from Arlington had worked all day helping set up the department's technical rescue team, the TRT, then was named the team's night-shift commander. After the standoff with Kent Watts and the FEMA leadership, he had spent much of the day handling logistics—arranging for lumber and other supplies, setting up cut stations, and arranging for food to be delivered. Gray was working closely with Bobby Beer, who probably knew more than anybody on the team about working in collapsed structures. Beer knew people too. He trained with many of the FEMA specialists, and knew others in the field through the equipment business he ran.

At one point Beer introduced Gray to a man in a hard hat. "This is

Johnny," Beer said. "He's our go-between with PenRen, and he knows some of the military guys too." Johnny wasn't wearing any kind of badge or ID, but seemed to know what he was talking about, and by then an inner security perimeter had been set up to keep everybody out except those approved to work at the site. If he was inside the wire, he must be official.

Plus, he looked the part. Johnny was taut and serious, with a purposeful military stance. He even introduced Gray and Beer to a couple of buddies who said they worked for Special Forces.

Johnny told the Arlington pair that if they needed anything from the military, he'd help. He could facilitate their interactions with Home Depot too. "Whatever you need, let me know," he offered. Gray and Beer were impressed, and happy to have a contact on the inside who could get things done.

Gray spent some time on the night shift looking for victims with Beer and Sam Short, who had helped him carve through the third-floor window to reach the widowmaker earlier in the day. They worked near the E Ring, where shoring crews were building additional supports to keep the upper floors from falling down. The small group found a few bodies and marked them for recovery teams. Gray directed the removal of debris so further shoring could be done—airplane parts went in one pile, to be delivered to a huge bin out on the lawn, while building debris went in another pile. People trying to help were still wandering unaware into dangerous parts of the building, and Gray chased them out. To create an additional emergency exit, in case there was another collapse, he and Beer bashed out a window on a ground-floor office on the E Ring.

Mike Regan's FEMA team got one assignment, then another. Every time Regan began to brief his people on the mission, he'd get summoned to the command post and be given a different one. Tension rose as time passed and the group accomplished nothing. Finally, after several false starts, the plan was set. As VA-TF1 teams finally fanned out to remove debris, build more shoring, and search for victims, Regan led his group toward A&E Drive. Their job was to help FBI and NTSB officials sift through the debris near the punch-out hole so they could start recovering victims there and look for the black boxes.

Earlier crews ran pumps in the service road to drain the standing water that had been more than a foot deep. But they were still wading through a toxic moat. Leo Titus was with the group, and he was sure that water was going to start seeping into his boots at any moment. He dreaded the squishy sensation.

As the water receded, it revealed a grotesque, soggy tangle of airplane debris and body parts, reminding Regan of a low tide that leaves behind a trail of detritus. The thing Titus noticed was the smell—so rancid it was indescribable. As they panned through the wreckage, Titus was surprised that he barely recognized anything. There was nothing that looked like parts of an airplane, except for small pieces of twisted, melted metal. It was hard to spot body parts too—although everybody knew they were there.

Ron Sacra, a medic, began to point out what others couldn't see. Sacra had been a combat medic with the Army in Vietnam, and he had some of the sharpest eyes on the task force. As he identified body parts, some smaller than a finger, workers marked them, and before long there were several hundred flags planted in the debris. FBI agents began to photograph and document every piece of remains, slowing the pace of the work.

As the structural specialist, Titus's job was to step through the punch-out hole and determine if the charred, wrecked area inside was safe to work in. The hole was so big that he didn't even have to duck to get through it—but he still had to step gingerly. Just inside the hole, somebody had marked two sets of remains, which he wouldn't have noticed if not for the red tape around them. Other body parts could be anywhere. And the force of the airplane had crammed wreckage up against the walls backing to A&E Drive.

Titus decided it was safe for workers to go about ten feet into the hole. Beyond that, he couldn't tell. But ten feet would provide enough work space for clearing debris out of the area, and once they got that far, he'd go back in and gauge the stability of the structure farther in.

When Titus came out of the hole, there wasn't much for him to do except watch the evidence specialists do their work. He had to stay with the team, so he sat down on an overturned bucket in a spot where the water had drained. FBI agents used the area too, since it was relatively dry, and Titus watched with fascination as they laid out some of the things they were recovering. A briefcase. A wallet. A checkbook. Shoes. Bits of clothing. Wallet-size photographs. A suitcase. They were routine objects, unremarkable in ordinary life, yet it was hard to look at them. He felt a confusing mixture of sadness and anger that had been simmering inside, rapidly coming to a boil.

As he sat on the bucket, engrossed by the sight of the everyday belongings on the ground in front of him, Titus realized that his feet were still dry. He was grateful for the small comfort.

THE NAVY COMMAND CENTER

Thursday, September 13, 1:00 A.M.

Mike Regan's recon team was getting way ahead of the FBI. They were finding and marking remains much faster than the recovery teams could document and process them. And since everything was mingled, they couldn't just push the debris out of the way and start searching additional areas.

It seemed like a waste of manpower. Search crews were usually most effective at the beginning of a shift, when they were rested. As people got tired, their concentration flagged and they started to miss things they should have spotted. The protective Tyvek suits they wore were hot, which drained even more energy. It didn't make any sense to stand around doing nothing, especially in the early part of a shift. So while waiting in A&E Drive for the FBI to catch up, Regan decided to bring his group out of the building and head to the command post to get another assignment.

He developed a plan with the FEMA commanders outside. Based on what they were finding near the punch-out hole in A&E Drive, Regan knew there had to be numerous victims on the other side of the wall, inside the C Ring. They couldn't get to the area through the punch-out hole—Titus had only declared a small part of it safe, and the recovery of remains made it slow going. But they might be able to reach the same area by going down the C Ring and plowing through the wreckage on the back side of the wall that bordered A&E Drive. Commanders agreed.

Regan's group went in Corridor 4, to the right of the crash site. They followed hallways part of the way toward the C Ring, but as they got closer, they took the road less traveled, deliberately climbing through debris that looked like it hadn't been searched, to look for victims. Elizabeth Kreitler and her dog, Nero, were with Regan, along with another canine handler and her dog. Chris Matsos, a rescue specialist, rounded out the search party.

They started in an area that was completely dark, with few other people around, the only light coming from their helmet lamps or flashlights. Then Regan noticed something odd 25 or 30 yards to the side: an electric light. An exit sign, cracked, jarred, and hanging by a wire, was lit, and he could see a glow nearby that looked like it was coming from a computer screen. That was disconcerting. The power was supposed to be off so nobody could get burned or electrocuted by live wires, especially with so much water around—not to mention the jet fuel that still pooled everywhere, ready to ignite.

Regan called the command post on his radio. "Hey, we've got some power on in here," he said. "Why is that?"

Somebody outside tracked down a building engineer to find out. "They have these big batteries that can run for weeks," the command post reported after a few minutes. "That's their backup system."

"Well, we can't touch that," Regan responded. "We need an electrician to shut it off." It made the list of priorities at the command post, and Regan made a note to steer his crew clear of any areas where there might be electricity.

As they clambered and crawled closer to the C Ring, they encountered a lot of activity. Much of it centered on shoring, which was necessary to stabilize the entire damaged area before recovery crews or anybody else could get in to operate. The most difficult part of shoring was often the prep work—clearing a clean, level base to build from. And there was so much wreckage to clear that it would be days, weeks maybe, before the whole demolition zone could be shored and stabilized.

The Army had provided dozens of fit young soldiers from the Old Guard, who were doing a lot of the tough manual labor, lifting mangled furniture and broken pieces of concrete and carting it outside in wheelbarrows. In a few places small patches of flooring had been cleared, like landing zones cut in a jungle, enough to start some shoring work. In addition to the FEMA crews, FBI agents prowled here and there, along with lots of other workers. Many were hard to identify since they wore unmarked Tyvek suits and respirators that obscured their faces.

For the first time, Regan's team saw something they had expected to see all along but had been scarce until then: recognizable airplane parts. They all thought they would find big pieces of the airliner laying everywhere, the way car parts end up strewn across a highway after a crash. But the physics of an airplane crash were obviously different: Mostly there was just tons of shredded metal and melted plastic.

Finally, they found several airplane seats, piled among the usual mounds of upturned office furniture and random wreckage. A couple of the seats still had bodies belted into them, which had already been found and marked for the FBI. Most of the workers inside were conscientious about not gawking, yet the seats attracted a lot of attention. They were the first objects the nonaviation experts had seen that unmistakably belonged to an airplane.

An NTSB official was nearby, and Regan asked him about the strange patterns of destruction. "I don't understand why we're not seeing more airplane parts," he said.

The NTSB expert, more familiar with the dynamics of airplane crashes, described the plane as a projectile that self-destructed from front to back. "Imagine if you took a banana and pushed it through a grinder," he explained. "Everything goes through the part that's in front of it. That's what happened here. The only reason those seats survived is because they were from the rear of the plane."

The smell of jet fuel was overpowering, and Regan worried about the dogs being overexposed to chemicals and toxins that could penetrate their skin, so he sent the dogs outside to get cleaned up and breathe some fresh air. He and Matsos kept pressing forward, into an area where shoring crews were just starting to clear debris. They were deep into the Navy Command Center, although it didn't look anything like the secure, compartmented suite of offices it had once been. The walls were gone in every direction, and the debris was thick, tangled stuff. The command center abutted the wall at the edge of A&E Drive, but they couldn't see it. Regan guessed they were about 40 feet away from the punch-out hole. Most of the area hadn't been searched yet, and there were bound to be a number of victims up ahead.

They found themselves in an area where the top level of debris was relatively easy to move—building material, light and crumbly, that had fallen down from overhead. A couple of workers lifted a big piece of the ceiling off the top of a pile—and took a deep breath when they saw what they had uncovered. There were two bodies gathered around a table, which had collapsed as if the base had been severed. One of the victims was perched upright on the floor, with the table resting on his lap. Next to it the second body sat in a chair that tipped forward into the table. Clearly they had been sitting around the table, unaware of the airplane when it tore into the building.

For all of the training about compartmentalizing your emotions and detaching yourself from victims, it was virtually impossible to uncover a body without wondering how the person had died and whether it was painful. Regan guessed that these victims died instantly. The area was partially burned, in random, unpredictable patterns, but not torched. The disintegrating airplane had probably passed directly over the room, killing the victims from the concussion of the impact or the violent explosion that sucked every bit of air out of the surrounding environment. As horrific as the scene was, it was a tiny bit of consolation that the victims probably hadn't suffered.

To free the bodies, covered in ash and rubble, workers started cutting away the table with power saws. When they moved the table away, Regan saw a third victim underneath it. "We've got another one right here," he called out.

No FBI agents had arrived in the area yet, so Regan started gathering what information he could on the victims. While it was the FBI's job to formally document everything found inside the building, the FEMA crews kept records too, as a matter of standard procedure. Like the FBI, FEMA was marking the location of remains, when they could be identified, on a diagram of the building.

There were also unspoken personal reasons to meticulously document what they had found. The only solace that search or recovery crews could offer victims was to handle their remains with extreme care. Being on best professional behavior was a form of tribute, and no detail was too trivial to account for. So Regan and the others carefully documented what information they could gather.

The first body was that of a man wearing a Navy uniform. Regan found a wallet in the pocket of his tan trousers and carefully fished it out. There was a driver's license inside. It belonged to Dan Shanower of Naperville, Illinois. Being able to assign names to the victims made the whole situation seem that much more real.

The victim in the chair was a woman with dark hair, in civilian clothes. There was a badge around her neck. Regan unclipped it. The badge identified her as Angela Houtz.

The man on the floor was also a Navy officer, Lt. Cmdr. Otis Tolbert, according to the ID tag affixed to his shirt. Regan removed that too.[1]

The three victims were a major find. Most of what the search teams had discovered up till then were body parts, which would take weeks to identify by DNA. But these three victims were intact and identifiable, with ID, and the sooner Regan got the information out, the sooner their families would know with certainty what had happened. He decided to head for the command post right away so the information could get processed as quickly as possible. It wouldn't hurt to get outside and clear his head either—for all the training and discipline, he still felt emotions welling up.

He and Matsos left the building and went through a decontamination tent that resembled a car wash. "Decon," as it was called, had become standard procedure for anybody leaving the building, even if they were going right back in. Uniforms and boots were thoroughly scrubbed. If workers were wearing Tyvek suits, they were stripped off and thrown away. As workers moved through the tent, they underwent additional layers of cleansing until they were considered clean enough to interact with people on the outside. It was tedious but necessary, and the mere routine of it helped chase the gloom that had followed Regan out of the building.

Once through decon, he went to the command post and conveyed the contents of his notebook. He got some water and rested for a while. Then he found his two dog handlers, put on fresh Tyvek, and led his group back in to do more searching.

Nero was a "live-find" dog, not a cadaver dog—he was specifically trained to detect living people and give a distinct bark to alert rescuers when he did. Some dogs were trained in both types of search work, but Elizabeth Kreitler, Nero's handler, felt that that type of cross-training diminished the dogs' capabilities. Detecting human scents was hard enough in the dirty, noisy disaster sites they often worked in. She didn't want a dog that might miss a living survivor because it was confused.

Still, live-find dogs could often locate remains, although they wouldn't indicate a find with a bark signal. It was up to the handler to interpret the dog's behavior and figure out what it meant. When Nero found remains, Kreitler could usually tell because he stopped in place, sniffing curiously. He wouldn't move unless she called him.

As the group continued searching, Kreitler allowed Nero to free-range, sniffing around on his own, often ahead of the group, without a leash. Through years of experience, as both a firefighter and a rescue specialist, Regan had developed a sharp eye for remains. Several times he watched Nero trot right past body parts. Some of them had already been marked, but others hadn't, and Regan posted evidence flags wherever necessary.

The team went back toward the area where the three victims had been clustered around the table, then passed by to push a little deeper into the debris. Nero was sniffing around in one area when Regan saw him stop moving. The dog seemed to be staring at something. Regan walked over, peering into the rubble Nero was poised next to. "What's he looking at?" he wondered.

Then he saw it—part of a skeleton that looked like a rib cage, so ashen and obscured that it might have escaped detection by human eyes for some time. Kreitler caught up, and Regan called her over. "Do you see it?" he asked. Kreitler had been on the task force since 1997 and at several overseas disasters, but on-the-job training was always helpful—even if gruesome. Kreitler looked into the gray rubble for a moment, then spotted the bones. She praised Nero for a job well done.

As the night's work progressed, search teams found numerous victims and body parts. Some were unidentifiable, except by a trained eye. But others were grotesque and shocking. Regan's group moved on to an area where about 25 young soldiers from the Old Guard were tackling a massive job, removing a giant piece of wrecked machinery that looked like it might have been an old mainframe computer. The troops had pushed big wooden poles through the piece of equipment so that several of them could hoist the poles onto their shoulders, harnessing the strength of several men all at once. The scene reminded Regan of schoolbook drawings of workers building the pyramids.

It took awhile to get the machinery into position, and some of the soldiers stared, horrified, to see bodies surrounding them. Behind their respirators, Regan could see shock in the eyes of the young troops, most of them probably no older than 20. Many of the professionals working in the building had spent years working around such awful conditions. You never got used to it, but it eventually became less disturbing. He could tell by the young faces around him, though, that most of the Old Guard troops had never seen anything like the devastation inside the Pentagon. What teenager had?

A mortuary expert working on one set of remains delicately lifted it into a body bag and noticed the stricken eyes, gawking. "What are you staring at?" he lashed out. "Why don't you show some respect?"

That didn't seem right to Regan. He couldn't tell who the mortuary worker was, beneath the Tyvek suit, but he sympathized with the young soldiers. "Hey, why don't you back off, pal," he suggested. "They've never seen anything like this. They're just 18- and 19-year-olds."

Regan and Matsos had been working their way toward the back side of the punch-out hole all night. If everything that had spilled out of the hole was an indication, there would be a lot to find there. Regan sent his dogs and their handlers out again, to take another breather and get cleaned up. By then he guessed they were about 20 feet away from the punch-out hole—probably as close as they were going to get that night. Debris was jammed together and piled high, like the aftermath of an earthquake. Bumping or pulling on the wrong place could cause a deadly avalanche. Clearing crews hadn't made it that far yet, and there wasn't a lot a couple of search specialists could do alone.

They decided to call it a night, Regan left the building, went through decon for the final time, reported the latest activities to the command post, and wrapped up the shift with his crew. The sky was brightening, and the day shift would be coming on soon. His legs felt like lead, his neck hurt from his helmet, and his nose ached from the mask that had been strapped to his face. For the first time in hours he realized that he felt tired. Really tired.

TWELVE VICTIMS

September 13, 7:30 a.m.

By the time the day shift showed up on Thursday, Bob Gray had been working a full 24 hours. At first light on the twelfth he'd started out as one of the officers in charge of the Arlington-Alexandria technical rescue team. Next, he was assigned team leader for the night shift, spending most of the night getting logistics and other parts of the TRT set up. By daybreak on the thirteenth a sturdy operation was in place—the fire was essentially out, and engineers had been able to survey the whole damaged area, which set the stage for clearing and shoring crews to make steady progress.

After two consecutive 12-hour shifts on his feet, Gray felt trashed. He went to Arlington's medical tents to lie down on a cot for a few minutes and take a break. He felt guilty to be resting, since there was so much work left to do, and momentum for the job was finally building. But he needed a few moments to regain his strength. He closed his eyes—and promptly fell into a deep sleep.

The TRT's day shift commander, Scott McKay, was there with a fresh group, however, and they quickly merged into the flow of the clearing and shoring operation. The FEMA group from Fairfax had finished the night shift and was packing up to head back to the navy yard for food and rest. The principal FEMA team on the day shift was Virginia Task Force 2, from Virginia Beach—known as "the Beach" to those in the business. Bobby Beer and a few others on the Arlington TRT knew and liked many of the experts from the Beach, and there was less of the rivalry Arlington had with their neighbors from Fairfax. It was a good fit.

While the overnight crews had done more shoring inside the building, the area between Corridors 4 and 5 was still an enormous wasteland of debris. It was now clear that that section of the Pentagon would eventually have to be demolished and rebuilt. But the remains of all the victims would have to be painstakingly recovered first, along with any evidence the FBI still deemed important. For recovery teams to work safely and retrieve all the victims, nearly 50 support columns still needed to be rebuilt or reinforced. And most of those columns were still enmeshed in wreckage. Clearing that debris was the primary job.

The hunt for Flight 77's black boxes was a top priority too. The cockpit voice recorder and flight data recorders might contain vital information about the hijackers and the overall terrorist plot— intelligence the FBI needed as soon as possible.

The day-shift crews would be pushing into parts of the building that were still unstable and could come crashing down with little warning. As team leaders wrapped up their pre-mission briefings, they emphasized a few key points: Stay alert for signs of impending collapse, call the FBI whenever you find a body or body part, don't move or disrupt remains, and keep an eye open for the black boxes.

Dan Fitch and Bobby Beer led their group into the E Ring, to the left of the rubble pile. The debris field they found inside resembled a metallic jungle, with footpaths meandering through thickets of rubble. The crews that were hauling out debris, mostly near the outer wall, had been aiming to clear paths from column to column, so shoring crews could do their work. A few of the pathways that took shape were fairly straight, with debris piled on either side like the walls of a cave or tunnel. Other pathways were more erratic, snaking around particularly onerous boulders of wreckage or areas where remains had yet to be processed. Much of the standing water had drained away, but even on the narrow trails where debris had been cleared down to the floor slabs, there remained a slurry of ash, dirt, and fluids that clung to workers' boots like muck in a swamp.

On all sides there were massive amounts of chest-high, incinerated debris—and all of it had to be removed. To Beer, it resembled a complex moving problem, like packing up a cluttered house that had been accumulating junk for 30 years—only a hundred times worse. The only sensible way to attack the problem was to lift stuff off the top of piles and deal first with pieces that could be carried. Some of the crews went to work near the columns, clearing enough space for shoring crews to do their work, passing debris out bucket-brigade style. Heavier pieces went into wheelbarrows or onto dollies.

The whole business reminded Fitch of digging a hole at the beach: Every time they scooped out debris, more would fall in. There were moments when the job felt endless. Yet everybody was thankful that the Old Guard soldiers were there. When the work seemed overwhelming, their muscle helped produce measurable bits of progress.

It was like bizarre Industrial-era factory work, with power saws, blowtorches, pumps, generators, and other machines buzzing and clanging constantly. The building's concrete structure still held the heat from the fire like a furnace, and the masks and protective uniforms most of the workers wore made it feel 15 or 20 degrees hotter. As workers tried to untangle mangled pieces of the airplane, the friction of metal on metal created a penetrating screech. Cables and wires ran everywhere through the wreckage, entangling it. Often they had to be cut or unraveled, to loosen a pile, but tugging on a wire also risked destabilizing surrounding debris. At times, when workers pulled a cable out of the rubble, body parts would come with it.

There was danger in every direction, but the biggest risks were overhead. Fitch was concerned about a big chunk of concrete hanging from the wrecked ceiling just ahead of where they were working. A steel girder also poked out of the ceiling, jarred out of position. As the team inched forward, workers occasionally yelled "Stop!" if they thought they heard a creak or groan that might be the start of a collapse. Fitch, Beer, and the FEMA team leaders made sure there was always some kind of evacuation plan. But in such tight circumstances, the planning usually amounted to "run this way" or "run that way." Jim Anderson, the endurance athlete who had climbed to the roof with Ed Hannon on 9/11, was on Fitch's team, and as he looked at the concrete overhead, he knew there'd be little chance of escape if it broke loose and tumbled down on them. It would squash them like bugs, he thought.

FEMA and the FBI had decided it was important to separate airplane wreckage from everything else. So as crews pulled debris apart, they'd examine it to figure out if it looked like part of an airplane or something from inside the building. They were still working on the fringe of the impact zone, and most of the wreckage was shredded or in tatters. In fact, hardly any of the recovery crews had any idea how to identify portions of an airplane. Nor did the FBI agents. So workers would hold up a piece of metal, looking for rivets or highly machined aluminum to help them guess.

"Airplane?" they'd say to each other. "Airplane," a couple of voices would usually answer back.

Then the part would go into a special bin, which would be hauled outside once it filled up and emptied into a bigger container near the rubble pile. All the other pieces of debris went into separate bins, and then to a huge sifting lot set up in North Parking, where agents raked through the material once again, taking a closer look for evidence, remains, and personal effects.

Body parts were as shattered and scattered as remnants of the airplane. Shortly after they began working, Beer uncovered two feet in one of the piles he was sifting through. He briefly looked around at all the wreckage they had yet to dig through, thought about the airplane passengers, and added it up. "Man," he said to one of his colleagues, "there are bodies *everywhere* in here."

This dismal realization quickly became evident to everybody on the team. The people clearing debris found dozens, then hundreds, of body parts. A couple of clearing crews found nearly intact bodies, buried in rubble. But mostly they found pieces. Searchers learned that when they spotted a piece of clothing matted into a pile of rubble, more often than not there was part of a body inside it. Cadaver dogs probing deeper inside some of the piles added to the count. As the flags marking body parts multiplied, the clearing crews ran out of places to work and had to wait around for overtasked FBI recovery teams, or went out for extended breaks, aggravated by the delays.

People were moving everywhere throughout the building, their various roles occasionally conflicting. Garrett McKenzie, the FBI photographer who was now the Bureau's liaison to the PenRen contractors, saw the tension from several different angles. He knew the FBI's style—they wanted everything as pure and pristine as possible. Evidence, after all, had to be uncorrupted if it was going to stand up in court. Fire and rescue workers, in contrast, were accustomed to fast, rough work, breaking things or heaving them aside if that's what it took to get to a victim. Then there were the contractors, who were already thinking about how to demolish the mess and rebuild the structure.

McKenzie had formed a loose alliance with Allyn Kilsheimer, the brazen engineer who didn't mind stepping on the toes of his fellow structural experts. A few people complained to Arlington command about his brash insistence on walking in and out of the Pentagon at will, and poking into people's business while ignoring all the rules. Kilsheimer drew even more attention to himself by refusing to wear a hard hat, while everybody else was clad head to toe in protective gear. He obligingly explained that he hadn't bothered with headgear since 1967, when he saw a construction worker wearing a hard hat get decapitated by a falling piece of lumber. "Hard hats are for pussies," he sneered to anyone bold enough to ask.

Chief Schwartz asked the FBI to kick Kilsheimer out of the site, but McKenzie had become Kilsheimer's protector. He could tell that the engineer had been around a lot of collapsed buildings and knew what he was talking about. The PenRen officials respected him as well, and vouched for him, and McKenzie identified with Kilsheimer's blunt disdain for bureaucracy. The two men got along, and McKenzie quietly did what he could to make sure Kilsheimer was allowed to stay inside the wire.

The deal worked well, and it was totally unofficial—the way both of them liked it. McKenzie needed to go inside the building periodically, to oversee PenRen and FBI operations, and Kilsheimer helped him know which areas were stable enough to operate in. As McKenzie's structural advisor, meanwhile, Kilsheimer could survey the interior and develop plans for tearing down and rebuilding the wrecked portions of the building. Once PenRen was ready to sign a contract for the work, he'd have a detailed plan.

Kilsheimer helped McKenzie understand just how fragile the whole demolition zone was. For a while, McKenzie would ask him if a given area was "safe," until Kilsheimer told him, "To me, 'safe' means I can bring my wife and kids in. None of this is 'safe.'" They decided to evaluate a given area based on whether it seemed a collapse was imminent. If not, they considered it suitable to work in.

Kilsheimer's reputation as go-to guy grew. When he was out by the woodpile near the impact hole at one point, a Navy admiral in fatigues walked up to him and said, "We lost a lot of people in there. We want to go in and see what it's like. Can you take us in?" Kilsheimer agreed, and escorted the admiral and a few others to the area where the Navy Command Center had been, for an emotional look at the devastation.

Others were revisiting random places that now held what seemed sacred import. After recovering at home for a day, Ed Hannon, the Arlington fire captain who had collapsed on the courtyard grass on the night of 9/11, was back on duty as part of a fire watch crew, ready to tackle any spot fires that broke out. Ever since waking up in the hospital, he'd felt haunted by thoughts of the people he and the D.C. crews tried to reach in the thick fire early on. Somebody had told them victims were trapped in an office, and pointed toward a flaming hallway, but relentless flames drove them back before they could reach the office door. Had people really been trapped in there, and died? Could they have gotten out some other way? Or had the person who directed them been mistaken?

It was eating at Hannon, and he decided he had to find out. Most of the interior was now under the control of the FBI and FEMA. He asked Scott McKay to escort him to the part of the C Ring where they had been forced out before they could check for victims. McKay led the way. Search-and-recovery crews had already made their way into the area—and there was plenty to find. Somebody jotted some information onto a placard hanging on the wall, revealing that 12 bodies were found in the area. It was about the worst news Hannon could have learned. The guilt that had been nagging at him reared up. If he'd just been a little quicker, he kept telling himself, he might have gotten them out. McKay asked Hannon if he wanted to find out more—the victims' names, for instance—but Hannon chose not to. He knew enough.

While the search and shoring work was under way in the building, an epic logistical operation was being developed to support it. The Arlington County Fire Department wasn't organized for weeklong operations, and at first, duties fell haphazardly to whomever was available. Doug Insley, Chief Schwartz's aide at the command post, often got the assignment, and he would start tracking down stuff like a homeowner pursuing a do-it-yourself project. When someone at the command post decided golf carts were needed to ferry people and equipment around the sprawling area outside the Pentagon, Insley called a golf-cart company he found in the yellow pages and dialed the number.

"How many do you need?" the employee who answered the phone asked.

"Every one you've got," Insley replied. It took a few moments to explain that the call wasn't a prank, and six hours later a trailer filled with golf carts showed up. It seemed amazing—Insley had never had that kind of clout before.

He was swamped helping Schwartz keep track of dozens of priorities, however, and the operation needed a more formalized logistics staff anyway. Insley got help from some Fairfax County experts, who had a wide network of resources and laptops with preloaded requisition forms. They helped organize an official logistics branch.

Matt Herrera, the Arlington firefighter who stumbled through the fire in the C Ring and wretched at the noxious smoke on the roof, was assigned to the new logistics cell, even though he had no relevant experience. He found it amusing to be suddenly in charge of ordering thousands of dollars' worth of lumber or tools or firefighting equipment. He quickly learned that the spigots were open and he could get virtually anything as long as he followed a few basic rules: Get one of the commanders to approve every request. Do the paperwork and nobody will hassle you. And when you need something in a hurry, call the Home Depot guy.

The newly knighted logisticians requisitioned a truckful of John Deere Gators, rugged little four-wheelers with a small cargo bed that were ideal for hauling equipment too heavy for a golf cart. Another trailer arrived, unsolicited, with several Bobcat skid-loaders, small wheeled tractors able to maneuver and scoop up debris in relatively tight spaces. They were quickly employed to clear pathways inside the building, once clearing crews had sifted through various piles of debris and taken care of any remains.

The work still proceeded at a stutter-step pace, but the day shift laboring to stabilize the building managed to make grudging progress. The Arlington and Alexandria TRT group helped the FEMA crews construct a couple of shores in the E Ring, moving a few steps farther into the "dirty," more dangerous areas of rubble. Other crews started building heavy-duty chutes in A&E Drive, from the upper floors to trash bins on ground level. They'd be used to speed the clearing of debris from areas where it couldn't just be carted out of the building.

The crews became familiar with the rest of the job that lay ahead too. The wrecked columns had to be handled in a number of different ways. The columns in the direct path of the airplane were completely gone, presenting the riskiest challenge, deep into the demolition zone. But others were still in place, although some were bowed or distended. Engineers and workers referred to them as "bananas" or "palm trees," because of their shape. There were other columns where the spiral rebar was still in place but the concrete inside had crumbled. Those were "empty baskets." Every column that had to be rebuilt presented unique challenges, but there were commonalities from place to place, and the workers were trudging up the learning curve.

Beer and Fitch, frustrated by the slow progress, paid close attention to how the experienced FEMA crews did their work, pleased to feel like equal members of the team. Fitch was a novice at collapse work and was getting better training than any class or exercise could provide. Beer was an old hand but had never worked on such a huge job. There was a lot to learn, and a lot still to do.

★ 40 ★

FLARE-UP

September 13, early evening

Two days after the attack, tendrils of smoke still wafted up from the Pentagon, a warning sign for those seasoned enough to recognize it. The smoke—including the smell—was so pervasive that most of the firefighters had become oblivious to it. Yet experienced firefighters also knew that hot spots could lurk in a fire for days and reignite just when you thought everything was wrapped up. Smoke was often the most convincing indication that the job wasn't quite finished.

The collapse pile at the impact hole had continued to spew smoke, which was getting heavier instead of lighter. Randy Gray, one of the daytime commanders, was starting to worry. He mentioned his concern to Arlington battalion chief Jim Bonzano, who had just arrived to relieve him on the night shift. "You know, Bonzi," Gray said, "that smoke's getting heavier."

Bonzano agreed, and asked his staff why there wasn't a fire engine up near the smoking pile. It turned out an engine had been up there all day, ready to open its hoses if fire broke out, but rotated out along with all of the crews on the day shift. A replacement engine was due, but security had tightened, and it took longer than before to get into place. The delay made Bonzano anxious. For the moment there was no way to get water on the building if the smolder erupted. "I wonder where the hell that engine is," he fretted to himself.

———

As Tom O'Connor was organizing his own crews for the night shift, a supervisor from the Bureau of Alcohol, Tobacco, and Firearms walked up to him near the FBI tent on the Pentagon lawn and vented his frustration about remains recovery going so slowly. "This is an embarrassment to law enforcement that this is taking so long," he ranted, his voice drawing the attention of others standing nearby. "We need to be in those areas doing recovery right now."

Of all the interagency rivalries in the federal government, the one between the FBI and the ATF was among the most bitter. The ATF considered the FBI arrogant and insular. FBI agents, on the other hand, felt the ATF suffered from an inferiority complex and was constantly reaching beyond its jurisdiction. Had it been any other agency, O'Connor probably would have brushed off the suggestion. But not when it came from the ATF.

"Well, we're not doing that yet," O'Connor snapped, "and that's the way it is. But just so you know—suit up."

The ATF supervisor hadn't been inside the Pentagon yet, so he and O'Connor pulled on protective gear. Then O'Connor led him in for a look at some of the areas that hadn't been stabilized yet. Water was still ankle deep in some places. Wires, cables, and pipes were poking out everywhere, like dozens of booby traps. Moving through the mess was like climbing a soggy barricade. Through the morass, they could see firefighters battling an outbreak of fire.

"So whaddya think?" O'Connor snorted. "Should we go in there and start sloshing around?"

The ATF man quieted down, and they backed out of the Pentagon. A short while later the supervisor came up to O'Connor. "Hey, I'm sorry," he apologized. "You were right."

"Well, that's great," O'Connor barked, unpacified, "except you were very vocal complaining to me in front of all those other agents. And now you're apologizing to me in private. You've got a ways to go." They parted ways, the interagency rivalry as tense as ever.

O'Connor once again needed volunteers for the morgue. One of the hand-raisers was Jennifer Farmer, an FBI photographer who had been a sporadic presence at the Pentagon till then. Farmer lived just a couple of miles from the Pentagon, and figured she'd end up working there soon enough. But her top priority on September 11 had been retrieving her four-year-old son Logan from a day-care center that overlooked the Pentagon, directly beneath the path Flight 77 had followed into the building.

After the attack, desperate to reach her son, she'd driven to the day-care center with Jen Hill, a fellow FBI photographer. It was a maddeningly slow chug, and they veered around inching traffic with lights flashing and siren blaring. A single mother, Farmer felt panic rising with every lurch of the car. I'm all he has, she kept worrying. There was no one else who could pick him up, since her family lived out of town, but then she thought of one person she could lean on: Chris Combs, the FBI agent, whom she had dated for a couple of years. They'd broken up eight weeks earlier and barely spoken since, but suddenly the pride and frostiness didn't matter. She dialed Combs's cell phone number. The lines were jammed; she couldn't get through.

After an interminable drive, Farmer finally raced in and retrieved Logan herself. "Mommy, I heard something go boom," he told her excitedly. "I think it was a bomb." Back home, Farmer called her ex, who was visiting family in Indianapolis, and said he needed to drive to D.C. and pick up Logan so she could go to work. They agreed that he'd bring the boy back to Indianapolis, away from the pandemonium in D.C.

Logan had gotten to know Chris Combs when the agent was dating his mom, and he knew that Combs had been a firefighter before joining the FBI. "Mommy, is Christopher dead?" Logan asked while waiting for his father to arrive. "They say on TV that firefighters are dead." She explained that Christopher was fine—and meanwhile wished she could call her old boyfriend and ask him to reassure her worried son.

Farmer finally reported for duty at the Pentagon on the night of September 11. She spent the night shooting some pictures outside and helping get the operation set up.

On the morning of the twelfth, she went home and slept before returning later for the night shift, but instead she got called away for another job. The FBI had found the car driven by the five hijackers on Flight 77 parked at Dulles International Airport, in suburban Virginia, and transported it to an FBI warehouse nearby. Farmer would be the photographer who documented all the evidence inside the suddenly significant rattletrap, a blue 1988 Toyota Corolla.

It was nearly noon by the time she got home on the next day, after a good 15 hours of work. She had never felt so tired—yet sleep was elusive. Construction crews at her condo were repaving the parking lot, undeterred by events just two miles to the north. The hiss and bang of the machines were unwelcome stimulants. She also felt lonely with Logan so far away and no other family nearby. If only she could sleep.

Farmer got what rest she could and returned for duty the evening of September 13. She arrived at the morgue around nightfall, unsure what to expect or how she would react. When she watched body bags being unzipped for the first time, it literally took her breath away. There was a moment of gut-wrenching suspense as the contents of each bag were revealed and she wondered if she was about to see something that resembled a person, or an intangible mass of flesh and bone.

Farmer quickly learned her own tolerance levels. As she focused her lens on the material inside the blue bags, she felt reasonably comfortable dealing with indistinct lumps of remains. But all of the things that evoked the unique individuals the victims had been—facial features, fingers, a shoe, jewelry, even a burned scarf—she found deeply upsetting. Fatigue intensified the emotion. For reassurance, Farmer watched Tara Bloesch, who was running the whole morgue operation with the businesslike demeanor of a school principal, yet the occasional soft touch when needed.

There were plenty of other weary people inside the Pentagon adjusting to long, unusual hours while finding adrenaline in the intense, demanding work. Arlington fire captain Bob Gray had returned to the job after spending the afternoon at home watching his two kids and getting a few fitful hours of sleep. As the technical rescue team's night shift commander, he was overseeing three crews removing debris and constructing shores. As commander, there was plenty to be concerned about. They were working close to the collapse pile, and Gray knew that if it broke loose, it would slide right into them, burying them instantly in a concrete avalanche. Yet despite the danger, it was hard to stay alert to all the risks. Jackhammers, generators, and power tools kept up an incessant, distracting roar, and the respirators that everybody wore deepened the sensory deprivation. The environment was jarring and numbing at the same time.

For no obvious reason, the air horns on the fire trucks parked outside started to blare. The blasts came in threes—the evacuation signal. Then one of the commanders announced over the radio, "We need everybody to evacuate. The building is on fire again." Gray and his group looked around and wondered where—they didn't see any sign of flames or smoke. But you didn't stand around and speculate about the reasons for an evacuation—you got out, fast. So Gray quickly spread the word, and his teams spilled out onto the helipad lawn.

Everyone in the group was astonished to see big flames blazing atop the collapse pile, which was less than 50 feet from where they had been working. Gray could tell what had happened: Something reignited deep in the pile, probably when the rubble shifted and fresh oxygen found a hot spot where debris had been smoldering. And judging by the height of the flames, there was obviously plenty of material in there to feed the fire.

The flames looked to be contained to the rubble pile, however, with little threat that they'd spread much farther. "So why are they stopping us?" somebody asked in jest. "Why can't we keep working?" With the fire concentrated in one place, at the exterior of the building, Gray hoped it would be extinguished quickly so workers could get back inside and continue clearing and shoring.

But for a while nothing happened. There were still dozens of firefighters at the Pentagon, but no engine or ladder truck up near the building—the crew that was supposed to rotate in still hadn't gotten through security. As the flames grew bigger and began to brighten the night sky, a throng developed on the lawn, everybody transfixed by the sight of the Pentagon burning—*again*.

While fire commanders bellowed for their crews, others hastily cleared a path for them. A rough-terrain crane, with huge knobby tires, had been helping move construction materials near the front of the pile. When the fire erupted, the operator jumped down and ran off, afraid the flames would reach the crane and set him on fire. Earl Shughart, one of the Fairfax FEMA team members, ran after the man, trying to coax him to move the crane out of the way. "Come on, dude," he pleaded. "The firefighters will keep the fire off of you." Shughart wasn't entirely sure of that, but he persuaded the operator to return to the crane and back it away. Now all they needed was a fire engine.

At the command post, Bonzano and his staff had barely settled in for the evening, and now the leaping flames were getting national attention. CNN showed live footage of the blaze, and a viewer from San Francisco even managed to get a call through to one of the phones in the command post. The caller wanted to know if the fire chiefs were aware that the Pentagon was burning. And shouldn't they be doing something about it? Chief Plaugher was in the bus, and he cringed when he heard the call. This is getting embarrassing, he thought.

A Fairfax ladder truck finally snaked through the complex of tents, construction materials, and work vehicles to battle the blaze. Once the crew parked the truck, they connected the proper hoses, raised the aerial device, and started drowning the fire. It took a while, but they made steady progress, and about two hours after it first flared, the fresh fire was out.

Bonzano, meanwhile, had ordered a second alarm, and half a dozen vehicles led by Bob Cornwell arrived shortly after the Fairfax crew had gone to work. Bonzano sent those fire crews inside the building, to make sure the fire wasn't spreading on the interior. Cornwell eventually reported that there seemed to be little extension of the fire; it had remained contained to the rubble pile.

Bonzano rejoiced once the flames were finally extinguished. He'd been picturing himself as the man responsible for burning down the Pentagon. Seeing the ladder truck finally pull into place made him feel like he had personally been plucked from disaster.

Shoring and search crews hustled back into the building, eager to return to the job. But it was hard to get into a steady work rhythm. The delay caused by the fire was a setback, and they were also pushing deeper into the demolition zone—what had been the core of the fire—where it was increasingly difficult to work. Since the force of the airplane swept everything in its path forward, the debris got denser as workers plowed their way toward the punch-out hole. Hot spots flared as clearing crews delayered the rubble, which meant firefighters had to rush in to douse the flames. In the C Ring, not far from the punch-out hole, one flare-up was big enough to force an evacuation of the area until firefighters put it out.

There was still plenty of work for the search teams, who would tag remains as they found them and move on. Mike Regan was back on the overnight shift, along with other FEMA crew members, including medic Carlton Burkhammer, who helped get Regan back on his feet after getting sick on the eleventh, and another medic, Brian Moravitz. The group passed the airplane seats and found dozens of body parts, often with the help of search dogs. Most were indistinguishable, which made the grim discoveries somewhat bearable.

Then Moravitz saw something awful: a toddler's hand. It enraged him—his own son Nathan was four years old. Why God? Why? he wanted to scream. But he didn't. He felt an overwhelming desire to go home and hug his son and his wife. But of course he couldn't do that either. There was a job to do.

The medics were there in case anybody got hurt, but the crews were in good shape. So Burkhammer and Moravitz pitched in with the debris clearing and other tasks. They were both eager to do anything that would keep their minds and bodies busy and awful thoughts at bay.

They'd all been briefed about the black boxes, and Moravitz decided to hunt for the crucial machinery, making it his personal crusade. He relayed his plan to Regan and a few others standing nearby.

"Worry about that later," Regan said. "We've got all these bodies we need to get out, and all this debris. Forget about the black boxes."

But Moravitz persisted, and he and Burkhammer began pushing debris around, looking for objects that resembled the pictures they were shown during their briefing at the beginning of the shift. It wasn't long before Burkhammer uncovered something unusual. "Hey, look at this," he said to Moravitz. "That's not office machinery."

"Maybe it's the black box," Moravitz said. "We should get the FBI."

They sent a runner out to summon an agent. Regan and a few others went and looked.

"I don't know," Regan said as he studied the object. It was a piece of machinery, charred and splintered, the size and shape of a small suitcase. "It looks like a desktop computer."

"I'm telling you, I think that's it," Moravitz insisted.

"Well, let's wait till somebody comes by, and we'll ask," Regan said.

They went back to work, but Moravitz kept saying, "That's got to be the black box," over and over. He was needling Regan, since the search team leader had told him not to bother looking. The banter defused some of the stress, so Regan didn't mind. But he was relieved when an FBI agent finally came by about 45 minutes later.

"Is this the black box?" several people asked him at once.

"Nope," he answered after looking at it for a second, then left.

But Moravitz had become convinced. "I'm *telling* you," he pestered Regan, "that's it!"

A while later another agent came into the area, and they asked him.

This agent scrutinized it for a moment and declared, "That's it!" Moravitz looked around triumphantly as the agent picked up the device and a couple other pieces nearby and carried them away.

"I'll be damned," Regan groaned. "The sonofabitch was right." He knew Moravitz would be telling the story and razzing him about his naysaying for months. There were a few laughs, but the levity didn't last long in the dismal surroundings.

Outside, the engineers had come up with several schemes for dealing with the fallen portion of the building where the rekindled fire had just been extinguished. The wrecked area stretched about 80 feet across, and reached into the interior nearly as far. The biggest concern was removing the rubble without creating a slide that could take out additional parts of the building, including areas where FEMA teams had already built shoring. One option was to use a crane and wrecking ball to knock everything down to the ground, then scoop it out with bulldozers, like a typical demolition.

A wrecking ball had already been delivered, in fact, by one of the contractors. But most of the engineers hated the idea. A "headache ball," as they called it, would probably do more harm than good, sending powerful vibrations through the building that would likely bring down other fragile sections. And when Chief Plaugher heard about it, he vetoed the idea—he wasn't about to allow TV footage of crews knocking down the Pentagon. It was the wrong image at a vulnerable time for the nation. Plus, there were victims in the pile. It wasn't the right way to treat them either.

Another possibility was attaching a cable to the roof slab on top of the pile and pulling the layers off one by one with a crane. But that wasn't very appealing, since the crane operator wouldn't have a lot of control over the pile if it slid in the wrong direction, into the intact part of the building.

Then a better idea surfaced. Earl Shughart, the heavy rigging expert for the Fairfax FEMA team, mentioned a machine known as a multiprocessor, or "pulverizer," that had a mechanical arm that could reach as high as 72 feet. The very top of the Pentagon was a bit higher than that, but the crane sounded like an ideal tool for the job. A jaw at the end of the arm could be worked like a pincer to lift objects off the pile, bring them to the ground, cut through steel and rebar if necessary, and sweep debris to the side. It turned out there were only two such machines in the country, but one of them happened to belong to Potts & Callahan, a construction firm in Baltimore, just 50 miles away. Shughart made the arrangements, and the pulverizer was at the Pentagon, ready to go, by Thursday afternoon.

Before the hulking machine went to work, however, engineers and search crews needed to scrutinize the pile closely, to gauge the most vulnerable areas, identify any visible bodies, and devise a plan for dismantling the pile with minimal risk to people, the rest of the building, and identifiable remains.

They used the man-basket to check out the pile from the front, but it was harder to examine the debris from the back side, inside the building, and the sides. So search teams were assigned to peer into the pile from every vantage point they could find. Mike Regan ended up there later during the overnight shift, overseeing a couple of rescue specialists. They scanned the pile from the upper floors, on the

Corridor 4 side, looking into the higher part of the sloping pile, where it still clung to the intact portion of the building like a cracked tree limb.

The pile was still smoldering from the fire, but one of the rescue specialists, Mike Davis, thought he could make out the telltale signs of a body wedged into the rubble—the shape of a torso, the slightly brighter colors of clothing that stood out amidst the gray. Regan got out his binoculars for a closer look. "Yeah, that's a guy," he confirmed.

Davis wanted to climb down onto the pile, to make sure and to mark the remains. "No way," Regan ordered, marveling at the gumption of somebody so gung-ho. Instead, they balled up a wad of yellow fire-line tape, with a piece of stone inside as a weight. Then they wrapped the whole thing in sticky tape, with the adhesive facing out, so it would cling to the pile when they threw it. If the aim was good, that would mark the body sufficiently.

Davis lined up his throw and let it fly. The tape ball whiffled through the air for about 25 feet, hit the rubble about three feet from the body, and stuck. "Good enough," Regan declared. Like so much else at the Pentagon, it wasn't perfect. But it got the job done.

"A GREAT FIND"

Friday, September 14, 2:30 A.M.

The black box found by the FEMA searchers turned out to be a false alarm. Once it was hauled outside and examined closely, it quickly became clear that the initial assessment was wrong. It was nothing more than a charred chunk of machinery. The black boxes were still in the wreckage somewhere.

On the third night, there was still a lot of work to do documenting remains, but many areas remained too fragile for evidence crews to work in. The punch-out hole, however, was buzzing with activity. FBI agent Mark Whitworth had been in that area on the day of the attack, with some NTSB experts, and they recognized pieces of the tail section from Flight 77, along with lots of other airplane debris. In addition to his expertise with explosives, Whitworth had a degree in aerospace engineering. He'd worked with the NTSB before, at other crashes, and spoke their language. He and the NTSB experts agreed that the punch-out hole would be a good place to look for the black boxes, since they were located near the back of the plane.

FEMA crews had expanded the safe area inside the hole, and several dozen people from the FBI and other agencies took turns picking through the densely matted debris, scouting for the elusive airplane recorders. When the fire flamed up out front and everybody evacuated, most of the crews in A&E Drive decamped to the courtyard to wait it out. Finally, word came that crews could resume their work inside, and the group continued picking through the rubble. One of the people in the group was FBI photographer Jen Hill, who spent some time snapping pictures. When she felt she was finished, she asked Whitworth if she could help with the hunt for the black boxes. Why not? he figured.

Agents had thoroughly combed through the debris in A&E Drive by then, and most of the searchers were working inside the hole in the remnants of the C Ring. Some portable lights on poles lit the area, but when Hill ducked inside to help, she still found it dark, damp, and depressing. In addition to the crazily stacked debris, there was fractured rebar sticking out everywhere, and as she stumbled over the uneven floor, her main concern was not getting hurt. She had already banged her head a couple of times and probably would have ended up bleeding, or worse, if she hadn't worn a helmet.

Hill still had her camera slung over her shoulder, which limited her maneuverability. Plus, she tried to help without getting in the way of agents with more expertise and a better idea about what they were looking for. Mainly she helped clear stuff out of the way by picking up light pieces of rubble and carrying them to a trash bin nearby.

Whitworth had positioned himself at the edge of the punch-out hole to eyeball everything searchers were hauling out. Hill walked by with a square object, blackened with soot, headed for the bin, when he stopped her. "Hey, gimme that," he said, pulling the burnt object out of her hands.

The device was roughly the size of a shoe box, melted on one end. It was ashen-colored and looked nothing like the pictures of the black boxes—which were orange—but Whitworth could tell that it wasn't part of the building. "We need to let the NTSB look at this," he declared.

Whitworth found one of the NTSB analysts. "Oh, fuck," she groaned when she looked at the mangled device. She identified it as the airplane's cockpit voice recorder, which captured sounds in the cockpit. It looked to be nearly demolished—there was a marginal chance they'd be able to get any information from it.

Still, it was a breakthrough. Whitworth returned to the punch-out hole a moment later, empty-handed. "Hey, that was a great find," he told Hill. "That was one of the black boxes. Where'd you find it?"

"Right over here," she said, pointing to a stack of jumbled rubble. Searchers formed a circle around the pile and started digging, since the black boxes on 757s were both in the same section of the airplane.

About half an hour later another NTSB expert uncovered a device that looked like it could be the other black box. It turned out to be the flight data recorder, which collected electronic information about the operation of the jet. Both of the black boxes had finally been found, pulled like two broken shells from an ocean of debris.

Since he was in charge of evidence recovery, Tom O'Connor took possession of the recorders, and promptly drove them through the dark to the NTSB's laboratory in downtown D.C. The immediate hope was that the cockpit voice recorder would yield a playback of conversations in the cockpit during Flight 77's last 30 minutes, the duration of the looping tape. That would give investigators the best insights yet into who the hijackers were, how they had taken over the plane, who their accomplices might have been, and whether the Pentagon was their intended target. But as the NTSB expert suspected, the voice recorder had been damaged beyond repair. They tried to extract the recording, but all information had been destroyed by the crash and the intense fire.

The data recorder survived, however, and O'Connor watched as NTSB technicians downloaded the data into a computer. They were able to quickly reconstruct Flight 77's circular flight path as it descended toward the Pentagon, and confirm that it was traveling extremely fast when it slammed into the building. Once the NTSB conducted a more detailed analysis, the experts hoped, the data would help produce a fairly complete picture of Flight 77's entire flight path.

The sun was up when O'Connor returned to the Pentagon. Jen Hill had come outside after finding the first black box, and met up with her friend and fellow photographer Jen Farmer. They both laughed as Hill described how she'd almost thrown the black box away. Then Hill took Farmer into the Pentagon for a look around, her first tour inside the building. The darkness, the destruction, and the foul water plinking down everywhere made Farmer think of a dungeon. "This is like a horror flick," she said.

Hill and Farmer lived near each other in suburban Virginia, just a couple miles southeast of the Pentagon. They were both single, and Farmer had sent her son to Indianapolis for the time being, so they were going to empty homes, alone, after the end of each shift. That was tolerable. But there were new rumors that one of the Flight 77 hijackers had lived in a condo nearby, which made them both feel skittish. With her son Logan away, Farmer already felt dreadfully lonely at home. When she heard about the local hijacker, her sense of isolation became overwhelming. As the night shift ended and began to pack up, she felt uncomfortable going to her own home.

There was a powerful sense of camaraderie at the Pentagon, and it was actually comforting for many to be there, especially as the operation became less frantic and more structured. Most agencies had established scheduled shifts, so workers could pace themselves for a sustained operation without burning out. People couldn't just walk in and out of the building anymore—strict security limited access— so everybody inside the wire was a member of the team. Camp Unity, in South Parking, had become the equivalent of an open-air mall, with all of the food and clothing anybody would need during the course of the mission. There were counselors and chaplains for anybody who wanted to talk to one. You could even get a haircut. And everything was free. As awful as the incident was, for Farmer and Hill work had become a more comfortable place than home. But the workday was over, it was time to rest, and they both headed home for a few hours of uneasy sleep.

Though it was now three days after the attack, tension was still mounting over the repetitive delays as search-and-clearing crews waited for FBI recovery teams to process remains. FBI agent John Adams, in charge of evidence recovery on the day shift, had been working with the FEMA daytime commander, Buddy Martinette, to synchronize FEMA's work with the FBI's. But remains recovery was turning out to be an overwhelming job. The Defense Department knew by then that probably fewer than 200 victims had died in the attack. But that didn't equate to 200 bodies. There were thousands of pieces of remains in the wreckage, and the FBI was treating all of it as valuable evidence. The painstaking work meant that the FBI's gears were turning much more slowly than everybody else's.

Around midday on September 14, Agent Chris Combs walked up to Adams near the FBI tent on the Pentagon lawn. The two agents knew each other, but Adams didn't even know Combs was there—in the chaos, they hadn't seen each other at all since 9/11. After a quick greeting, Combs said, "What are you doing, man? Your guys are killing me."

"What do you mean?" Adams asked, perplexed.

"Evidence is taking too long," Combs answered. "We're not responding fast enough." He explained how the command group had meetings every four hours, and at the most recent one, Buddy Martinette complained that FEMA's debris-clearing and shoring operation had been severely bogged down by FBI procedures. The whole pace of progress, in fact, was generating intense interest from Defense Department leaders, and even the White House. Government officials watching TV noticed cranes operating in New York, pulling wreckage apart, and wondered why there were no cranes at the Pentagon to speed up the removal of debris. A four-star general hovered at the FEMA command post, urging Martinette and other commanders to hurry up and finish the job so the military could reclaim their building.

The structural engineers, meanwhile, were warning commanders to slow down and be careful, or more people might get killed. There were continual, intense negotiations over the pace of the work, bordering on confrontation.

One thing that would speed up the work—safely—was devising a more efficient way to handle the recovery of remains. So Combs and Adams agreed that the FBI needed to work better with FEMA. "Here's what we're going to do," Adams said. "We'll put an evidence guy on every search team." He'd also make sure FBI crews were on standby, ready to go the moment search crews called for them. And they'd see about loosening the recovery rules. If search teams got far ahead of recovery crews, it might be good enough to flag pieces of remains and continue working around them, even if that meant moving them slightly. Combs returned to the command bus, confident he'd be able to report a solution.

Other concerns surfaced as the operation matured. One issue that got the FBI's attention was firefighters bringing in cameras. Firefighters routinely wanted to document the many unusual things they saw on the job. Some took pictures for training purposes, to help educate new recruits or junior firefighters. Others just wanted to show their friends, or add to their career memorabilia. And there were always one or two who might be tempted to claim the spotlight by providing pictures to the press or posting them on the Internet.

Combs wasn't going to tolerate any of it. As firefighters chatted about the pictures they had taken inside the Pentagon showing the destruction, the FBI agent clamped down. "Listen, this is a crime scene," he told Schwartz. "If I see any goddamn pictures of this on

406 PATRICK CREED AND RICK NEWMAN

the news, I guarantee you I will prosecute whoever took them." He didn't want to embarrass any firefighters, but was determined to prevent the Pentagon from becoming a spectacle for tabloid journalists or whoever else might exploit the gruesome images of victims.

The issue percolated up to Schwartz and Plaugher, who both agreed with Combs. Plaugher sent out a message to fire crews that anybody who had taken pictures and agreed to turn in their cameras would be granted amnesty: Nothing would happen. A couple of firefighters stepped forward with their cameras. Then Plaugher said that he planned to axe the firefighters. Chris Ramey, his aide, strongly objected. "Man, you can't do that!" he protested. "You told those guys nothing would happen to them!"

"Well, I meant nothing criminally," Plaugher explained.

Ramey was alarmed. Afterward, he told all the firefighters he knew that if they had a camera, they shouldn't turn it in—they might get fired. "If you took a picture," he advised, "just throw the camera away."

Plaugher got the hint and realized he might have overreacted. He told Schwartz and other commanders to grab whatever cameras they could and talk tough, but let the troops off the hook. As long as no pictures got out, it was one problem they could sweep under the rug.

★ 42 ★

THE JAWS OF LIFE

September 14, afternoon

Plaugher was unsympathetic toward VIPs. He had little tolerance for dignitaries who felt the rules should be bent just for them, and would have preferred that he and his department stayed out of the limelight altogether. Special requests annoyed him. But he also realized that September 11 was a national event, and that the world was watching. Besides, as General Jackson reminded him, when it came to the military, rank often got its way.

Jackson fielded one call that was especially delicate, from Gen. John Keane, the Army's number-two officer, the vice chief of staff a hulking career paratrooper known for his forceful demeanor. Lt. Gen. Tim Maude, the Army personnel chief, had been in an office on the second floor of the E Ring, directly above the path of the airplane. He and about a dozen others in the same area, at the edge of the rubble pile, were presumed dead. As far as anybody knew, Maude was the highest-ranking victim among Pentagon officials. He had also been a personal friend of Keane, who had a special request: to escort Maude's wife Terry up to the edge of the rubble pile so she could lay a wreath and honor the place of her husband's death.

Jackson was dubious. "I don't think that's a good idea," he told Keane.

"Why not?" Keane asked.

"No matter how strong those workers are," Jackson said, "if they see a woman collapse, especially with people around her, it would be really upsetting."

"She'll do fine," Keane insisted. His persistence indicated he was not going to give up, and the four-star general wasn't accustomed to being told no by subordinates. Plus, the Army had lost several dozen people in the Pentagon, and while mourning personal friends, Keane was also one of the senior officers bearing the stress of leading the institution through an awful ordeal. He was in no mood for negotiation.

"Okay," Jackson relented, aware that the conversation was quickly souring. "Let me talk it over with Plaugher."

Jackson met with Plaugher and Schwartz at the command post and laid out his dilemma. Plaugher agreed it was a bad idea to allow victims' families into an area where bodies were still heaped in the rubble and workers were trying to deal with the carnage. Jackson wanted to make sure Plaugher knew that Keane could be very forceful. If Jackson told Keane no and then Plaugher reversed the decision, Jackson's credibility would crumble.

Besides, Jackson had provided pivotal support to the fire chiefs since Tuesday morning. He'd backed them up in meetings with the Pentagon's top brass, and now he needed some of that support back. "Listen," he told Plaugher, "when I tell Keane what your decision is, I'll bet he's gonna want to talk to you. If you're going to give in on the phone, then you need to tell me, and let me be the one to give in."

"I'll stand my ground," Plaugher assured him. "Don't worry."

Keane called Jackson back a few minutes later. "What does Plaugher say?" the vice chief wanted to know.

"He doesn't think it's a good idea," Jackson told him.

"Let me talk to the chief," Keane demanded. Jackson handed over the phone.

Plaugher reiterated Jackson's concerns: If his workers were exposed to the grief of a family member, it would puncture the professional detachment required to do a gruesome job. "They'd be decimated," he told Keane, calmly explaining his logic. "Sorry, Vice Chief, but it's not gonna happen." Then he gave the phone back to Jackson.

"Okay," Keane told Jackson, "I agree with the chief." Jackson was relieved when he hung up, and the fire chiefs felt a break in the tension too. They worked out another plan. Construction crews were building a VIP viewing stand up by the Citgo station so dignitaries could inspect the scene and get a personal briefing from Plaugher or one of the other chiefs without interfering with work at the site. They'd bring the general's wife there, along with a couple of chaplains and other Army officials who could offer support.

With better access to the most-damaged areas of the building, military teams also started to retrieve some of the sensitive classified material from the Pentagon, including safes, file cabinets, and other containers that held secret or top-secret documents. The unattended classified data had become a major concern. Foreign agents from Russia, China, and other countries were known to case the Pentagon regularly—usually through electronic means—and counterintelligence officials assumed they'd be clustered around the Pentagon in one form or another, gathering whatever information they could. If some of the most important classified data couldn't be collected or accounted for, Pentagon officials would have to assume it had fallen into unfriendly hands. Vital military secrets might be revealed and covert operations even compromised.

The Defense Protective Service, headed by John Jester, had teams of classified-information specialists working since the evening of 9/11 to secure all the sensitive information they could find. Within a couple of days they had hauled about 300 safes out of the building, along with dozens of classified computers. Material that seemed damaged beyond repair was fed into the Pentagon's classified-waste incinerator. Many of the safes had been fused shut by the heat, with markings burned off. The only way to tell who the safes belonged to was to open them and see whose documents were inside. Then they'd be stored in a Pentagon vault until the appropriate agency claimed them.

For a while the classified containers were being hauled to an area in the North Parking lot, where they could be handled away from the commotion inside the building. Many of the safes and filing cabinets had dial-combination locks that no longer worked. Others seemed to be in working order, but whoever had the combination died in the attack or couldn't be located. One way or another, the military needed to get inside the heavy-duty containers, and they didn't have the kind of equipment it would take to pry them open.

Arlington sent a few crews to help. Cub Lyon, the son of battalion chief G. O. Lyon, had spent 9/11 with a crew battling flames near the C Ring, where many of the classified containers had been located. He was now assigned to Rescue 109, with Capt. Charlie Winchester in charge. Their unit was assigned to head over to North Parking, to help retrieve the classified material. When they got to the parking lot, a row of safes and filing cabinets was lined up, surrounded by armed guards belonging to the DPS.

The firefighters used hydraulic Hurst tools, commonly known as the "Jaws of Life," to break open the cabinets, but it was hard work. A Hurst tool resembles a big chain saw on one end, where the handle is, with pincers instead of a cutting chain at the other end. Firefighters wielded the tool by hand, securing the jaws in place, while a generator pumped hydraulic fluid through a hose, allowing the jaws to close with thousands of pounds of force. The safes and cabinets had to be partially crushed with the jaws to create gaps or holes that would allow the firefighters to pry open safe doors or cabinet drawers. It was tedious and tiring to manage the heavy tools by hand, and progress was slow. The firefighters tried to figure out a better way.

When the Hurst tool punctured a cabinet, Lyon noticed that there was a locking mechanism inside whose arms secured the drawers to the frame. He quickly calculated that instead of prying apart the entire cabinet, they could simply make a few small cuts on the outside of the drawers with a handheld torch, which would cut the locking mechanism and allow them to yank open the drawers. Charlie Winchester agreed with the logic, and they decided to give it a try.

With the gun-wielding DPS officers hovering over them, Lyon lit a cutting torch called a Slice Pack, and used the flaming tip to cut through the steel on the front and sides of one of the cabinets. It worked. He could hear the locking arms falling away inside the metal frame. After making the final cut, he stood up and proudly yanked open the drawer—which promptly set off a minor panic. The papers inside had caught fire from the heat of the cutting torch, and flames leapt from the drawer. The DPS officers raced for fire extinguishers and desperately tried to pat out the burning files.

Lyon glanced sheepishly at Winchester, who was struggling to suppress a grin. Lyon felt an uncontrollable giggle rising up as well. The vital files had survived the terrorist attack and raging fire, only to be incinerated by a clumsy firefighter. Maybe that wasn't his greatest idea, Lyon admitted to himself.

The military changed its procedures, and acquired its own Hurst tools; they'd open the rest of the safes and other containers themselves. When Lyon and Winchester rejoined their colleagues, there were roars of laughter over the story. Scott Hagan brought down the house mimicking Lyon's great idea: "Hey, buddy, safe's open. Where do you want these ashes?"

Dean Tills, Earl Shughart, and a few other stalwarts who had been working around the clock finally left the site and got some meaningful sleep. They had tried to sustain themselves with two- or three-hour naps in one of the FEMA tents, or out on the grass by Washington Boulevard, but exhaustion finally overwhelmed them. At one point Titus even fell asleep—standing up.

Tills and Shughart had told the FEMA commanders not to use the pulverizer—the huge crane—to dismantle the collapse pile until they got back and thoroughly examined conditions in the pile. But when they returned for the night shift on Friday, September 14, there was an urgent problem. FEMA officials rushed them up to the edge of the building, where the pulverizer had been ordered into action ahead of schedule. The result was a near catastrophe.

One of the FEMA commanders had told the operator of the huge crane to start pulling debris off the pile, and before long a huge piece of the roof, big enough to cover a town house, came tumbling down, nearly toppling the base of the crane; pinching off one piece of debris, it turned out, had destabilized the whole pile. Part of the debris slid into one of the key shores at the edge of the collapse zone, the one Kent Watts had constructed using additional wood and a more robust design than Dean Tills had ordered. Those precautions now looked brilliant—the slide had kicked out a corner of the shore but it still held. It was an awfully close call, though. Shughart stared at the damage, fuming—it was as if somebody up the chain was *trying* to take out a couple of crews.

This time the FEMA commanders listened to Shughart and Tills. Pulverizer operations were put on hold while they thoroughly analyzed the vulnerabilities in the pile and gauged the best way to limit the chances of another dangerous slide. There were plenty of unusual complications. One of the building engineers told Shughart that there was a roomful of big, heavy safes on one of the upper floors, just to the edge of the pile. If that part of the building gave way, the safes could come tumbling down the front of the pile and take out the crane itself, or anybody standing nearby. Shughart worked with the crane operator to construct a kind of pocket in the pile, so if the safes dropped through, they'd fall into a hole instead of rolling out where people were working.

With most aspects of the Pentagon operation in capable hands, it was time for the last of the round-the-clockers to finally go home and sleep in an actual bed. Doug Insley, Chief Schwartz's aide, had been shadowing Schwartz nonstop, tending to a mushrooming list of duties that could have kept him occupied for a week if it were humanly possible. He hadn't seen his wife, Donna, in four days, and had a new baby girl in addition to a three-year-old son. As he was nearing the point of exhaustion, Insley got a worrisome phone call—his daughter, just four weeks old, had gotten a bump on her head and Donna rushed her to the hospital.

Insley left the Pentagon in a hurry. When he got to the hospital, it turned out his daughter was fine. Donna could tell he was running on empty. "Go home," she told her husband. "Everything's okay."

Insley complied and got back in his car. After a couple of minutes, a cop pulled him over. Insley had been weaving like a drunk driver. The officer peered suspiciously into the car, then noticed Insley's uniform. "Hey, do you work for the fire department?" he asked.

"Yeah," Insley nodded.

"You been at the Pentagon?" the officer probed.

"Yeah," Insley said in a weary monotone.

"Go home," the officer told him, closing his notebook and walking back to his car. Insley redoubled his concentration and made it the last few miles to safety, and a bed.

Schwartz burned out at around the same time. Like Tills, Insley, and a few of the others, he had scarcely slept in four days, relying on adrenaline and continual movement to keep him awake and alert. The strategy worked for a good long while, but finally ran its course. He had a crushing headache, the worst he'd ever endured. He finally checked out and drove to his home in Alexandria, just a few miles south of the Pentagon. He was returning to an empty house, since the place was being renovated, with contractors adding a third floor. His wife and two daughters were staying with relatives.

Schwartz headed straight for bed, on the second floor. As he collapsed on the mattress, he looked up, and for a brief moment it seemed as if he hadn't come home at all. He was staring at a blue tarp, left by the contractor after they had removed the roof. I'm back home, but I'm still outside, he thought. He could just as well have been sleeping in one of the tents out on the Pentagon lawn, and for a bleary second he wondered if he was. But then he noticed something: It was quiet. No, it definitely wasn't the Pentagon.

★ 43 ★

TRAFFIC

September 14, evening

Mike Regan started the night shift on Friday evening with a strange, anxious feeling. His father was in the hospital on Long Island, dying of bladder cancer. The elder Regan, a retired cop for the Port Authority of New York, had told his son, "Don't come here just because I'm sick. You're not going to do anything for me here." And family members in the hospital were saying that Pops seemed okay for the time being, all things considered. But for some reason, Regan didn't think so.

There was still a lot of clearing and shoring to be done in the Pentagon, but as a search team leader, Regan felt his job was winding down. Except for piles of debris that workers hadn't reached yet, most of the office spaces had been thoroughly searched, some multiple times. Regan had never left a deployment before it was over, but this was different. He found Ed Brinkley, one of the Fairfax FEMA leaders. "My father is really sick," Regan explained. "I've got a bad feeling. I'm gonna go home."

When he finally got there, around 1:00 A.M. on September 15, there were hundreds of candles lining the streets near his neighborhood. He didn't understand why. After giving his wife, Janice, a clenching hug, he led her to the front door and pointed to the candles. "Come look at this," he urged her. "What's going on?"

She explained that since 9/11, people everywhere had been waving flags, lighting candles, volunteering, doing anything to feel like they were reaching out and connecting with other Americans. Regan realized how isolated he'd been at the Pentagon. He'd been at the epicenter of one of the attacks, but had little idea what was going on in the outside world.

He still felt the same urgency as before. "I need to go see my father," he told Janice.

"Do you want to go tomorrow?" she asked.

"I don't know," he said.

Janice made the decision: "Okay, we're going to New York." She told the couple's two girls to pack their bags. Regan said he needed a quick power snooze and then they'd go. "Wake me up in an hour," he requested.

Back at the Pentagon, the mission was steadily progressing, with new people arriving and some of the early hands rotating out. When the night shift began, Bob Gray and Bobby Beer found their helpful friend "Johnny," the badgeless official with the Special Forces buddies, whom they had come to rely on. They asked the well-connected wheel-greaser for help with a number of things, like getting some supplies from Home Depot and arranging for Old Guard troops to help with the heavy lifting inside the building. Johnny had come through repeatedly before, and sure enough, as the shift moved forward, their requests were fulfilled.

Later in the shift, one of Gray's teams found two bodies deep in the E Ring, and they called the FBI, as usual. There was no response, and after a while Gray walked over to the FBI tent to see what the holdup was. Then he noticed that the white panel truck used to transport bodies to the temporary morgue was pulling up to Corridor 5. What are they doing here? Gray wondered, since they hadn't even made contact with the FBI yet. He rushed over to the truck to make sure nobody removed the bodies before agents photographed and documented them.

The confusion got sorted out, and evidence teams finally came in and did their work. But later in the shift, Gray and Beer couldn't find Johnny. They looked around and asked for him, but nobody knew anything. He seemed to have vanished.

They went back to work, both men puzzled by Johnny's disappearance. As the shift wound down, they dug a little deeper, asking if anybody knew who he worked for. A number of contractors and FEMA officials had interacted with Johnny, but nobody seemed to know exactly who he was—or even what his last name was. None of the agencies claimed him. Contractors thought he worked for the government, and vice versa. Since he had never worn a badge or name tag, there was no way to tell for sure.

Then Gray learned that Johnny was the one who called for the body truck—prematurely—and he and Beer began to piece together a theory. Maybe "Johnny" had no official standing at all and was faking it all along. He would have required some kind of clearance to get through the concentric security perimeters that sprung up around the building—unless he'd been inside the wire before security tightened. It was possible that he had wandered in at the very beginning and simply stayed—there was enough food, water, and basic support on the scene to survive for days. Somebody who was determined enough to sleep inside one of the tents, or even on the grass, could easily have bypassed security.

If Johnny had indeed been an impostor, then the mishap with the body truck might have been his undoing. Security had become strict, and the FBI was scrutinizing everybody who didn't have airtight credentials. It wasn't unusual at high-profile crime scenes for law-enforcement pretenders to show up and insinuate themselves into the work.

But with criminal evidence throughout the building—and classified material literally floating through the air—the FBI had gone around and ushered out any volunteers. Others were being checked out. Gray and Beer figured that Johnny might have tripped some kind of alert when he called the body truck, prompting the FBI to ask who he was. After scratching their heads over the mysterious character, they laughed. "Well, whoever he was," Gray said, "I think we're going to miss him."

The night shift was winding down, but the pulverizer was back at work, plucking huge chunks of debris off the collapse pile. The massive machine—technically, a Caterpillar ultra-high-reach excavator—was quickly branded the "T-Rex," on account of its gargantuan size and weird resemblance to some kind of prehistoric carnivore. Two crane operators had come from Baltimore with the T-Rex, one to work the day shift and one the night shift. Workers at the site found themselves transfixed as they watched the huge contraption manhandle concrete slabs or steel beams, yanking them from the pile and twirling them around effortlessly.

Dean Tills and other engineers had been able to examine the collapse pile from the man-basket and other vantage points, which let them study part of the problem. But it was too dangerous to get close enough to key pressure points—like those under the roof—to gauge with confidence whether the pile was likely to stay in place as workers dismantled it, or whether it would come tumbling down the moment somebody disturbed a pebble at the bottom. It wasn't even clear what was connecting the roof to the rest of the building—beams, steel rebar buried in the concrete, or nothing but friction.[1]

Every movement of the T-Rex carried the risk of starting another rubble slide without warning. Menacing chunks of concrete and steel—widowmakers—threatened anybody who walked near the pile, and the first priority was clearing them off. The T-Rex was an ideal tool for that job, working in concert with backhoes and bulldozers, which would scoop up the rubble from the outside in, steadily reducing the pile.

The massive machines rumbled back and forth like elephants. Earl Shughart, dubbed "the maestro" by Kent Watts, was the man choreographing the movements. In his ordinary job, Shughart rebuilt heavy equipment damaged in accidents, which gave him an acute understanding of what could go wrong in a complex clearing operation. The Pentagon job required continual coordination too. As the T-Rex pulled debris from the building, the operator laid it out on the ground at the foot of the huge crane. Then a backhoe or loader would spread it around, so cadaver dogs and FBI agents could go over it, checking for remains. Once that was done, the earthmovers would pick up the debris and drop it into dump trucks, which transported everything to the sifting lot in South Parking, where agents would spread everything out and pore over it once more.

As the sky was just starting to brighten on Saturday morning, September 15, the T-Rex reached into the pile and snatched a piece of fractured concrete five or six feet wide. It turned out to be one of the linchpins holding the mass in place. When the T-Rex yanked out the piece of concrete, about half of the pile came tumbling down into a fresh heap at the base of the big machine. For a couple of seconds the gnashing of steel and concrete overwhelmed the usual din of machines, and the workers on the lawn turned to see what was causing the awful screech. Everybody held their breath as they waited to see if the slide would take out any other portions of the building, especially the parts that shoring crews had already reinforced.

Dean Tills and some of the other structural specialists rushed up to the pile, to inspect the damage and assess whether more debris was likely to come crashing down. Since the area had been clear of people, nobody got hurt. Perry Bowser, the crane operator, had pushed the head of the machine into the slide, which slowed its descent. The slide was an abrupt scare, but it turned out there was no major damage. Yet it proved that the crippled structure was getting weaker, and becoming even less stable as the wreckage settled. Forging ahead with the clearing and shoring operation was an urgent priority.

As the day shift began to ramp up on Saturday morning, Jennifer Farmer, one of the FBI photographers, was just coming off duty. She decided she needed to do something awkward: track down her ex-boyfriend, Chris Combs. Every time she talked with her son, Logan, on the phone, he was worried about "Christopher" and asked if he was dead. Combs's voice seemed to be the only thing that would put the boy's mind at ease.

Chris Combs was spending most of his time at the command bus or the joint operations center, and he was easy to find. Although they had both been at the site on and off for four days, Combs was working days and Farmer nights. It was the first time they saw each other there. The encounter felt uncomfortable, but Farmer quickly got to the point. She explained that Logan was worried. "Will you call him and tell him you're okay?" she asked. "He's really upset."

Combs said sure, and dialed the boy on the spot. "Hey, Logan," he said, "It's Christopher. I'm all right. I'm fine. I'm here with your mother. Everything's okay."

Once Logan was reassured, the two adults talked for a few minutes. Farmer mentioned the hijacker she'd heard about, who had supposedly lived near her neighborhood. Combs could tell she was unnerved. His own parents had driven to D.C. from their home in Ridge, New York, on Long Island, to stay with him indefinitely, offering company, support, and anything else they could. It was great just to have somebody to talk to when he went home after 12 or 14 intense hours on the job. He imagined how lonely it must feel, working at the Pentagon and then going home to nobody.

"Listen," he said, "my parents are here. Why don't you come sleep at my place? My parents will take care of you. They'd be happy to do it."

Farmer wasn't about to ask for help—but was grateful that he offered. She thought it over for a moment. She knew Combs's parents well, and liked them. Since she and Combs were working opposing shifts, she could stay at his place with his parents without actually having to be there with *him*. That was a plus. When she thought about going to her own home—alone once again—that clinched it. She said yes.

Combs set the arrangement, and Farmer headed over to his town house on Capitol Hill. His parents were happy to see her.

While Farmer was starting to feel comfortable for the first time in five days, Mike Regan was inching toward New York on the New Jersey Turnpike.

After going home on Friday night and lying down for a brief power snooze, he had conked out till daylight. When he woke up he was unsure what time or even what day it was. His urgent desire to get to New York had faded—until his wife Janice reminded him that they needed to get in the car and go. Then, as he remembered about his father in the hospital, he became irritated. "I told you to wake me up in an hour!" he barked. He calmed down when she explained that she'd done exactly as he asked—shaking him, jostling, jabbing, and finally practically shouting at him, for 45 minutes in the middle of the night, with no success. So she gave up and let him sleep.

About halfway to New York, the highway became choked with traffic. After spending the days after 9/11 sequestered at home, everybody on the eastern seaboard suddenly had someplace to go, it seemed. Regan's anxiety grew. The more urgently he felt the need to see his father, the slower they seemed to go.

As they crawled along the highway, his brother Tim called on the cell phone. "Where are you?" he asked. "You better get here in a hurry." Their father had taken a worrisome turn and was sinking fast.

They reached the Verrazano-Narrows Bridge, which crosses the mouth of the Hudson River, from Staten Island into Brooklyn. The family had made the trip from Virginia to Long Island dozens of times, and Regan always used to make sure his kids noticed the striking view of the Manhattan skyline in the distance. "Look at the city," he would say, pointing to the shimmering buildings across the water. He always highlighted the twin towers, soaring over everything else.

Now there was only smoke—a black swirl of it, drifting ever upward, still surprisingly thick more than four days after the attack. Even from the bridge eight miles to the south, there was a palpable hole in the cluttered skyline, like a chunk of the city had just been carpet bombed. The breeze carried a burnt, pungent smell that made their throats contract. Inside the car, nobody spoke, but they all thought the same thing, as tears formed in eight eyes: The towers are gone. They're not there. How can that be?

Regan knew he was racing the clock. Finally, by late afternoon, they made it to New Island Hospital and raced in. When they got to the room, Regan's mother was holding his father's hand, rubbing it softly. Regan took his hand in his own. "I'm here, Dad," he said. There was no response, but it didn't matter. He had made it.

Fifteen minutes later his father died.

★ 44 ★

THE T-REX

Saturday, September 15, evening

The Red Cross and Salvation Army had been roaming the Pentagon grounds for days, delivering food, dry socks, clothing, counseling services, and other things people requested. Volunteers kept asking, "Is there anything we can do?" So one evening FBI agent Tom O'Connor made a flip suggestion.

"How about some massage therapists?" he joked.

When he arrived for the night shift on Saturday the fifteenth, to his astonishment, there was a tent with several massage therapists kneading the necks and backs of workers. But it wasn't just O'Connor's request that had brought the therapists. With so much support staff on hand, several people had thought of marshaling local therapists to work at the Pentagon. Dodie Gill, Arlington's director of employee assistance, had arranged for a couple of massage therapists to work on her charges, in the Arlington tents. There was nothing funny about it—anything that would help relieve tension for people working 12-hour shifts under hot, dangerous conditions was a welcome addition to the operation.

Perks like these, while the product of a lavish support system, were also a reward for work that was rapidly gaining momentum. FEMA and the FBI had streamlined procedures yet again for dealing with the body parts scattered throughout the wreckage. After dozens of frustrating work stoppages, commanders worked out a system where only certain types of remains, above a certain size, needed to be individually documented. The rest would still be carefully collected, but work crews were now permitted to move them aside and continue working.

A quicker pace would allow workers to fully harness the muscle provided by the Old Guard. With so many agencies involved, making decisions and requesting outside resources was becoming a bureaucratic tangle. But the Army's ceremonial unit continually showed up in force, with no strings attached. O'Connor was working with a captain from the regiment, Steven Nerenberg, and every evening, the young officer asked him what he needed. "How about 25 guys?" O'Connor would say, expecting to hear that that was too many.

But Nerenberg wouldn't flinch. "Okay, 25 guys," he'd say, and a short while later they would show up, ready to go.

With the young soldiers applying their muscle, parts of the demolition zone, once clogged with chest-high debris, were emptying out. The Old Guard troops functioned as all-purpose laborers. Sometimes they'd pick through piles of debris that search crews had marked as "areas of interest," because they might contain key airplane parts or something else the FBI cared about. Other times the soldiers just removed everything in sight, using picks, shovels, rakes, and buckets, all of it brand-new and in seemingly endless supply.

Specialist Dakota Gallivan, a strapping, recruiting-poster soldier, was among the Old Guard troops who gathered near the building like part of a standby labor pool, ready to do whatever was needed. Someone might call out, "I need two!" or "Gimme three!" and the right number of soldiers would jump to their feet. At the beginning, Gallivan helped carry stacks of six-by-six lumber from the cut stations outside to the spots in the building where FEMA crews were constructing shores. At other times, he and his comrades pawed through piles of debris the search crews had asked them to inspect for evidence or remains, then hauled it out in buckets or wheelbarrows.

The terrorist attacks and the gruesome work with the remains left Gallivan, who was ordinarily quiet and serious, seething with anger behind his respirator. He had grown up in New York, and the destruction in his hometown felt personal. Like others in the Old Guard, he also felt frustrated to be in a ceremonial unit that would almost certainly remain Stateside during whatever war ensued. The only relief he felt at the Pentagon was the camaraderie with the firefighters and other rescue workers, who would stop by the Old Guard tent and thank the soldiers for their help. Firefighters would joke with them, asking to try on their helmets. "These things are too damn heavy," one firefighter groused. "Here, try mine on. It's much more comfortable."

The energy of the Old Guard troops amazed some of the supervisors, who were accustomed to a more bureaucratic pace of work. At one point the FBI asked four Old Guard soldiers to clear the debris from a room that had been thoroughly searched for victims. O'Connor figured it would take a few hours. He came back a little while later to check on their progress and to see if they needed any help. The room was completely empty, the soldiers leaning against a pole, waiting for their next assignment. He marveled at their youth and strength—it made him and his FBI colleagues look like a bunch of geezers, he thought.

As clearing crews dug deeper into the debris, they encountered random materials fused by intense heat. Steel, aluminum, rebar, concrete, chunks of furniture, seat springs, and all kinds of unidentifiable objects were mashed together. Bits of clothing ran through everything, somehow binding the jumble even tighter. Instead of simply delayering the piles, clearing crews had to cut much of the debris free with hand or power saws.

The airplane had nearly disintegrated, but Dan Fitch's group found several huge cogs, bent and blackened, that weighed a couple hundred pounds each; it took a couple of workers to handle each one. Other objects nearby looked like large gears, and strips of metal that appeared to be fan blades. Workers realized they were pulling apart the remnants of one of the aircraft's two engines. The aluminum cowling that had encased it all had been torn away, but the guts of the engine were there.

FEMA crews used a blowtorch to free the core of the motor from the column in which it was embedded. Then Fitch and several others used pieces of six-by-six to pry the motor loose from the column and push it off the pile. With the help of some Old Guard troops, they rolled the heavy piece of machinery onto a dolly and finally managed to push it outside. The whole effort took the better part of an entire shift.

As crews dug deeper, unmistakable remnants of a passenger plane were everywhere. Wallets, shoes, jewelry, and the everyday items that had been stuffed into dozens of suitcases were littered throughout the debris. Virtually every worker came to know the jarring sensation of sifting through the gray, indistinct scraps of metal and concrete and discovering something small and personal like a ring or a photograph.

But the most relentless reminder of the carnage was the smell. In the first day or two after 9/11, it was the greasy odor of jet fuel, infused with smoke, that overpowered workers, clogging throats and making eyes water. That scent seemed fragrant, however, compared to the stench of remains after a few days in the wet, warm building. One worker called it the "wet-dog-on-fire smell." Others were more blunt. Many of the workers got in the habit of smearing Bengay or mentholated cream under their noses; others quickly learned to breathe through their mouths.

The odor intensified closer to the punch-out hole, since there were so many body parts there. Investigators knew by then that the passengers on Flight 77 had been herded to the back of the plane; the wrecked cockpit voice recorder produced no clues, but a passenger and a flight attendant were able to place cell phone calls in the moments before the flight crashed, describing what was happening on the aircraft.[1] Since the contents in the rear of the plane had generally traveled farther than what was in the front, many of the passengers' bodies came to rest amidst the wreckage near the punch-out hole.

As rancid as the smell was, it helped in the hunt for remains. It was no longer just the dogs who could sniff out body parts. Most of the humans working in the building could now do it too, and they kept the recovery teams busy by following their noses. They were astounded at some of the things they uncovered. Crash experts explained to the work crews how the forces of high-speed collisions tend to tear apart the human body, which consists mostly of water and soft tissue. All around them were the bizarre, gruesome results. There were feet without bones, the outcome of forces powerful enough to separate flesh from the skeletal structure supporting it. One group of workers found a scalp of long red hair. Other body parts had been transmogrified into shapes nobody could identify.

Even with the new FBI procedures, there were constant delays near the punch-out hole, which were more frustrating than ever—everyone was desperately eager to finish the awful work. Crew members paused frequently when a discovery took them aback. A few went outside to seek counselors and talk about what they'd seen. Others shunned the counselors, while relying on their own coping techniques.

Dodie Gill nudged some of the sterner, old-fashioned firefighters, like Bobby Beer, to open up and let some emotion out. "I don't have time for that, Dodie," he replied. But he was glad she was there—it felt reassuring just having someone looking after them like that. Meanwhile, Beer and a few others got in the habit of going to Jay's Saloon, a mile or so from the Pentagon, after their shifts. They weren't supposed to drink, but they'd have a few beers anyway and talk about everything they'd done that day—*real* therapy, they all agreed.

428   PATRICK CREED AND RICK NEWMAN

The T-Rex was making rapid progress too, steadily reducing the collapse pile that had seemed a deadly, unapproachable tangle just a couple of days earlier. After the slide that occurred the morning of September 15, the engineers gingerly reinspected the pile—and concluded that the biggest danger was gone. Since much of the pile had already come tumbling down, any further collapses would likely stay isolated to the area around the pile and not endanger the rest of the building.

With the T-Rex quickly dismantling the pile, FEMA set up a round-the-clock watch detail to scan for body parts, evidence, and anything that might signal the onset of another slide. Everything in the pile was the same earthen color—the dusty gray of ground concrete. It was difficult to distinguish bodies, or anything else, from the crushed stone that encrusted everything. Floodlights lit up the pile in the dark, but the shadows they cast made it more difficult to distinguish anything besides concrete or steel.

As the watchers' eyes adjusted, however, recognizable objects began to materialize. Earl Shughart knew that Lieutenant General Maude's office had been in the area of the collapse, and he found a couple of objects that he guessed came from the general's suite, like a flag, wound around debris. He also found a wide-brimmed, Teddy Roosevelt–style Rough Rider hat, which looked like a memento that might have hung on the wall in somebody's office.

As with other clearing operations, the T-Rex had to stop frequently, so teams could document and retrieve the remains, most of which were gathered near the bottom of the pile, only reachable once the T-Rex pulled off the debris that had buried them. But in some instances remains were so precariously tangled with other material in the pile that getting them out pitted the safety of the recovery teams against the sanctity of preserving the remains.

At one point the T-Rex came to a sudden halt. Shughart called

Perry Bowser, the operator, on his headset to ask what was up, while spotters in the man-basket zoomed in for a closer look. There was a body in the rubble, and it represented an intricate problem. Part of the body was exposed and clearly visible. But another part was pinned into place by several tons of sandwiched concrete.

Shughart, Dean Tills, and some of the others puzzled over what to do. There was too much concrete weighing down on the trapped portion of the body for workers to dislodge it on their own. They would need help from the T-Rex, but the machine might trigger another slide—with workers right at the base of the pile. Chunks of concrete were perched everywhere on the heap, and while the T-Rex could pluck off the biggest widowmakers, a falling piece of concrete as small as a softball could still be deadly if it came careening out of nowhere. If they tried to dig out the entire body, and triggered even a minor slide, Shughart estimated it could kill three or four workers.

There was another complication: The whole scene was unfolding in plain view, and there were continual worries about grisly photographs showing up on the news or the Internet. The body was obscured by dust, but the sudden activity at the edge of the pile would surely attract attention. No doubt there were telephoto lenses trained directly on numerous parts of the work site. There was nothing illegal about filming a delicate body recovery, but it was not the kind of thing anybody wanted to see aired on the evening news.

The FEMA commanders sent a staff member up to the press area by the Citgo station to gauge whether the body was visible from that vantage point. It turned out that the cab of the T-Rex itself blocked the view. Still, that was a small margin for error, and just in case there was a clearer perspective from someplace else, the FEMA workers held up a tarp as they began some unpleasant work: a surgical amputation, conducted by a physician who was a FEMA team member, to free all but the arm of the victim. The remaining part was marked so it could be retrieved once the debris holding it in place had been removed.[2] Then the T-Rex went back to work, reducing the debris around the limb as gently as a lumbering giant with a crushing bite could.

There were continual shifts in the debris pile as the heavy equipment pulled wreckage away, and toward the end of the night shift the T-Rex went motionless once again. FEMA officials started chatting on their headsets, wondering what was going on. At the edge of the rubble pile, Bowser had unwittingly dislodged a body with the T-Rex, and he found it especially upsetting. He stopped for a moment and lowered his head—to show a bit of respect and take a moment to compose himself.

One of the FEMA officers called Bowser on the headset. "Are you all right?" he asked.

"Yeah, I'm okay," Bowser answered hesitantly.

But the FEMA commanders were concerned about the T-Rex operator, whom they couldn't afford to lose. Bowser had no experience working around bodies and the human aftermath of catastrophes, so they devised a diversion to help take his mind off of it. They asked him to use the T-Rex's massive jaws to knock a couple of holes in the Pentagon's outer wall, to be used as entryways for front-loaders and other equipment. Bowser fulfilled the request quickly, and by then the night shift was just about over. FEMA arranged for a doctor and a counselor to talk with Bowser. What he'd seen disturbed him, but he would show up for the next shift.

With much of the first floor stabilized, clearing and shoring crews were able to begin work on the upper floors of the Pentagon. There wasn't as much damage or debris on the upper floors, but there were still plenty of dangerous areas. On the second floor, in the D Ring, a section of the floor slab—20 feet wide and 60 long—had been deflected upward by the force of the exploding plane, and buckled so severely that workers could see the first floor clearly through a number of large fractures.

There were several victims on the second floor, including Lieutenant General Maude, most of them clustered near the breach where the collapsed section of the E Ring had broken off. But search crews also found some remains scattered deeper in the building, including one set on the shaky floor that had been blown upward. Tom O'Connor had to decide which agents should handle the risky recovery. Once again he chose his wife, Jean, who was small and light.

FEMA officials led a recovery contingent to the spot and pointed out the remains, which were thoroughly burned and reduced to little more than a pile of ash. They decided that just one person at a time should work on the remains. Jean went first, tiptoeing across the disintegrating floor. She tagged the remains, documented their condition and location, then returned to the group. Next, photographer Jen Farmer, who was about the same size, edged over to the remains to do her work. The floor felt like it might give without warning as she moved around, working her camera. She was scared, but the slab held.

When she was finished, a two-man military mortuary team moved in to collect the remains. Traditionally, they worked as a pair, one at the head of the victim and one at the foot. Despite the danger—and the minimal remains—they insisted on following custom. They both inched across the floor and retrieved the victim together, evoking a mass exhalation from the group when they finally backed out onto firmer ground.

Though it was now a grotesque distortion of an office building, parts of the Pentagon began to take on a casual familiarity to the FBI crews and other workers who rotated inside frequently. Bent columns and punctured walls became landmarks that workers used to navigate through the maze of debris. In place of orderly, marked hallways, there was a growing network of pathways plowed by the Bobcats.

Some of the workers found comfortable places to rest that became unofficial break rooms during the course of a shift.

Tom O'Connor discovered a general's office on the third floor that he used as a place to plan and think when he was inside the building. It was one of the rooms that had been close to the impact point, but mysteriously survived, with little more than a light coating of ash and some jarred picture frames as evidence of the conflagration. A hat with two silver stars pinned to it sat on the desk. There was a coffee cup, half full, that O'Connor left in place. On a memo pad, somebody had written, *9:15: Your daughter called.*

The office had a stately formality that O'Connor found soothing. A flag stood in one corner. On the wall were pictures of Dwight Eisenhower and George Marshall from their days in uniform, each overlooking the occupants of the room with the grave authority of four-star generals. Sitting at the desk, O'Connor could look across the collapse zone into an office on the other side of the hole, where a statue of a saluting soldier stood on top of a filing cabinet. With the floodlights from outside shining on it, the statue created a nearly life-size shadow on a wall, as if a phantom soldier, arm crisply raised to forehead, were honoring the victims. O'Connor found it strangely inspiring.

The Pentagon was still a dreadful place, however. Few workers said much about it, but to many the horror around them felt penetrating. At one point Dean Tills found himself alone in the center of the damage, in the middle of the night, with no light except for the beam from his headlamp. It seemed to him the scariest place a person could ever be. There were bodies everywhere in the debris, and everything was dark.

Tom O'Connor finally decided to take advantage of the massage therapists, and visited the tent where they were plying their trade. He laid down on a table, where a woman who looked to be about 60 told him, "When the pain hits nine on a scale of ten, I want you to tell me." She started kneading his shoulders with powerful fingers. Right away he sounded the alarm.

"Hey!" he howled. "That's a nine!" She dialed back the pressure slightly, and before long the pain wasn't pain anymore. For the first time in days he felt something vaguely familiar: a moment of relaxation.

★ 45 ★

THE VIPs

Sunday, September 16

Chris Combs now knew that he had lost his two firefighter cousins in
New York. His sister, Cathie, had called to confirm: Kenny and Richie
were among those who died in the collapse of the twin towers.
Combs's bosses had told him to leave, to go to New York. "What am
I gonna do there?" he argued. "Go up there and do nothing? Or stay
here and do my job?" After he got the news, he found an empty room
at the joint operations center and sat there for a few moments by
himself, absorbing the tragedy and thinking about his cousins. Then
there was nothing else to do but return to work.

As the dust began to settle in the aftermath of the terrorist attacks,
the toll became clearer. The devastation reached far beyond three office buildings in New York and Washington, and suddenly life and
death intersected in ways nobody could have expected.

The firefighters from Alexandria, many of them still working on
the technical rescue team, carried their own burden from shift to
shift. They had been worried about one colleague, Joel Kanasky, who
moved to New York and started working with the FDNY. It turned
out Kanasky had been assigned to a training academy on 9/11 and
was okay. But another former Alexandria firefighter, Andy Fredericks, responded with FDNY's Squad 18, a special operations unit
based in Manhattan's West Village. The whole unit was missing and
presumed dead.[1]

When Alexandria's Dan McMaster had been in New York, he lived in the same town as Kanasky and Fredericks. Kanasky and a couple others had been calling him with updates on the New York firefighters, as they gathered fragments of information. Fredericks was the driver for Squad 18 and was slightly behind the rest of his crew as they entered the north tower and started climbing the stairwells. There was an evacuation order, and he probably could have gotten out in time. But he waited for the rest of his group. None of them made it out.

McMaster's old FDNY company, Ladder 35, from Manhattan's Upper West Side, was missing too, along with many other New York firefighters he knew. McMaster was usually intense, and now only seemed more so to his fellow team members, as he worked with a quiet, energetic resolve. He didn't say much, and nobody asked. But his colleagues wondered what kind of guilt or rage he must have felt, with so many friends dead while he survived.[2]

Like the Trade Center site, the Pentagon had rapidly become a totemic place that for some people represented sacred ground and for others had become a lurid tourist attraction. The officials running security and controlling access to the grounds had their hands full fending off gawkers, while being mindful of others who were mourning family members or loved ones who'd died in the building.

At one point Chris Combs got a call from an FBI agent manning one of the gates. "Man, you gotta help me out," the agent pleaded.

"What's going on?" Combs asked.

"I've got an Army chaplain here with some family members," the agent explained. "They want to get in. He's giving me a really hard time."

Combs headed down to the gate, familiar with the strains faced by people on both sides of the fence. His own cousins were dead in New York, so he understood what it felt like, having family members buried in the rubble somewhere. But he also knew that the workers recovering victims needed considerable distance from those mourning the very same people.

Combs found the chaplain and brought him inside the fence. "I understand what you're trying to do," he said, "but you've got to listen to me. I've got FBI agents in that building putting pieces of bodies in bags. Heads. Arms. Feet. Right now, it's not personal. They're doing a job. It's tough work. But if you go in there with family members, suddenly you're gonna make it personal. They can put bodies in bags, but they can't put dads and moms in body bags. If you go in there and people are crying and my agents have to see kids crying, you just wrecked everybody in there."

Combs was persuasive. "Okay, I got you," the chaplain deferred. "I understand. I'm sorry."

VIP visits were another distraction that commanders tried to protect workers from. Early in the mission, the appearance of top government officials and other dignitaries was a morale booster. But the visits quickly became tedious. So many members of Congress and Virginia politicians and Defense Department bigwigs asked for tours of the site that after a while they became a nuisance rather than a shot in the arm.

Team leaders would have to stop their work to give personal briefings to politicians in hard hats. It wasn't long before some of the firefighters' irreverence surfaced. When Senators Hillary Clinton and John Warner visited several days after the attacks, one of the men in the crowd shouted out, "What are you gonna do for the New York firefighters?" The appearance seemed like political grandstanding, while colleagues up north were in desperate need of genuine help.

Another time, a congressman's aide came up to Plaugher holding an airplane part that the FBI had overlooked. "My boss wants to know if he can keep this as a souvenir," he said.

"I recommend that you put that back exactly where you found it," Plaugher said, scowling.

"Why?" the aide asked.

"This is a crime scene," Plaugher informed him, "and you just tampered with evidence."

The aide began to protest, but Plaugher lost patience. "One, two, three—go!" he barked, ordering the aide to put the piece of wreckage back where he'd found it. The startled man scampered away.

Several generals and other officials wanted to visit the temporary morgue, at the loading dock, to examine the condition of the victims and pay their respects. Counselors and religious people also wanted permission to enter the morgue, to comfort the workers. Tara Bloesch, the FBI agent in charge of the morgue, held off virtually all of them. The last thing the morgue workers needed was a parade of spectators gawking at the contents of the blue bags and disrupting the somber rhythm of the work. Yet Bloesch and the others working there noticed that they never got requests for a visit from the President or vice president, or senators, or any of the other name-brand officials who were prominent visitors elsewhere at the Pentagon. "None of the *real* VIPs want to come here," they joked. Their work environment was too grisly for the people in fancy suits, they figured.

A few military commanders became fixtures near the command bus, and once the fire bosses realized they weren't facing a coup by the military honchos, they became comfortable with them. They were more suspicious of the civilian officials, though. Defense Secretary Rumsfeld and his deputy, Paul Wolfowitz, often came by the command bus early in the morning to see how things were going. Plaugher understood that the Pentagon was Rumsfeld's building, and of course the SecDef would be intensely interested in following the shoring and recovery work. But the Incident Command was doing just fine on its own, and Plaugher would have preferred to be left alone. Besides, the Defense Secretary's visits tended to disrupt the flow of operations, since there was always an additional security burden, and fire commanders working in the bus would have to stop what they were doing to answer all his questions.

"Can't we keep him out?" Plaugher asked Jackson at one point.

"It's the Pentagon!" Jackson reminded him. "How do you tell the SecDef that he can't come in?"

"Yeah, you're right," Plaugher sighed.

Still, there were moments when Rumsfeld seemed to overstay his welcome. At one point during the weekend Rumsfeld showed up with his wife, and ended up hanging around much longer than usual. It became uncomfortable. General Jackson finally pulled one of Rumsfeld's aides aside. "Doesn't he have anything else to do?" Jackson asked. The aide explained that there was a bomb scare at Rumsfeld's house and they were waiting for the all-clear from the Secret Service.

Another time, Rumsfeld went out to Camp Unity in South Parking to visit with the work crews relaxing over some food. Dakota Gallivan, the Old Guard soldier who had been helping clear debris inside the building, was in the crowd, and he found himself next to Rumsfeld. "Everyone taking care of you?" the SecDef asked. Gallivan said yes, and they exchanged a few cursory words. Then Gallivan decided to keep moving. The entire incident—the attacks, the grim work inside the Pentagon, the fact that his country was preparing for war—had put him in a surly mood. He didn't feel like talking to anybody, not even the Secretary of Defense.

A moment later, as Gallivan was working his way through the crowd, he ended up near Rumsfeld again—almost as if the guy was following him around, he thought.

Then the SecDef asked him again, "How are things going? Is everyone taking care of you?" The soldier gave a terser answer than before and moved along.

He decided to work his way back to the Old Guard tent near the helipad. While crossing the parking lot, he glanced to his side, and there was Rumsfeld for a third time. "How do I get away from this guy?" Gallivan mumbled to himself, quickening his pace. When he finally found his Army buddies and told the tale, they immediately branded him as the soldier being stalked by the SecDef.

Vice President Cheney paid a visit on Monday, September 17, and as an emissary from the White House, he attracted more attention than the run-of-the-mill VIPs who had become commonplace at the Pentagon. Since it was daytime, the Fairfax FEMA team was off-duty, resting and sleeping at Washington Navy Yard. But when they learned of the vice president's visit, commanders decided to rev up the buses so that whoever wanted to take part would be able to.

Cheney's appearance was more formal than some of the other VIP visits. Personnel from various organizations lined up so the vice president could shake hands, and he worked his way from unit to unit. Elizabeth Kreitler, the dog handler, was there with Nero, waiting in line. When Cheney was about three people away, a yellowjacket started buzzing around Nero's nose. The German shepherd had been sitting at attention right next to Kreitler, but the wasp was an irresistible distraction.

Nero had a habit of snapping at bees, and his head began to swivel as he waited for the right moment. Kreitler started to sweat. Several things were about to happen at once, and they added up to a minor disaster. The wasp was hovering at waist level, the vice president was about to stick out his hand, and Nero was about to lunge for the wasp. Kreitler envisioned the headline: "Dog Bites VP's Hand." But just as Cheney reached her, the wasp buzzed off, and Nero let the vice president pass unmolested.

Plaugher, the reluctant tour guide, spent some time showing Cheney around, and the two men walked up toward the building so Cheney could have a close look at the damage and the repair work. The vice president wanted to go through the innermost security perimeter, where only approved workers with red badges were allowed. Even though it was the vice president, security was airtight, and Plaugher knew there'd be a holdup while the U.S. marshals manning the checkpoint sorted it out. Besides, a VIP poking around would disrupt the pace of the work.

Plaugher had a quick idea. As they approached one of the gates, he said, "Mr. Vice President, now, if you go through there, I'm going to have to decontaminate you when you come out." The notion of getting scrubbed down in the human car wash dissuaded Cheney, and he agreed to stay outside the fence.

By the end of the weekend, the pace of work inside the building had quickened significantly. FEMA and the FBI had finally gotten into a rhythm that allowed the clearing and shoring work to move along briskly. With the military manpower and the Bobcats, large areas of clear floor appeared. The shoring work had moved into some of the most vulnerable parts of the building, and the Pentagon was becoming a safer place to work.

FEMA policy was to limit task-force deployments to seven days, and the time was coming for the Fairfax team to head home. There was also concern about additional terrorist attacks, either in the United States or overseas, and FEMA wanted to make sure VA-TF1 would be able to respond if necessary. So top officials decided that the group would pack up and head home on September 18, a week after they had arrived. Another FEMA task force, from New Mexico, had been mobilized, and they'd take the baton from the Fairfax team.

It felt like it was time to go. The uniquely outfitted task force was designed for the early, chaotic stages of a disaster, when there was little conventional support to help find victims. In less than a week the Pentagon had become a superduty construction site, with all the equipment, specialists, and support services money could buy. After a week of intense 12-hour shifts, many of the team members were tired, and eager to see their families. Like many others, Leo Titus felt ready to go home. Their work had been vital, but they'd done just about all they could do.

The task force would work one more shift, on Monday night, September 17, then break down their base of operations, pack everything up, and get on buses back to Fairfax. As the group assembled for the last shift, Kent Watts, the shoring expert, decided there should be a small ceremony to mark the end of the deployment. Watts hated the word "closure"; he felt it was a phony buzzword that didn't apply in real life. But he also felt there should be an event to mark the solemnity of the work they had done there, something to convey to task force members the significance of their efforts. And he wanted an opportunity for everyone to say the Pledge of Allegiance at the place where dozens of Americans had been killed.

The Fairfax commanders agreed, and Watts began organizing a small event. The task force had no standing procedure for closing ceremonies, but Watts had been at Oklahoma City with the group when a couple of members organized an impromptu silent march after the last shift, as a show of respect for the victims. It had felt right, and gone over well with local citizens. Something similar seemed appropriate at the Pentagon.

Watts had gotten to know an Army chaplain working at the site, and the man agreed to officiate at a short ceremony. As the task force members were organizing for the night, Watts stood on a lumber pile near the VA-TF1 tent and announced there would be a small ceremony. "Participate if you wish," he said. "If not, stay back here."

There were a few retired military personnel on the task force, and they helped organize the members into a column, three abreast. There was no attempt at military precision, but the group looked distinctive, even reverential, as it formed up. Everyone was dressed in the same uniform—a gray jersey with blue military-style fatigues, black work boots, and yellow hard hat—and since the shift was just starting, everybody was clean. Faces were solemn and weary. The task force members strode silently up toward the hole in the building, then fanned out along the outer wall, facing some of the shores they had built. With their uniformity and loose cohesion, they could have been a company of soldiers after a battle, fatigued and saddened but still maintaining order and discipline. Nobody stayed behind.

The rubble pile had been reduced, but it still spilled out of the building like the aftermath of a wrecking ball. The chaplain stood at the edge of it and said a few words about the importance of the work everyone had done, then offered a short prayer while the members bowed their heads. When that was finished, the group turned to their right, faced the garrison flag draped over the building, and said the Pledge of Allegiance.

The ceremony was meant to be self-contained and informal, for VA-TF1 alone. Nobody was seeking an audience. The chaplain spoke without amplification, addressing only the 60-odd task force members assembled before him. Yet everybody at the work site noticed the activity and stopped what they were doing to watch. Arlington's Bob Gray was getting ready for his own night shift with the technical rescue team when he saw the Fairfax group assembled up by the building. He couldn't hear what the chaplain was saying but was impressed with the solemnity of the quiet little service. If Arlington got the chance, he vowed, they should do something just like it.

After the Pledge of Allegiance, the group turned around and walked back to their tent the same way they walked up, three abreast. The whole ceremony took less than ten minutes, yet suddenly VA-TF1 was the center of attention. Other rescue workers, government officials, PenRen contractors, and military personnel crowded in around them, applauding or reaching out to shake hands. The path ahead remained clear, but on both sides people pressed in around them. To Kent Watts, it felt like they were walking through a human hallway.

The outpouring capped off the weeklong experience the way Watts had hoped it would. It felt good and gave meaning to the work they'd done. Leo Titus realized he had made many new friends that week. Dean Tills felt tears coming on, and fought to keep them back. A burly Fairfax firefighter was marching stoically next to Tills, and by the time they got back to their tent, tears moistened the man's cheeks. "I'm glad I'm wearing safety glasses," he told Tills, "so I can hide my emotions."

★ 46 ★

A CEREMONY

Tuesday, September 18

The crews working at the Pentagon were no longer living in a bubble. Unlike the first couple of days, when the battle at the Pentagon was so consuming that firefighters got little news from the outside world, they were now closely following events in the rest of the country. Most of them devoured the news when they finished their shifts and went home, or decamped to the hotel rooms that had been booked for them. The news from New York was still stunning a week after the terrorist attacks: Authorities estimated that more than 5,000 people died in the destruction of the twin towers.[1]

The nation was starting to get back to normal, or at least adapting to a "new normal," as commentators were starting to say. After locking down all commercial flights, the FAA allowed planes to start flying again. The stock markets reopened after a week-long hiatus. Major League Baseball, which had suspended play, resumed its season. People were going back to work.

But the nation was also girding for war. President Bush promised that Osama bin Laden, thought to have masterminded the attacks, would be brought to justice "dead or alive." There was fervent speculation in the papers and on TV about an invasion of Afghanistan. News crews were camped out at Fort Bragg, North Carolina, where the 82d Airborne Division was based, waiting for signs of a combat deployment. And Bush and other leaders were warning Americans to prepare for casualties.

Firefighters and other workers at the Pentagon noticed something different about their own role in the nation's business too. When they left the Pentagon at the end of a shift, there were still people along the streets who would applaud or wave flags. Strangers walked up to firefighters and thanked them in public. Instead of blending into the backdrop of daily life, as they usually did, firefighters and police officers were now "brave" and "fearless." The recognition was gratifying—but off-putting too. "Suddenly we're all heroes," Bobby Beer griped, suspicious of the sentiment. He preferred the old way, just doing his job without all the fuss and attention.

Unlike New York, the job at the Pentagon was now moving briskly. Defense Department officials had a precise list of the missing, and estimated that 125 Pentagon employees had been killed, in addition to 64 people on the airplane.[2] More than a hundred sets of remains were shipped to Dover Air Force Base, where the military had a sophisticated forensics lab, and about 20 victims had been identified. And the work inside the Pentagon was actually ahead of schedule. Commanders originally estimated it would take until September 25 to clear and stabilize the building. But they had moved that date up by a few days, thanks to the tireless Old Guard soldiers, the Bobcats, the T-Rex, and a lot of determined workers.

With the work finally picking up steam, and the Fairfax team heading home, it was probably time for the Arlington TRT to pack it in too. Those crews had been there just as long as the original FEMA teams, working under the same duress. Arlington medical officials were concerned about toxins inside the building, and the longer the exposure, the more dangerous it would be for the workers. The fire department needed all of its crews back on normal rotations. And more FEMA workers were scheduled to arrive—commanders figured they would be able to finish the job.

But when Schwartz told Scott McKay, the daytime TRT commander, that the team would be demobilized, McKay protested strongly. The Pentagon was Arlington's responsibility, and everybody on the team, he insisted, wanted to see the job through to the end. Schwartz said he'd think it over—and wanted to know how the other TRT members felt. McKay surveyed the group that was on duty and reported to Schwartz: There was 100 percent agreement; everyone wanted to stay. So Schwartz allowed the deployment to continue.

The Arlington-Alexandria group developed a kind of studied coolness as their confidence grew, and they grew more familiar with the quirks of the damaged structure. By the time the New Mexico FEMA team arrived on Tuesday, September 18, a full week after the attack, the Arlington-Alexandria group had become the resident experts on the clearing and shoring operation. They ended up tutoring the fresh FEMA crew, instead of the other way around. They also noticed that compared to Fairfax, the New Mexico team seemed pretty green. It had only been formed a couple of years earlier, and the Pentagon was its first major deployment.

As the local boys showed the newcomers around, the huge heaps of debris near the punch-out hole were finally dwindling, with large patches of clear floor emerging. Crews began to tackle shoring work on the upper levels, including the tricky second story where the floor slab had been blown upward and where Jean O'Connor and Jen Farmer tiptoed up to a set of remains. The fragile structure required some delicate construction, and the first priority was making sure nobody fell through the ruptured floor. But the crews handled it without incident.

There were still signs of wreckage all over, though the building was being cleared out. Broken girders, tangled pipes, and torn wires protruded everywhere. Charred insulation and deformed ductwork hung from the ceiling. The remnants of a few support columns lay toppled on the floor, twisted rebar extending from the crumbled shafts like the tentacles of a giant squid. It remained an unforgiving workplace. Strung lights and portable lamps were the only source of illumination, other than daylight that found its way through the E Ring windows or the hole at the impact point. Mold, fed by ample moisture and hothouse warmth, began to form on many of the remaining walls and other exposed surfaces, posing a fresh hazard for safety experts to sort out.

But there were unmistakable signs of progress, and the vast, damaged area of the Pentagon was being transformed into something that resembled a disheveled warehouse. Most remarkably, workers could see from one end of the destruction zone to the other. For the first time, it was possible to view the whole expanse of the wrecked portion of the building, which stretched longer than a football field from Corridor 4 to Corridor 5, and nearly as long from the inner side of the C Ring to the outer side of the E Ring. On the first floor alone, workers had cleared wreckage from an area of more than 50,000 square feet.

As the piles got smaller and the floor cleaner, crews went back over the whole area several times in successive sweeps, looking for remains and other evidence they might have missed the first or second time through. There was still plenty to find. Dan Fitch was shoveling out some rubble when he uncovered something that looked unusual. He pushed and prodded to see what it could be, then realized it was a woman's body, obscured by dust and grime after several days beneath debris. How it had gone unnoticed for a whole week, he had no idea. But it startled him to find the body, just when he'd started to think there would be no more gruesome discoveries. Almost involuntarily, he stopped what he was doing and spent a moment regaining his composure.

One of the last areas workers reached was a computer room on a raised platform near the punch-out hole. It was framed by the ruins of a metal cage, which signified that it had been a SCIF, a sensitive compartmented information facility, hardened to prevent electronic eavesdropping. Clearing the room and pulling up the platform to check for remains or other material underneath was one of the last major jobs for the search-and-rescue crews. After that would come basic clean-up work: gathering up the tools scattered throughout the building, tidying up the work site, packing up, and going home.

Except that the Pentagon was far more than a routine work site. Brian Spring was a Civil War buff who had explored historic sites like Gettysburg and Fredericksburg, using a metal detector to unearth pieces of rifles and other artifacts. The Pentagon reminded him of those battlefields, which had been unremarkable places until conse-crated by those who gave their lives so that the nation might live, as Abraham Lincoln said at Gettysburg. To Spring, there was a perpetual pall inside the Pentagon, a combination of smoke, dust, gloom, and history. It gave him the same heavy sensation he felt when he walked some of the old battlefields, as if the souls of the victims hung in the atmosphere, thickening the air.

By Thursday morning, September 20, Schwartz decided he needed all of his fire crews back on normal duty, for good. In the aftermath of 9/11, fire and rescue crews in the D.C. area were busier than ever, re-sponding to calls that nobody would have phoned in before. There were concerns about chemical or biological attacks in D.C. and other urban centers. Nobody knew if the terrorist plan had been fully car-ried out or if there was a second phase coming. The Arlington Fire Department was stretched thin, so Schwartz told his TRT leaders that Thursday would be the team's last day at the Pentagon. The New Mexico FEMA crew would wrap things up, then hand the mission over to the FBI. Once the Bureau finished its work, contractors would raze the damaged portions and start rebuilding.

This time, Schwartz got no argument. Most of the TRT members were finally ready to get back to their regular lives. But just packing up and leaving, as if quitting a routine job, felt too abrupt. They'd have to hustle to get all their work completed and their gear packed up by the end of the day. Bob Gray and Scott McKay, the TRT team leaders, agreed they should have a ceremony at the end, the way the Fairfax FEMA team had.

They started scrambling to put it together. They enlisted Arlington firefighter Mike Staples, head of the local firefighters' union, to call all the TRT members who weren't on duty and make sure they knew about the ceremony. Gray commandeered a flag they could use for the ceremony, and got a couple of others to start putting together a large plywood plaque that would memorialize the TRT's work.

Chief Schwartz, however, had other ideas. There were plans to hold a ceremony for the entire Arlington County Fire Department a few days later, and he didn't want any of the separate divisions holding their own events. There were already minor rivalries over which specialty was more prestigious—TRT, the Arlington hazardous materials unit, EMS, or other divisions. A bit of competition boosted morale, and Schwartz didn't have any problem with that. But he didn't want any elitists in the department, and he also didn't want the duties and accomplishments of one particular group to overshadow the contributions of others. When he heard that the TRT leaders were organizing their own ceremony, he called Staples. "*Do not* have a closing ceremony especially for the TRT," he ordered.

Staples promptly passed the message to Gray and McKay. They had a dilemma. After talking it over, both agreed: They needed to have a ceremony, no matter what the chiefs said. Gray had been particularly impressed by the solemnity of the Fairfax event. It was quiet and unpretentious, allowing the people who had toiled in the building, among the dead, a chance to make peace and cut ties before returning to their regular lives. He felt his own team members needed that. *He* needed that. To deflect the heat from Staples, who wasn't an officer, McKay and Gray said they'd take the blame if Schwartz or other commanders came looking for heads. "I'll take the hit, Mike," Gray told him. "But we've got to do this."

Staples continued making calls, alerting the off-shift crew members, while Gray and McKay went to work closing down the TRT deployment. Word got around that the ceremony was "unauthorized," which heightened interest. There were rumors that the ceremony had been called off, then was back on. The confusion, rather than discouraging attendance, generated more enthusiasm. Everybody, it seemed, wanted to be there.

The crews working on Thursday spent the day checking over the shores one last time, and making sure vehicles and other logistical necessities were in place to transport all the equipment back to home stations once the shift was over. By late afternoon the work was winding down, the off-shift team members starting to filter back onto the Pentagon grounds. They gathered around the TRT "camp," where the group's tent and command post had been. Most of it was broken down by now, and packed up. Compared to the balmy weather on 9/11, it was more like fall, with cooler air and a cloudy sky. And the whole place was starting to look more like a conventional construction site than a federal emergency. Contractor trailers and heavy machinery had replaced many of the emergency vehicles, and virtually all of the fire and rescue equipment had been sent home.

It was time to get the ending started. Bob Gray sent somebody to get the chaplain who worked with the Old Guard. He arrived, and the team members assembled, then made the short walk up toward the building, just to the left of the impact hole. Gray stood up to say a few words, framed by the Pentagon's charred facade. He looked out at about 60 faces, most of them drawn with exhaustion. Virtually every team member from Arlington was there, and many from Alexandria. Most of the off-duty crew members had arrived home after the night shift, gotten the word about the ceremony, and headed straight back to the Pentagon. A few who lived far away had driven as far as 90 miles to get there.

Gray also saw Chief Schwartz standing near the big command bus, about 100 yards away, watching the gathering. Schwartz didn't gesture, he just watched, expressionless. Oh, shit, Gray thought. It occurred to him that among other things, the ceremony might mark the moment he got demoted.

He began to speak, thanking everyone for coming on short notice, especially those who had traveled from far away. "As you've probably heard," he said, "today is the last day of TRT and fire department operations. We decided to have this closing ceremony to pay final respect to those who perished here and in New York City. You should all be very proud of what our team has accomplished over the duration of this event."

The words became difficult. Tears formed in Gray's eyes and spilled onto his cheeks. He stopped for a moment and swallowed. Then he continued. "I am personally very proud to have served with each of you," he gulped. "Each of us will carry this experience for the rest of our lives. We will never forget."

Heads nodded heavily out in the small crowd. Gray introduced the chaplain, who said a short prayer. Then the group edged up closer to the spot where Flight 77 had crashed through the E Ring, for a moment of silence. The monstrous pile of debris, five floors pancaked down on one another, was virtually gone. All that was left was a layer of crushed stone and concrete, no different than the detritus that littered the ground at any big construction project. The danger zone that had once threatened anybody in the vicinity was now a large entryway to the building. As they peered into the hole, the team members could see the matrix of shores they and other workers had constructed, holding up the building.

After a moment of reflection, a few of the team members brought forward the plaque they had prepared, a four-by-eight-foot piece of plywood with a flag nailed to it, stretched tightly. At the bottom it read, ALWAYS REMEMBER. They nailed the board onto one of the E Ring shores, built to support the most fragile part of the building the first night after the attack. Then they all backed away a few steps, contemplating the flag and what it had come to mean.

That was all. The ceremony was over. A few of the team members drifted away, but most milled around for a while at the edge of the building, talking quietly, exchanging pats on the shoulder, sizing up the flag, and looking into the Pentagon one last time.

Dan Fitch was awed and humbled. It felt eerie to gaze into the building, now so clean and empty, which just a few days before had housed dozens of bodies and a couple acres of chest-high debris. He was immensely proud of the work he and his colleagues had done. Still—he couldn't wait to leave. He had barely seen his wife and four kids since the eleventh, and the gravitational tug of home was intense. It was time to go.

Bobby Beer battled a creeping sense of emptiness. Something profound had begun ten days earlier, and he and the others had given it everything they had—not for glory, or money, or any kind of reward, but just because it was their job. Now it was ending. He knew he ought to feel relieved to get away from the death and destruction, but he found it difficult to leave.

As everybody turned around and peeled away, Brian Spring and Bob Gray walked next to each other. Gray still had tears on his cheeks. Spring caught the emotion. Both felt a kind of unease they didn't have the words to explain. But they didn't have to. The two men shared a hesitant hug. "There's part of me in there," Spring said to Gray. "All of us left a part of ourselves in that building."

Gray nodded. Yes. They were all leaving something behind.

★

EPILOGUE

On September 21, the Arlington County Fire Department formally relinquished control of the Pentagon incident site to the FBI. The following day, search-and-rescue operations officially concluded and the remaining FEMA teams went home.[1] The mission ended with no deaths or serious injuries to fire and rescue workers. The FBI spent another two weeks gathering evidence and finishing its own work at the crime scene, ultimately deploying more than 700 agents to the Pentagon.[2]

In early October the FBI turned the site back over to the Defense Department. By then, the government was able to confirm that 189 people had died in the attack on the Pentagon: 125 people who had been working in the building, 59 passengers and crew members aboard Flight 77, and five hijackers. Of more than 100 patients transported to area hospitals with burns and other injuries, only one died.[3] Capt. Ed Blunt's "load-and-go" decision early on the eleventh probably saved lives, by getting the most-injured patients to area hospitals as quickly as possible and bypassing additional treatment on the scene.

Lee Evey, who was in charge of the Pentagon Renovation office, hired Allyn Kilsheimer to lead the reconstruction effort. On October 5, Evey announced that the Defense Department planned to rebuild the Pentagon within one year of the attack. On October 18, crews began to demolish the damaged portion of the building. Workers poured concrete for the rebuilt portion of the structure on November 7, nearly two weeks before the demolition work was even completed.[4] The rebuilding effort came to be known as the Phoenix Project, after the mythical bird that grows from the ashes after its nest has been set ablaze.

On September 11, 2002, the first anniversary of 9/11, the Defense Department hosted a crowded, solemn ceremony on the Pentagon's west lawn, overlooking the spot where Flight 77 smashed into the building. Thirteen thousand people gathered to listen to remarks by President Bush and Defense Secretary Rumsfeld.[5] The Pentagon's western facade had been completely rebuilt, with a stone from the original wall laid at the base of the impact point. The stone was blackened by fire but intact. It was inscribed simply with the date: September 11, 2001.

People had already gone back to work in parts of the Pentagon that were destroyed and rebuilt. By then U.S. and allied forces had also invaded Afghanistan, seized the capital, Kabul, routed Taliban and al Qaeda fighters in much of the rugged central Asian country, and begun a prolonged hunt for Osama bin Laden. At 9:37 A.M., on the Pentagon lawn, there was a moment of silence to mark the instant, one year earlier, when Flight 77 blasted through the Pentagon, part of the September 11 onslaught that triggered America's war against terrorists.

Two months later a group of clergy and military chaplains dedicated a somber, spare memorial chapel inside the Pentagon, built at the very spot where the nose of Flight 77 punctured the Pentagon. The names of the 184 victims were inscribed on the wall, with a book beneath the names containing a picture and short biography of each victim.

In the year following the 9/11 attacks, the Army Corps of Engineers began planning for a memorial to honor the victims who died at the Pentagon. In 2003 a memorial foundation, run by victims' family members, selected a winning design out of more than 1,000 entries. It featured 184 sleek benches, each representing a victim, with a small reflecting pool beneath each. The Defense Department would set aside two acres of the Pentagon's western lawn for the memorial, nestled along Washington Boulevard, close to the spot where Bob Cornwell and other commanders first pulled up to the fire on 9/11. The small tract would be 165 feet from the impact point, immediately beneath the path Flight 77 followed into the building.

The benches would be organized to reflect the age of the victims—which ranged from three to 71—and also to differentiate between victims who were on the plane and those who were in the Pentagon. The memorial benches representing Pentagon workers would face toward the building, while those representing people on the airplane would face the opposite direction, toward the open sky where Flight 77 had come from. The groundbreaking for the memorial took place in 2006, with construction expected to be completed in the fall of 2008.[6]

It goes without saying that the events of 9/11 changed the lives of many Americans. Here are a few of the notable ways that the attack on the Pentagon affected people who were there that day:

About 15 firefighters left the Arlington County Fire Department for reasons related to post-traumatic stress disorder stemming from the 9/11 incident. While the number seems small, it represented nearly nine percent of the entire force. Capt. Mike Smith, who made several sorties into Corridor 5 on 9/11, later reflected that "9/11 tore through the department like a bowling ball. It took out a lot of people." Many other members of the department were treated for PTSD and stayed on the job.

Steve Carter, Kathy Greenwell, Dan Murphy, and all of the other members of Carter's staff who continued working in the Pentagon on

9/11 were awarded the Medal for Valor, an honor the Defense Department created after 9/11 to honor civilians who labored valiantly that day.

FBI photographer Jennifer Farmer and Special Agent Chris Combs reconnected after meeting on the Pentagon grounds a few days after 9/11. The reasons they broke up several weeks earlier suddenly seemed trivial. "I didn't know what I was doing, just being a guy," Combs recalled later. "My thinking changed. I thought, 'Hey, I love her. What am I doing?'" Combs and Farmer married in 2003. Farmer's FBI colleague Jen Hill took the wedding photos, and Special Agent Tara Bloesch was a bridesmaid. The Combs's daughter, Caroline, was born in November 2004.

Army nurse Jennifer Glidewell, who found herself running triage in the Pentagon courtyard on 9/11, had been divorced for three years at the time of the terrorist attacks, with a six-year-old son, Justin, who lived with her in Virginia. On September 12, her ex-husband, Jared, who was living in Texas, called her and said, "My son needs me." The two eventually reconciled, and they married for the second time in May 2006.

Arlington fire captain Bob Gray was promoted to battalion chief in 2004. He never heard a word from Chief Schwartz about organizing a closing ceremony for the technical rescue team against Schwartz's orders.

Army Maj. Dave King, badly burned from the fire in the Pentagon, suffered injuries similar to many surviving victims. He underwent six operations, to repair burn damage to significant portions of his body. Five weeks after 9/11 he was released from the hospital. For about a year King wore spandex gloves and sleeves on his hands and arms, to keep constant pressure on skin that had been grafted on. The two colleagues who had been working in the same area with King, Staff Sergeant Maudlyn White and Lt. Col. Jerry Dickerson, died in the attack.

Navy SEAL Craig Powell, who caught the jumpers in A&E Drive, developed a persistent cough after 9/11. More than three months later, on December 30, 2001, he passed out in the middle of the night in the kitchen of his home. At the hospital he was diagnosed with infectious pneumonia—most likely caused by toxins he ingested at the Pentagon on 9/11. After a priest discussed last rites with him, Powell recovered. He received a Navy and Marine Corps Medal for his actions at the Pentagon on 9/11, and was eventually selected for field command. Powell retired in 2007 as a captain.

FEMA search specialist Mike Regan happened to know a firefighter, Chuck Wehrli, who lived in Naperville, Illinois—the town where Dan Shanower, the victim Regan discovered in the Navy Command Center, was from. Wehrli knew Shanower's parents, and asked Regan if it was okay for them to contact him. Regan said yes, though he never expected to hear anything. To his surprise, Don and Pat Shanower called him about nine months after 9/11. Regan and his wife, Janice, eventually traveled to Naperville to meet with the Shanowers, and the two families became unlikely friends. "They have a lot of the same emotions we have," Regan discovered. In 2006 the Regans and the Shanowers spent the fifth anniversary of 9/11 together, in Naperville.[7]

Jim Schwartz, the ACFD Assistant Chief for Operations, was promoted to fire chief in 2005, replacing Ed Plaugher, who retired.

★

ACKNOWLEDGMENTS

There were thousands of people involved in the effort to put out the fire and salvage the Pentagon after Flight 77 tore the building apart. We have told the stories of a small number of them. We regret that our narrative does not include more of the firefighters, rescuers, government agents, and structural experts who served with distinction at the Pentagon. We have done our best to distill the remarkable stories of a few representative characters into one tale that encapsulates the efforts of ordinary people in the midst of an extraordinary event.

In addition to the documentary evidence we've cited as source material, we have relied on the memories and personal records of more than 150 people interviewed for this book. Memories, of course, can be incomplete and faulty, which is why we made extensive efforts to corroborate and confirm every detail. We checked personal recollections against official documents wherever possible, and triangulated our reporting with additional sources, to make sure memories were credible. We asked more than 50 people familiar with events at the Pentagon on 9/11 to review portions of our manuscript. They made numerous suggestions that improved the accuracy of this account.

There are a number of official documents, which we've cited in endnotes, that were essential to reconstructing this story. But it's also important to note the resources we did not have. The "Arlington

County After-Action Report," for instance, provides a thorough overview of the incident at the Pentagon. But it was based on a trove of officer reports, internal memos, interview transcripts, and other documents from the Arlington County Fire Department that were either destroyed or misplaced afterward, and were unavailable to us. So to gather deeper detail, we had to rely almost exclusively on the recollections of individuals, without the benefit of any further formal documentation.

The people named in these pages obviously helped construct our story. There are many others who deserve recognition. Arlington firefighter Rick Goddard was one of the first to describe the remarkable operation inside the Pentagon, launching what would become nearly five years of research. John Delaney, another Arlington firefighter, helped us navigate the Arlington County Fire Department during the early days of the project and gain access to key people. Tom Hawkins, who served as fire chief in both the Arlington and Alexandria fire departments, provided historical background that helped frame the story. Maj. Brian Zarchin, a pilot who led a unit of Army helicopters to the Pentagon shortly after the attack, described what he saw from the sky in such compelling detail that it made us determined to learn more.

Bob Rossow, an Army Reserve officer who made it his personal mission to write a detailed account of everyone in the Army's personnel division who was killed or injured, provided a wide range of assistance. Navy historian Randy Papadopoulos, one of the authors of the Defense Department's official history of 9/11, helped us understand how the incident affected various individuals, agencies, and departments inside the building. Army historian Frank Shirer recounted how various Pentagon officials reacted in the minutes and days following the attack. Paul Mlakar of the U.S. Army Corps of Engineers patiently explained, in plain English, the physical and technical details of what happened when Flight 77 struck the Pentagon.

Former Pentagon officials Craig Quigley, Denny Klauer, and T. Mc-Creary guided us to several key sources and helped corroborate important aspects of our story.

In addition to sharing his personal story, Dean Tills of Virginia Task Force 1 spent many hours reviewing portions of the manuscript and helping us make dozens of improvements. At the FBI, Debbie Weierman displayed unflappable good humor as she arranged numerous interviews and handled follow-up questions that must have seemed endless at times. FBI photographer Jennifer Combs (formerly Jennifer Farmer) went far out of her way to pull hundreds of photographs from archives and narrate all of them, which helped us better understand what it must have been like working in the shattered building.

It is thankless work to read a lengthy, unedited manuscript and offer meaningful suggestions without discouraging the authors. We were lucky to have at our disposal several deft critics who both cheered and improved our work, including retired Air Force general Don Shepperd and his wife Rose, Cathy and Trevor Weiss, and Richard and Gertrude Creed. Philip Creed applied his journalistic skills to help us fine-tune many details that otherwise escaped our notice.

We are both indebted to our agent, Jane Dystel, who brought us together and made this book happen. Ron Doering incubated the book at our publisher, Ballantine. Our editor, Laura Ford, applied firm judgment and a delicate touch that helped bring the core story forward and make it far more accessible to readers. Paulette Garthoff, who fact-checked the manuscript, helped tighten up accuracy even further with her keen eye. If any mistakes remain, we alone bear responsibility.

Patrick owes special thanks to David Morrell, author of *First Blood,* who listened to a stranger describe a book idea at a late-night party and helped turn concept into reality. Army Lt. Col. William

Mason allowed valuable extra time to conduct research after Patrick was mobilized for a tour in Iraq, midway through the production of the book. Torrey Creed was the biggest—and sometimes the only—booster behind this project during the early months, and a source of support all the way to completion. Pat's son Jeremy was a source of inspiration throughout, and a constant reminder to keep hunting for the best stories.

Rick gives a shout-out to his children, Jessica and Robert, who motivate without ever meaning to. Carol Newman is a marvelous mom and subtle mentor who inspires through uncommon curiosity and intelligence. Ted Slafsky and Diane Prescott offered their home, hospitality, and boundless support during many trips to Washington, D.C. Debbie Stier and Kelly Leonard O'Keefe provided invaluable advice about how to navigate the book-publishing business, along with plain old great friendship. At *U.S. News & World Report*, Rick's employer, Brian Duffy, Brian Kelly, Tim Smart, and Jim Bock allowed a degree of flexibility that any writer would envy, while always setting an example by practicing the highest standards of journalism. These are great people all and we feel lucky to know them.

★

NOTES

CHAPTER 1. THE TOWERS

[1]Baron, Jeff, "Discontent in the Air," *Washington Post,* Sunday, Sept. 9, 2001, C2.

CHAPTER 2. AA 77

[1]National Commission on Terrorist Attacks Upon the United States, "The 9/11 Commission Report: Final Report of the National Commission on Terrorist Attacks Upon the United States," 2004, 8.

[2]Unless otherwise indicated, information in this chapter on communications with air traffic controllers is from National Transportation Safety Board, "Air Traffic Control Recording, Specialist's Report," by Joseph A. Gregor, Dec. 21, 2001.

[3]"The 9/11 Commission Report," 24, 460.

[4]Ibid, 24-25.

[5]Ibid.

[6]Ibid, 25.

[7]Agence France Presse, "Text of Bush's remarks after World Trade Center attacks," Sarasota, Florida, Sept. 11, 2001.

[8]A few minutes after the last routine transmission from the pilots, at about 8:50 A.M., five hijackers had stormed the cockpit, using knives and box cutters to overwhelm the flight crew and seize control of the aircraft. They herded passengers and crew members to the back of the plane. Somebody claiming to be the pilot came on the public address system to announce that the plane had been hijacked. The hijackers then turned off the transponder that sent airspeed and position data to FAA receivers on the ground. FAA ground radars could still track airplanes without this data, but coverage was sporadic, and data from the radars was not automatically transmitted to air traffic controllers. "The 9/11 Commission Report," 8, 16.

[9]Unless otherwise noted, information in this chapter on the flight path of AA 77 is from National Transportation Safety Board, "Flight Path Study—American Airlines Flight 77," February 19, 2002.

[10]As with all commercial airplanes, Flight 77's airspeed was measured in knots, not miles per hour. For the benefit of nonpilots (including ourselves), we have converted all airspeed measurements from knots to miles per hour.

[11]"The 9/11 Commission Report," 39.

[12]Ibid, 39–40.

[13]Carroll, James, *House of War: The Pentagon and the Disastrous Rise of American Power.* Boston, 2006: Houghton Mifflin Co., ix.

[14]Goldberg, Alfred, *The Pentagon: The First Fifty Years.* Washington, D.C., 1992: Historical Office, Office of the Secretary of Defense, 47, 89.

[15]*The Pentagon,* 183.

[16]Ibid, 34.

[17]Ibid, 58.

[18]Ibid, 175.

[19]By law, only the National Command Authority, which consists of the President and the Secretary of Defense, or their authorized subordinates, can authorize a nuclear strike, and they must do so jointly. In turn, they must jointly inform the Chairman of the Joint Chiefs of Staff, who will begin the process required to carry out the order.

[20]Department of the Army, Office of the Deputy Chief of Staff, G-1, "Uncommon Strength: The Story of the Office of the Army Deputy Chief of Staff for Personnel During the Attack on the Pentagon, 11 September 2001," n.d., 35, 39–40.

[21]Ibid, 39.

[22]Like many people who were at the Pentagon on September 11, Alan Wallace was featured in various press reports. The material here comes from a first-hand account he provided to the authors.

[23]"Uncommon Strength," 14–15.

CHAPTER 3. 0.8 SECONDS

[1]Mlakar, Paul E., et al, "The Pentagon Building Performance Report," Reston, Virginia: The American Society of Civil Engineers, 2003, 13. There are other anecdotal sources for this.

[2]"The Pentagon Building Performance Report," 12–13, 35–36. This report generally presents facts related to the damage caused to the Pentagon, without drawing conclusions about the behavior or intent of the hijackers on Flight 77. The authors have combined material in this report with other research to present as clear a picture as possible of what happened when Flight 77 struck the Pentagon. Any inferences should be attributed to the authors.

[3]Ibid, 6, 34-35, 45, and other research.

[4]Ibid, 35.

[5]Ibid, 36.

[6]From an interview with Paul Mlakar, U.S. Army Corps of Engineers.

[7]"The Pentagon Building Performance Report," 12, 36.

[8]Ibid, 50. For easier reference, we have converted pounds of fuel, as presented in the report, to gallons, using the conversion ratio 1 gallon of fuel = 6.83 pounds.

[9]From an examination of footage from a Pentagon security camera that captured the initial explosion.

[10]"The Pentagon Building Performance Report," 50, using the same conversion ratio noted in earlier footnote.

[11]Ibid, 33, Figure 5.27.

[12]*The Pentagon,* 32–34.
[13]Ibid, 49, 53.
[14]Ibid, 12, 46.
[15]"Arlington County After-Action Report on the Response to the September 11 Terrorist Attack on the Pentagon," Titan Systems Corporation, 2004, 9.
[16]"The Pentagon Building Performance Report," 53.
[17]From an interview with FBI Special Agent Tom O'Connor, one of the officials in charge of collecting evidence at the Pentagon on 9/11.
[18]Based on eyewitness accounts from numerous sources.
[19]Information on the location of bodies found inside the Pentagon comes from an FBI exhibit, "Summary Presentation of Damage to Pentagon and Location of Bodies Found Inside," prepared for *United States* v. *Zacarias Moussaoui,* Criminal Case No. 01-455-A, U.S. District Court, Eastern District of Virginia.
[20]From multiple eyewitness accounts.
[21]"The Pentagon Building Performance Report," 28, 40, 58.
[22]More precisely, 79/100 of a second. From an interview with Paul Mlakar.

CHAPTER 4. "BUMP IT TO A THIRD"

[1]"Uncommon Strength," 14–15.
[2]The authors transcribed an audiotape of the Arlington County dispatch recordings for the morning of September 11, 2001. Unless otherwise noted, quotes over the radio network are taken from that transcription.

CHAPTER 5. JUST LIKE VIETNAM

[1]Ward, Michael J., "Attack on the Pentagon: The Initial Fire & EMS Response," JEMS, April 2002, 24, also, http://info.jems.com/911/pdf/jems0402.pdf

CHAPTER 10. HELLHOLE

[1]"The Pentagon Building Performance Report," 49.

CHAPTER 11. CIGARETTE BREAK

[1]"Arlington County After-Action Report," A-66.

CHAPTER 14. 1,000 DEGREES

[1]The plane the FAA thought had been headed toward Washington obviously did not strike Camp David. This was one of hundreds of shards of misinformation passed through official channels throughout the day. The aircraft in question was United Flight 93, originally scheduled to fly from Newark to Los Angeles. The flight went off radar because it had crashed in Shanksville, Pennsylvania, which the FAA did not know at the time. They had estimated its flight time to Washington based on the plane's airspeed, heading, and altitude when it went off radar, and the assumption that it was simply flying low, to avoid radar detection.

[2]"Pentagon Building Performance Report," 43. Experts estimate the fire inside the Pentagon may have gotten as hot as 1,740 degrees Fahrenheit.

CHAPTER 16. UNTENABLE

[1]Maj. Stephen Long and Lt. Col. Dennis Johnson, who were attending the Army personnel meeting with Colonel McNair at the time of the attack, both died in the Pentagon. Evidence, including interviews with firefighters, suggests the two men tried to rescue others nearby rather than fleeing the fire. In instances where we have named victims whose bodies were found by rescue crews, we have consulted with family members to assure they are comfortable with the way we have mentioned their loved ones.

CHAPTER 17. THE NMCC

[1]The National Military Command Center and other sensitive offices have since been relocated.
[2]This feature of the building has since been modified.
[3]None of these things turned out to be true.
[4]"The 9/11 Commission Report," 37.
[5]The National Command Authority consists of the President and the Secretary of Defense, or their authorized subordinates. By law, only these civilian leaders may authorize military action.

CHAPTER 19. EVERYBODY OUT OF THE POOL

[1]"Arlington County After-Action Report," A-25–A-26.
[2]At the time, of course, nobody knew how many firefighters had died in New York. The final tally of firefighters killed in the twin towers was 343. More information is available at the FDNY's Web site, www.fdny.org.
[3]More misinformation, typical of the confusion that day. The Sears Tower was not attacked on 9/11. And by early afternoon there were no longer any hijacked airplanes flying.
[4]Media analysts guessed that as many as 800 people may have been killed inside the Pentagon, based on the typical occupancy of a portion of the building the size of the impact area. Those estimates did not take into account the fact that much of the impact area was under renovation and therefore uninhabited. "Arlington County After-Action Report," A-31.
[5]The unidentified airplane had been a U.S. government jet carrying Attorney General John Ashcroft back to Washington from an out-of-town trip. It had a fighter-jet escort. The "Arlington County After-Action Report" concluded that this evacuation could have been avoided through more timely information-sharing among the FAA, the Department of Transportation, the FBI, and the commanders on-scene at the Pentagon. One problem was that Chris Combs and the FBI had set up their own command post, and an FBI representative was not available to advise Chief Schwartz, directly and in person. "Arlington County After-Action Report," A-30–A-31.

CHAPTER 20. MAKING THE TEAM

[1]More misinformation.
[2]Even more misinformation.

CHAPTER 22. "DADDY'S THERE"

[1]An acronym, popular among military and law-enforcement officials, meaning "fucked up beyond any recognition." There are other variations.

CHAPTER 25. OPEN FOR BUSINESS

[1]Varley, Pamela, "Command Performance: County Firefighters Take Charge of the 9/11 Pentagon Emergency," Kennedy School of Government Case Program, Taubman Center for State and Local Government (2003: President and Fellows of Harvard College), 24–25.
[2]Federal and Virginia law makes clear that responding to emergencies is the responsibility of local governments, which can ask for help from neighboring jurisdictions if needed. The state governor, in turn, can ask for federal help. One provision of federal law states that the federal government can assume jurisdiction over an emergency if it is the result of a foreign attack, and the attack took place on federal property. That was in fact the case at the Pentagon. But since the federal government did not have a firefighting force capable of responding to an incident of this size, there was never serious discussion of seizing jurisdiction from Arlington County. From "Command Performance," 2–3.

CHAPTER 27. NIGHT OPS

[1]"Arlington County After-Action Report," A-57.
[2]Ibid, A-53.

CHAPTER 34. THE TILLER CAB

[1]The plane turned out to be a federal government aircraft. "Arlington County After-Action Report," A-30.

CHAPTER 35. STRESS MANAGEMENT

[1]The office mates King had gone looking for right after Flight 77 hit the Pentagon—Staff Sgt. Maudlyn White and Lt. Col. Jerry Dickerson—were both killed in the attack.

CHAPTER 38. THE NAVY COMMAND CENTER

[1]In instances where we have named victims whose bodies were found by rescue crews, we contacted family members to assure they were comfortable with these references.

CHAPTER 43. TRAFFIC

[1]Collins, Larry, "Collapse Rescue Operations at the Pentagon 9-11 Attack: A Case Study on Urban Search and Rescue Disaster Response," n.d., 9–10.

CHAPTER 44. THE T-REX

[1]The flight attendant was Renee May, who was able to reach her mother in Las Vegas. The passenger was Barbara Olson, who was able to reach her husband, Solicitor General Ted Olson, in Washington. "The 9-11 Commission Report," 9.

[2]Collins, Larry, "Collapse Rescue Operations at the Pentagon," 12.

CHAPTER 45. THE VIPs

[1]Seven members of FDNY's Squad 18 died on 9/11. For more information: www.fdnysquad18.com/memorial.php

[2]Six members of FDNY's Ladder 35 were killed on 9/11.

CHAPTER 46. A CEREMONY

[1]The final death toll in New York turned out to be just over 2,600 dead and missing. "The 9-11 Commission Report," 1.

[2]The final death toll at the Pentagon was 189: 125 people who were working in the building, 59 passengers and crew members aboard Flight 77, and five hijackers.

EPILOGUE

[1]"Arlington County After-Action Report," A-27.

[2]Ibid, C-56.

[3]Ibid, A-8, A-14.

[4]Vogel, Steve, *The Pentagon: A History.* New York, 2007: Random House, 474–77. Vogel's book provides a detailed account of the rebuilding of the Pentagon.

[5]Ibid, 489–90.

[6]For more information: http://memorial.pentagon.mil

[7]Newman, Rick, "Ties That Truly Bind," *U.S.News & World Report,* Sept. 11, 2006, 41-42. Also posted at www.usnews.com/usnews/news/articles/060903/11pentagon.htm.

INDEX

G

ABOUT THE AUTHORS

PATRICK CREED is an amateur historian, volunteer firefighter, and U.S. Army Reserve officer who recently returned from a tour in Iraq as a civil affairs officer with the Army's Special Operations Command. Creed has one son and lives in Havertown, Pennsylvania, where he is a member of the Bon Air and Landsdowne fire companies.

RICK NEWMAN is an award-winning journalist and staff writer for *U.S. News & World Report*. He has also written for the *Washington Post* and many other publications and is the co-author of *Bury Us Upside Down: The Misty Pilots and the Secret Battle for the Ho Chi Minh Trail*. Newman has two children and lives in Westchester County, New York. Visit his website at www.rickjnewman.com.

www.firefightthebook.com

ABOUT THE TYPE

The text of this book was set in Berkeley, designed by Tony Stan in the early 1980s. It was inspired by and is a variation of University of California Old Style, created in the late 1930s by Frederick Goudy for the exclusive use of the University of California Press at Berkeley. The present face, in fact, bears influences of a number of Goudy's fonts, including Kennerly, Goudy Old Style, Deepdene, and Booklet Oldstyle. Berkeley is notable for both its legibility and its lightness.